ARCHAEOLOGY AFTER INTERPRETATION

ARCHAEOLOGY AFTER INTERPRETATION

RETURNING MATERIALS TO ARCHAEOLOGICAL THEORY

Edited by
Benjamin Alberti
Andrew Meirion Jones
Joshua Pollard

Walnut Creek, California

LEFT COAST PRESS, INC.
1630 North Main Street, #400
Walnut Creek, CA 94596
http://www.LCoastPress.com

ISBN 978-1-61132-341-2 hardback
ISBN 978-1-61132-343-6 institutional eBook
ISBN 978-1-61132-725-0 consumer eBook

Library of Congress Cataloging-in-Publication Data:

Archaeology after interpretation : returning materials to archaeological theory/ edited by Benjamin Alberti, Andrew Meirion Jones, Joshua Pollard.
    pages cm
 Includes bibliographical references and index.
  ISBN 978-1-61132-341-2 (hardback) — ISBN 978-1-61132-343-6 (institutional eBook) — ISBN 978-1-61132-725-0 (consumer eBook)
 1. Archaeology—Methodology. 2. Antiquities—Analysis. I. Alberti, Benjamin, 1968- II. Jones, Andrew, 1967- III. Pollard, Joshua.
  CC80.A664 2013
  930.1—dc23
                          2013022284

Printed in the United States of America

☉ The paper used in this publication meets the minimum requirements of American National Standard for Information Sciences—Permanence of Paper for Printed Library Materials, ANSI/NISO Z39.48–1992.

Contents

Illustrations

TABLES

FIGURES

Preface

The idea for this volume arose from a train journey shared between two of the editors, Andrew Meirion Jones and Joshua Pollard. We were both traveling to work in Southampton through the beautiful Wiltshire countryside of southern England; naturally our minds were on archaeology (Wiltshire is full of archaeological sites, and several important prehistoric monuments are visible from the train), and we began discussing the prospect for future approaches in archaeological theory. We both agreed that there seemed to be a new ontological turn developing in archaeology. We decided that it would be useful to bring together people working in this area for a small conference or workshop. We also decided that the best work on ontological approaches in archaeology was being undertaken by Ben Alberti.

We approached Ben and contacted the list of prospective contributors. Happily, most of the people we contacted were interested in developing these approaches to archaeology, and Ben Alberti readily agreed to jointly organize a workshop or meeting. In order to facilitate an informal discussion among contributors we hired a cottage in the small village of Cote, Oxfordshire; informality was the order of the day, and on the two days of the workshop most contributors presented their papers as casually as possible—shoes were off, and socks were proudly displayed! The workshop, held in May 2012, was generously funded by a small grant from the Faculty of Humanities, University of Southampton, and we would like to thank the Head of Research (Humanities), Professor Mark Everist, for supporting the project. The aim of the workshop was to produce discussion papers. These would then be presented, critiqued, and polished for final publication. The workshop was a tremendous success and a very enjoyable experience; the contributor biographies in this volume reflect the informal nature of the gathering.

The attendees at that meeting included Andrew Meirion Jones, Joshua Pollard, Ben Alberti, Chantal Conneller, Lesley McFadyen, Dave Robinson, Sarah Baires, Amanda Butler, Chris Fowler, Marcus Brittain,

13

Emilie Sibbesson, Andrew Cochrane, Ben Jervis, Sara Perry, and Bill Walker. Sadly, Tim Pauketat, Alejandro Haber, and Gavin Lucas were unable to attend. The volume underwent minor changes prior to publication. Unfortunately, due to pressure of work, Bill Walker was unable to contribute to the final volume and Andrés Laguens was added to the list of contributors.

We are grateful to all the contributors for their hard work, belief in the project, and for rapidly turning around the papers for the workshop and publication. We are also grateful to Mitch and Caryn at Left Coast Press, who have been helpful and constructive throughout the editorial process.

CHAPTER ONE

Archaeology after Interpretation

Andrew Meirion Jones and Benjamin Alberti
(with contributions from Chris Fowler and Gavin Lucas)

What do we mean by "archaeology after interpretation"? The purpose of this introduction is to explain this phrase and introduce some of the themes of the book. To be clear, in discussing an "archaeology after interpretation," we do not reject the utility of theoretical discussion in archaeology (*contra* Bintliff & Pearce 2012); indeed we would argue that archaeology (or any scientific or scholarly discipline) without theory is an oxymoron. Instead, "archaeology after interpretation" is a statement by theoretically oriented archaeologists about the current shift in archaeological thinking from questions of interpretation as a *post hoc* in a continuous enterprise to a position that accepts the fully relational and constitutive character of all practices.

We intend the phrase "archaeology after interpretation" to denote two things. First, it distinguishes contributions to this book from the intellectual outlook known as interpretative archaeology (or interpretive archaeology) that characterized the early 1990s (e.g., Tilley 1993; Shanks & Hodder 1995; Thomas 2000); in that sense, our phrase signifies "archaeology after *interpretation*." Second, it highlights the elusive and changeable nature of archaeological interpretation. We recognize that archaeologists are always *after* interpretation, in the sense that they are attempting to grasp or get at interpretation(s). In fact, what interpretation is becomes an open question. In highlighting a distinction from Interpretative Archaeology we intend to foreground and take stock of developments in archaeological thought by addressing fundamental changes in the epistemological and ontological character of archaeological thought over the past decade. In that sense our aims are closer to the

Archaeology after Interpretation: Returning Materials to Archaeological Theory, edited by Benjamin Alberti, Andrew Meirion Jones, and Joshua Pollard, 15–35. ©2013 Left Coast Press, Inc. All rights reserved.

"quiet revolution" imagined by anthropologists Amiria Henare, Martin Holbraad, and Sari Wastell (2007, 7), who argued for a shift away from epistemological questions.

Perhaps contradictorily, what we are after is what happens *during* interpretation, which is where the question of ontology lies: What kind of work is involved in the co-emergence of interpretation and reality, and what role do materials play in this process? Like Henare et al. (2007), we see the fundamental shift in archaeological thinking as a reorientation from questions of an essentially epistemological nature—what constitutes archaeological knowledge and how we go about securing it—to concerns of an ontological kind: What *are* archaeological entities and what is the real character of archaeological thought and practice? Certain key themes have percolated to the surface in archaeological work and signposted this shift. The "brute materiality" of given matter has been questioned, and is now understood to be imbued with vibrancy and enlivened by innate energy (Conneller 2011; Hodder 2012; Jones 2012). Bergson's claim (1999) that it is material stability, not movement, that has to be explained exemplifies this position. This is a world of fluidity, process, change, and contingency. We see, consequently, a return to materials and a rethinking of the notion of "material agency" beyond the confines of human exceptionalism. "Relationality" is another key term, which challenges any claims to preexistent fixed substances. The modernist substance ontology of "mind" and "matter" gives way to relational ontologies; essentialist "objects" and "subjects" give way to relational identities, persons, and entities, in which dividing lines are not pre-drawn (Alberti et al. 2011; see contributors to Alberti & Bray 2009). The new direction in archaeology, then, has much in common with posthumanism—the critique of the reduction of explanation in the social sciences to the human, and the recognition that there is no ontologically marked category of the human that can serve *a priori*—as the basis of natural philosophy (Haraway 2008). Linked to this is a critique of the necessity of mediation by humans or culture in understanding the nature of the world, which brings post-humanist scholars to lean towards non-representationalist thinking. How can we understand belief, image, memory, society, and other apparent abstractions without resorting to the representationalist gambit of an interpreting subject/culture quite distinct from the world she/he interprets, but also without resorting to the opposite side of the same coin, the natural scientists' steadfast belief in a correlative theory of truth? Work in this line has produced analyses that stress the necessarily non-reductive material nature of such ideas (e.g., Jones 2007 in the case of memory; Lucas 2012 in the case of the archaeological record; see also Edgeworth 2012 for the process of interpretation in archaeological fieldwork).

All this work can be characterized by a desire to integrate the best thinking and categories available to us from the hard sciences with the type of social theory that came out of the archaeology of the 1980s and 1990s. Earlier post-processual efforts to integrate the sciences and humanities in archaeology were very much about using both traditions for a common goal derived from the humanities and humanist thinking (e.g., Hodder 1999). More recently, though, archaeologists have stressed the common goals of theoretical traditions in the hard sciences, social sciences, and humanities, all of which move beyond humanism (e.g., Jones 2004, 2012; Lucas 2012). The hard and natural sciences are no longer seen just as a source of techniques for data production but as theoretically sophisticated. A balanced account requires considering theoretical perspectives from both, not using results from scientific techniques in an "interpretative" approach.

INTERPRETATION AND DIVERSITY

There is no radical intellectual break heralded by *Archaeology after Interpretation*. Rather, there is a return to theoretical influences long felt in archaeology but now reread alongside new voices. During the late 1970s and early 1980s, British, Scandinavian, and American archaeology witnessed a major paradigm shift from an approach dominated by positivist scientific outlooks—new or processual archaeology—to one characterized by constructivist approaches drawn from the humanities and social sciences—post-processual archaeology. With the publication of seminal volumes such as *Symbolic and Structural Archaeology* (Hodder 1982), the later publications of Shanks and Tilley (1987a, 1987b), and the reappraisal of pioneering books such as *In Small Things Forgotten* (Deetz 1977), archaeologists were introduced at a stroke to a diversity of approaches including neo-Marxism, structuralism, feminism, and a variety of post-structuralist positions. The significance of these volumes cannot be overstated, as they heralded a phase of experimentation and creativity in archaeology; indeed, the eclectic and contradictory nature of post-processual archaeology was actively promoted (Hodder 1992, 86–87). Arguably, the diversity of approaches began to ossify towards the end of the 1980s and the beginning of the 1990s as certain themes began to be emphasized over others; it is during this phase of development that we witness the emergence of interpretative archaeology. In what follows we will critically review a series of concepts that have emerged from this discourse. We will revisit some familiar philosophical figures that have underpinned the development of post-processual and interpretative archaeology, including Michel Foucault, Jacques Derrida, and the less familiar Gilles Deleuze and Felix Guattari, Karen Barad, and Bruno Latour. In readdressing the works of these philosophers and their application in post-processual and interpretative archaeology we do not wish to imply that there is a correct way to read these authors, but rather that certain themes have been emphasized by post-processual and interpretative archaeologists at the expense of others (see also Olsen 2003, 2007). In this introduction, our primary focus is on the nature of the interpreting subject, but we also discuss the analysis of context in archaeology and the notion of material symbols and material culture studies. In each case our argument is that despite their rhetoric post-processual and interpretative archaeologies have in many cases produced surprisingly static and formal visions of past life. Our aim, in returning to these key intellectual figures, is to bring to light elements of their work that in fact stress the importance of fluidity and process. We are therefore able to trace the origins of the type of thinking represented by contributors to *Archaeology after Interpretation*, which rests on a reconsideration of the position of the human subject as the preeminent figure in archaeological analyses.

FROM THE INTERPRETING SUBJECT
TO THE RELATIONAL PERSON

The key emphasis in early formulations of the post-processual approach was on the nature of interpretation, that is on the interpretative position of the archaeologist in relation to excavated artifacts from the past. Shanks and Tilley (1987a, 107–8) proposed a hermeneutic (or interpretative) position for archaeology in which archaeologists not only interpret between "our" world and "their" world, as anthropologists do, but also interpret historically between the past and the present (see also Shanks & Hodder 1995, 10). Both Tilley (1993) and Shanks and Hodder (1995) describe the importance of the archaeologist as the person who sifts the indeterminate nature of evidence from the past to produce plausible statements about that past; the primary goal of the archaeologist is to interpret. We do not wish to argue that the primary goal of archaeology should not be interpretation, although we will question the character of that interpretative process and the role of archaeologists in it. The significance of interpretation was perhaps forged in the early days of post-processual archaeology in contradiction to the criticisms of processual archaeologists; interpretation emerged then as an important mission statement for post-processual archaeologists. One of the consequences of this was that the centrality of interpretation to the archaeological project was mapped onto archaeologists' understanding of the human subject in the past. Like the archaeologist in the present, the human actor in the post-processual past is ultimately an interpreting subject. Witness the individual patrolling past prehistoric landscapes in Tilley's accounts, constantly aware of the changing circumstances of the environment, always aware of the symbolic significance of distant mountain views in relation to built structures (e.g., Tilley 1994, 2004). In another example, the literature on agency in archaeology includes interpreting subjects (or knowledgeable agents) who make informed—if limited—decisions concerning their ability to alter and change the worlds they inhabit (e.g., Dobres & Robb 2000; Gardiner 2004).

The interpreting subject of archaeology exists in a world of representations, dominated by the meaning and significance of the world; the world only has significance to the subject in that it is converted to meaningful symbols. The consequence is a reification of the separation and a privileging of the role of the human subject. An alternative view is to see the person as always being in a process of interaction with the world, as was emphasized in phenomenological approaches in archaeology (e.g., Gosden 1994; Tilley 1994; Thomas 1996); though—as noted above—there remains a tendency in phenomenological accounts to retain a distinction between world and interpreting subject (see Olsen 2007; Fuglestvedt 2009). Instead, we argue that action should not be seen simply as a unidirectional process running from the actor to the acted upon, from the active to the passive, from mind to matter (Anderson & Harrison 2010, 7). With geographers Beth Greenhough (2010) and Sarah Whatmore (2008), and political theorist Jane Bennett (2001, 2010), we argue that rather than placing primary emphasis on the interpreting subject as having the sole capacity for action and interpretation we need to remember that action takes place with and alongside other active agencies in the world. These are not surrogates for humans—their agency a derived form of human agency, as much material agency theory in archaeology would have it—nor the active material culture conceived by Hodder (1986), but are rather constituted by the same processes as humans and are therefore coproductive of the world. The idea of a meaningful and ongoing relationship between subject and world is not new in archaeology; it is the nature and the prominence given to that relationship in relation to other relationships that changes.

This perspective is presaged to an extent in the work of Michel Foucault (1972, 1981). Interestingly, whereas the work of Foucault was utilized by earlier writers in archaeology to discuss the significance of power as discourse (e.g., Miller & Tilley 1984) and the body as site of discourse (Meskell 1996), we also observe in his work a disquiet about the violence done to the world by a recourse to symbolic analysis. Foucault (1981, 67) writes: "We must not imagine that the world turns towards us a legible face which we only have to decipher; the world is not the accomplice of our knowledge; there is no prediscursive providence which disposes the world in our favor." The agency of the world therefore intersects or even crosscuts human understanding, a point taken up and developed in Karen Barad's "new materialist" (2007) development of Foucault's work.

In this respect we highlight the important work of Julian Thomas (2002) in examining the problematic emphasis on humanist perspectives in recent archaeological interpretations. He associates humanism with the notion of the autonomous and rational individual, and traces its relationship to the political philosophy of modernity and liberalism. He calls for an antihumanist perspective, drawing on the work of Judith Butler (1990, 1993), to suggest that bodies and individuals are materialized, or continually undergo a performative process. This perspective radically questions the security and integrity of the essential individual or identity, and it leads us to reposition the human subject as a relational and performative construction (Fowler 2004). Rather than viewing the interpreting subject as the seat of reason and cognition, we shift then to an image of the relational and fractal person positioned in a set of unfolding relationships. As Chris Fowler (2010, 141) notes, "The image of the 'fractal' illustrates that there are really no social 'wholes,' only unfolding relationships which can be viewed at different scales." Such an image allows the person to be viewed as situated in a complex field of interactions with the environment; an environment inhabited by both human and other-than-human forces and entities that interact with and impinge upon the person (Ingold 2000, 2011). This view resonates with the concept of the rhizome, as articulated by the philosophers Gilles Deleuze and Felix Guattari (1987). The use of rhizomes as vegetal metaphors for a set of intersecting and crosscutting links offers an alternative to the hierarchical metaphor of the tree. Whereas the tree of knowledge is dominated by its trunk, a solid foundation upon which to build further branches of knowledge, rhizomes—those interconnecting fungal mycelia—promote a sense of the partial connections generated by many forms of scholarly knowledge, with various interconnected sites of knowledge production. Curiously, Tilley (1993), Shanks (1992), and Shanks and Hodder (1995) all draw on Deleuze and Guattari to promote their sense of interpretation. Shanks and Hodder (1995, 27) discuss the rhizome as an appropriate metaphor for interpretation: "Rhizomes thinking does not aim to reproduce an object in thought, image or words, but to connect with it, construct with it." Tilley (1993, 18), on the other hand, lists a series of principles derived from Deleuze and Guattari to aid his interpretative project. The deployment of Deleuze and Guattari to promote interpretation is especially strange, since these authors explicitly eschew interpretation, describing representational thinking as a form of "interpretosis," a pathological condition that afflicts those who assume that there is some meaning or truth that awaits interpretation, revelation, or disclosure. In this belief Deleuze and Guattari (1987) cleave to a position earlier discussed by Foucault (1972). Arguably, this trend of thought did not become central to post-processualism, losing ground to structuralist and post-structuralist approaches that placed emphasis on meaning, and then to largely phenomenological approaches prioritizing human experience and the effects of material media.

Both Foucault (1972) and Deleuze and Guattari (1987) argue against utilizing the thinking subject as a basis for argument and analysis; it is for this reason that Deleuze and Guattari promote the idea of the interconnecting rhizome. What concerns these authors is any search for absolute truths, for something that we feel we can know or interpret and which will give us a foundation. Abstract foundational concepts such as God or Truth have been rejected in the modernist era. However, since the work of Descartes and Kant, the human subject as the object of foundational knowledge has replaced these abstractions. Consider Descartes *cogito ergo sum*, "I think therefore I am": this is a foundational statement par excellence. The knowledgeable and interpreting human subject is a problematic entity. It is consequently surprising that interpretative archaeology figures both the archaeologist and the human subject in the past as primary loci of interpretation. This can clearly be seen in Tilley's assertion that "without the interpretative work of the archaeologist the past would remain dead and gone" (Tilley 1993, 20; see Fowler, in this volume, for a critical analysis of this point). Here it is the interpreting archaeologist that provides the meaning for past artifacts and objects. In these accounts the interpretative archaeologist acts as a foundation for archaeological knowledge; and archaeological knowledge is figured primarily in terms of symbolic meaning. This perspective is all the more surprising when we consider that, as Hodder (1999) points out, in practice archaeological excavation and analysis is a group endeavor that involves several people analyzing different aspects of the evidence and making interconnections between pieces of evidence (see also Jones 2002), rather than the preserve of the lone individual.

We argue instead that interpretation involves understanding the interconnections between archaeological remains, tools of archaeological excavation, survey, and recording (trowels, total stations, etc.), and the archaeologists themselves, rather than positing either the archaeologist or the past human subject as the primary site of interpretation. Interpretation arises from multiple sites rather than a single location. Further, these interconnections are always changing; they are immanent and in a constant process of becoming. Rather than arriving at interpretations that fix meaning, it is important that we are aware of the changing character of these interconnections. Rather than focusing primarily on symbolic meaning, we also need to acknowledge the physical and material characteristics of the artifacts and contexts that we excavate. In addition, we would argue that the material qualities or properties of the evidence play an active role in their interpretation, and interpretation should take place with and alongside materials. In the next section we consider this latter issue in more detail.

FROM MATERIAL SYMBOLS TO VIBRANT MATERIALS

Archaeology after Interpretation challenges the straightforward representationalist notion of a material symbol and attempts to think through materials as inherently agentive. Meaning and productivity come from the nature of the interaction among all such vibrant materials—"the force of things" (Bennett 2010)—of which the human is one example, and not from the imposition of meaning by a singular and exclusively human subject.

As we have argued, interpretative archaeology figures the archaeologist as the primary locus of interpretation. This perspective is mapped onto the conceptualization of the human subject that inhabits the past, often figured as a knowledgeable individual or agent (Robb 1999; Dobres & Robb 2000). One of the concepts that underpin this conceptualization is the idea of material symbols. From the inception of post-processual archaeology, material artifacts were understood as signs or symbols; they were thus "meaningfully constituted" (Hodder 1986, 1989, 1992). Of course, the difference between linguistic signs and material signs was acknowledged (Hodder 1992; Tilley 1999; Preucel 2006), and Hodder (1992, 201) notes that in their materiality, material artifacts and their use participate in the construction of their significance: "Material culture references are motivated and non-arbitrary." Nevertheless, it was felt to be appropriate to discuss material artifacts in terms of their signification and symbolism. The material world encountered by the knowledgeable agents of interpretative archaeology is therefore a world replete with symbolism; materials are to be understood as conceptually motivated (Hodder 1992, 202). Interpretation is therefore interpretation of the symbolic dimensions of material artifacts.

Of course, the notion of material symbols reproduces a philosophical distinction between material and ideal, despite several attempts to overcome this distinction—whether through Daniel Miller's (1987) adoption of Hegel to argue that subjects are constituted as cultural subjects through the appropriation and use of external objects, or through Chris Tilley's (1994) use of Merleau-Ponty to argue for the body as a modality of the physical world. Whereas Miller established a space between the subject and the object only to bridge it, Tilley collapsed subject and object into the same conceptual scheme (Rose 2011, 113). In both cases the philosophical distinction remains: Tilley's phenomenological analysis still retains a focus on the search for meaning, and the abilities of materials to actively participate in interactions with subjects are overlooked (Olsen 2003, 2010).

For this reason we are sympathetic to the approach that has come to be known as "symmetrical archaeology" (Witmore 2007; Olsen 2010, 2012). Drawing on the Actor-Network Theory of Michel Callon and Bruno Latour, symmetrical archaeologists argue that humans are characteristically enmeshed with things and other-than-human entities (see also Hodder 2012 for a similar argument); or that indeed humans do not stand apart from things, but they emerge from such relationships (Olsen 2012, 209). We strongly agree with this argument and the underlying premise that things are not significant only because of their relations to humans (Olsen 2012), though the approach has been criticized for human exceptionalism in its claims on how humans and things come to be "mixed" (Ingold 2012). There remains a danger of replacing one form of representational approach in which materials are significant as symbols with one in which materials are significant because of their relationships with humans. In addition, an emphasis on networks and nodes, if not built in to the model, can produce a mobile network made up of static things (Ingold 2012, 436–37). It is important that we forefront the vitality and vibrancy of materials in and of themselves (Bennett 2010). It is also critically important that we examine how materials and persons are assembled and articulated together, constituting boundaries as they do so. This is a topic discussed in greater depth in the "Assembling the Social" section of this book.

Usefully, Tim Ingold (2007) draws our attention to the properties of materials as opposed to the concept of materiality. Whereas the concept of materiality presupposes that materials are meaningful only because they are made meaningful by humans, a focus on materials *per se* enables us to consider how material properties actively participate in the interaction between people and materials; it is for this reason that Jane Bennett draws our attention to the force of material things, "thing-power" (Bennett 2010; see also Jones 2012; Lucas 2012). The concept of materiality disguises (poorly) a continued reliance on a dualism that actually reinforces the separation between human and objects (see also Ingold 2007). Similarly, the notion of material or object agency, very popular in the past decade, attempts to grapple with the animacy of the world, but suffers from an overly human conception of agency. Notions such as "secondary agency" (from Gell 1998; see Robb 2005) and some examples of the taking up of Latour's non-human actants, or his parliament of things, in archaeology introduce metaphors of human agency into a material world essentially unchanged. The thing as material object is rarely considered (Tilley 1990; Schiffer 1999; Olsen 2010; Hodder 2012, 14). As such, the notion of "object agency" or "material agency" and the field of material culture studies can be seen as transitional between post-processualism and a new approach to the agentive character of materials not modeled on human agency (for attempts to employ the idea of "material agency," see Jones 2002, 2007; Knappett 2005; Knappett & Malafouris 2007; Boivin 2008; Garrow & Gosden 2012).

Thus, in line with Bennett's thesis, we perceive a desire in recent work to treat materials or archaeological remains as efficacious, meaningful, or affective in their own right (Thomas 2004; Lucas 2012). The concept of "material culture" does not acknowledge the meaning of materials beyond their adoption into culture. In *Understanding the Archaeological Record*, Lucas (2012) exemplifies the new approach. Through a reconfigured notion of "materialization"—"a process in which objects and people are made and unmade, in which they have no stable essences but are contextually and historically contingent" (ibid., 166)—he attempts to account for the dynamism and tension inherent in the archaeological record. What transitional work on material agency lacks is a model of "materiality in the making" (ibid., 165). Materiality is, at bottom, a relational process rather than a kind of substance. Ultimately, the difference between this notion of materialization and the more common idea of materiality, critiqued by Ingold (2011, 2012), is that "qualities already inherent in matter itself but not actualized" (Lucas 2012, 167) are materialized, not abstract beliefs and ideas.

In another recent example from the archaeological literature, and probably the most sophisticated book-length treatment of the new approach to materials, Chantal Conneller (2011) draws on Deleuze and Guattari, among others, to investigate how materials are known and how they exhibit different qualities in different circumstances. It is not that a material contains a finite list of inherent properties that are elicited by a knowing subject; rather, properties or qualities are the product of the interaction among subject, technology, and material.

So far we have argued for a shift away from an interpretative project that conceives of material artifacts as symbols, in favor of an approach motivated by ontological concerns about the properties of materials and the way these properties articulate with people. In this sense we are motivated by a desire to reconsider what this relational understanding means for our conceptualization of ontology (this issue is discussed in greater depth in the "Relational Ontologies" section of this book).

Almost a defining feature of new theoretical approaches to archaeology is the explicit and reflexive ontological register of their arguments. In fact, the language of ontology has proven extremely useful in highlighting the key movements and changes introduced by these new approaches. Lucas (2012) refers to ontology frequently to mark the distinctions he needs; Hodder (2012) makes similar claims. As Lucas (2012, 3) points out, this shift—what he terms the "current interpretive dilemma"—questions the underlying metaphysical assumptions of archaeological discourse. It is not that previous approaches were unaware of the ontological grounding of their position; they simply did not see it as problematic or as a possible resource for analyzing and fixing some key conceptual issues in archaeology. Clearly, ontologically informed archaeologists had drawn for some time on authors such as Heidegger (e.g., Gosden 1994; Tilley 1994; Thomas 1996) and Butler (Thomas 1996; Joyce 2000; Alberti 2001) in discussions of topics such as landscapes and bodies. Although Heidegger's insights about the prediscursive makeup of our worlds has inspired the dwelling perspective in landscape archaeology (Ingold 2000; Thomas 2008), and Butler's (1993) undermining of the prediscursive fixity of sex has influenced strongly how we understand bodies and gender in archaeology, it could be argued that neither approach has been successfully developed in its more profound insights. There is a tendency to continue to treat landscapes as social constructions and bodies as willfully performed or, indeed, socially constructed.

Where the difference seems to lie is the nature of the use of ontological sources. Previous attempts were aimed at producing a new "Ontology," a better one that would replace the defunct sort. These "meta-ontologies" are themselves problematic as they cannot countenance other possibilities, a real problem when faced with non-Western intellectual traditions (Alberti & Marshall 2009). They are, in fact, further examples of foundationalist thinking (see also Henare et al.'s [2007, 6–7] critique of Latour's ontology). Now, we argue, archaeologists are both taking ontology as a tool to challenge such overarching ontologies (Alberti & Marshall 2009; Alberti in Alberti et al. 2011) and are attempting to reconstruct more accurately the "world as it really is." That is, an ontological focus can bring with it the search for a new, better metaphysics (e.g., Witmore in Alberti et al. 2011; Ingold 2011), a new conceptual production on the basis of the search for alterity, and the recognition of some kind of material agency or vibrancy (Alberti et al. 2011). The question remains whether any of these approaches actually escapes the assumption of an underlying meta-ontology.

The shift to questions of ontology in archaeology follows a path inspired by Bruno Latour's critique of the "wholesale conversion of ontological questions into epistemological ones" in *We Have Never*

Been Modern (1993). Other influential authors such as Viveiros de Castro echo Latour's concerns, adding to it an informed anthropological critique. In archaeology, papers and position statements in Alberti and Bray's edited volume (2009) and Alberti et al.'s dialogue (2011), as well as recent book-length treatments (Olsen 2010; Lucas 2012), have opened the way for an explicit disciplinary conversation on the merits of ontologically oriented inquiry. Thinking ontologically, as opposed to epistemologically, is shorthand for leaving no stone unturned. The interpretive dilemmas presented by the debate between processual and post-processual archaeologies, as well as the critique of post-processualism, are mostly based on explicitly epistemological grounds: Who has the correct interpretation of the archaeological record? Can we be fully objective or are we doomed to subjective ambivalence in our storytelling? These may not always be the most salient questions for archaeology, and they may fail to grasp the possibilities that the material residue of the past entails for productive new "past-presents." The move to ontological questions is, then, about not presupposing a given ontology, substantivist or relational. Focusing on ontology as a varied thing opens up the possibility for new things to emerge (Alberti et al. 2011; Lucas 2012, 168; Lucas, in this volume).

The focus on ontology stresses the relational rather than essential constitution of the world, which brings us back to how archaeologists are thinking about materials in a fundamentally new way. What appears to be primary to the new ontological focus on materials in archaeology is the idea that there are properties unactualized in matter. Materials are no longer quantifiable in terms of a list of inherent properties based on which social actors add, extract, or interpret meaning. Rather, any property is only present when actualized through specific relations. Archaeologists seem to take this assertion more or less literally. Some, like Conneller (2011) and Lucas (2012), argue for a notion of matter as containing unactualized potential. Lucas (2012, 167) describes this notion as objects "holding something in reserve" (see also Harman 2009). Hodder (2012, 48–50) leans more on Gibson's notion of affordances—the properties of materials that enable some outcomes. Alberti and Marshall (2009), based on feminist philosopher and physicist Karen Barad, articulate a more radical notion in which all properties are properties of things-in-relation, not of things themselves (see Fowler 2013; Marshall & Alberti 2014). As such, it is not possible for properties to be inherent or even potential.

The focus on ontology may be the dividing line between the approach we are promoting in this book and other similar projects, such as Hodder's recent *Entangled* (2012). The move back to materials is controversial, as we see in the response to Ingold's 2007 article, because it becomes very difficult to conceptualize the line between materials and simple physicality (as something shorn of meaning). Hodder's entanglements fail, ultimately, to account for the social in the same breath as the material because they don't show convincingly how meanings emerge from or are connected to material entanglements. Lucas (2012) is perhaps more successful in coming up with a set of terms that mobilize the relationship between materials, although the question remains: Are all abstractions to be done away with? We hope that the contributions to this volume go some way towards developing ways to think about that relationship. In the following section we outline how this might be accomplished by reconsidering the significance of this relational approach for contextual archaeology.

FROM CONTEXTUAL ARCHAEOLOGY TO AN ARCHAEOLOGY OF ASSEMBLAGES

In this section we will examine two quintessentially archaeological terms: context and assemblage. We will argue for a shift in emphasis away from context and toward assemblage. We will examine the distinctions between these terms below. One of the ways in which post-processual archaeologists sought to examine meaning was through a definition of archaeological context. Contexts were established as a mechanism for building up an understanding of meaning. As Hodder (1992, 128) argues, "In beginning to systematize the methodology for interpreting past meaning content from material culture, it seems that archaeologists work by identifying various types of relevant similarities and differences, and that these are built up into various types of contextual associations." Hodder's systematic analysis of context utilizes the similarities and differences in association to define meaning.

This need not be the only definition of context (see McFadyen, in this volume). Of course, we need to remember that contexts may simply relate to a set of relationships. Barrett and Kinnes (1988, 1) argue, quite simply, for an "archaeology of context" that attends to the details of material conditions; it is from a detailed appreciation of these material contexts that an understanding of the past will arise. We can take this observation further to consider a relational archaeology of context. If we assume that material contexts provide the means to understand the past, it is because these contexts articulate together to give us knowledge of the past. Understanding, therefore, arises from looking at how multiple material contexts articulate. We can consider contexts either in terms of similarities and differences—the contextual associations discussed by Hodder—or as the material conditions discussed by Barrett and Kinnes. The notion of context is, of course, useful and one we do not seek to abandon or reject. Instead, we wish to place emphasis on another equally useful term: assemblage.

Assemblages are curious entities, and differ substantially from contexts. Drawing on the philosophy of Deleuze and Guattari, Wise (2011) remarks on the peculiar character of assemblages. Using archaeological examples, he explains:

> These examples illustrate that an assemblage is a collection of heterogeneous elements, but what is especially important is the relation between the elements. These elements could be diverse *things* brought together in particular relations, such as the detritus of everyday life unearthed in an archaeological dig: bowls, cups, bones, tile, figurines and so on. This collection of things and their relations express something, a particular character: Etruscaness, for example. But the elements that make up an assemblage also include the *qualities* present (large, poisonous, fine, blinding etc.) and the affects and effectivity of the assemblage: that is, not just what it *is*, but what it can *do*. (Wise 2011, 92, original emphases)

We have shifted our understanding here from contexts that frame meaning to assemblages that actively produce meaning and affect. We can chart this changing perspective by considering Hodder's use of the terms "similarities and differences" as a device for understanding contextual meaning. These terms carry a resonance, since they are of signal importance in the philosophy of both Jacques Derrida and Gilles Deleuze. Hodder (1992) utilizes the terms as a means of tying down or fixing archaeological meaning through an analysis of contextual associations; however, he recognizes that Derrida's work radically questions the fixity of meaning (Hodder 1992, 179), a position also acknowledged by Yates (1990). Derrida's work was especially concerned with context; an understanding of context is fundamental to his analysis of deconstruction. For Derrida no meaning can be determined out of context, but no context permits saturation of meaning (Derrida 1988, 136). In order for meanings to be understood they require contexts, but in so doing that meaning must be able to escape its context. In the archaeological field, then, we cannot consider contexts purely as static frames or containers for meaning, we also have to acknowledge that contexts are active participants in the generation of meanings (Jones 2007, 78–81; Lucas 2012). Derrida's work captures the sense of a movement of meaning, which is also encapsulated in Gilles Deleuze's deployment of the terms "difference and repetition." Deleuze (1994) considers difference as "difference from the same" or difference from the same over time: difference as the variation between two states. Like Derrida, he is concerned to overturn the primacy given to identity and representation in Western thought by theorizing difference as experienced; this marks a shift from attempting to grasp the essential "identity" of an entity toward emphasizing how entities change over time, how they differ and become. Rather than looking at static contexts that frame meaning, the aim is to examine the changing properties of things as they are articulated in ever-changing assemblages and configurations; the emphasis is on the process of becoming, and on the immanent and open-ended nature of the world (DeLanda 1999; Grosz 1999; Conneller 2011; see also Barad 2007). There are important differences between Derrida's discussion of difference in terms of context and Deleuze's discussion of difference in his development of the notion of assemblage. Whereas Derrida's project is concerned with understanding difference as a system of organization that makes signification possible, Deleuze is less interested in what he describes as "managing" difference and more concerned with the "dramatization" of difference—with understanding how things are differentiated and change. Whereas an analysis of context focuses on the displacements of meaning that occur in placing things in context, an analysis of assemblage focuses on how things are composed or assembled. If the notion of context concentrates on arrangement and organization, the notion of assemblage relates to the arranging, organizing, and fitting together of heterogeneous components.

In archaeology, Lucas (2012, 193–214) has recently examined and reworked the notion of assemblage through a series of contrasting terms. He is at pains to make this assemblage archaeological: he draws on the two received meanings of assemblage in archaeology—depositional and typological—in order to capture something of the dynamism and durability of archaeological entities. The outcome is entities in constant flux, assembling and disassembling, materializing and dematerializing, in an open-ended ontology that refuses a distinction between entities on the basis of a putative distinction between material and ideal. We have arrived then at a completely different conception of the role of the archaeologist. Rather than interpreting the meaning of the artifacts they excavate through contextual analysis, archaeologists shape and compose the assemblages that they excavate; through this process of composition, interpretation and evaluation arises (Lucas 2012; see also Fowler 2013). We have shifted then from a conception of archaeological interpretation as a largely cognitive or cerebral endeavor to a recognition of the physical and material aspects of archaeological interpretation. Archaeologists are not cognitively distinct from the archaeological record; rather, they actively assemble that record. Here we do not wish to simply suggest that archaeologists construct the past: archaeologists are situated within the changing assemblage, and they are only part of what gives it its shape (see also Fowler 2013).

In many ways this perspective closely resembles the process described by the science studies scholar Karen Barad (2007) as "agential realism." Barad notes that there are no unambiguous ways of differentiating between the "object" and "agencies of observation." There is no prior distinction that can be made between objects and the methods we use to observe them; we cannot describe the world without acting on it and shaping it. Although Barad's analysis uses the example of particle physics, it could equally apply to the archaeologist shaping the archaeological record through excavation (see Marshall & Alberti 2014).

CONCLUSIONS

So far we have suggested a shift from the epistemological concept of context, concerned with defining the meaning of artifacts in specific archaeological settings, to the ontological concept of assemblage, concerned with examining the changing character and affect of materials as they shift from one grouping and set of relationships to another. The move "beyond" the interpreting subject we have charted here is not the same as the infamous death of the subject as proclaimed by Foucault. Questioning ontological foundations is a way to take a step back, to inquire about the constitution of the subject before it has emerged. It is not a matter of refusing its existence; rather, it means questioning the conditions of emergence of a specific subjectivity, humanity, in the past and present. Much like Fowler's (2004) insistence on the relational underpinnings of personhood, the posthumanism of recent work is not about ignoring the subject. We are perfectly entitled to focus on the human as our subject of inquiry, as long as we do not assume the human to be central to or play an exceptional role in our ontologies or our theories of the world.

And this begs the question of reflexivity: What is the role of the archaeologist in these archaeological entanglements? Our current concern is to understand the archaeologists' responsibility as productive parts of assemblages (or actants, phenomena, etc.) that are in themselves ontologically generative. Reflexivity becomes less a question of recognizing the cultural bias or partiality of the observer, and more of understanding the productive nature of our involvement at the level of "reality." As Niels Bohr put it, "we are part of that nature we seek to understand" (in Barad 2007, 26). Here the crossover between what we imagine to have been the experience of past peoples and what we do as archaeologists is most obvious. This has implications for the way we conceive of the archaeological project, our fieldwork, and the broader conceptualization of our research. This concern is as much a part of writing and fieldwork as it is of interpretation and theory building. And the answer is the same in both cases: if we are indeed arguing that we understand materials as significant in their own right, without reference to human exceptionalism, then it follows that the archaeological process itself must be equivalent to the means of intervention in the world undertaken by past peoples. This is the case whether we are speaking of the need to "ontologically suture" the gap between methodological and interpretive concepts (Lucas 2012, 5) or arguing for a radical procedural equivalence between the theories we deploy and the worlds we produce (Alberti et al. 2011, 905). Thus, Lucas (2012, 16) argues that learning to see archaeological features is an ontological act; and Conneller (2011) makes the point that qualities are possibilities that only emerge as such—for us and for the material—through the ontologically productive mediation of technology (see also Barad 2007).

We are not so much promoting a new position as gathering and helping to crystallize work that exemplifies the current state of archaeological theory. As we emphasized at the beginning of this introduction, the types of questions asked, analyses undertaken, and methodological assumptions adopted by archaeologists are now firmly rooted in an intellectual tradition that shares the concerns of post-processual, feminist, and interpretive archaeologies. There is an important change, which has not to do simply with the importation of a whole new set of theorists and ideas into archaeology. Rather, it has to do with the diffractive effect of returning to similar sources but with new sight, new questions, and hence new possibilities.

The key themes discussed above crosscut the contributions to this volume in true rhizomic fashion. In what follows, contributors address: the importance of questioning ontological assumptions and the utility of thinking relationally about such ontologies (Part I, Relational Ontologies); the importance of materials and how we work with them (Part II, Working with Materials); the ways in which the social is put together in a post-humanocentric archaeology (Part III, Assembling the Social); and the way we talk about representation once we have refused the representational premise of an ontological gap between meaning and matter (Part IV, Beyond Representation). Because of the ontological and material character of our discussion, it is particularly important that the contributors to this volume present their arguments using well-developed case studies as opposed to abstract theoretical statements. Each section, therefore, includes contributions that discuss a particular issue through specific material examples.

In ending, we stress that we do not expect *Archaeology after Interpretation* to be programmatic. In the spirit of becoming, we expect our positions to radically change in the future, just as we anticipate our arguments and materials to be taken up and assembled in novel ways.

REFERENCES

Alberti, B. 2001. Faience goddesses and ivory bull-leapers: the aesthetics of sexual difference at Late Bronze Age Knossos. *World Archaeology* 33(2), 189–205

Alberti, B. & Bray, T. 2009. Introduction. Special section "Animating Archaeology: of Subjects, Objects and Alternative Ontologies." *Cambridge Archaeological Journal* 19(3), 337–43

Alberti, B., Fowles, S., Holbraad, M., Marshall, Y. & Witmore, C.L. 2011. "Worlds Otherwise": archaeology, anthropology and ontological difference. *Current Anthropology* 52(6), 896–912

Alberti, B. & Marshall, Y. 2009. Animating archaeology: local theories and conceptually open-ended methodologies. *Cambridge Archaeological Journal* 19(3), 344–56

Anderson, B. & Harrison, P. 2010. The promise of non-representational theories. In B. Anderson & P. Harrison (eds.), *Taking Place: Non-Representational Theories and Geography*, 1–36. Farnham, UK: Ashgate

Barad, K. 2007. *Meeting the Universe Halfway: Quantum Physics and the Entanglement of Matter and Meaning*. Durham, NC: Duke University Press

Barrett, J.C. & Kinnes, I.A. 1988. Introduction. In J.C. Barrett & I.A. Kinnes (eds.), *The Archaeology of Context in the Neolithic and Bronze Age: Recent Trends*, 1. Sheffield, UK: Department of Archaeology & Prehistory Monographs, University of Sheffield

Bennett, J. 2001. *The Enchantment of Modern Life*. Durham, NC: Duke University Press

Bennett, J. 2010. *Vibrant Matter*. Durham, NC: Duke University Press

Bergson, H. 1999. *An Introduction to Metaphysics*. Indianapolis, IN: Hackett Publishing Co.

Bintliff, J. & Pearce, M. (eds.) 2012. *The Death of Archaeological Theory?* Oxford, UK: Oxbow Books

Boivin, N. 2008. *Material Culture, Material Minds*. Cambridge: Cambridge University Press

Butler, J. 1990. *Gender Trouble*. London: Routledge

Butler, J. 1993. *Bodies that Matter*. London: Routledge

Conneller, C. 2011. *An Archaeology of Materials: Substantial Transformations in Early Prehistoric Europe*. London: Routledge

Deetz, J. 1977. *In Small Things Forgotten: The Archaeology of Early American Life*. New York: Anchor

DeLanda, M. 1999. Deleuze, diagrams, and the open-ended becoming of the world. In E. Grosz (ed.), *Becomings: Explorations in Time, Memory, and Futures*, 29–41. Ithaca, NY: Cornell University Press

Deleuze, G. 1994. *Difference and Repetition*. Translated by P. Patton. London: Continuum

Deleuze, G. & Guattari, F. 1987. *A Thousand Plateaus: Capitalism and Schizophrenia II*. Translated by B. Massumi. London: Continuum

Derrida, J. 1988. *Limited, Inc.* Evanston, IL: Northwestern University Press

Dobres, M.-A. & Robb, J. 2000. *Agency in Archaeology*. London: Routledge

Edgeworth, M. 2012. Follow the cut, follow the rhythm, follow the material. *Norwegian Archaeological Review* 45(1), 76–92

Foucault, M. 1972. *The Archaeology of Knowledge*. Translated by A. Sheridan. London: Routledge

Foucault, M. 1981. The order of discourse. In R. Young (ed.), *Untying the Text: A Post-Structuralist Reader*, 48–79. London: Routledge

Fowler, C. 2004. *The Archaeology of Personhood*. London: Routledge

Fowler, C. 2010. Relational personhood as a subject of anthropology and archaeology: comparative and complementary analyses. In D. Garrow & T. Yarrow (eds.),

Archaeology and Anthropology: Understanding Similarity, Exploring Difference, 137–59. Oxford, UK: Oxbow Books

Fowler, C. 2013. *The Emergent Past: A Relational Realist Archaeology of Early Bronze Age Mortuary Practices*. Oxford: Oxford University Press

Fuglestvedt, I. 2009. *Phenomenology and the Pioneer Settlement on the Western Scandinavian Peninsula*. Lindome, Swed.: Bricoleur Press

Gardiner, A. (ed.) 2004. *Agency Uncovered: Archaeological Perspectives on Social Agency, Power and Being Human*. London: UCL Press

Garrow, D. & Gosden, C. 2012. *Technologies of Enchantment: Exploring Celtic Art 400 BC to AD 100*. Oxford: Oxford University Press

Gell, A. 1998. *Art and Agency: An Anthropological Theory*. Oxford, UK: Clarendon Press

Gosden, C. 1994. *Social Being and Time*. Oxford, UK: Blackwell

Greenhough, B. 2010. Vitalist geographies: life and the more-than-human. In B. Anderson & P. Harrison (eds.), *Taking Place: Non-Representational Theories and Geography*, 37–54. Farnham, UK: Ashgate

Grosz, E. 1999. Thinking the new: of futures yet unthought. In E. Grosz (ed.), *Becomings: Explorations in Time, Memory, and Futures*, 15–28. Ithaca, NY: Cornell University Press

Haraway, D. 2008. *When Species Meet*. Minneapolis: University of Minnesota Press

Harman, G. 2009. *Prince of Networks: Bruno Latour and Metaphysics*. Melbourne, Aus.: Re.press

Henare, A., Holbraad, M. & Wastell, S. (eds.) 2007. *Thinking Through Things: Theorising Artefacts Ethnographically*. London: Routledge

Hodder, I. (ed.) 1982. *Symbolic and Structural Archaeology*. Cambridge: Cambridge University Press

Hodder, I. 1986. *Reading the Past*. Cambridge: Cambridge University Press

Hodder, I. (ed.) 1989. *The Meaning of Things: Material Culture and Symbolic Expression*. London: Unwin Hyman

Hodder, I. 1992. *Theory and Practice in Archaeology*. London: Routledge

Hodder, I. 1999. *The Archaeological Process*. Oxford, UK: Blackwell

Hodder, I. 2012. *Entangled: An Archaeology of the Relationships between Humans and Things*. Oxford, UK: Wiley-Blackwell

Ingold, T. 2000. *The Perception of the Environment: Essays in Livelihood, Dwelling and Skill*. London: Routledge

Ingold, T. 2007. Materials against materiality. *Archaeological Dialogues* 14(1), 1–16

Ingold, T. 2011. *Being Alive: Essays on Movement, Knowledge and Description*. London: Routledge

Ingold, T. 2012. Toward an ecology of materials. *Annual Review of Anthropology* 41, 427–42

Jones, A. 2002. *Archaeological Theory and Scientific Practice*. Cambridge: Cambridge University Press

Jones, A. 2004. Archaeometry and materiality: materials-based analysis in theory and practice. *Archaeometry* 46, 327–38

Jones, A. 2007. *Memory and Material Culture*. Cambridge: Cambridge University Press

Jones, A.M. 2012. *Prehistoric Materialities: Becoming Material in Prehistoric Britain and Ireland*. Oxford: Oxford University Press

Joyce, R. 2000. *Gender and Power in Prehispanic Mesoamerica*. Austin: University of Texas Press

Knappett, C. 2005. *Thinking through Material Culture*. Philadelphia: University of Pennsylvania Press

Knappett, C. & Malafouris, L. (eds.) 2007. *Material Agency: Towards a Non-Anthropocentric Approach*. New York: Springer

Latour, B. 1993. *We Have Never Been Modern*. Harvard: Harvard University Press

Lucas, G. 2012. *Understanding the Archaeological Record*. Cambridge: Cambridge University Press

Marshall, Y. & Alberti, B. 2014. A matter of difference: Karen Barad, ontology and archaeological bodies. *Cambridge Archaeological Journal* (forthcoming)

Meskell, L. 1996. The somatization of archaeology: institutions, discourses, corporeality. *Norwegian Archaeological Review* 29(1), 1–16

Miller, D. 1987. *Material Culture and Mass Consumption*. Oxford, UK: Blackwell

Miller, D. & Tilley, C. (eds.) 1984. *Ideology, Power and Prehistory*. Cambridge: Cambridge University Press

Olsen, B. 2003. Material culture after text: re-membering things. *Norwegian Archaeological Review* 36(2), 87–104

Olsen, B. 2007. Keeping things at arms length: a genealogy of asymmetry. *World Archaeology* 39(4), 579–88

Olsen, B. 2010. *In Defense of Things: Archaeology and the Ontology of Objects*. Walnut Creek, CA: AltaMira Press

Olsen, B. 2012. Symmetrical archaeology. In I. Hodder (ed.), *Archaeological Theory Today*. Second edition, 208–28. Cambridge, UK: Polity Press

Preucel, R. 2006. *Archaeological Semiotics*. Malden, MA: Wiley-Blackwell

Robb, J. 1999. Secret agents: culture, economy, and social reproduction. In J. Robb (ed.), *Material Symbols: Culture and Economy in Prehistory*, 3–15. Carbondale, IL: Center for Archaeological Investigations, Southern Illinois University. Occasional Paper 26

Robb, J. 2005. The extended artefact and the monumental economy. In E. DeMarrais, A. Renfrew & C. Gosden (eds.), *Rethinking Materiality: The Engagement of Mind with the Material World*, 131–39. Cambridge, UK: McDonald Institute for Archaeological Research

Rose, M. 2011. Secular materialism: a critique of earthly theory. *Journal of Material Culture* 16(2), 107–29

Schiffer, M. 1999. *The Material Life of Human Beings: Artifacts, Behaviour and Communication*. London: Routledge

Shanks, M. 1992. *Experiencing the Past*. London: Routledge

Shanks, M. & Hodder, I. 1995. Processual, postprocessual and interpretative archaeologies. In I. Hodder, M. Shanks, A. Alexandri, V. Buchli, J. Carman, J. Last & G. Lucas (eds.), *Interpreting Archaeology: Finding Meaning in the Past*, 3–29. London: Routledge

Shanks, M. & Tilley, C. 1987a. *Reconstructing Archaeology*. Cambridge: Cambridge University Press

Shanks, M. & Tilley, C. 1987b. *Social Theory and Archaeology*. Cambridge, UK: Polity Press

Thomas, J. 1996. *Time, Culture and Identity: An Interpretative Archaeology*. London: Routledge

Thomas, J. (ed.) 2000. *Interpretative Archaeology: A Reader*. Leicester, UK: Leicester University Press

Thomas, J. 2002. Archaeology's humanism and the materiality of the body. In Y. Hamilakis, M. Pluciennik & S. Tarlow (eds.), *Thinking through the Body: Archaeologies of Corporeality*, 29–45. New York: Kluwer Academic/Plenum Press

Thomas, J. 2004. *Archaeology and Modernity*. London: Routledge

Thomas, J. 2008. Archaeology, landscape, and dwelling. In B. David & J. Thomas (eds.), *Handbook of Landscape Archaeology*, 300–6. Walnut Creek, CA: Left Coast Press

Tilley, C. 1990. *Reading Material Culture*. Oxford, UK: Blackwell

Tilley, C. 1993. Interpretation and a poetics of the past. In C. Tilley (ed.), *Interpretative Archaeology*, 1–30. Oxford, UK: Berg

Tilley, C. 1994. *A Phenomenology of Landscape*. Oxford, UK: Berg

Tilley, C. 1999. *Metaphor and Material Culture*. Oxford, UK: Blackwell

Tilley, C. 2004. *The Materiality of Stone: Explorations in Landscape Phenomenology*. Oxford, UK: Berg

Whatmore, S. 2008. *Hybrid Geographies: Natures, Cultures, Spaces*. London: Sage

Wise, J.M. 2011. Assemblage. In C.J. Stivale (ed.), *Gilles Deleuze: Key Concepts*, 91–102. Durham, NC: Acumen

Witmore, C.L. 2007. Symmetrical archaeology: excerpts of a manifesto. *World Archaeology* 39(4), 546–62

Yates, T. 1990. Jacques Derrida: "There is nothing outside of the text." In C. Tilley (ed.), *Reading Material Culture*, 206–80. Oxford, UK: Blackwell

PART I
Relational Ontologies

Benjamin Alberti

Understanding the fundamental questions in archaeology as ontological questions is a hallmark of the approaches adopted by the authors in this volume. They operate from the position that understanding materials, practices, and interpretation implies questioning ontological assumptions. The chapters in this section make evident the difference that grappling with ontological questions can make in archaeology from several different perspectives. There are quite different ways to understand ontology in archaeology, depending on what the author wishes to achieve. Incorporating ontology into an approach can improve interpretations of past ways of life (**Robinson**), refine methodologies and practices (**Haber, Laguens**), or challenge archaeological concepts (**Alberti**). "Relational ontologies" is a catchall for ontological theories that challenge the atomism of modern substance ontologies. As such, much recent scholarship that addresses archaeological questions from an ontological perspective takes ontology to be open-ended (thus plural) and in constant processes of flux, and it considers relational rather than essential entities to be primary. Major differences in explicitly ontological work in archaeology can be traced. Some authors are interested in providing a better understanding of how the world is actually constituted (e.g., Conneller 2011; Olsen et al. 2012); others do not look for general theories but rather want to provoke novel realities or ontologies to emerge from the material (e.g., Alberti & Marshall 2009). There are authors who work at a conceptual level and those for whom the question of ontology is a crucial political issue of the present time that must be understood in the context of everyday experience, practice, and negotiation (Alberti et al. 2011).

Approaches that search for an improved metaphysics and a better grasp of ontological processes draw from existing trends in Western philosophies, represented by thinkers such as Bruno Latour, Alfred Whitehead, and John Law. They recognize that archaeological entities are ontological by nature and therefore productive of reality; they do not simply aim at coherence with an external reality. Work in this vein includes the symmetrical archaeology approach, which is concerned with founding the analysis on an essential ontological unity between domains usually separated by the presumptions of modernity, such as human and nonhuman or social and material (e.g., Witmore 2007; Olsen et al. 2012). The focus here is on archaeological entities and fieldwork practices in which all possible elements of the process must be understood as active and creative. Working closely with these questions, in his chapter **Laguens** argues that the descriptive language of archaeological entities and the conceptualization of fundamental notions that allow the material to be translated through interpretation lag uncomfortably behind recent thinking on the constitution of social life and materiality. If relational ontologies are posited as able to get at the processes that constitute materials and past societies, then we require a concept of material matrices that is far more complex and better able to grasp the multiple, heterogeneous, fluid, and relational nature of the archaeological context.

Ontological difference as alterity—the constantly shifting terrain of things that do not make sense to us (Holbraad in Alberti et al. 2011, 902)—offers the opportunity for other archaeologists to fundamentally challenge any claim to a singular set of processes or generalized theory. In such approaches, anthropological theory, Western philosophies, and the practices and thoughts of scientists and Indigenous peoples are treated with parity (Alberti & Marshall 2009; Haber 2009). A central tenet is that we must take seriously the claims and practices of peoples who appear to be thinking and acting in nonsensical ways. From an ontological and conceptual perspective, "to take seriously" means to accept at a fundamental level the truth of a claim and to doggedly follow its consequences (see Henare et al. 2007). In this volume, **Alberti** is concerned with using ontological difference as a tool to theorize archaeological material and challenge the meaning of general concepts in a particular case. Alberti reworks the concept of scale in an archaeological case study of first-millennium AD anthropo- and zoomorphic ceramic pots in northwestern Argentina in relation to miniaturization. Through a reading of the theory of perspectivism developed on the basis of Amazonian ethnographies, Alberti argues that the conventional understanding of scale as dependent on a default and self-evident human biological body is challenged when perspectivist notions of bodies are introduced. In this case, bodies are measured on the basis of their visibility/invisibility in relation to a soul. The play of figure and ground that this constant relationship (i.e., the measure of scale) produces is signaled through the relative intensity of the body. Although the body stays relatively constant (it is always recognizably human), its size can change radically. It is more or less of a body depending on the degree of intensity—brilliance, adornments, excess, monstrosity, and so on. Alberti argues that the scale of the pots is not a function of size, but of the intensity of their markings and grotesque forms.

Other ontologically oriented research is marked by the use of Indigenous concepts that hold an ontological valence and seem to fit the archaeological material, yielding improved interpretations. Animism, as a catchall for non-Western relational ontologies, has been a popular term for unifying a series of beliefs and practices that can be recognized archaeologically (e.g., Brown & Walker 2008; Alberti & Bray 2009; Harrison-Buck 2012). Such work, though, often lacks the specificity that comes from the analysis of a particular concept and of its possible use in archaeology (however, see Bray 2009; Haber 2009; Wilkinson 2013). In a case study that makes use of Indigenous concepts that seem to better explain elements of the archaeological record, **Robinson** develops the notions of "transmorphism of being" and "correspondence" to interpret the Chumash pictographs of south-central California. Robinson is critical of the tendencies to read archaeological material in unselfconsciously Western terms, most clearly illustrated by the de-historicizing effect of imposing psycho-cognitive shamanic models on the art. The ontological shift in focus for Robinson is about allowing us to better explain the art from an Indigenous perspective and to understand the social rather than purely cognitive significance of rock art. Guided by these key notions, Robinson demonstrates that the rock art was driven by the ontological premise that humans can affect what in conventional Western terms might be considered as fixed relationships. Ultimately, Robinson shows that the ontology of the Chumash explains the relationships established in rock art not just in terms of representation, as in a document, but as agentive relationships meant to bring about change through the combination of substances with transformative potential.

In his chapter, **Haber** develops the politics that comes from working with ontological questions in archaeology and explores the consequences for archaeological thought and practice of such an engagement between ontologies. It is not sufficient to work at a purely conceptual level, his work shows, as an ontological approaches encompasses us as "dwellers" in the world and not merely as isolated "knowers." His work refuses the structures of authority and canons of archaeological representation because when one thinks ontologically, nothing less than total commitment to that position will reduce the inherently colonial nature of the archaeological enterprise. Haber works from the assumption—learned during his study among the Andean community of Antofagasta de la Sierra—that the researcher is not outside of the relationships in which he works. This is a key moment in the turn to an ontological approach: the recognition of a fundamental equivalence between what we theorize and how we live and practice archaeology. This gives Haber's project a relevance for the local community that would be missing from a conventional account, which might simply collude in the reproduction of relations of domination. The chapter is centered on the contrast between an historical Indigenous mining settlement and the practice of contemporary multinationals, a contrast in which distinct ways of living reveal distinct ontological commitments. However, his account does not simply reiterate the premises of the relational ontologies that underlie local peoples' commitments to land, practices, and archaeological materials. Rather, he argues for the necessity to occupy the borderland, a place on the move from where to practice an archaeology that is no longer simply a search for disinterested knowledge; a place where knowing is transformed as multiple subjectivities become agentive, reducing the importance of the role of author in these "conversations across ontologies."

The different objectives of these ontological approaches to archaeology convey different understandings of what ontology means. Technical definitions are all but absent in the archaeological literature, a trend continued in this volume where none of the chapters offers more than a passing definition. Inquiring into the nature of "what is" from a philosophical perspective is clearly not the goal. Careful definitions may not be what are needed, though they might help clarify the differences among approaches. The lack of definitional specificity spills over into other terminological issues, such as the use of "world," "reality," and "ontology" as synonyms in some accounts.

The question of whether we are dealing with a singular world or plural worlds, a single ontology or multiple ontologies, has shadowed the debate about ontologies in archaeology (Alberti et al. 2011; Harris & Robb 2012). There are weaker and stronger claims regarding how much "reality" we share and how much is subsumed within general processes of becoming that nonetheless have the potential to generate distinct realities or ontologies. Some authors argue that there is a material common ground—one world—that forms the basis of all our arguments. Garrow and Gosden's (2012) concept of "social ontologies" does not challenge the fundamental constitution of a singular world or reality. These authors understand ontologies as the manner in which societies in the past understand the nature of the world: different cultural engagements with "the multiplicity of the universe . . . [highlight and render] differing aspects of the world" (ibid., 22). Matter itself is singular; it becomes apparent to people in different ways depending on how they engage with it through practice and skilled action. Harris and Robb (2012) argue for an understanding of ontologies as multiple and suggest that contradiction can operate within a single cultural context or even a single person. In their example, bodies are ontologically multimodal, their various modes coexisting alongside one another. People are able to experience their bodies in accordance with these differing modes at different times.

Others insist that arguing for a single world undermines the legitimacy of worlds that do not conform to the modern, Western model of matter (Alberti et al. 2011). Yet others challenge the idea of a singular world on the basis of current theoretical approaches in the hard sciences and philosophy, such as the work of Karen Barad, and by drawing on Indigenous ontologies (Alberti & Marshall 2009; Jones 2012; Fowler 2013; Marshall & Alberti 2014).

Each chapter in this section demonstrates the potential for archaeology of a focus on ontological questions, be it by employing Indigenous ontologies as a source for alternative concepts to better interpret art or ceramics (**Robinson, Alberti**) or by reconceptualizing context and relationships in archaeological fieldwork (**Laguens**). Finally, as Haber pushes us to concede, our very knowledge practices and the position of archaeology in relation to the materials and peoples studied are changed if we take seriously the generative nature of relationships when understood as ontological. As archaeologists, we do not simply interpret and represent the world. Rather, the world is a coproduction of all its constituents: material, conceptual, human, nonhuman, animal, and so on. How we integrate our various influences and theoretical approaches—more satisfying philosophies, accounts from the hard sciences, or Indigenous thought—without collapsing one into another will be crucial to ongoing work in this area.

REFERENCES

Alberti, B. & Bray, T. 2009. Animating archaeology: of subjects, objects and alternative ontologies. *Cambridge Archaeological Journal* 19(3), 337–43

Alberti, B., Fowles, S., Holbraad, M., Marshall, Y. & Witmore, C.L. 2011. "Worlds otherwise": archaeology, anthropology and ontological difference. *Current Anthropology* 52(6), 896–912

Alberti, B. & Marshall, Y. 2009. Animating archaeology: local theories and conceptually open-ended methodologies. *Cambridge Archaeological Journal* 19(3), 344–56

Bray, T. 2009. An archaeological perspective on the Andean concept of *Camaquen*: thinking through Late Pre-Columbian *Ofrendas* and *Huacas*. *Cambridge Archaeological Journal* 19(3), 357–66

Brown, L.A. & Walker, W.H. 2008. Prologue: archaeology, animism and non-human agents. *Journal of Archaeological Method and Theory* 15(4), 297–99

Conneller, C. 2011. *An Archaeology of Materials: Substantial Transformations in Early Prehistoric Europe*. London: Routledge

Fowler, C. 2013. *The Emergent Past: A Relational Realist Archaeology of Early Bronze Age Mortuary Practices*. Oxford: Oxford University Press

Garrow, D. & Gosden, C. 2012. *Technologies of Enchantment: Exploring Celtic Art 400 BC to AD 100*. Oxford: Oxford University Press

Haber, A. 2009. Animism, relatedness, life: post-Western perspectives. *Cambridge Archaeological Journal* 19(3), 418–30

Harris, O.J.T. & Robb, J. 2012. Multiple ontologies and the problem of the body in history. *American Anthropologist* 114(4), 668–79

Harrison-Buck, E. 2012. Architecture as animate landscape: circular shrines in the ancient Maya lowlands. *American Anthropologist* 114(1), 64–80

Henare, A., Holbraad, M. & Wastell, S. 2007. Introduction: thinking through things. In A. Henare, M. Holbraad & S. Wastell (eds.), *Thinking Through Things: Theorising Artefacts Ethnographically*, 1–31. London: Routledge

Jones, A.M. 2012. *Prehistoric Materialities: Becoming Material in Prehistoric Britain and Ireland*. Oxford: Oxford University Press

Marshall, Y. & Alberti, B. 2014. A matter of difference: Karen Barad, ontology and archaeological bodies. *Cambridge Archaeological Journal* (forthcoming)

Olsen, B., Shanks, M., Webmoor, T. & Witmore, C. 2012. *Archaeology: The Discipline of Things*. Berkeley: University of California Press

Wilkinson, D. 2013. The emperor's new body: ontology and the Inka sovereign. *Cambridge Archaeological Journal* 23 (forthcoming)

Witmore, C.L. 2007. Symmetrical archaeology: excerpts of a manifesto. *World Archaeology* 39(4), 546–62

CHAPTER TWO

Archaeology and Ontologies of Scale: The Case of Miniaturization in First-Millennium Northwest Argentina

Benjamin Alberti

ENCOUNTERING MINIATURES, STUMBLING ACROSS ANALOGIES

In the spring of 2011, while tracking down old sites excavated by Osvaldo Heredia in the 1960s in Northwest Argentina, my Argentinean colleagues and I were shown objects that had been found in burial urns on local properties. Included were two "miniature" vessels and a beautifully polished, miniature stone axe with its distinctive three-sided collar (see Figure 2.1).

Figure 2.1   Miniature pots collected by locals near La Candelaria locality

Archaeology after Interpretation: Returning Materials to Archaeological Theory, edited by Benjamin Alberti, Andrew Meirion Jones, and Joshua Pollard, 43–58. ©2013 Left Coast Press, Inc. All rights reserved.

Miniature objects of this kind are common archaeological finds. Interpretation has proven a challenge, but it usually focuses on ritual activities, such as grave offerings or sympathetic magic, where something of the power of the original is captured by the miniature, as in the case of architectural models widespread in pre-Hispanic South America (e.g., Moseley 2001; Moore & Mackey 2008). The size of the object is often related to the person it accompanies in a burial, so that miniature objects are assumed to accompany children or infants. I want to think about these objects in a different way, one that reorients our concept of miniaturization. Here is something suggestive to start with. In her account of the Indigenous northwestern Amazonian Wari', Beth Conklin (2001, 135) writes:

> When dissociated from their bodies, people's spirits are apt to wander off to the forest, where they may be captured by a sorcerer. . . . Sorcerers can capture someone's spirit only when it leaves its body in a dream, and they attract their victims by manipulating individuals' selfish desires. To lure a spirit into the forest, the sorcerer builds a miniature traditional bed (*tapit*) and a small palm screen upon which he hangs attractive gifts of meat, fish, honey, and other tempting foods and miniature objects. If he wants to capture a man's spirit, the sorcerer also offers bows and arrows and, these days, cigarettes and shotgun shells. If he wants to capture a female spirit, he might add baskets, cooking pots, cloth, perfume, or needles and thread.

The reason the trap works is because the Wari' draw a contrast between the body as the site of sociality and personality and the spirit as the undifferentiated (i.e., non-individuated) desire to be free of the "patterns of mutualism" that constitute Wari' society. The Wari' provide us with a rich interpretive clue for the La Candelaria miniatures. They suggest an analogy between miniatures and spirit traps meant to lure spirits away from bodies so that they can be captured by another being. Immediately, we are presented with a number of possibilities that rest on further ethnographic details from the Wari' and other Amazonian societies.

I think it would be an error, however, to pursue this example as a simple analogy. Instead, this case can usefully illustrate an approach to understanding material from first-millennium AD Northwest Argentina that starts from questions of an ontological nature. The issue revolves around the concept of "scale" as understood archaeologically. In archaeology the default measure of scale has tended to be the body: miniaturization is an artifact of scale change in relation to the self-evident human body. In this chapter I argue that careful attention to alternative ontologies of scale introduces new interpretive possibilities for such miniature objects. I work through the implications of the Amazonian perspectivist notions of scale, size, and dimensionality in relation to human bodies. My conclusion is that these pots are in fact spirit traps but, paradoxically, they are not necessarily miniatures, because scale operates through intensity and not size.

AN ONTOLOGICAL RESEARCH PARADIGM

The approach I take has been called ontological, which refers to the act of trying to think in new ways about reality and our ontological commitments (Alberti et al. 2011). The word "ontology" has some performative value. It carries the sense of a real, solid world—unlike the word "culture," for example—and challenges us to explore the possibilities of different worlds. It is about leaving open the possibility of finding something new by avoiding overly strict metatheoretical frameworks about "the substance of the world" (see Alberti et al. 2011). Feminist philosopher Elizabeth Grosz (2005, 113) formulates this concept in terms of the importance of asking the right questions: unless we do, the answers make no difference. She argues, for example, that feminism must contend with the question of "the substance of the world," an ontological question, because "without broader and different concepts of the real, the ontological . . . feminist theory is unable to invent or develop its own cosmologies" (Grosz 2005, 115). Otherwise, we are simply reiterating the versions of reality that already make sense to us. Ontology is about giving credibility to the possibility of other worlds; not as a relativizing gesture, but quite literally to force the production of new concepts and materialities (Viveiros de Castro 2003).

As a theorist oriented to ontological questions, Brazilian anthropologist Viveiros de Castro (2010, 2012) has developed general theoretical propositions on the basis of his readings of Amazonian ethnographies. Precisely along the lines argued for by Grosz, Viveiros de Castro challenges us to take the Indigenous metaphysics of "multinaturalism" as a serious philosophical intervention and to trace out its effects on anthropological theories and concepts. Multinaturalism is the metaphysics that lies behind the theory of perspectivism and is formulated by Viveiros de Castro in contrast to multiculturalism. Multiculturalism presupposes a single objective universe and many cultural interpretations of it; multinaturalism reverses this formula, positing multiple universes and a single mode of interpretation (Viveiros de Castro 2012, 46). Therefore, a perspective is not a different "point of view" on a singular, natural world, but is the same "point of view" on—the same way of knowing or seeing—qualitatively different worlds.

In this chapter I use the theory of perspectivism to think through miniature pots from the La Candelaria archaeological culture of first-millennium AD Northwest Argentina. In common with other theorists,

I argue for a form of ontological symmetry or equivalence between the theory we bring to bear on our evidence and the way that material acts as evidence (Alberti et al. 2011; Jones 2012; Olsen et al. 2012). As a consequence, we cannot approach the La Candelaria material with a standard theory of representation in mind. Viveiros de Castro (2010) makes it clear that the conventional sense of representation does not exist in perspectivist thought; as a consequence, archaeological materials cannot represent general principles in the sense of making them visually manifest, but instead must be instances or embodiments of them. The pots exist in a state of ontological equivalence with other bodies and thought. Likewise, Indigenous thought is treated as a theoretical discourse on the nature of reality, and not as an interesting interpretation of it.

THE SETTING: CHRONICALLY UNSTABLE BODIES

The archaeological material involved in this reconceptualization is a corpus of zoo-, anthropo-, and biomorphic ceramic pots from the La Candelaria archaeological culture of northwestern Argentina (see Figure 2.2). The material is dispersed throughout central Tucuman and

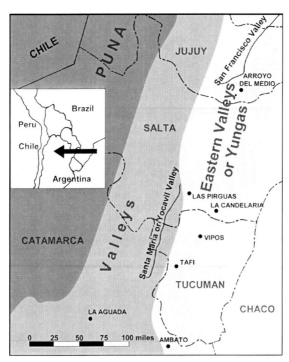

Figure 2.2   Map of Northwest Argentina

south-central Salta, although examples are found in a wider area. There is little evidence of settlement type or subsistence activities from the core area; the sites are often superficial sherd scatters, with the occasional indication of a stone foundation or cluster of burials (Rydén 1936; Heredia 1975). There is considerable affinity with neighboring regions in terms of the patterns and types of some of the anthropomorphic ceramics, especially with the Santa Maria valley to the west and the La Ciénega culture to the south.

Geographically, this area is the southern extent of the Argentine *yungas*, semitropical forests. Its position—a bright swath of green between the dry, high Andes and the flat lowlands of the Chaco to the east—indicates its transitional status. In fact, the area has been considered a geographical and cultural intermediary zone between the lowlands and highlands: depending on the theory, either positive influences work their way through the zone, often from the Andes to the Amazon, or it is war and devastation that travel across it, most frequently from the Amazon to the Andes. This area is rarely considered itself a region of innovation or origin (Heredia 1975). All sorts of dualisms are at work in the archaeological imaginary of the region, including a geo-archaeology of gender in which male warrior imagery is seen to dominate the highlands and female imagery the lowlands, with subsequent research bias (Scattolin 2004).

There have been few good excavations in this region, and fewer still published reports (Rydén 1936; Heredia 1975; Berberian et al. 1977). The extant materials were mainly recovered by collectors, so contextual information is often lacking. It is clear, however, that many of the pots were found in direct burials, burial urns, and occasionally cists. Pots vary enormously in terms of form and decoration. Common themes among the zoo- and anthropomorphic corpus include some standard shapes such as "globular," an "asymmetrical" variant, and some upright larger urns (see Figure 2.3). Anthropomorphism is manifested in distorted corporeal forms and appendages, most commonly the ubiquitous "bulge," but also plenty of humanoid, peccary, fox, amphibian, and random limb or limb-like forms. There are many anomalous cases; this is not a carefully controlled canon.

Associated skeletal material includes articulated single burials but also many disarticulated bodies and secondary burials—including evidence of reuse and reburial in urns, multiple burials, burials of adults and children, and partial or full cremation. Evidence of modified bodies includes cranial modification and piercings, including labrets, as well as body ornamentation (necklaces of shell, stone, and feather). The better-preserved burials from the cave sites of Las Pirguas, in Salta province, contained accompanying materials. Apart from ceramic vessels, there

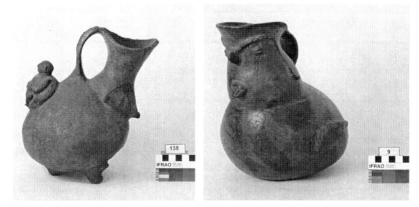

Figure 2.3 La Candelaria globular and asymmetric anthropo- and zoomorphic vessel forms

were textiles, pendants, shells (Spondylus and other conches), feathers, seeds, and some small metal objects (González 1972; Alberti 2007).

In previous work I have suggested that the acts of modifying a body and shaping and decorating a pot marked an ontological equivalence across these domains of practice. Marks on a pot were a result of the same action, with the same goal, as marking a body and not a representation of that act (Alberti 2007, 2012; Alberti & Marshall 2009). If the aim of body modification was to bring about a change or fix some features of the person marked, as is common among many Amazonian groups (McCallum 2001; Viveiros de Castro 2012), then marking a pot did not represent a body being marked but should itself be considered a body being changed or fixed. My argument has been that the fantastic forms, bulges, protuberances, and other modifications of bodies and pots express a general concern with "shoring up" or "fixing" a world conceived of as inherently volatile. Bodies—both pots and people—were thus considered "chronically unstable" (see Vilaça 2005).

These interpretations were based on the Amazonian theory of perspectivism (Vilaça 2009; Viveiros de Castro 2010) and ethnographies of the Wari' (Conklin 2001; Vilaça 2005, 2009). According to perspectivism, all species potentially share a way of knowing with humans. Their "essence" or "soul" is human; they see themselves as human and others as animals. This is because species or groups are differentiated on the basis of the bodies they have. To occupy a body is to have a perspective on the world, to see and be in the world in a particular way. Bodies, however, are bundles of affects and not simply objective biological states. Carrying out specific tasks, sensing the world in a particular way, sharing capacities and habits with others is what keeps a body as it is and maintains its similarity to other bodies in a group. The notion of "soul" rather than an essence denotes the capacity to transform. And transformation is always a matter of changing bodies. Changing one's body, therefore, necessarily means changing one's perspective and world.

Bodies with the potential for souls (i.e., humanity) are always in danger of transforming into others. In their ordinary condition, bodies do not "have" souls. Souls are only present in moments of danger. To have a soul among the Wari', for example, is a sign of danger, a sign that some transformation (of perspective) is imminent (Vilaça 2009). Transformation is an ontological event because humans transform into animals, the dead, spirits, and ghosts. Under normal conditions, when the work of affective attention is in full effect, the soul is not present "in" the body because it is eclipsed by the body. The chronic instability is due to the fact that despite the care taken, one's soul is always vulnerable to ontological predation by another spirit or person and therefore one's perspective can always change.

MINIATURE POTS AS SPIRIT TRAPS

The interpretive challenge here is to approach these miniature objects and the hypothesis of their being "spirit traps" in a way that opens up the possibility that they do not correspond easily to our conventional ontological modes but should rather be thought of in the terms established by perspectivism. The suggestion that miniature pots are spirit traps works as an analytic strategy insofar as it gets us thinking about what that suggestion would imply. What are the consequences if we take it as an ontological possibility and not merely an analogical one?

There are other miniatures in the La Candelaria corpus, though they are not particularly common. In general, size is not tightly controlled—the same forms occur at various different scales. The general assumption about miniatures has been that their size is dimensionally related to the size of the dead with whom they are interred (see discussions in Bailey 2005; Back Danielsson 2007; Jones 2012). More than a simple relationship of scale, however, Douglas Bailey (2005) demonstrates that miniaturization has powerful and often unsettling—because paradoxical—cognitive and perceptual effects. In the case of figurines, these effects enable people to enter "other worlds," to think about their own worlds, or to manipulate or influence others. All the senses are implicated, which makes figurines "perceptually explosive objects" (Bailey 2005, 42). Similarly, Jones (2012, 32) demonstrates that scale is "emergent and performative"; juxtapositions of scale produce "interesting psychological and phenomenological effects."

Bailey's (2005, 42) "paradox of multiple worlds" has another meaning when "other worlds" are precisely what is expected by an audience for whom the world is inherently unstable. Though Bailey's observations draw our attention to the potentially powerful cognitive effects of miniaturization, their general relevance is circumscribed by Bailey's own ontological commitment to a particular type of human body and its perceptual apparatus. As Jones (2012, 32) has pointed out, work on miniaturization has taken as the scale the environment as perceived in relation to the human body. Indeed, the biological human body is the default scale in Bailey's work, whether in relation to the onto-transformative effect of miniaturization (i.e., new worlds) or as the scale against which dimensional changes are measured. Bailey (2005, 29) clearly recognizes the anthropocentrism of "the scale of the human" but not, perhaps, the anthropocentrism of what is the human scale. The default ontological scale is the perceiving human in a self-evident human-sized body (Bailey 2005, 42). By starting from multinaturalism we are forced to reconsider that default. Even though perspectivism agrees that perception is a human capacity, anything can be a human from its perspective. This perceptual apparatus is therefore a generalized ontological mode of knowing that is not exclusive to "us," whereas alternative worlds for Bailey appear to be alternative settings for human minds.

FINDING THE CORRECT SCALE: AMAZONIAN SPIRITS

If the human body is the default scale in Bailey's (2005, 42) work, what is the scale adopted by perspectivism? Will an ontological shift in scale reveal new ways of conceptualizing the miniatures? I argue that we cannot assume the same scale, especially if the terms of our theory dictate otherwise. The pots must be part of an instantiation of scale rather than respond to an imposed scale (that of the self-evident human body). A scale must "grow indigenously," to paraphrase Wagner's (1991, 160) comments in relation to the Melanesian person. Melanesian persons "keep their scale" through all possible permutations. This is "scale retaining" as opposed to the anthropological heuristics that rely on "scale shifts." Changes are changes in magnification: the scale stays the same. The task, then, is to find the scale in each case, not impose it.

Amazonian notions of spirits offer clues to the scale appropriate to the pots in two ways. First, the scale applicable to Amazonian body-pots has to do with the relationship between bodies and souls, a single relationship that maintains its scale through various permutations. Second, Amazonian spirits can be of the same scale even though in our quantitative universe in which the tangible human body is the de facto scale, they are considered chaotically scale-changing. Their scale is one of intensity and excessiveness in relation to the figure-ground relationship between the visible/invisible and the body/soul. In Wagner's terms, spirits are magnified or diminished in size but the scale or relation does not change. Therefore, a very small but intense body is of the same "scale" as a very large, excessive body. The effect is the same.

In Amazonia, souls designate a condition of transformability, so that all bodies contain the potential to transform into other bodies; each body, therefore, contains all bodies. This is expressed in myth: each being contains the possibility of all other beings, since it contains an "intrinsic capacity to be something else" and therefore differs infinitely from itself (Viveiros de Castro 2007, 158; 2010, 46). Viveiros de Castro refers to this as "intensive difference"; nonhuman spirits "denote [this] ontological mode of the 'intensive multiplicity type'" (Viveiros de Castro 2007, 155). Spirits are less a distinct type of being and more "a moment of indiscernibility between the human and the non-human" (ibid.). This moment or "region" invokes "a background of molecular humanity, hidden by non-human molar forms" (ibid.). This is the intensive multiplicity, the "super-divided being," made up of the full complement of generalized background affects out of which all specific forms emerge.

Spirits, then, are a sign of the "immanent universal background" that is obscured by the actualization of current forms (i.e., bodies). Spirits are not conceived "in opposition" to a body, but are themselves "a dynamic and intensive corporality" (ibid., 161). They are not the negation of the body; they are both more and less than a body. They keep their general human form but can be as minute and multitudinous as specks of dust or excessive—brilliantly adorned and sometimes anomalously huge and grotesque. These issues of size—the tiny and the huge—are actually two complementary ideas: both refer to the "'excessive' intensity of [all] spirits" (ibid.).

From an ontological perspective, then, to suggest that the miniature pots are spirit traps is to posit that they respond to a different scale than that imposed by phenomenological concerns with the self-evident human body as the default yardstick. The key is not size but intensity or excess.

PERSUASIVE POTS: MAKING OBJECTS INTO SUBJECTS

Drawing on perspectivism, I have argued elsewhere that anything in the immediate, intimate vicinity of people can be subjectivized or personified through exchange and shared affects (Alberti 2013). In this view, the addition of appendages and incisions to pots is the intentional activation of affective capacities in the clay. Thus activated, the zoo- and anthropomorphic pots had specific tasks to perform in the burials in persuading spirits and souls to linger or move on. This goes for any sized material. The explanation of why the miniatures are small does not rest on a scale in relation to an original, biological human body, but rather on what makes that pot or body more or less a body.

I have argued that both pots and bodies are "grown" in the same way (Alberti 2013). Neither are considered self-evident, natural facts, even though the process of fabrication, as Vilaça (2002) has argued for Amazonian peoples, is a natural act. The fashioning of pots from materials and their marking through incisions and modeling are quite concretely the same as acts of growth. This parallelism is noted in Amazonian ethnographies. Erikson (2009, 187; see also McCullum 2001; Hugh-Jones 2009, 49) writes that the Matis mark pots with incised parallel crisscrossed lines, called *musha*. These he interprets as "tattoos," which mark pots as persons. This personhood is not symbolic or secondary, and the clay, temper, and water are not merely the prop for such marks but are themselves fully subjectivized. In other words, pots are not objects in the ordinary sense. As Phillipe Descola has remarked, it would be impossible to differentiate a theory of objects among Amazonian peoples, since the notion of subjectivity is all-encompassing (Erikson 2009, 185). Viveiros de Castro (2010, 51, emphasis in original) comments that perspectivism confirms an "intensive difference that carries the human/nonhuman difference *to the inside of every existing thing*," which strongly suggests that there is no a priori reason preventing anything from being a subject. As Santos-Granero (2009, 18) has argued, Amazonian craft production is always about the making of object-as-subject. Anything, therefore, is a potential subject.

Bodies are coincident with subjectivity. You need a body to know. All things can be bodies or subjects, but not because their bodies look like the natural object, the biological body. The La Candelaria corpus consists of pots, *pucos*, and bowls with incised and decorated marks, bulges, moldings, appendages, and zoo/anthropomorphic and non-zoo/anthropomorphic forms. I argue that the relationship between potters and materials established by the fabrication process instilled specific capacities for action in the pots and allowed their subjectivity to emerge. The general background to the forms the ceramics and bodies take is a juxtaposition of shapes and appendages in which zones are demarcated through cinching, piercing, incising, and modeling (Figure 2.3). The appendages and modeling recall limbs, wings, and faces, with an emphasis on eyebrows, noses, and ears. On the pots, the incisions and appendages serve to differentiate the basic form. The differentiation occurs in relation to all parts of bodies, so that what we might consider parts of a basic body template are not essential features. Bodies are, after all, bundles of affects. So, for example, when a pot is marked by sex, that is not a representation of maleness or femaleness, but a particular differentiation of a body (Alberti & Marshall 2009). Similarly, body ornaments, clothing, and other so-called cultural markings are no different in kind from the so-called natural markers of bodily difference and capacity. Clothes, like claws, are affects: both "sign and substance of capacities and dispositions" (Hugh-Jones 2009, 46: after Viveiros de Castro 2004, 474).

The purpose of marking, molding, painting, adorning, clothing, piercing, and otherwise working on the body is not just to elicit a particular kind of subject, but it is to fix a body and therefore to stabilize an otherwise wildly unpredictable perspective and world. The deliberate attention those makers paid to pots in the same way that attention is paid to other bodies encouraged the pots to develop a perspective. And the reason for such attention has to do with the reciprocal relationship between knowing and subjectivity. To know a thing, as Viveiros de Castro (2010, 36) argues, is not to objectify it, to strip away all subjective bias, but rather to subjectivize it—to add the maximum amount of intentionality to it. Communication is only possible between subjects because knowledge is about occupying a perspective congruent with the thing you wish to know. The addition of appendages and incisions to pots is the intentional activation of affective capacities in the clay. It is noteworthy that the organs of knowledge are emphasized—eyes, ears, mouths, and skin (see Alberti 2013). The addition of eyes, ears, incisions, piercings, and so on, endowed the pots with the capacity to know and influence others from their perspective. The pots, then, were made to communicate to an audience, to establish relationships, to persuade others of their point of view.

The idea that pots were endowed with affective capacities for specific purposes fits a particularly striking characteristic of the La Candelaria archaeological corpus: the presence of pots that resemble each other closely in form yet differ in anthropomorphizing details. These take the form of pots without faces where faces are expected or pots with bulges replacing arms or legs. Some bulges are mounted with frogs, foxes, or human bodies; many are bare, and others show partially complete figures. The forms are identical, but the details are glaringly absent. It is possible that objects were deliberately left only partially subjectivized, semi-potent, stunted in their subjective potential and therefore in their potential to know and be known. Partial subjectivization or de-subjectivization of prior artifact-persons has been noted among Amazonian peoples. For example, the Matis remove the eyes of masks to "decommission" them and reduce their potency before they are sold (Erikson 2009). Domestic ware in the La Candelaria corpus was also sometimes marked in simple ways as potentially anthropomorphic. Such pots were clearly used and contain less dense anthropomorphic markings, often just crude eyes or the indication of a tail or wings. They are just "subject" enough, having been given their minimum complement of affects.

An argument can be made that the more intensely subjectivized pots were potent beings entrusted with specific kinds of tasks, to both impede activity and enable knowledge. Perhaps their role was to convince others of a shared perspective, or to activate a capacity to know. Some pots have round, wide-open eyes, recalling the staring eyes that mark out a ghost or specter among some Amazonian peoples (Conklin 2001; Viveiros de Castro 2012). Eyes wide open indicate an inability to see the invisible. The communicative assistance they provided could be to turn a blind eye to the soul emerging from the recently defunct person's body. They may have operated as traps, offerings of an animal-like body for a human soul. As such, they were a protection for the living against the wandering ghosts of the dead but perhaps also a means of ensuring a successful transition for the dead. Other forms of convincing the dead spirit of its need to move on include the very common use of incised "tears," which recalls practices such as keening and ritual tears that make the changed state of affairs clear to the recently dead and so protect the living (e.g., Conklin 2001).

An alternative explanation emphasizes the play of perspectives and the hiding/revealing of body/spirit. As Viveiros de Castro (2007) notes in relation to spirits, to see is to be seen. One must be seen first by the spirits in order to activate one's own sight. Do the eyes of the pots work to "activate" the sight of other spirits in the vicinity, perhaps enabling the dead spirit to complete its separation from the body, to see things as they really are? Endowed with sight, the buried pot teaches the dead to see properly, to maintain a perspective. As complex beings, with their relational bodies (that is, capacities) firmly in place, the pots worked to convince spirits and others of a particular perspective on the world.

CONCLUSION: TRAPS, MINIATURES, AND INTENSITY

The notion of a spirit trap seems to imply that the spirit gets caught inside the pot. But the metaphor of containment does not work here. The basis for multinaturalist metaphysics is the idea of the radical and infinite superposition of states: insides and outsides are simply figure and ground to each other (Vilaça 2009). There is no interior space to the body, just an invisible body. Even so, I do think the pots are traps. Douglas Bailey (2005) and Alfred Gell (1998) alert us to the cognitive effects of confusion and paradox brought on by miniatures and artwork traps. They can impede passage, and their indecipherability alludes to complex intentionalities that lie behind them. These pots, however, work on the basis of a much broader spectrum of intentional beings. They are not only left by agents so that they can do their work for them, ensnaring and confusing malignant spirits; rather, they themselves as bodies fully engage in perspectival communication and battles of will. These bodies, variously constructed and provided with affects and capacities, were capable of knowing different things and of inciting different kinds of knowledge through the types of relations they entered into.

Andy Jones (2012, 36–37) argues that previous work on scale has reinforced an ontological distinction between the macro and micro. He advocates, instead, a "flat" approach to scale that does not separate the social and material, or the micro from the macro. Similarly, Conklin's sorcerer is operating on the basis of an ontological scale the measure of which is not size. Size emerges as a possibility, as one means of enacting the potential of another scale, but a scale that retains its key relation—body/soul—through all permutations. In other words, size is not the most important scalar thing going on here. As we have seen, identical forms such as the bulges exist in many sizes without changing their essential shape; and the same pot form can manifest at different sizes. In this case, the body as natural object is not a good predictor of scale, since the body itself is not a stable object divided into sensing parts but is rather a collection of affects bundled into an unstable bodily form.

The scale here is about intensity and excess, which refer to the potential for visibility/invisibility and proximity to the original condition of undifferentiated, intensive difference. The body surfaces of spirits and humans are often brilliant and intensely marked (Viveiros de Castro 2007), which creates an "excessive corporeality." Likewise, some pots are, like spirits, intensively embodied, as shown by the density of their markings and especially the care with which the smallest of piercings were executed. I think the intensively worked surfaces are gauges of the potency of the embodied subjects: their "scale" as efficacious beings, dense with affective capacities. If the miniatures do work as traps, they do so along this scale. A small pot from the Arminio Weiss collection, perforated down to its lip and ears, which are pierced clean through, is an example of that scale (see Figure 2.4). Multiple incised marks on its face, miniature legs sprouting from a perfectly globular corpulence: it is indeed intense—the combination of small size, intensity of effect, and the perfect formless form.

Size does matter, but it is an accidental effect of intensity. It is thus the wrong register for thinking about the scale of the pots. Small size is important only insofar as it can be a potent site for the materialization of intensity and excess and therefore humanity.

Figure 2.4 Intensively perforated miniature anthropomorphic vessel

ACKNOWLEDGMENTS

The research for this chapter was partially funded by a 2011 Fulbright teaching and research grant for Argentina, where I was hosted by the Museo de Antropología of the Universidad Nacional de Córdoba. I am extremely thankful to my host Dr. Andrés Laguens, with whom many of the ideas presented in this chapter were developed. I am grateful to staff at the Museo Municipal de Rafaela for facilitating access to the Arminio Weiss collection and for permission to publish photographs of material from the collection.

REFERENCES

Alberti, B. 2007. Destablizing meaning in anthropomorphic forms from Northwest Argentina. *Journal of Iberian Archaeology* 9/10, 209–29

Alberti, B. 2012. Cut, pinch and pierce: image as practice among the Early Formative La Candelaria, first millennium AD, Northwest Argentina. In I.-M. Back Danielsson, F. Fahlander & Y. Sjöstrand (eds.), *Picture This! The Materiality of the Perceptible*, 23–38. Stockholm, Swed.: Stockholm University

Alberti, B. 2013. Designing body-pots in the Formative La Candelaria Culture, Northwest Argentina. In E. Hallam & T. Ingold (eds.), *Making and Growing: Anthropological Studies of Organisms and Artefacts*. Aldershot, UK: Ashgate

Alberti, B. & Bray, T.L. 2009. Animating archaeology: of subjects, objects, and alternative ontologies. *Cambridge Archaeological Journal* 19(3), 337–43

Alberti, B., Fowles, S., Holbraad, M., Marshall, Y. & Witmore, C.L. 2011. "Worlds Otherwise": archaeology, anthropology and ontological difference. *Current Anthropology* 52(6), 896–912

Alberti, B. & Marshall, Y. 2009. Animating archaeology: local theories and conceptually open-ended methodologies. *Cambridge Archaeological Journal* 19(3), 344–56

Back Danielsson, I.-M. 2007. *Masking Moments: The Transitions of Bodies and Beings in Late Iron Age Scandinavia*. Stockholm, Swed.: Stockholm University

Bailey, D.W. 2005. *Prehistoric Figurines: Representation and Corporeality in the Neolithic*. London: Routledge

Berberian, E., Azcárate, J. & Caillou, M. 1977. Investigaciones arqueológicas en la región del Dique El Cadillal (Tucumán-Rep. Argentina). Los primeros fechados radiocarbónicos. *Relaciones de la Sociedad Argentina de Antropología* 11, 31–53

Conklin, B. 2001. *Consuming Grief: Compassionate Cannibalism in an Amazonian Society*. Austin: University of Texas Press

Erikson, P. 2009. Obedient things: reflections on the Matis theory of materiality. In F. Santos-Granero (ed.), *The Occult Life of Things: Native Amazonian Theories of Materiality and Personhood*, 173–91. Tucson: University of Arizona Press

Gell, A. 1998. *Art and Agency*. Oxford, UK: Clarendon

González, A.R. 1972. Descubrimientos arqueológicos en la Serranía de Las Pirguas, Pcia. de Salta. *Revista de la Universidad Nacional de La Plata* 24, 388–92

González, A.R. 2007 [1977]. *Arte, estructura y arqueología*. Buenos Aires, Arg.: La Marca

Grosz, E. 2005. *Time Travels: Feminism, Nature, Power*. Durham, NC: Duke University Press

Heredia, O. 1975. Investigaciones arqueológicas en el sector meridional de las selvas occidentales. *Revista del Instituto de Antropología, Universidad Nacional de Córdoba* 5, 73–118

Hugh-Jones, S. 2009. The fabricated body: objects and ancestors in Northwest Amazonia. In F. Santos-Granero (ed.), *The Occult Life of Things: Native Amazonian Theories of Materiality and Personhood*, 33–59. Tucson: University of Arizona Press

Jones, A.M. 2012. *Prehistoric Materialities: Becoming Material in Prehistoric Britain and Ireland*. Oxford: Oxford University Press

McCallum, C. 2001. *Gender and Sociality in Amazônia: How Real People are Made*. Oxford, UK: Berg

Moore, J. & Mackey, C. 2008. The Chimú. In H. Silverman & W. Isbell (eds.), *The Handbook of South American Archaeology*, 783–808. New York: Springer/Plenum/Kluwer

Moseley, M. 2001. *The Incas and Their Ancestors: The Archaeology of Peru*. 2nd edition. New York: Thames & Hudson

Olsen, B., Shanks, M., Webmoor, T. & Witmore, C. 2012. *Archaeology: The Discipline of Things*. Berkeley: University of California Press

Rydén, S. 1936. *Archaeological Researches in the Department of La Candelaria (Prov. Salta, Argentina)*. Göteborg, Swed.: Etnografiska Museet i Göteborg (Ethnological Studies 3)

Santos-Granero, F. 2009. Introduction: Amerindian constructional views of the world. In F. Santos-Granero (ed.), *The Occult Life of Things: Native Amazonian Theories of Materiality and Personhood*, 1–29. Tucson: University of Arizona Press

Scattolin, C. 2004. Categorías indígenas y clasificaciones arqueológicas en el Noroeste Argentino. In A. Haber (ed.), *Hacia una Arqueología de las Arqueologías Sudamericanas*, 53–82. Bogotá, Col.: Universidad de los Andes

Vilaça, A. 2002. Making kin out of Others in Amazonia. *Journal of the Royal Anthropological Institute* 8, 347–65

Vilaça, A. 2005. Chronically unstable bodies: reflections on Amazonian corporalities. *Journal of the Royal Anthropological Institute* 11(3), 445–64

Vilaça, A. 2009. Bodies in perspective: a critique of the embodiment paradigm from the point of view of Amazonian ethnography. In H. Lambert & M. McDonald (eds.), *Social Bodies*, 129–47. New York and Oxford: Berghahn Books

Viveiros de Castro, E. 2003. Anthropology (AND) science. At http://abaete.wikia.com/wiki/. (Also published in *Manchester Papers in Social Anthropology 7*.)

Viveiros de Castro, E. 2004. Exchanging perspectives: the transformation of objects into subjects in Amerindian ontologies. *Common Knowledge* 10(3), 463–84

Viveiros de Castro, E. 2007. The crystal forest: notes on the ontology of Amazonian spirits. *Inner Asia* 9(2), 153–72

Viveiros de Castro, E. 2010. *Metafísicas Caníbales: Líneas de Antropología Postestructural.* Buenos Aires, Arg.: Katz Editores

Viveiros de Castro, E. 2012. Cosmological perspectivism in Amazonia and elsewhere. *HAU: Journal of Ethnographic Theory* 1, 45–168

Wagner, R. 1991. The fractal person. In M. Godelier & M. Strathern (eds.), *Big Men and Great Men: Personifications of Power in Melanesia*, 123–35. Cambridge: Cambridge University Press

CHAPTER THREE

Transmorphic Being, Corresponding Affect: Ontology and Rock Art in South-Central California

David W. Robinson

This chapter examines the ontology of Indigenous South-Central California with a focus on the colorful pictographs of the Chumash. I argue that interpretations of rock art from shamanic perspectives have dehistoricized the art and cast imagery within essentialist cognitive terms, effectively curtailing the possibility of interpreting the images as something more than the standard outward expression of a universal neuropsychological function. By contrast, considering Indigenous ontologies affords a much better understanding of both rock art and Native perceptions of their environment, allowing us to move closer to an emic perspective and to appreciate Indigenous social dynamics and rock art in social rather than cognitive terms.

Since Lewis-Williams and Dowson's seminal paper, "The Sign of All Times" (1988), shamanism has become a dominant, though certainly contentious, explanation for the making of hunter-gatherer rock art. Starting with Whitley's (1988) supporting comments in the discussion section of that same publication, the rock art of the American Far West has since been interpreted within this shamanic paradigm (Whitley 2000; Pearson 2002). Of course, from the beginning there has been a strong critique of both the model and its application to rock art across the world; at times, this debate has descended into unproductive hyperbole and shrill polemics (see Chippindale 2003). Although Dowson (2007, 2009) has recently questioned the usefulness of the model and called for a move beyond Cartesian notions of shamanism, and despite considerable

Archaeology after Interpretation: Returning Materials to Archaeological Theory, edited by Benjamin Alberti, Andrew Meirion Jones, and Joshua Pollard, 59–78.

criticism in California and the Great Basin (Quinlan 2000; Quinlan & Woody 2003), interpretations of rock art based on the shamanic model of the American Far West remains the dominant theory. It is pertinent to point out that because of the historical use of the term by anthropologists in their ethnographic fieldwork, the term has a long tradition of usage in California and the Great Basin. Since the start of ethnographic recording, anthropologists called certain Indigenous practitioners "shamans," so it is inescapable to refer to shamans when utilizing the ethnographic literature.

However, the use of a theoretical model derived from the word shaman raises fundamental issues. First, it is problematic and highly questionable that we continue to employ a late nineteenth- and early twentieth-century term that was formulated within very different theoretical understandings than those of twenty-first-century anthropology. More to the point, applying shamanism as a theoretical lens can actually obscure rather than reveal. As painstakingly argued by scholars such as Whitley (2000), shamanism as an anthropological term is defined by a set of characteristics; in particular, the "structural characteristics of ASC" (Altered States of Consciousness) are considered fundamental in identifying shamanism as the origination of rock art (Whitley 1998). Following the multiple stages of the trance model (or neuropsychological model), it has been argued that if these characteristics can be identified in either the ethnographic literature or the rock art imagery, then the causal link can be established and the rock-art production can be confidently interpreted as shamanic or shamanistic. This "check-list" approach has serious drawbacks. First, its foundational assumption is that rock art images are visionary in origin. In other words, the shamanic model purports that rock art depictions are either direct representations of images seen in visionary states or shamanic self-portraits representing bodily sensations experienced during stages of the trance experience. As Whitley (1998, 25) states, the depiction of this visionary imagery is "the unifying characteristic of Native Californian rock art." Below I will question this assumption, suggesting that, although trance may have played a partial role, the design characteristics of the art itself likely have a more complex origin than the simple reproduction of visions.

A further issue with the shamanic model (or at least, with the way it has been applied) is that it has distracted research from the art's associated archaeology. In other words, because of this emphasis on cognition and image, the archaeological context and placement of the art have often been ignored. An example of this from South-Central California has led to the erroneous interpretation that rock art imagery was separate from public contexts (see Robinson 2010b for discussion). Archaeological research has clearly demonstrated a consistent public placement for the art, which directly contradicts any assertion that the space art occupies is the exclusive domain of the shaman and is somehow taboo to the rest of society (Robinson & Sturt 2008; Robinson 2010b, 2011; Robinson et al. 2010). More significant, and perhaps surprising, is the effect that the shamanic model has had on limiting interpretations of element design and characteristics. Since the neuropsychological model explains the cognitive origin of the imagery, and just about any geometric forms matches some aspect of the model, the images themselves are immediately explained by a universal model of the human mind. The effect is to superimpose the model over the art, thus reifying the model itself. The art is effectively consumed by the model. In California, this has resulted in a dearth of interpretations of the rock art imagery itself (other than to illustrate shamanistic characteristics). Since we know what shamanism is, and we know how to identify its manifestation in rock art imagery, all this perspective does is find the characteristic traits in the art that match the expected characteristics of the shamanic model. There are exceptions, however: the Coso rock art of Eastern California and much rock art of the Great Basin have profited by a closer consideration of the rock art imagery, including detailed analyses of anthropomorphic and zoomorphic elements (see recent discussion in Garfinkel & Austin 2011; Eerkens et al. 2012; Hildebrandt & McGuire 2012). In particular, bighorn sheep imagery has received sustained attention since the 1960s (Grant 1968). However, the compelling images from South-Central California (see Figure 3.1), particularly those of the Chumash linguistic peoples, reveal an entirely different corpus, especially in the prevalence of pictographs (i.e., paintings) over petroglyphs, but also in an entirely different manner of depiction.

Characterized by "fantastical" imagery (see Grant 1965), Chumash design elements are diverse, depicting insects, reptiles, birds, bears, humans, and more often therianthropic (or more properly "transmorphic," see discussion below) combinations, often with upturned

Figure 3.1 Linguistic groups of South-Central California

appendages or embellishments with fine lines and delicate dots. Other images, painted in vibrant reds, look like mandalas or sun disks with radiating spokes. There are also abstract compositions and wide palettes of color—showing careful pigment processing and skillful application. Chumash elements do not lend themselves to easy interpretation. Even zoomorphic "representational" forms are difficult to identify in terms of species. It is for this reason that it may be easier to simply classify those images as "shamanic," as in the case of an element from Pleito (see Figure 3.2) that has been called the "exploding human" undergoing a shamanic transformation (Whitley 2000, 121).

Indeed, many Chumash rock art elements represent beings of some sort, and even those that cannot be identified as a specific species do include "real world" attributes of humans, animals, plants, or insects within their design matrix. I submit that rather than relying on a general model of shamanism, considering Chumash relational ontologies affords a much better understanding of both the rock art and Native perceptions of their environment. Fortunately, a wide body of Californian ethnographic literature exists that enables us to understand Chumash ontology (see Robinson, in press). This is important because understanding ontology promotes an appreciation of the active role of rock art

Figure 3.2   Transmorphic polychrome Chumash composition at Pleito

within Chumash power and ideology. Two interrelated principles are key: transmorphism of being, or the elision of certain characteristics of plants, animals, humans, and other sentient "beings"; and correspondence, a principle that affords connections between sentient and less than sentient materials and substances. These principles in part explained the operation of power in specific places of the Chumash environment, whereas the mystique associated with the display of such power contributed to the justification of authority within society at large.

CORRESPONDENCE AND TRANSMORPHIC AFFECT

The underlying substructure of the Chumash environment was defined during a mythic past, beginning with a vast flood and followed by the formation of geological topography (mountain ranges in particular). The building of the world occurred through the agency of mythic animals during the time when "animals were people" (Robinson 2013a). During this mythic time, many of the rock formations visible today emerged via supernatural events, typically following episodes in which mythic animals were turned into stone due to various supernatural stunts, conflicts, or other actions. Thus, the visible geology of the Chumash territory was constituted by a kind of dormant animal agency in the form of petrified mythic beings. It is important to note that not all rock formations seem to have been ascribed this personality, but only certain ones. Thus, potential power was differentially distributed across landscapes.

Just as animals in the past had the ability to affect the world before humans existed, power imminent in a personalized environment could be coaxed through various means to affect the Chumash world. According to Blackburn (1975, 70), a fundamental postulate of Chumash ontology was that of "affectability": "Because of the personalization of causative agencies, it is possible for man to affect or influence those agencies directly. He is not at the mercy of completely impersonal, unaffectable forces beyond inexorable laws." The concept of affectability was possible because the physical world was conceived of as inhabited by different forms of sentience that enabled dialogue between human and non-human actors to occur.

The ability to wield some kind of influence was not universally attributed to all matter, but seems to have been concentrated in sentient forms, which included animals, plants, natural phenomena such as fog or thunder, supernatural entities, celestial bodies, and specific minerals and stones. Thus, non-human agency was not restricted to a mythical origin but was distributed throughout the environment in various manifestations. For instance, one stone used in curing was called 'alipte, derived from the term *kipte*, meaning "I am alive" (from Harrington, in Walker & Hudson 1993, 50). The ability of this stone to be used by humans to cause an affect was activated through an alchemical treatment with substances derived from other sentient powers, such as "hummingbird blood mixed with fine, powdery grass; or oil from an eel mixed with powdered *yerba santa*" (ibid.). Stones such as plummet-shaped charmstones were ascribed sentience and the potential power to cause earthquakes or rain (Blackburn 1975, 223–24, 272–73); *Toshaawt* (or "sorcerer stones") stones purportedly had similar powers, as did "vulture stones" and other stones retrieved from birds' nests (Timbrook 2000). The Harrington notes record a rain ceremony that involved soaking a stone pipe in oil extracted from poisonous animals or fireflies, or from a weasel's or skunk's gallbladder; this pipe would then be put in a basket of water to create "vapor," a correspondence to create rain (Hudson & Underhay 1978, 33). Rain ceremonies often required the use of water, so that a small amount of water, employed in the proper manner with other paraphernalia, had corresponding affect on water in the form of rain. The principle that "parts represent wholes" was fundamental to the operation of affectability; for instance, activating the power of an animal did not require the entire animal, since "simply a portion of animal or plant could make an effective talisman: a claw, feather, piece of skin or hair" (Walker & Hudson 1993, 50). It appears that a process of change was necessary to enact correspondence, and this was made possible, in part, by notions of transmorphism—i.e., the process whereby physical form undergoes a process of change. This could be reductive, as in preparing a body part for use as a talisman, and/or additive, as in combining different processed substances to create a composite effect. Blackburn (1975, 40) notes that within Chumash practice such transmorphism, or the modification or creation of physical form, is an expression of supernatural power: "The Chumash belief in transmorphism, it might be suggested, is part of a complex series of philosophical assumptions and postulates concerning the relationship between supernatural power and human nature on one hand, and man's interaction with his environment on the other. Transformation, it would seem, is regarded as a kind of natural phenomenon, an inherent part of the structure of reality potentially available to all."

Through their transmorphic applications, the composition of parts or substances appears to increase or multiply the affective power of the objects. Indeed, the ability to manipulate reality even from considerable distances was predicated upon principles of material correspondence, as "spatially separated parts of a whole can still affect one another" (Blackburn 1975, 72). Importantly, then, principles of correspond-ence allow knowledgeable individuals to be "technicians of power."

Hudson and Underhay (1978, 141–42) argued that highly influential "shaman-priests" partly derived their power from watching the movements of the sun, moon, and stars:

> The Chumash must have regarded the entire universe as a complex network of interaction involving man and these [celestial] beings, who caused all celestial phenomena and some natural (earthly) phenomena that could only be understood in causal terms. Because of this, the universe was seen as unpredictable and dangerous, but man could cope with this uncertainty if he undertook the proper rituals and correctly used the power which he had acquired from some of these celestial beings.

It seems therefore that power was obtainable by those who had the ability to acquire powerful things—certain constituent parts or objects—and the knowledge of the effects of certain compositions. In a very real social sense, power was a manipulatable resource within Chumash society. Since most of these principles are known to us today through the ethnographic recording of oral narratives, we know that these principles were widely known within Indigenous society because those same narratives were told to all of its members again and again. However, the specific correspondences arising from particular objects and parts might only be understood by the individual who owned or used that object (Applegate 1978). Thus, the visual employment of certain talismans (through the use of animal parts and other objects) was understood by people throughout society as an exercise of power, even if they did not know the specific correspondence in operation. A certain degree of mystique only enhanced the social power of such objects, since the ambiguity surrounding their potency and effects suggested a certain amount of judicious respect lest the object, and therefore its owner, be underestimated. Ethnographically, this manner of encouraging a circumspect awareness was promoted by the ceremonial and political multivillage group called the 'antap. This elite group performed ceremonies using a secret language and constructing a brush enclosure, called a *siliyik*, which was not visible and accessible by the rest of society, who were called the 'emechesh (Librado 1981). The display of ritual prowess was important, as was the control of its knowledge. As the Chumash informant Fernando Librado (1981, 19) put it, "The 'antap do not like the 'emechesh, for the 'emechesh will learn the secrets of their mysteries." These mysteries attributed to the 'antap included the use of objects and the public performances associated with the *siliyik* (ibid., 40).

Objects imbued with agentive characteristic could also be personal items called 'atiswin, which I have discussed elsewhere (Robinson 2004; see also Applegate 1978). These objects were often said to have been "obtained" in a dream and to be carriers of a particular animal power. They were the material manifestation of the relationship between an individual and that animal power, and usually they could only be "employed" by the original owner: again, except to the owners, such objects were inherently ambiguous.

This ambiguous mystique was further amplified by the belief that particular substances could be supernaturally dangerous or even toxic. One such substance was called '*ayip*, which may have been used as a medicine and was certainly used as a poison (Timbrook 2007). Agentive power substances were also used in paint and binding admixtures, particularly for body paint but also quite likely for paint used in the production of rock art (see Robinson 2004). Ethnographic information conveys that the pigments comprising the pictographs were considered to be highly potent material (Robinson 2004, 2010b): they were "carriers" of correspondences to the raw materials used in concocting the paint, contributing to its potency. Thus, the power of rock art was not solely based on images: this explains the employment of pigment at sites where little recognizable form was produced, such as the red swath of pigment at the Beehive and Rattlesnake Shelters on the Vandenberg coast (see Robinson 2004). However, the materiality of the pigment does not in any sense reduce the importance of the image itself; instead, the images likely enhanced the efficacy of the affect. The form of the image likewise conveyed allusions or correspondences to the various sentient beings that were depicted; or, as suggested above, perhaps even to parts of beings.

An example of paintings being used in this manner can be found among the Gabrilieno (Tongva) just to the south of the Chumash territory. In 1801, an outbreak of sickness on the mainland was attributed to three sorcerers on Santa Catalina Island. The following account shows how pigment enacted long-distance affective powers and demonstrates how the use of pigment and the creation of zoomorphic designs activated a correspondence between dangerous animals and their ability to cause injury:

> There in the canyon, where none save the three [sorcerers] could see it, they painted the world on the level ground. They painted it like the world is, and they painted all, outdoors in the canyon . . . When they were finished painting the world, they began to paint infirmities and blood, as well as such dangerous animals that cause pain by biting, clawing, and so on . . . all of these things for sickness. . . . Meanwhile the people in San Gabriel were dying. They had headaches, and blood came out of the mouth . . . (Hudson 1979, 357)

Given this situation, an expedition was launched to the island, the sorcerers were killed and the painting destroyed, thus ending the epidemic (ibid., 358). A similar account documented by Blackburn (1975, 276) details how a drought was caused by the use of a painted portable rock; the drought ended when the rock with the "evil figures" was submerged in water. Another account (in Hudson 1979, 360) suggests that some Chumash pictographs images were agents of sickness: "Luisa Ygnacio, Barbareno Chumash, told Harrington that a Santa Barbara Indian shaman named Andres used to go up into a canyon behind the mission to paint figurines for the purpose of making his enemies sick."

Thus, rather than simply creating a record of a trance event, the pictographs activate different forms of agency; they interrelate a range of correspondences, the location of the painting in relation to water bodies and other environmental attributes (including the geological surface), the material used in production, and references within the designs themselves. In total, this suite of correspondences presented Chumash artists (and audiences) with a wide latitude of affects and outcomes.

CHUMASH DESIGN AND TRANSMORPHISM

The images produced by the Chumash made allusions to a collective range of parts, particularly human and animal but also vegetable, and quite probably to personified astronomical bodies (Hudson & Underhay 1978). Many images show characteristics that elide anthropomorphic traits with parts from these other categories.

Indeed, various rock art elements appear to represent transmorphic beings, either during their process of transformation, or more commonly as a collage of different forms, each part of which seems to be representative of some form of sentience. The combinations are indeed creative—human/animal, human/celestial, human/plant, animal/celestial, animal/plant, etc. A simple example of animal/celestial can be seen at Piedra Blanca (see Figure 3.3): a monochrome red bird figure has a celestial pinwheeling element replacing its head and beak. Elements found in Sierra Madre and Mutau sites appear to be anthropomorphic figures with celestial extensions (see Figure 3.4). At Three Springs is the element known as Blue Boy (see Figure 3.5), which elides the human/animal in a classic example of an anthropomorphic figure (seen in its upright posture) with bird-like feet.

Readily identifiable plant imagery is rare, but it may be that pinwheel elements are metaphorically linked to the opening of flowers such as the hallucinogenic datura (see Robinson & Sturt 2008). Thus, elements may make allusions across forms: a pinwheeling element may be a double metaphor, evoking at the same time the power associated with a celestial body and that of the datura plant (see Hudson & Underhay 1978).

Figure 3.3   Monochrome red pictograph at Piedra Blanca

Figure 3.4   Monochrome red Chumash pictograph at Mutau

Figure 3.5 Polychrome transmorphic design known as Blue Boy at Three Springs

Of course, there are inscrutable elements that defy a simple classifica-tion into recognizable categories of human/animal/plant/celestial. The ubiquitous so-called aquatic motif is such an example (Hudson & Conti 1981). This element is characterized by bifurcating ends—it sometimes appears straight like a bone but is more often curved to some degree (see Figure 3.6).

Some have projections that appear to be "fin-like" and may refer to parts of some species of fish (hence the term, aquatic). Although its main form remains enigmatic, at times this figure includes body parts that add a valence of sentience to it. This compositional aspect illustrates how important the constituent parts of individual elements appear to have been to Chumash artists. Some elements have artistic flourishes that emphasize particular parts of the body. For instance, circular embellishments on appendages are not uncommon, and zigzag elements may radiate from torsos. Joints are often emphasized, as illustrated in an element from Alder Creek (see Figure 3.7).

To this point, I have focused mostly on individual elements, and it is clear that even a single element may be comprised of multiple indi-vidual parts. Elsewhere, I have discussed how the creative combining of a set of stock elements (or motifs) into multiple composition ele-ments or panels resulted in widespread "set pieces" that allowed for

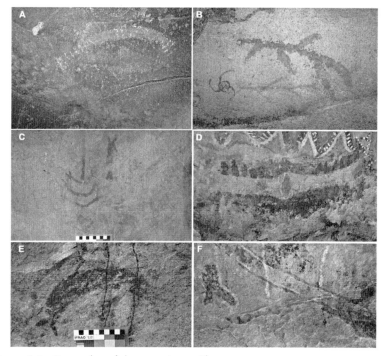

Figure 3.6   Examples of the aquatic motif

Figure 3.7   Monochrome red design from Alder Creek

a modular use of symbols (Robinson 2006, 2013a). Although there is great variation within these set pieces, there are common, recognizable combinations that imply analogous meanings. For instance, a common trope is to position a central figure (often a transmorphic figure such as Blue Boy, see Figure 3.4) between pinwheel or radial elements that connect to or are near the elbows. We don't know the specific metaphor or correspondence alluded to, but it is clear that the combinations being employed are not simply a record of an individual trance experience. There is a purposeful utilization of particular elements to construct a visual narrative that shows specific similarities across the Chumash geography.

SHAMANIC SELF-PORTRAITS OR AFFECTIVE IMAGERY?

The neurophysiological shamanic model remains contentious in explaining Chumash rock art. At issue here is the extent to which images are depictions of specific trance experiences. Sequence is a first problematic question. When is the art supposed to have been made, exactly—during trance experience? This is unlikely, if the debilitating effects of datura are in effect. Immediately following? This is possible, but again recovery time may be needed; certainly, some images might have been made after the event, but some of the pigment preparation and the skills involved in applying the art (such as at Pleito) require planning and preparation (Reeves et al. 2009). Likewise, the common suite of elements and set piece compositions suggests a societal set of visual rules employing common metaphors rather than a replication of individual neurophysiological imageries. In other words, each artist worked with a conventional "toolkit" of stock images, employing them creatively but within a common manner.

Of course, it is impossible to rule out that some rock art imagery was related to trance, especially as datura ingestion was integral to Chumash perceptions of the supernatural (see Applegate 1975; Blackburn 1975). Datura was mythologized as an old grandmother figure in Chumash mythology and was taken in response to a variety of situations to cure sickness, to access supernatural power, or to counteract potentially supernatural dangers. Even so, the representation of datura in a pinwheel form (if that is what is represented) may acknowledge the sentient power of that plant to induce trance and activate supernatural power rather than represent an image seen during a trance experience. And, most importantly, why make images representative of an individual trance experience? For what reason or purpose would such shamanic self-portraits have been made? Of course many humans have had, or have, trance experiences but do not record those experiences by painting on walls. The making of rock art requires further motivation (i.e., explanation) beyond the trance experience itself. Considering the ontology of the Chumash in regard to correspondence and affect, and their use of multicomponent material culture in power objects and talismans, it is more likely that rock art was meant to actively *do something* rather than passively represent an image. Much of the rock art was likely to be an agentive visual and material medium that was employed to play an active role in the Chumash world rather than to simply document an internal vision. Datura provided an ontological connection to the supernatural world, but there is yet little or no evidence that Chumash rock art was a direct depiction of specific trance images (see Quinlan 2000 for related debate).

Returning to the image that Whitley (2000, 121) terms the "exploding human" at the site of Pleito (see Figure 3.1), a close examination reveals that it is comprised of a variety of parts, most of which are animal. The top of the element has lines radiating upward; eyes are outlined on either side of the head, similar to pictographs found at sites such as Pinwheel Cave and the Carneros Rocks. This manner of depicting eyes may represent owl eyes (Sanger 1987, 34). Below, the torso is complicated by polychrome imagery including multiple appendages and a possible beaver tail. More importantly, this element is not a unique, one-off self-portrait: near identical images have been identified, including a recently discovered arborglyph interpreted as a mythic celestial being associated with the North Star (Saint-Onge et al. 2009). Sprague (2005) has identified this element as part of a common motif (what I term a "set piece") across South-Central California that combines a circular (solar?) element with a trailing element underneath, perhaps representing lightning or rain. These compositions may or may not represent a personification of the North Star, but certainly the element at Pleito is a composite transmorphic image with multiple allusions to a wide tradition of imagery rather than a direct representation of a single human trance episode; it is also a complex example of a common regional set piece. Indeed, the circular polychrome "celestial" image above it contains a blue hue that is likely to be an "optical blue," which is the result of a delicate process of combining white and black pigments to create an optical illusion of grey-blue. The artistic skill needed to produce this image, and many of the other images at Pleito, required precise application of pigment and intensive pigment preparation (Scott et al. 2002). This certainly could not be achieved by someone undergoing the profound effects of datura. In sum, the evidence points to an imagery redolent with correspondences rather than a shamanic self-portrait immediately related to an individual trance experience.

ONTOLOGY AND INDIGENOUS IDEOLOGY

The argument presented so far suggests that much of Chumash rock art can be interpreted as images that activated power through affective transmorphic combinations that drew upon complex correspondences based upon materialities, place, and imagery. These images were less about documenting a specific trance experience and more about influencing the Chumash physical, supernatural, and most importantly, social worlds. Certain substances and types of sentience had potential transmorphic qualities: this principle shows strongly in rock art imagery, but also in oral narratives concerning animals such as coyote or bear that may transform into alternate forms (Blackburn 1975). The ability to effect transformations in a visual format such as rock art was likely considered a highly powerful enactment, just as were healing, weather manipulation, and other forms of transformative practices.

With its overreliance on cross-cultural applicability and its erroneous insistence that rock art sites were the exclusive domain of the shaman, the shamanic debate has been slow to move the interpretation of Chumash rock art beyond the cognitive concept. By seeing rock art essentially as a recording of individual cognitive imagery, for the last twenty years this perspective has largely overlooked the agentive role of rock art within Chumash society; only recently the ideological and social aspects of it have been revisited (see Whitley et al. 2006; Robinson 2010a, 2011; Whitley & Whitley 2012). Although aspects of what is termed shamanism certainly overlap and resonate with ideas expressed in this chapter, the overemphasis on brain function and the pursuit of an internal origination of specific imagery has resulted in limited attention to the associated archaeology and the constituent characteristics of the design. Rock art is too often used simply to illustrate the model of shamanism, reifying both the model and the individual shaman as the sole owner and user of rock art locales. Such exclusionary interpretations, which stand in direct contradiction to the archaeological record, have unfortunate side effects in contemporary politics and are deeply problematic if used to exclude people from visiting rock art sites.

Indeed, scholars such as Thomas Blackburn (1975, 1977), Richard Applegate (1975, 1978, 1980), and Travis Hudson and Georgia Lee (1984), who largely published their work before the "shamanic turn" in rock art interpretation, all recognized to some degree the importance of the agency of rock art within Chumash society. Like other anthropologists of their era, these scholars employed the term "shaman" in their writing largely because the term is deeply embedded in the language of the discipline. However, all of these scholars recognized the integrated relationships between private and public ceremonial practices and the political makeup of Chumash and other South-Central Californian groups (Blackburn 1976). Hudson and Underhay (1978, 147) argued that "the very process of depicting certain symbols activated supernatural power." Hudson and Lee (1984) published a largely ignored article on the ideology of Chumash rock art in which they argued that the visual consumption of Chumash rock art by the wider society performed a positive ideological role, integrating both individuals and groups into the social and cosmological order. In his study of the neighboring Yokuts, Gayton (1930) viewed ideology from a more negative viewpoint, and he detailed how Yokuts chiefs allied themselves with shamans to control the wider populace through the threat of supernatural coercion. Besides the particular use each author makes of the term "shaman," what is pertinent here is the ideological role that the supernatural played in authority structures within the wider public realm. Archaeological survey and excavation of rock art sites clearly shows that rock art was visibly integrated into Chumash land use patterns, workspaces, and habitation areas (see Robinson 2010a, 2011). Likewise, as the ethnographic record shows, rather than being an exclusive esoteric knowledge, the fundamental principles of Chumash ontology were known to all members of society (Robinson 2013a). It is in this respect that this discussion of ontology matters: Chumash rock art was visually consumed by the public, and notions of the manipulability of the supernatural were widely shared through oral narratives and the common usage of talismans.

Rock art established a relation between the makers of the art and wider society. Its value was in the ability of individuals to demonstrate their skills in manipulating notions such as correspondence and in the others' ability to recognize that skill. In this sense, rock art was an ideological tool that made value statements about particular places, highlighted the value of particular materials, demonstrated the causal links between sentient power and the ability of humans to negotiate those personified powers, and therefore allowed for the differential employment of power within Indigenous society. However, it is unlikely that everyone in Chumash society made rock art; it appears that rock art was made by people of skill and authority (Robinson 2013b), and this concept resonates with what is known ethnohistorically about ceremonial and political leadership among the Chumash (Gamble 2008). As with individually owned talismans and the secretive language of the ʻantap, it is likely that individual rock art elements were imperfectly understood by those who did not make the art. This probably ascribed a mystical aspect to the paintings and enhanced their ambiguity as powerful images whose specific affects may remain obscure.

CONCLUSION

The ontological understandings touched upon here focus on notions of affect as they relate in particular to objects of special power and painted rock art. This focus is only partial, and there are certainly other aspects of agency related to Chumash rock art that need to be explored more deeply, including perceptions of agency in the environment and how onto-logical knowledge is transmitted within Indigenous societies (Robinson 2013a). Ultimately, interpreting rock art is important not in itself, but because of how rock art may have acted as a fulcrum for ideological relations to become enacted. This allows rock art to be appreciated as one strategy within a range of practices integrating ceremonialism with economy and social status (Blackburn 1976). Thus, rock art was part of how relationships were maintained, and even manipulated, through the agentive property of animals and other sentient powers. It was part of wider uses of material culture that provided the underpinning for Chumash ideology and authority (see Gamble 2012). Aspects typically associated with shamanism (such as trance and dreams) certainly played a role within Chumash society, and they were undoubtedly a factor in rock art. However, the shamanistic and neuropsychological model does not account for similarities in element design, placement in public space, or even the motivation to make the art itself. Indeed, Lewis-Williams (2001, 346) puts forward that "reaching out to touch powerful mental images in an attempt to possess them and fix them on the surfaces on which they were projected was very probably the initial motive for the production of two-dimensional, representational images." This explana-tion seems entirely too cursory and simple to explain not only the original motivation to make rock art in the Paleolithic, but also the making of rock art since. In this sense, and in the spirit of this volume, this chapter follows Dowson's (2009) call to "move on" from the intractable shamanic debate and to go after more satisfactory interpretations by analyzing rela-tional ontologies of Indigenous peoples.

In conclusion, this chapter is not a proposal for a new interpretive "model" of rock art. Indeed, Chumash rock art cannot be encapsulated by any singular explanation, theory, or perspective, and multiple interpretations are simultaneously possible. Relational ontology in Indigenous terms was explicitly and implicitly a fluid means of enacting malleable transformations, and as such singular explanations will never hold for very long. On one end of the spectrum is the remarkable complexity of the metaphors, allusions, correspondences, and the sheer imagination of the Chumash and their perception of the world. On the other end of the scale, pictographs are simply paint-on-rock, and therefore a number of motivations may lie behind the swaths of pigment and variety of images depicted. As valuable as the extensive ethnographic record is, it should also be kept in mind that it is necessarily fragmentary and lacking in time depth (see Robinson 2010b). Even the most basic of designs have polyvalent possibilities that exponentially increase in time and space. Ultimately, the study of rock art will profit more by focusing on the society within which rock art images were created and the role they played within that society than by focusing on grand models and universal cognition. By paying close attention to the ethnography, the archaeology, and the images themselves, the integrative potential that rock art enacted within societal dynamics can be appreciated.

ACKNOWLEDGMENTS

I would like to thank the editors for the invitation to participate in this volume, as well as the rest of the contributors for the very useful discussion we had in a cottage in Oxfordshire. I would also like to thank the Rock Art Documentation Group (Rick Bury, Antoinette Padgett, and Dan Reeves), plus the staff of the Wind Wolves Preserve in California for their support of my research. Thanks also to Julienne Bernard, Christopher Chippindale, Vicki Cummings, John Johnson, Richard Peterson, Duncan Sayer, Fraser Sturt, and Unika Delpino-Mark, as well as Ben Jervis for his useful comments on the initial draft of this chapter. All photographs are by the author.

REFERENCES

Applegate, R.B. 1975. The datura cult among the Chumash. *Journal of California Anthropology* 2(1), 7–17

Applegate, R.B. 1978. 'Atishwin: the dream helper in South-Central California. *Ballena Press Anthropological Papers* 13. Santa Barbara, CA: Ballena Press/Santa Barbara Museum of Natural History

Applegate, R.B. 1980. Ethnosemantics of the dream helper in South-Central California. In K. Klar (ed.), *Trends in Linguistics: American Indians and Indoeuropean Studies*, 3–9. New York: Mountain Publishers

Blackburn, T.C. 1975. *December's Child: A Book of Chumash Oral Narratives*. Berkeley: University of California Press

Blackburn, T.C. 1976. Ceremonial integration and social interaction in aboriginal California. In L.J. Bean & T.C. Blackburn (eds.), *Native Californians: A Theoretical Perspective*, 225–43. Romona, CA: Ballena Press

Blackburn, T.C. 1977. Biopsychological aspects of Chumash rock art. *Journal of California Anthropology* 4(1), 88–94

Chippindale, C. 2003. Trying to test a trance hypothesis in its social context. *Cambridge Archaeological Journal* 13(2), 218–19

Dowson, T. 2007. Debating shamanism in Southern African rock art: time to move on. *South African Archaeological Bulletin* 185, 49–61

Dowson, T. 2009. Re-animating hunter-gatherer rock-art research. *Cambridge Archaeological Journal* 19(3), 378–87

Eerkens, J.W., Dinkel, R. & Ormsbee, C. 2012. A land of style: a quantitative and cultural transmission approach to understanding Coso rock art. In T.L. Jones & J.E. Perry (eds.), *Contemporary Issues in California Archaeology*, 237–53. Walnut Creek, CA: Left Coast Press

Gamble, L.H. 2008. *The Chumash World at European Contact: Power, Trade, and Feasting among Complex Hunter-Gatherers*. Berkeley: University of California Press

Gamble, L.H. 2012. A land of power: the materiality of wealth, knowledge, authority, and the supernatural. In T.L. Jones & J.E. Perry (eds.), *Contemporary Issues in California Archaeology*, 175–96. Walnut Creek, CA: Left Coast Press

Garfinkel, A.P. & Austin, D.R. 2011. Reproductive symbolism in Great Basin rock art: bighorn sheep hunting, fertility and forager ideology. *Cambridge Archaeological Journal* 21(3), 454–71

Gayton, A.H. 1930. Yokuts-Mono chiefs and shamans. *University of California Publications in American Archaeology and Ethnography* 24(8), 361–420

Grant, C. 1965. *The Rock Paintings of the Chumash*. Berkeley: University of California Press

Grant, C. 1968. *Rock Drawings of the Coso Range, Inyo County, California*. China Lake, CA: Maturango Museum

Hildebrandt, W. & McGuire, K.R. 2012. A land of prestige. In T.L. Jones & J.E. Perry (eds.), *Contemporary Issues in California Archaeology*, 133–51. Walnut Creek, CA: Left Coast Press

Hudson, T. 1979. A rare account of Gabrielino shamanism from the notes of John P. Harrington. *Journal of California and Great Basin Anthropology* 1(2), 356–62

Hudson, T. & Conti, K. 1981. The "aquatic motif" in Chumash rock art. *Journal of California and Great Basin Anthropology* 3(2), 224–31

Hudson, T. & Lee, G. 1984. Function and symbolism in Chumash rock art. *Journal of New World Archaeology* 6(3), 26–47

Hudson, T. & Underhay, E. 1978. Crystals in the sky: an intellectual odyssey involving Chumash astronomy, cosmology, and rock art. *Ballena Press Anthropological Papers* 10. Santa Barbara, CA: Ballena Press/Santa Barbara Museum of Natural History

Lewis-Williams, J. 2001. Brainstorming images: neuropsychology and rock art research. In D.S. Whitley (ed.), *Handbook of Rock Art Research*, 332–57. Walnut Creek, CA: AltaMira Press

Lewis-Williams, J.D. & Dowson, T.A. 1988. The sign of all times. *Current Anthropology* 29(2), 201–17

Librado, F. 1981. *The Eye of the Flute: Chumash Traditional History and Ritual as Told by Fernando Librado Kitsepawit to John P. Harrington*. Edited by T. Hudson, T.C. Blackburn, R. Curletti & J. Timbrook. Banning, CA: Malki Museum Press

Pearson, J.L. 2002. *Shamanism and the Ancient Mind: A Cognitive Approach to Archeology*. Walnut Creek, CA: AltaMira Press

Quinlan, A.R. 2000. The ventriloquist's dummy: a critical review of shamanism and rock art in far western North America. *Journal of California and Great Basin Anthropology* 22(1), 92–108

Quinlan, A.R. & Woody, A. 2003. Marks of distinction: rock art and ethnic identification in the Great Basin. *American Antiquity* 68, 372–90

Reeves, D., Bury, R. & Robinson, D.W. 2009. Invoking Occam's razor: experimental pigment processing and an hypothesis concerning Emigdiano Chumash rock art. *Journal of California and Great Basin Anthropology* 29(1), 59–67

Robinson, D.W. 2004. The mirror of the sun: surface, mineral applications and interface in California rock-art. In N. Boivin & M.A. Owoc (eds.), *Soils, Stones and Symbols: Archaeological and Anthropological Perspectives on the Mineral World*, 91–106. London: UCL Press

Robinson, D.W. 2006. *Landscape, Taskscape, and Indigenous Perception: The Rock Art of South-Central California*. Unpublished PhD dissertation, Department of Archaeology, University of Cambridge

Robinson, D.W. 2010a. Land use, land ideology: an integrated Geographic Information Systems analysis of the Emigdiano Chumash rock-art, South-Central California. *American Antiquity* 74(4), 792–818

Robinson, D.W. 2010b. Resolving archaeological and ethnographic tensions: a case study from South-Central California. In D. Garrow & T. Yarrow (eds.), *Archaeology and Anthropology: Understanding Similarities, Exploring Differences*, 84–109. Oxford, UK: Oxbow Books

Robinson, D.W. 2011. Placing ideology: rock art landscapes of inland and interior South-Central California. In D.W. Robinson & J. Perry (eds.), "Landscape Archaeology in Southern and South-Central California." Special issue, *California Archaeology* 3(1), 31–52

Robinson, D.W. 2013a. Drawing upon the past: temporal ontology and mythological ideology in South-Central Californian rock-art. *Cambridge Archaeological Journal* 23 (forthcoming)

Robinson, D.W. 2013b. Legitimizing space: art and the politics of place. Special issue "Art Makes Society." *World Art* 3(1) (under review)

Robinson, D.W. In press. From ethnohistory to ethnogenesis: a historiography of hunter-gatherer cultural anthropology in California and the Great Basin. In V. Cummings, P. Jordan & M. Zvelebil (eds.), *The Oxford Handbook of the Archaeology and Anthropology of Hunter-Gatherers.* Oxford: Oxford University Press

Robinson, D.W. & Sturt, F. 2008. Towards articulating rock-art with archaeology: an interim report of the Pinwheel Cave rock-art and bedrock mortar complex (CA-KER-5836 & 5837), Kern Country, California. *Kern County Archaeological Society Journal* 10, 25–44

Robinson, D.W., Sturt, F. & Bernard, J. 2010. Enculturating environments: rock-art and the interior of South-Central California. *Antiquity* 84, 232 (Project Gallery at http://antiquity.ac.uk/projgall/robinson323/)

Saint-Onge Sr., R.W., Johnson, J. & Talaugon, J.R. 2009. Archaeoastronomical implications of a northern Chumash arborglyph. *Journal of California and Great Basin Anthropology* 29(1), 29–57

Sanger, K.K. 1987. *Carneros Rocks: Rock Art at a Cultural Boundary.* Unpublished Master's thesis, Department of Anthropology, University of California, Los Angeles

Scott, D.A., Scheerer, S. & Reeves, D.J. 2002. Technical examination of some rock art pigments and encrustations from the Chumash Indian site of San Emigdio, California. *Studies in Conservation* 47(3), 184–94

Sprague, J. 2005. *Icons and ideograms: rock-art within the interior region of South-Central California.* Paper presented at the American Archaeological Society Seminar, McDonald Archaeological Institute, Cambridge

Timbrook, J. 2000. Search for the source of the sorcerer's stones. In D. Browne, K. Mitchell & H. Chanes (eds.), *Proceedings of the 5th California Islands Symposia*, 633–40. Santa Barbara, CA: Santa Barbara Museum of Natural History

Timbrook, J. 2007. *Chumash Ethnobotany: Plant Knowledge among the Chumash People of Southern California.* Santa Barbara, CA: Santa Barbara Museum of Natural History

Walker, P.L. & Hudson, T. 1993. *Chumash Healing: Changing Health and Medical Practices in an American Indian Society.* Banning, CA: Malki Museum Press

Whitley, D.S. 1988. Comment on "The Sign of All Times." *Current Anthropology* 29(2), 238

Whitley, D.S. 1998. Cognitive neuroscience, shamanism and the rock art of Native California. *Anthropology of Consciousness* 9(1), 22–37

Whitley, D.S. 2000. *The Art of the Shaman: Rock Art of California.* Salt Lake City: University of Utah Press

Whitley, D.S., Simon, J. & Loubser, J. 2006. The Carrizo collapse: art and politics in the past. In R.L. Kaldenberg (ed.), *A Festschrift Honoring the Contributions of California Archaeologist Jay von Werlhof*, 199–208. Ridgecrest, CA: Maturango Museum Publications 20

Whitley, D.S. & Whitley, T.K. 2012. A land of vision and dreams. In T.L. Jones & J.E. Perry (eds.), *Contemporary Issues in California Archaeology*, 255–72. Walnut Creek, CA: Left Coast Press

CHAPTER FOUR

Carnival Times and the Semiopraxis of the Snake: Mining and the Politics of Knowledge

Alejandro Haber

This chapter mines the ontologically intricate history of my involvement with an archaeological mining site, a site at which one of the earliest anticolonial uprisings started during the carnival of 1775. Beginning with the usual involvement of an archaeologist with prior research, and expanding to incorporate diverse historical agents, the chapter rapidly diversifies to include not only my intellectual consideration of agency but also my being as a political agent and living creature. The very place from where archaeology is carried out shifts when its own foundations become part of the conversation, transforming it from an enterprise related to the search for knowledge to an interculturally relational endeavor. Even accepting the impact of being a dweller in the scenarios in which I am also the knower, the latter role is not ruled out but rather transformed. In this sense, this piece explores the semiopraxis that develops in the course of the history told. Only occasionally does my writing or authorship—whether as performance, oral discussion, or as part of collective and heterogeneous subjectivities—intervene in the conversation. Just as during carnival time, what is said (with or without words) is said in conversations across ontologies, in which locations and characters are inverted in surprising ways. This piece of writing explores the position of theory within a broader conversation concerned with places on the move.

Archaeology after Interpretation: Returning Materials to Archaeological Theory, edited by Benjamin Alberti, Andrew Meirion Jones, and Joshua Pollard, 79–95. ©2013 Left Coast Press, Inc. All rights reserved.

WRITING IN/ON CARNIVAL TIMES

In retrospect, this story appears to have been led by an invisible hand. One of the difficulties of committing it to writing, then, is to narrate it as a series of events. This would convey the idea that these events simply occurred sequentially along a timeline, and therefore overlook the entire issue. Instead, events happen in an undulating fashion; they appear from underground, from the inside of things. However, to make a start, I will commence near the beginning (but maybe not right at the beginning). This text, at least, has a beginning, and perhaps the reader will believe that my story has a beginning after all. I am in Cuenca, Ecuador, and it is carnival. People are feasting in town, and I am in a dark cybercafé trying to answer Ben's call[1] for papers on ontological difference. Writing is a disproportionately difficult task if we think of the world of relations that always remain outside it. People are happy and drinking outside this text.

MINING AND DRINKING ON THE BORDER

On the eve of a day of fieldwork I drove the group of students who were surveying the archaeological mining site of Ingaguassi back to Fenix, the lithium mine camp belonging to a multinational company where we were staying, but not before an anticipated stopover at the La Aguadita primary school.[2] The teacher, José María,[3] would be there waiting for us with a cup of tea, some nice conversation, and a shot or two of whisky or *aguardiente*, after which we would enter the alcohol-free zone of the mine camp. That evening we arrived late at the school because along the dirt road leaving Ingaguassi we were delayed by a man whom we saw moving toward the area of a ruined house. He was hesitant and seemed suspicious when I got out of the car and approached him, and his stammering speech initially confirmed my impression (until I learnt that his powerful eloquence needed more time). The man, Andrés, was on his way to pan for gold from the discarded sediment at the now-abandoned 1960s lower mine of Mina Incahuasi (near the older Ingaguassi site), and he suspected—I suspect—that I would inform the police about his illegal activity (mines, like other land, are owned by people who paid for a title, not by the people who look after them). Over the next few days, as I demonstrated complicity by asking him to teach me to pan for gold and by bringing him fresh water every day from the school, we started a long, deep, and friendly conversation, part of which is enmeshed in the story I relate here. Andrés was very interested in my being an archaeologist and university professor, and he pushed me, slowly and insistently, to the borders of my knowledge, asking me simple and deep questions. Initially, these concerned my knowledge of certain phenomena, but eventually they led to questions about my relationship to the knowledge I had.

SEARCHING FOR INDIGENOUS AGENCY: AGAINST EMPIRES

I spent several field seasons at Ingaguassi, searching the area for the Incas. Even though archaeologists who had worked there assured me that Ingaguassi was the main Inca site in the southern high plains (Raffino 1981; Olivera 1991), my research ended with the conclusion that all evidence of Inca state agency was as evanescent as the thin air of the Andes. Archaeologists used to (and still do) speak of "empire" when referring to the Incas, who, according to them, conquered the Kollau (the southern territory encompassing the high plains or *altiplano*) in search of precious metals. Such a large-scale strategic operation, which would have included the building of roads and administrative centers and the diffusion of architectural features and standardized objects, is read through the lens of the narrative of empire. That is, the interpretive model of the "Inca Empire" assumes that the existence of certain features (roads, planned settlements, and architectural and craft styles) was integrated within a system of domination. As such, the observation of any of these features is generally read as belonging to an "integrated whole" or system that would confirm the Inca Empire model. Because Ingaguassi was a gold ore mine, the presence of architecture and finds of an Inca type had been rapidly recorded by those who visited the site before me. After a systematic search at Ingaguassi and two other contemporary sites, I could confirm nothing of the Inca presence: either the diagnostic features were nonexistent or they weren't diagnostic at all. The only thing that remained was the imaginary association between metal mining, empire, and precolonial times that formed part of the bedrock of the Inca model. The purely imaginary character of the association was the first discovery I made at Ingaguassi.

Even documentary historians who researched the site (without really knowing where it was located) were contradicted by my research (Hidalgo Lehuedé & Castro 1999). Neither did I find evidence of the Spanish colonial state at the foundation of the settlement. According to my research, the history of the settlement began with the placement of several single-roomed rectangular houses aligned north-south directly on top of quartz veins rich in gold ore. Their single doorways faced east; each house had a mine entrance, a stone mill (*maray*), and a kiln (Haber 2004, 2007a, 2007b). These houses (see Figure 4.1), built by local families during the late seventeenth and early eighteenth centuries,

Figure 4.1 Ruins of Loreto de Ingaguassi, Antofagasta de la Sierra, Catamarca, Argentina

constituted an Indigenous mining hamlet founded just after the demise of the armed Indigenous resistance in the area, part of the so-called Calchaqui (warrior) rebellion that took part in the southern end of Spanish Peru.

REVOLUTION AND CARNIVAL: THE SNAKE

My search for Indigenous agency (instead of that of the Inca Empire or the Spanish Empire, privileged by archaeological and historical literature) went beyond the initial settlement of the site. In fact, one of my central interests was its abandonment. Ingaguassi was the scene of one of the first anticolonial uprisings in 1775 that eventually developed into the great highland rebellions against European colonialism in 1781, led by Tupac Amaru, Tomás Katari, and Tupac Katari (Hidalgo Lehuedé 1996). I was delighted, then, when I discovered a concordance of meaning between the leaders' military names (*katari* means snake in Aymara, and is *amaru* in Quechua) and the only figurative decoration I found on the Indigenous-made pottery at the site (and at two other related sites): small, modeled snakes applied on the lip-joined handles wind their way towards the mouths of the jars (see Figure 4.2).

Historians' interpretations of the rebellion ranged from a growing resistance to "*repartimientos*" (a compulsory distribution of overpriced European goods to Indigenous peoples) (Hidalgo Lehuedé 1987) to the role inversion adopted during carnival time (the rebellion erupted at Ingaguassi during the 1775 carnival) (Hidalgo Lehuedé & Castro 1999). My own interpretation of the rebellion was related to the architectural

Figure 4.2   Examples of decoration applied on lip-attached handles, typical of the Indigenous pottery of the nineteenth-century Ingaguassi area

sequence of the site (Haber 2004, 2007a, 2007b). A first phase consisted of Indigenous peasant occupations, during which Indigenous families managed their own access to the extraction and processing of minerals. They retained control of the mine shafts and of the milling and reduction equipment by placing their houses directly over the veins of mineral. The subsequent architectural phases demonstrated a history of increasing European intervention in the form of colonial officers, businessmen, and priests, apparent in the transformation of former peasant houses into complex compounds and internal walled spaces, including a church oriented west and several compounds oriented towards the church in a grid plan of streets and plaza (see Figures 4.3 and 4.4). The rebellion, I argued, was resistance to the loss of control of the mine by the Indigenous population. The threat was that the Europeans would make Ingaguassi another Potosí; that they would gain control over the mines *and* the labor force through the *mita* forced-labor scheme established in 1570 by viceroy Toledo, as occurred at Potosí.

A QUESTION ABOUT THE VEIN

At this moment (in the argument, if not in time) comes the question Andrés asked me a year after I first met him. We met by chance at the La Aguadita school, where we continued our conversation of few and difficult words: "What do you think, as archaeologist and professor:

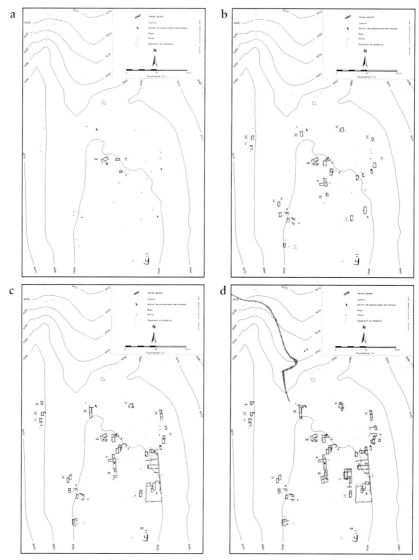

Figure 4.3 Phases of architectural renewal in the upper part (the hamlet) of Loreto de Ingaguassi

Is it true or not that the mineral vein grows overnight?" This shocking question required several years of reflection from me—about the concrete fact of the vein growing, the meaning of the night as a time for the vein's agency, the correct and expected relationship to the vein, the concept of truth, my relation to truth and the gods, and the consequences of my

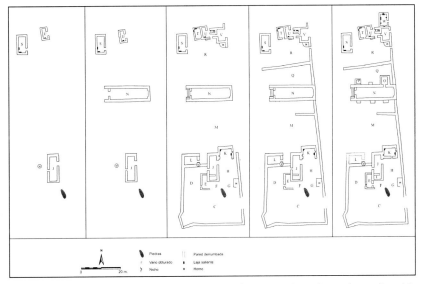

Figure 4.4 Building phases of Indigenous houses oriented north-south with eastward-facing entrances; building of the Nuestra Señora de Loreto de Ingaguassi Chapel; and reorientation and refurbishing of the houses around the chapel as colonial residences.

being part of that conversation. I understood with time that the vein was not merely an object to be mined but a potent living being to which one must relate properly. Placing the houses on top of the vein was as much an act of social and domestic appropriation of the mineral resources as it was an act of nurturing the vein (and thus of nurturing the families living there). I also understood why Indigenous houses were oriented eastward in the first place (towards the rising sun), while relations with the god of the mine were carried out in underground darkness. But my involvement with this local ontology was not merely about knowing, as a conventional ethnographer would assume his/her role to be. In the meantime, other interrelated processes—which were other in appearance only—were developing in the area. These processes involved me not only as a knower (my relationship with truth) but also as an inhabitant (my relationship with the world, which included my relationship with truth).

LOOKING AFTER THE *ANTIGUOS*

We spent several summer months during our third fieldwork season excavating one of the houses considered to be early in the settlement sequence. The team slept at the La Aguadita school and walked forty minutes to the site every morning and back in the evening. Ubalda, who

Figure 4.5 Pile of white stones (*apacheta*) by the side of the excavated house at Ingaguassi

was looking after her granddaughter after school, accompanied the team every day. She learnt to read numbers on the measuring instrument, and taught us—among other things—to pick up a white stone at the start of the walk and add it to a pile near the excavation. The tiredness of the walk would remain in the stone and not with us, and the *apacheta* (the name of the stone pile) that grew day after day became the place where coca leaves and alcohol were offered before starting work each morning. We were there to conduct an excavation but, thanks to Ubalda, we ended up developing a different relationship to the *antiguos* (the archaeological site/object/being).[4] To be involved in that unexpected conversation was the main event of that summer, and the *apacheta* was its most visible outcome (see Figure 4.5). No words were needed.

MINING AGAIN: INDIGENOUS AND SOCIAL MOVEMENTS

A year after the beginning of my research in the Hombre Muerto area, a group of local people visited me at home in the Catamarca valley, asking for advice regarding their plans to present themselves to the state as an Indigenous community and thus claim formal communal property titles to land and resources. Local people live in dispersed settlements around the Hombre Muerto salt lake, breeding llamas and sheep, and carry on a number of traditional productive activities classified as illegal by the state (such as mining, hunting, and so on). The salt lake area is completely covered in mining properties, several of which are exploited by big companies, including at the time RTZ (Rio Tinto) and FMC. Mining companies occupy the people's territory, cut off their roads (even making local people apply for permits at the mining property gates), exploit their resources, and demonstrate ongoing hostility towards locals. They have demanded the depopulation of the area because, they claim, there is nothing to do there except mine. This hostility was even directed at the local school, where the teacher kept the only record of the lithium mine's productivity (by drawing pen marks on the wall by the little window in the kitchen from where the trucks loaded with mineral could be seen passing). The teacher revealed that the mining companies had not declared the doubling of mineral production during a one-year period to Argentine authorities, hence keeping royalties and taxes at the level of the lower production rates. Eventually, the school building itself was rented out by the provincial state to another mining company as a base camp for a campaign of exploration (which included drilling in the Ingaguassi archaeological site, supposedly protected as a National Historic Monument). The community organization process was eventually deactivated, and local leaders temporarily emigrated to other provinces.

My denouncement in the media of the conversion of a primary school into a mining camp was supported by other university professors and paralleled the social movements for life and against large-scale mining in Catamarca (Machado Aráoz 2009; Svampa & Antonelli 2009). Local educational authorities countered that the few students that remained were at least fed by the mining campaigns catering service in exchange. This was one of the last occasions that local newspapers published anything against the abuses of the mining companies. The state merely genuflected as the media blockade turned openly impermeable to any kind of critical word regarding the new colonial conquest. The denouncement was, at least, picked up by the well-known journalist Mona Moncalvillo from Radio Nacional Buenos Aires. Mona interviewed me by telephone while simultaneously talking to the Director of Education of Catamarca province, who argued that the children I saw sleeping at the back of the school under zinc sheeting and discarded wood from the mining supplies packaging did not exist; in her words, "there were no enrolled pupils." I had the opportunity to speak of the omnipresence of the mining companies in western Catamarca, where they control school supplies, hospitals, and basic community services. Such activities are included by companies under the subheading of "social responsibility," which refers inescapably to duties of the state. The state's complicit withdrawal from such responsibilities sets a trap of complacency for local populations from which it is extremely risky to escape. Mona did not seem convinced of the truth of what I said, exaggerated as it sounded through the speakers of the radio studio in Buenos Aires. My words may be read with the same skepticism here.

KNOWING AND LIVING ON THE BORDER

To relate to another ontology is not simply a matter of knowing; neither is it a matter of being involved with radical cultural difference. Because cultural difference is colonial difference in the first place (Thomas 1994), to be involved with a non-Western ontology implies inhabiting a borderland (the colonial border). On the border, the West's knowledge project is challenged, as are its projects of intervention. In this sense, to inhabit the border is not just a strategy for obtaining control over a section of the world (at least through knowledge of it). Inhabiting the border, one is transformed not only as a knower but also as an inhabitant; or, one is transformed as a knower because one is transformed as inhabitant (Haber 2008). In the story I bring to light here, colonialism (and particularly mining) is implicated both as the target of the history to be known and in the social relationships out of which one attempts to understand that history. In both contexts—historical (the known) and present (knower)—colonial relationships are only one side of the coin. The other is the colonial character of knowledge, or the alleged superiority of one type of knowledge (Christianity, science, archaeology) over another (local ontology) (Haber 2008). The colonial character of knowledge creates the conditions for continued colonialism: local practice is illegal, local concepts of rights to land are neglected, whereas expert knowledge feeds the state's and companies' colonial projects. In this postcolonial scenario, even to understand a particular thing as an archaeological object (naming it as such, and applying to it the pertinent legislation) is an act weighted towards the continued renewal of colonialism. The relationship between mining and science cannot be reduced to ethical correctness alone or to the assumed need to protect an independent sphere of critical thought. The postcolonial and postmodern contexts wrap science and academia in the entanglements of the colonial border, where political meanings are provided by relational histories and discursive positions. Attempting to acquire some autonomy from these contexts, protecting oneself by a simple will-to-knowledge, and modulating the relationship according to assumed ethical standards are different ways of avoiding the terrible fact that we are already at the battlefront, acted upon epistemically by disciplinary mechanisms. One can focus on one's "own business," provide one alibi or another, or alternatively be grateful for the opportunities that interpellation can offer to address one's thought towards either science or the snake.

There is always another side that remains hidden from the outside, an internal side that lives within a completely different network of relationships (Haber 2009); though its difference does not mean it is independent or isolated. Though sometimes kept independent and in isolation, this other side is always related to the dominant culture through relations of hegemony and subalternity. Difference is built on intercultural relations (Grosso 2010), that is, colonial/cultural difference is a constitutive relation of both hegemonic and subaltern positions.[5]

Hegemonic discourse conflates local ontology with cultural diversity, objectified in knowledge projects and managed by multicultural politics. Beings in relation are dissected and put at the disposal of projects of colonial expansion: land, water, minerals, animals, human labor, landscapes, crafts, and customs are formulated by science, made available to the state, and exploited by capital. Archaeology makes a central contribution to these processes of colonial border expansion. But at the border, far from the light of reason, another kind of relatedness lives; obscure and resistant, that relatedness is busy reproducing relations that are, above all, nurturing (Haber 2007a).

CARNIVAL TIME AND THE SEMIOPRAXIS OF THE SNAKE

There is a living ontology on the inside of the world. This ontology, like a snake, comes to the surface at particular times, such as carnival, when relations of care to the mine gods are renewed. In this sense, carnival is not just an inversion of normal life but also the exposure to daylight of an ongoing living network of relationships. Populations of sacred beings—*antiguos*—are included in this network, not as objects of knowledge relating to the past but as potent beings that live and reproduce underground, demand obligations, and protect the living. This has powerful implications for archaeology: time and matter, as constitutive of disciplinary metaphysics, mean something quite different. Time is never linear, even if it is related sequentially; the past lives heterogeneously in the present. Material culture is not merely material and cannot be manipulated as if it were inert matter without offending its sensibility and potency. These understandings of matter as soulful and animated, and time as nonlinear, imply a departure from core modern Western principles that take "the West" as a theory of history. Those principles, consolidated by Western historiography, are guarded and reproduced by the discipline of archaeology in its role of expanding

Western theory beyond its own borders—that is, the West as civilization and writing as its record.

To approach the interior of things implies communicating both as inhabitant and as knower through relationships that are visible only during carnival, and usually with the aid of alcoholic toasts (*ch'alla*) that feed the underground gods and liberate historical memory (Abercrombie 1998; Arnold & Yapita 2005). During carnival time, however, things are not merely said or articulated in literary form. Dance, movement, gestures, music, and even the materiality of the utterances proffered are more eloquent than the linguistic communication involved. In this sense, as much remains outside the text as within it. A departure from the West implies, first of all, a departure from a place of normality and a relocation to the borderland.

DRINKING WITH THE GODS

In April 2006 I returned to Ingaguassi with about sixty people from Antofagasta de la Sierra, the closest town, where I had been involved with school students, teachers, and the general public at the museum. This was not the first time that I had been invited to develop community activities concerned with local culture and history. In fact, in October 2005 I delivered a course on the topic to almost fifty interested people from Antofagasta de la Sierra. Continued self-reflection on the epistemic violence implied in explaining local history to local people pushed me to develop other dialogic methodologies for this subsequent opportunity. On the second occasion, then, along with the results of several years of research I presented my work at Ingaguassi. My spelling the site "Ingaguassi" and not "Incahuasi" (which I took from a document from the colonial period and the twentieth-century spelling of Mina Incahuasi) was challenged by some people. My pictures of the ruins of the church of Nuestra Señora de Loreto, the first Christian church in the area and the original location of the image of the Virgin of Loreto, currently patron of the church at Antofagasta, were observed with interest (see Figure 4.6). In fact, my first surprise on returning to Ingaguassi was to see the rows of whitened stones that marked the road from the entrance of the ruins to the door of the church. The explanation was that the Virgin of Loreto had been taken some months earlier to visit her original home at Ingaguassi.

I was surprised again when our little *apacheta*, next to the archaeological excavation from the summer before, was chosen as the site to dig the hole for the mouth of Pachamama in order to share with the earth the picnic lunch. One by one, the attendees gave coca leaves and alcohol to Pachamama (see Figure 4.7). This exemplifies the nonlinguistic aspect of

Figure 4.6 Remains of the eighteenth-century Chapel of Nuestra Señora de Loreto de Ingaguassi

Figure 4.7 *Ch'alla* (offering or toast) to Pachamama beside the *apacheta*

intercultural communication: our being there as archaeologists and communicating with the gods was seen by the locals as much more efficient in its materiality than anything interesting we might have found there or might have said about the excavations.

CODA: ONE MORE TOAST

Mining, drinking, and colonialism are related on these pages in different ways, one of which is usually unseen, unexpected, nonlinear, and carnivalesque. This implies a poetics of the world that expresses a set of relations that are distinct from colonial and capitalist relationships. Such a poetics is enacted ("written") from an ontologically different place, though one that exists in relation to hegemonic relationships (embodied by the state, science, and capital). Carnival times are not delimited by a particular pair of dates but by their relationship with hegemonic culture. Archaeology itself is already located within the hegemonic set of cultural dispositions and power relations. But something happens (or may happen) when one is touched as much by ontological difference as by colonial difference; when one decides to abandon hegemonic intentions towards normality (West, science, discipline, linguistic expression, state, development, and so on). Such conversations become constitutive, and the place of writing (archaeology), free from its former attachment to the position of normality, moves to different settings in the borderland. It is not that a different ontology is discovered and one moves to it. Ontological difference, built on colonial difference, has always been in relation; different ontologies are built on their mutual relations of difference. But these relations of difference (of which, again, colonial difference is part) are not just a matter of diversity. Colonial difference implies asymmetrical hegemonic relations: the hegemonic position is the place of utterance, the place of normality, and the other is the place to be known, the place of abnormality. Both positions have always been intercultural in their relationship. Thus, it is not that we travel from one side to discover the other. It may rather be the case that, touched by the other, we discover the assumption of normality that fixes us in the hegemonic position and then move away from it. Such a movement implies a displacement of writing and writing that is about displacement.

Science, archaeology, and academia should examine carefully their roles in colonialism, not only because they occupy a privileged place of critical knowledge that ought to be preserved but also because they are ways of inhabiting the colonial border. These contexts and the reflections they necessitate may imply shifts in position that question, displace, and depart from colonialism. Condemnation of and opposition to financial, political, and cultural links to transnational mining companies that academia, archaeology, and science have either tolerated or actively promoted are no different from the necessary theoretical work of detaching ourselves from categories and assumptions that recapitulate the colonial character of knowledge and make possible the expansion of the colonial border (Shepherd & Haber 2011). The theory of history that is a given for the discursive mobilizations that continuously reactivate the border is, after all, the same theory of history that archaeological research reads into the world as if it were a constitutive part of the objective world. But there are other theories of relatedness that live on the other side of things, as the counterpart of the normal world. Their power is as tactical interpellations of modern colonial assumptions.

What are the consequences for knowledge when one is displaced as inhabitant as well as knower? One of the consequences is that knowledge becomes enmeshed in complex ways with forms of relatedness for which the canons of validation are completely unprepared. This is one reason for the incongruences of texts such as the present one: writing cannot be expected to represent all that happens during research when knowledge moves to the border. Nevertheless, it can produce hints, partial pictures, and evocations. At the very least, writing may convey the idea that there is another reality in another time, constructed out of relationships that form on the inside of things—and that such a reality, like the snake, resists domination and, just as during carnival time, reappears and captivates us.

NOTES

1. A first version of this essay was read at the "'Worlds Otherwise': Archaeology, Theory and Ontological Difference" session chaired by Ben Alberti and Yvonne Marshall at the 2010 Theoretical Archaeological Group conference in Providence, Rhode Island. Here I am addressing the material (and social and cultural) context of writing on ontological difference. Even when academic writing is oriented towards a qualified audience, the ontological difference implied within its own context is, ultimately, one of the axes of this text. Ontological difference cannot merely be an object of writing without becoming also the place of writing, unless we opt for the multicultural domestication of difference. I retain the original reference even though this is a substantial rewriting of the presentation. Many people contributed in different ways to this text, and I'll mention only a few of them. The Kolla people from the Salar del Hombre Muerto (Incahuasi) community, in the first place, taught me whatever knowledge these pages may contain. Many students from the Universidad Nacional de Catamarca were part of the research team. Ben Alberti extended his invitation to the session to contribute to this volume, and helped—as usual—with the final shape of the text. Ben Alberti, Sonia Archila, Brian Boyd, Zoë Crossland, Mónica Espinosa, Cristóbal Gnecco, Herinaldy Gómez, Alfredo González-Ruibal, José Luis Grosso, Almudena Hernando, Alex Herrera, Martin Holbraad, Mario Santucho, and Jairo Tocancipá, among others, commented on this text, which remains my sole responsibility.

2. The events described here took place during the first field season at Ingaguassi, in November 2003. The research was funded by Fundación Antorchas (Project 14116/167, "Enclave landscapes in the Antofalla area, second half of the second millennium AD"). Ingaguassi, Mina Incahuasi, Fénix, and La Aguadita are places within the Hombre Muerto area, Antofagasta de la Sierra department, in the northwestern end of Catamarca province, northwest Argentina.
3. Individuals' names are fictitious in order to protect the identity of local people.
4. *Antiguos* are what archaeologists refer to as archaeological sites or objects, but they are also living, or dead but agentive, beings. They act upon other beings and demand action in return. They correspond to another space/time but also exist in the present because space/time is relational rather than dimensional.
5. Difference is used differently here from the multicultural notion of diversity.

REFERENCES

Abercrombie, T.A. 1998. *Pathways of Memory and Power: Ethnography and History among an Andean People*. Madison: University of Wisconsin

Arnold, D.Y. & Yapita, J. de D. 2005. *El Rincón de las Cabezas: Luchas Textuales, Ecuación y Tierras en los Andes*. La Paz, Bol.: Universidad Mayor de San Andrés e ILCA

Grosso, J.L. 2010. Constitutivo, construido: símbolo, espacio-tiempo y praxis crítica. In J.L. Grosso & M.E. Boito (eds.), *Cuerpos y Emociones desde América Latina*. Córdoba: Centro de Estudios Avanzados CEA, Programa de Acción Colectiva, Universidad Nacional de Córdoba—Doctorado en Ciencias Humanas, Facultad de Humanidades, Universidad Nacional de Catamarca

Haber, A.F. 2004. *Paisajes de Enclave en el Área de Antofalla, Puna de Atacama. Segunda Mitad del Segundo Milenio D.C. Informe*. Buenos Aires, Arg.: Fundación Antorchas

Haber, A.F. 2007a. Arqueología de *uywaña*: un ensayo rizomático. In A.E. Nielsen, M.C. Rivolta, V. Seldes, M.M. Vázquez & P.H. Mercolli (eds.), *Producción y Circulación Prehispánicas de Bienes en el Sur Andino*, 13–34. Córdoba, Bol.: Brujas

Haber, A.F. 2007b. Reframing social equality within an intercultural archaeology. *World Archaeology* 39(2), 281–97

Haber, A.F. 2008. ¿Adónde están los 99 tíficos? Notas de campo de arqueología subjuntiva. In F.A. Acuto & A. Zarankin (eds.), *Sed Non Satiata II. Acercamientos Sociales en la Arqueología Latinoamericana*, 103–20. Córdoba, Arg.: Universidad Nacional de Catamarca, Encuentro, Universidade Federal de Minas Gerais & Universidad de Los Andes

Haber, A.F. 2009. Animism, relatedness, life: post-Western perspectives. *Cambridge Archaeological Journal* 19, 418–30

Hidalgo Lehuedé, J. 1987. Tierras, exacciones fiscales y mercado en las sociedades andinas de Arica, Tarapacá y Atacama, 1750–1790. In O. Harris, B. Larson & E. Tandeter (eds.), *La Participación Indígena en los Mercados Surandinos: Estrategias y Reproducción Social, Siglos XVI a XX*, 193–231. La Paz, Bol.: CERES

Hidalgo Lehuedé, J. 1996. Rebeliones andinas en Arica, Tarapacá y Atacama, 1770–1781. In C. Walker (ed.), *Entre la Retórica y la Insurgencia: Las Ideas y los Movimientos Sociales en los Andes, Siglo XVIII*, 173–204. Cusco, Peru: Centro de Estudios Bartolomé de Las Casas

Hidalgo Lehuedé, J. & Castro, N. 1999. Rebelión y Carnaval en Inguaguasi (San Pedro de Atacama) 1775–1777. *Estudios Atacameños* 17, 61–90

Machado Aráoz, H. 2009. Minería trasnacional, conflictos socioambientales y nuevas dinámicas expropiatorias: el caso de Minera Alumbrera. In M. Svampa & M.A. Antonelli (eds.), *Minería Trasnacional, Narrativas del Desarrollo y Resistencias Sociales*, 205–28. Buenos Aires, Arg.: Biblos

Olivera, D.E. 1991. La ocupación inka en la puna meridional argentina: Departamento Antofagasta de la Sierra, Catamarca. *Comechingonia: Revista de Antropología e Historia* 9(2), 31–72

Raffino, R.A. 1981. *Los Inkas del Kollasuyu: Origen, Naturaleza y Transfiguraciones de la Ocupación Inka en los Andes Meridionales*. La Plata, Arg.: Ramos Americana

Shepherd, N. & Haber, A.F. 2011. What's up with WAC? Archaeology and "engagement" in a globalized world. *Public Archaeology* 10(2), 96–115

Svampa, M. & Antonelli, M.A. (eds.) 2009. *Minería Trasnacional, Narrativas del Desarrollo y Resistencias Sociales*. Buenos Aires, Arg.: Biblos

Thomas, N. 1994. *Colonialism's Culture: Anthropology, Travel, and Government*. Princeton, NJ: Princeton University Press

CHAPTER FIVE

Unstable Contexts: Relational Ontologies and Domestic Settings in Andean Northwest Argentina

Andrés Gustavo Laguens

Order and Chaos, a 1950 lithograph by M.C. Escher,[1] is perhaps one of the best syntheses of the illusion of archaeology: the fragmentary chaos of everyday debris reflected in a perfect, crystalline object that attracts us unavoidably (see Figure 5.1). It depicts both the most accepted modes of thinking about the archaeological record—Binford's (1977)

Figure 5.1   *Order and Chaos*, by M.C. Escher

Archaeology after Interpretation: Returning Materials to Archaeological Theory, edited by Benjamin Alberti, Andrew Meirion Jones, and Joshua Pollard, 97–114.

present statics and past dynamics and Schiffer's (1972) archaeological and systemic contexts and their transformations—and the more general assumption that archaeological objects are substitutes for something else that exists beyond their physical presence.

In the same way as Escher's polyhedron (a platonic solid), and in a new sort of idealism or contemporary Platonism, objects and their contexts are reduced to intermediaries between their physicality as mere remains or traces and the nonmaterial. Time, ideas, functions, meanings, identities, genders, adaptations, evolution, and so on, are the nonmaterial elements that archaeologists must animate. In one sense, objects do represent. They stand for something else. But, as Lucas (2012, 9) asserts, it is a matter of recognizing the ontological constitution of the archaeological record. The associations and contexts of the objects collaborate in this endeavor. Even contextual and textual approaches move in an Escherian world, between the chaos of the palimpsests of material traces and the order of lost meanings.

Although archaeology, and the social sciences in general, have adopted new ways of thinking about humans, things, and their interrelationships, objects and their contexts still seem to be thought of more as technological objects than as objects of material culture. In some cases, when connections between objects and contexts are made, the artifacts themselves are analyzed as morphological and functional units; once characterized, they are put in relation to other items and information from the context in circles of successive inclusion. Such is the case, for instance, of many hunter-gatherer studies in Early Holocene South America, where other dimensions of inference are permitted (i.e., social or nonmaterial) once the artifacts have been typologically characterized and put in contextual relationship (see Bayón & Flegenheimer 2003; Laguens 2009). Like a latter-day Hawkes' ladder, relationships are considered more an inference than a perspective on things.

The archaeological definition of context implies relationships by its very nature, it is a relational concept *per se*. But surprisingly, if context is thought of relationally, objects usually are not. Objects are put in relation as part of the context. It is as if things were treated as bounded objects in themselves that subsequently come into relation through observations of association and relative proximity. It is my aim in this chapter, then, to contribute to rematerializing—in the sense proposed by Lucas (2012)—the archaeological record and to try to think through objects in themselves and within their contexts: not simply as intermediaries but based on their own materiality, which means trying to think about them dynamically and relationally from the start.

If we can break with the limitations imposed by current conceptions of the archaeological context, we may be able to research in greater detail the ways in which associations in the archaeological record came about, and ask, for instance, how roles, functions, categories, meanings, and the relative positions of people and objects in the material world are ascribed and fixed. This chapter begins with an invitation to rethink things and objects as parts of a relational web. I argue that multiple agencies coincide in such relationships; the archaeological record can thus be conceived of as a configuration of multiple parts in relation. A case study of ceramic assemblages used for cooking and consuming food in northwest Argentina during the ninth century will illustrate the archaeological possibilities of this argument. The boundaries of material contexts are discussed in relation to an ethnoarchaeological study of Bolivian urban *chicha* makers residing in Córdoba, Argentina.

THINGS, OBJECTS, STRANDS, NETWORKS[2]

Sociologist John Law (2000) claims that any object is the effect of a durable disposition of relations. In other words, an object is a particular effect of a heterogeneous and dynamic network of humans and nonhumans (Latour 1996b). As long as those relationships do not change, their effect will remain stable or immutable (Law 2000, 1). Although an object can participate in further relationships, its constitutive relationships will remain stable. For example, the molecular bond of clay in a vessel is not the simple effect of chemical and physical interactions, but the convergence and articulation of many other relationships in which artisans, processes, actions, agencies, artefacts, other networks, and so on participate. The result is a particular material effect: the manufactured object.

To talk about the durable effects of relationships is not to talk of causes. In fact, those relationships are what makes effective a series of possibilities brought about by particular social and/or individual practices that put in play material and nonmaterial resources (such as Bourdieu's capitals) available to individuals according to their position (Bourdieu 1984; Laguens 2006). In some ways, things can be seen as the materialized effect of social dispositions—though to talk of such effects in Bourdieu's terms means not seeing things as mere epiphenomena of a social realm. Rather, just as *habitus* can be said to be "society made body" (Gutiérrez 2009, 36), objects, as constitutive parts of those *habitus*, can be said to be "society made material." At the same time, things in their materiality affect those social dispositions and social structures, constructing and reproducing them as individuals do.

These seemingly fixed and durable relationships allow objects to participate in different contexts while maintaining some sort of material identity (see Fowler, in this volume). However, objects can take part in other networks consisting of multiple relationships among people and things, which makes them unstable. Any web of relations, contexts, and things in context will never be completely fixed; despite our efforts to capture them in some form of record at the beginning of our fieldwork, such webs are inherently unstable. Even though for practical and theoretical reasons we usually emphasize and fight for a single perspective on "things," things are singular and multiple at the same time. Singular, because we believe that a thing "is" a something (a vessel, a stone, an axe, a technological fact, a sign, an adaptive medium, etc.); multiple, because many perspectives can converge at the same time and on the same thing. However, what if things were simultaneously networks, technological facts, and behavioral by-products, meaningfully constituted, multidimensional, multitemporal, and more? What they appear to be and what we prioritize in our concepts of them depends on how they are put in relation (in the past or today), because it is cognitively impossible for us to hold on to many dimensions simultaneously, and methodological and theoretical constraints mean that things are conceptualized as unidimensional.[3]

It is not a matter of conciliatory standpoints trying to hold many dimensions—and theories—of things simultaneously. To think of things as one and many at the same time rather than only as nodes in a web of webs, parts of a meshwork, or the durable effects of a series of relations, can lead to new interpretive possibilities. The impact on multifactorial or multivariable analysis in terms of artifact classification, for example, would be considerable.

AGENTS AND AGENCIES

Objects, then, are parts and effects of a series of relationships, some of which are durable, and they are incorporated into heterogeneous networks in which humans participate and multiple interrelationships are established between parts. Relationships imply active links between parts in a form of mutual agency in which humans and nonhumans are co-constituted (as in Karen Barad's notion of "intra-action"; see Alberti & Marshall 2009). This notion of agency challenges the idea that objects can hold agency and exercise the same type of agency as humans do, or that there are two distinct types of agents (Breslau 2000). From a relational point of view, agency can be understood as one effect of an underlying structure (Fuchs 2000, 34), or as the *habitus* in a structured system of socially embodied dispositions. In these senses, agency is closer to being a variable dependent on situational dynamics, and it will manifest itself more in some networks. Thus, not all people and objects at all times and in all relationships have agentive capacities, since this depends on the dynamics of particular situations and inter-relationships.

Objects' properties are in part the effects of their durable relationships, which include those intentionally attributed to them when they are made (such as their shape, color, raw material, and so on), and are in part generated within those relationships in the networks in which they participate (such as their meaning, function, value, etc). By virtue of their properties, objects potentially have the power to influence other entities with which they enter into relationship. A vessel generates a space of inclusion and exclusion due to the physical locus that it occupies, and it may produce a visual impact on viewers that may surpass the intentions of its creator or user (much in the same way as distributed agency as proposed by Gell [1998]). The notions of *influence, incidence,* or *non-inherent agency* may be more appropriate terms for these possibilities related to the power of objects, which are redolent of the notions of "active material culture" (Hodder 1994, 16) and "affordances" (Gibson 1971, 406). Agency can be thought of as a product of the same network of relationships that constitutes entities; humans and nonhumans are therefore both capable of becoming agents. As Serrano and Argemí (2005, 11) argue, any entity that produces a relational effect can be considered an agent (see also Normark 2006 on polyagency). Additionally, an object is always linked to other agentive objects. Relations between these objects result in other kinds of agency that overlap. Likewise, we must consider the agency of the objects put in motion by the relationships between people and things during excavation. Objects are not passive, and archaeologists and things mutually modify one another in the practice of excavation (Yarrow 2003, 71–72).

In sum, objects have the potential to be points of convergence of a simultaneity and multiplicity of agencies. Objects are multiagents. But our thinking about agency is limited to a few dimensions, as if it were mainly a dyadic relationship between an agent and a patient. Usually one agency in particular is prioritized, such as the influence of built space on people's attitudes, which generates different *habitus* and, for example, gender differentiation.

An ethnoarchaeological study of traditional Andean maize beer preparation by Bolivians living in an urban context in Argentina will help to elucidate these issues (Pazzarelli & Vargas 2008; Laguens & Pazzarelli 2011). Many human and nonhuman—both material an nonmaterial— agencies come into play when making the beverage. A large number of Bolivians reside in Cordoba, Argentina: approximately 50,000 migrants and native descendants, mostly concentrated in one neighborhood of the city, Villa El Libertador. Many traditional practices are maintained. Every year on August 15th they celebrate the feast of the Virgin of Urkupiña; the feast is an opportunity to gather and reassert socio-identitary, ideological, and political aspects of the local community. The celebration is an opportunity for the consumption of *chicha*, the fermented corn beverage native to inhabitants of the Andes.

Our study investigated the making of chicha by Bolivian women (*chicheras*) in domestic settings (Pazzarelli & Vargas 2008). The beverage's manufacture involves a series of successive steps, with many regional variations across the Andes, which include preparing the corn flour paste that is the basis for the fermentation (*q'ora* or *wiñapu* flour made from sprouted corn), adding water, cooking (repeated over three days and two nights), and brewing for two weeks. Each of these steps requires a specific type of vessel (Menacho 2007), many of which are used only for this purpose. Given the lack of Indigenous vessels (Bolivia is more than 1,000 kilometers away), plastic containers were used; these were chosen for their morphological similarity to the original ceramic ware. We observed that many areas of the chicheras' houses, such as the yards and kitchens, as well as other neighborhood homes, entered into relationship as a consequence of the practice of making chicha.

A particularly interesting fact is that the raw material used—the wiñapu—had been brought especially from Bolivia. Thus the wiñapu is not a mere ingredient (i.e., an element resulting from the internal relationships that define its materiality and spatial boundaries), but it is also characterized by a wider network of relationships and agencies. It is Bolivian wiñapu; it is also wiñapu to be mixed; wiñapu for chicha; wiñapu for the celebration. All told, wiñapu is a thing-concept (Henare et al. 2007); as long as the wiñapu is not thought of as ontologically distinct from the associated concepts, it is more than an object and more than a concept (Holbraad 2007). In the hands of the chicheras, the wiñapu became an object whose effects made the recipe effective: its being the "original" Bolivian raw material generated a setting in which the chicha prepared could be considered "*buena*" [good] and "just like the one from over there" (Pazzarelli & Vargas 2008; Laguens & Pazzarelli 2011).

It was not only the wiñapu, but the making of Bolivian chicha in a city far from its place of origin, that put in motion many people and objects simultaneously and involved many different agencies—from the material agencies of pots, hearths, houses, spoons, and raw materials to the human agencies of cooks, homeowners, neighborhoods, to nonmaterial ones such as nationality, "good" chicha, local spaces, distances, and so on. In this case, the agencies of the raw materials and material implements for making chicha were so strong that chicha makers changed their attitudes and behaviors in an adjustment to local materialities and relationships.

This meant that non-Bolivian chicha could be "good" Bolivian chicha despite being made abroad with none of the original materials.

CONTEXTS WITHOUT CONTEXT

I begin with a conventional and provisional notion of archaeological context as the set of associations and objects in association that make sense of, or are the bases for, archaeological inferences. According to their variations and peculiarities, the different contexts in which objects are found acquire meaning and enable inferences to be made. There are various linear processes that archaeologists have adopted to think of objects as acquiring meaning through relationships, including the life cycle of an object in a behavioral chain (Schiffer 1972), the social life or biography of things (Gosden & Marshall 1999), the *chaînes operatoires* (Lemonnier 1992), and the contextual approach (Hodder 1999). In these approaches to the archaeological record, whether processual or interpretative, there is a tendency to view things as performative; that is, objects are thought of as embodying different cultural and historical possibilities that are activated when archaeologists put those objects in relation. Much in the same way as in human performativity (Butler 1990), objects have no inner essence: it is their concrete expression in the world that renders them specific and situated. The circulation of an object during its life cycle through a behavioral chain and its movement through different contexts, from manufacture to discard, result thus in a performance: according to the interactions or activities in which they are involved, objects acquire different identities, roles, functions, and biographies, which allow archaeologist to access nonmaterial realms of inference. This performance is also a kind of "ontological choreography" (Hitchings 2003) in which objects attain different characteristics. In the same vein, from a contextual perspective (Hodder 1982, 1999) the meanings of objects change according to changes in context, arenas of activity, and the other objects and actors involved. Relationships may change, but objects still stand for something beyond themselves.

Although such approaches enrich a relational view and are potentially non-essentialist, their conception of objects tends to be limited in two ways. First, objects are seen as closed entities, "blackboxed"[4] in ANT's terms (Latour 1990), as if they were stable and singular in their identities. Second, although some of the linear schemes can form intersecting webs of related processes, such as in behavioral chain analysis (Schiffer 1972) or in the technological systems of the *chaînes operatoires* (Lemonnier 1992, 20), all operate on one level, a single horizon or plane of relationships, or at most follow an ascending spiral through

successive planes. Although such approaches take into account different dimensions (material, social, temporal, spatial, etc.), it is as if these
were successively tied one to the other after the fact, like fabric, and not
constitutively interrelated. Nevertheless, despite the fact that we remain
with two conventional views sewn together—objects as both closed units
and open to substitution through representation—such approaches have
opened up interpretative possibilities. Thinking multirelationally means
capturing the simultaneity of planes, entities, and relationships that are
at play in each thing and in every interaction, thus recovering other fixed
and dynamic dimensions and properties involved in or generated by the
articulation of entities. This is not easy, since methodologically we tend
towards linearity, and tie everything together by adding, overlapping,
discarding, bonding; that is, by relating. But in practice we perceive,
think, and interpret simultaneously, as Hodder argues in his reflexive
methodology (Hodder 1997, 2000; Hodder & Berggren 2003), and as
Edgeworth (2012, 80) demonstrates in his claim that excavation is not
just a practical skill but is also an intellectual task. All such relationships
and agencies existed when making chicha and in chicha itself. As such,
locally produced chicha did not stand for Bolivian chicha: it was "true"
chicha because of the dimensions and entities that were at play simultaneously in the ensemble. Had it been different, perhaps the chicha would
have been mere maize beer.

From this perspective, the network of relations resembles more closely
the one generated in a ball of paper, such as the one in Escher's drawing.
Archaeological relations have been modeled as a series of interwoven
chains. I argue that these relations in fact confront us like a crumpled
piece of paper. Things that had been conceived as separate along a
single plane are now proximate or overlap as a series of infinite planes
that collide and intersect in endless lines of relationships, some shorter,
some longer, with hundreds of points of intersection and a multiplicity
of connections that did not exist before. We can try to flatten out the
paper, ironing it with our methodologies, but its wrinkles persist. Webs
of relations become evident.[5]

The question now concerns the limits of these networks. How far
does this multiplicity of coexisting relationships and agencies extend?
Thinking of objects in these terms poses a difficulty when we try to define
boundaries. Networks do not have a beginning or an end, warns Latour
(1996b). In this sense, and as in excavation, the limits of the context—
and even the very idea of context—are hard to grasp, since they become
diluted in an entanglement of materials with multiple relationships and
dimensions (Hodder & Berggren 2003; Edgeworth 2012). For example,
where does the procurement of raw material to manufacture an object
start? In the prior social representation of the things made from that

material? In the action of extracting it? In the act of collecting it? In the agent's intention to obtain it? In the agent's practical need? And where does it end? One possibility is to establish the boundaries of an object or a network where its effects are no longer felt, like the boundaries of social fields posed by Bourdieu (Bourdieu & Wacquant 1995; Laguens 2007). It is clear that the effect of the network of durable relationships that define an object sets a net limit to its physicality, such as the surface of a vessel, the base, the mouth, and so on. But the effects produced by a storage vessel used in a domestic context can be felt by a range of people, from the inhabitants of the house to all those who share or consume its contents in a communal celebration. A further problem of limits arises if matters are conceived as relationships and their effects rather than as substances. Defining an inside and an outside, something micro and something macro, becomes impossible. For instance, where is the limit of an activity area in a room if the raw material was brought in from outside? How far does the technology of a system of production reach? In short, rather than "limits," networks of relationships have *ranges* (Laguens 2007), that is, they incorporate the possibility of greater or lesser influence on other entities and networks of human and nonhuman entities.

The case of the chicha makers illustrates this point. The yards and kitchens where the chicha was made in the houses of the Bolivian chicheras entered into relationship with other homes as the processes unfolded and people in the neighborhood collaborated in the making of the chicha. A common area was constituted that lacked physical continuity, but which allowed the preparation of the drink to proceed effectively for the agents involved. Also, since the plastic containers that were used were similar in shape to the original ceramic ware, the effects of the Bolivian vessels reached the buckets used in Córdoba. The practice and its effects exceeded the immediacy of the physical location of the action (the stove, pots, yard) and generated a larger outline of other rooms, other houses, and other families (Laguens & Pazzarelli 2011).

In summary, the chicha was manufactured in a materially heterogeneous and spatially discontinuous relational context of blurred boundaries, carried out inside and outside, and simultaneously involving human and material agencies. Overall, both the object chicha and the actual production of chicha were effects of that entire wide-ranging network.

I have argued so far that objects are effects of relationships within multidimensional and heterogeneous networks in which both humans and nonhumans participate, and which in turn are the effects of other webs of relationships. All are interrelated and vary in scope with no clear beginning or end. Furthermore, these objects and relationships have agentive potential, which can manifest itself in multiple directions at the same time. How, then, can we understand archaeological contexts? Can we continue to think of them as products and by-products of processes or practices? Can we keep thinking of the archaeological context as something static, made up of distributions and physical associations in a given space, whose dynamism is given by the actions or meanings that humans imprinted on the material world in the past? We could go on thinking that this is indeed the case as long as we follow just one line at a time of the many strands of the web of objects and people, and then progressively relate one to another. I argue, however, that this cannot be the case once we accept that the distribution and physical proximity of objects are elements of a heterogeneous network of entities interrelated in ways that vary in scope and time. From a multirelational point of view, context no longer exists. There are no associations, there are only relations. In place of chains, processes, by-products, boundaries, substances, essences, and behaviors we have networks, multiplicities of agencies, effects, scopes, interrelationships, durable forms, and practices. That is, in a relational context, the idea of archaeological context lacks, precisely, a context.

OBJECTS IN NON-CONTEXTS

How do we proceed if we lose the idea of context, something so practical and incorporated into archaeological thinking? Shanks and Hodder (1995) anticipated the notion that the archaeological record is far from clear and, in fact, creates uncertainty. To say that the archaeological context is not a context is not to say that the archaeological record does not exist or that there is no other way to capture and understand past networks as contexts. In a multirelational context, the context is a *configured space*. I have argued that contextual relationships are unstable, in contrast to the more durable relationships of the objects themselves. A dynamic relational context, then, is closer to the idea of configured space. The Oxford English Dictionary defines configuration as an "arrangement of parts or elements in a particular form or figure" and "the form, shape, figure, resulting from such arrangement." Related parties are arranged in a particular way that results in the appearance of a thing with specific properties. Hence, the same parts disposed differently—for example, a change in the spatial arrangements within a context—can lead to different properties, that is, different things. In mathematics we speak of a "space of configuration" as a space of possible states: a configuration is one possible state among others.

Such configured spaces, identified and described in the archaeological record as "stages," "events," or other units are themselves networks with varying degrees of stability depending on the agents and practices involved. They are "frameworks for interaction": a complex and diverse network of people, places, and times (and things) behind all relations (Latour 1996a, 231). Networks, thus, are simultaneously webs and frameworks of relations. I prefer to define these situational frameworks for relationships as the *entorno* or "setting":[6] the set of extrinsic conditions that facilitates the relating of things. As we have seen, the production setting of chicha—its agents, spaces, objects, and their interrelationships—in a neighborhood of Córdoba enabled that chicha to be as good as the one made in Bolivia. From a relational perspective, then, we can rethink context as a configured space that functions as a setting where objects and their relations with other things and people vary in scope and extent.

Approaching the archaeological record from this perspective is not without problems, as it poses the challenge of capturing and communicating a simultaneity of events, entities, and relationships using a language and mental structures that impose linear or, at the most, dendritic, modes of writing and thinking. In previous work I have analyzed the configuring space of Piedras Blancas, a ninth-century site in La Aguada, in the Andes of northwest Argentina (Laguens et al. 2007). The site is a slightly hierarchical residential village in the Ambato valley. Work to date has analyzed how the material culture and its relationship with people constituted and reproduced a way of life that institutionalized social differences within a non-egalitarian society (Laguens 2006). The objective has been to elucidate the networks of relationships that came together in domestic food production in that particular social space. From a more general perspective, one purpose was to examine how different networks and entanglements (in the sense of mutual dependence put forward by Hodder [2011]) between humans and other materialities, past and present, are constructed, maintained, and transformed.

TO COOK AND LIVE AT AMBATO

My research initially examined the networks of relationships that ceramic objects established with people and things in a dynamic flow of actions, relationships, and mutual agencies at different moments in time. Eventually, the study incorporated different scales—from the micro, such as clay materials, to the macro, such as the landscape—across domains of interaction usually defined as economic, social, political, and ideological. This led immediately to a more extensive network involving entities beyond the immediate scope of the local and including other objects and relationships, such as other kinds of pottery, hearths, animal resources, plant resources, production structures, storage infrastructures, different types of sites, as well as technical gestures, activities, and production and extractive practices. Nonmaterial dimensions also became apparent, such as the possibilities of objects' agency or the natural annual cycles.

One of the (conventional) contexts at the site is an enclosure dated AD 760–1000: an earthen-walled room, slightly sunken from the outside, roofed and attached to a galleried courtyard. At least fifteen broken tricolor vessels were found in the yard (apparently several of them were left there intentionally), together with charred remains of wild fruit. Only one of these vessels was found inside the enclosure. The remainder of the pottery was related to cooking or consumption. Activities such as food consumption and small-item manufacture were carried out in defined spaces, both outside and within the enclosure. The enclosure and gallery were burned prior to abandonment, resulting in a well-preserved final deposition of objects protected by the fallen, burned house beams. In conventional terms, this is an abandonment context of a domestic area of the site.

The "Ambato Tricolor" ceramic urns (see Figure 5.2) form a standardized set of tempered pottery made with local raw materials fired in an oxidizing atmosphere. They are thick-walled, globular in shape, with conical bases and wide mouths; some include modeled anthropomorphic elements on their necks, and others are painted in red, black, and white. Their volume ranges from 60 to approximately 300 liters. They are large vessels and relatively immobile. Some were exposed to fire and used for cooking; others had vegetable and/or animal organic residues; and still others showed no signs of wet or dry content on their walls.

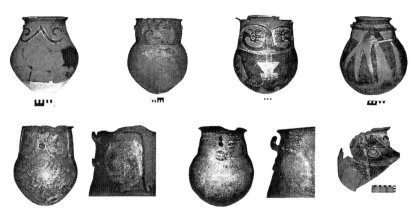

Figure 5.2   Tricolor ceramic vessels from the Ambato valley

The vessels are associated with various site types, both residential and ceremonial, and with another class of pottery known as "Ambato Negro Gravado" ("Ambato Black Engraved"). These were fired in a reducing atmosphere, lack temper, and were made from non-local clays from more than 30 kilometers away. They have thin walls and very standardized forms, including bowls (*pucos*) and vases with horizontal handles. These pucos and vessels characteristically display naturalistic and fantastic themes that express ideological and political concerns, such as jaguar-shamans, warriors, priests, leaders, scenes of human sacrifice, and fantastical beings (Laguens & Gastaldi 2008) (see Figure 5.3). The volume of a puco is close to half a liter; the other forms vary between 3 and 15 liters. Such pieces are found in all excavated sites, although in varying proportions. Differential access to these goods marked distinctions between people (Laguens 2006). Through the daily practices in which these elements were involved, we begin to understand one of

Figure 5.3 Black engraved ceramics from the Ambato valley

the multirelational networks—the one related to food—that linked all these elements together.

In addition to organic residues, the Ambato Tricolor pottery reveals traces of the gestures associated with specific actions (Gastaldi 2010). Circular motions produced by stirring left marks perpendicular to the central axis; other marks on the bottom of the pieces were produced by serving or transferring the contents to smaller pieces at a lower height. The clay matrix is worn inside too—temper has been exposed and left above the surface of the clay by the corrosive effect of fermented liquids such as chicha. Other pots were directly exposed to fire. All these properties refer to at least three interrelated elements: food and its forms of production and procurement; cooking techniques; and mobile objects such as pucos and vases. It is important to remember that each element involves a particular network—not just as object, but as a network of relationships among other elements, processes, and individuals.

Products stored and processed in these vessels, whether wild or cultivated, have different natural cycles. Moreover, different forms of processing may require pre-cooking, demand varying quantities of water, or may only be possible in specific seasons (Laguens et al. 2007). Highly fragmented animal bones indicate that animals were prepared prior to cooking, and although they were available year-round, procurement distances varied between domestic and wild animals, necessitating different time schedules. Wood used for cooking was from the vicinity of the site and was available year-round. Burn marks on the outer surfaces of the ceramics correspond to a low, flameless fire. They are concentrated on the lower parts of the vessel, as if coals or charcoal had been used for cooking, a technique that facilitates stirring, mixing, or adding ingredients without burning the contents. Restricted forms with relatively small-diameter mouths prevent excessive evaporation of water and require meat to be cut into smaller pieces—a typical Andean practice for food processing that remains widespread (Pazzarelli 2010).

Pucos have not been found in the same rooms as other vessels. They are more commonly found in courtyards and galleries rather than inside the habitations, where the black engraved pottery is more abundant. The smaller pucos may have been used as serving ware for food or drink made outside in the larger pots, whose size, volume, and relative immobility means their contents had to be transferred. Use wear on pucos includes a high degree of wear on the bases, corresponding to tilting and rotation movements on a rough earth floor (Gastaldi 2010).

The other black pieces—the horizontal-handle vases—show horizontal and inclined marks on the inside and signs of heavy wear on their bases, as if the contents had been stirred and removed with an implement that scraped the walls, rather than being poured. To date little trace of organic residue has been found, suggesting they were used as temporary containers. They were perhaps intermediaries between the pucos and the large cooking vessels, a function facilitated by the horizontal handles that enabled them to be carried from the place of production to interior rooms.

When the rich diversity of relationships is revealed we see that the tricolor vessels were complex forms made up of converging and intersecting strands in a heterogeneous and multitemporal tangle actualized through practice. Although I initially explored a single dimension (food), tracing the relationships involved by it has led to other coetaneous dimensions that go beyond the immediate spatial relationships usually understood as context. What emerges is a complex configuration of things, objects, natural elements and cultivated resources, actions, agencies, knowledge, temporal cycles of varying duration (from the minimum event—the gesture—to annual cycles of planting and cultivation), spaces of differing scope (from the microscopic trace of a gesture in a vessel to agropastoral systems and clay sources), and individuals actively involved in the daily practice of feeding.

The archaeological context of "courtyard and room" at Piedras Blancas has been blurred. Or, more accurately, it has become diluted in a particular configuring space among other overlapping and, perhaps, synchronous possibilities, such as the Ambato valley inhabitants' perspectives on nature that we can glimpse in the iconography of the domestic ware. The context transcended the enclosure's walls and reached a radius of many kilometers away from it. The tricolor vessels, without moving from their places, merged into networks of multiple interactions that led to a delinearization of the processes involved. The everyday use of these pieces as domestic ware constantly made present broader modes of understanding the world and social order. And temporalities—of various durations, linear, cyclical, routinized, synchronized, alternating—traversed relationships and entities. The context of the site expands into a relational configuring space, overwhelmed by networks of objects and both human and nonhuman possibilities of agency.

NOTES

1. The lithograph can be seen in detail at http://www.eschergranada.com/es/exposicion/item/134-contraste-orden-y-caos&Itemid=65.
2. These concepts are used synonymously, although I recognize there are many different perspectives on them.
3. Museologist Peter van Mensch (1990) has proposed a similar multiperspective approach to material culture in which different "identities" are simultaneously born by objects.

4. "Black-boxing" refers to a process of simplification that hides relationships as if they were given or stable. This facilitates network operation by not questioning its constitution.
5. Law (2000) holds that objects are like origami: a series of successive folds and overlapping relationships in which each fold makes sense in terms of the others. The model I present is closer to Michel Serres's circle drawn on a handkerchief that is then pressed and put in a pocket (see Smith 2003).
6. "Setting" may not be the best concept. There is no appropriate translation for the Spanish *entorno*. However, words such as "milieu" or "environment" carry too much theoretical baggage in archaeology.

REFERENCES

Alberti, B. & Marshall, Y. 2009. Animating archaeology: local theories and conceptually open-ended methodologies. *Cambridge Archaeological Journal*, 19(3), 344–56
Bayón, C. & Flegenheimer, N. 2003. Tendencias en el estudio del material lítico. In R.P. Curtoni & M.L. Endere (eds.), *Análisis, Interpretación y Gestión en la Arqueología de Sudamérica*, 65–90. Olavarria, Arg.: INCUAPA, UNICEN, Serie Teórica
Binford, L.R. 1977. General introduction. In L. Binford (ed.), *For Theory Building in Archaeology: Essays on Faunal Remains, Aquatic Resources, Spatial Analysis, and Systematic Modelling*, 1–13. New York: Academic Press
Bourdieu, P. 1984. Espacio social y génesis de las "clases." In P. Bourdieu, *Sociología y Cultura*. Mexico City: Editorial Grijalbo
Bourdieu, P. & Wacquant, L.J.D. 1995. *Respuestas: Por Una Antropología Reflexiva*. Mexico City: Editorial Grijalbo
Breslau, D. 2000. Sociology after humanism: a lesson from contemporary science studies. *Sociological Theory* 18(2), 289–307
Butler, J. 1990. Performative acts and gender constitution: an essay in phenomenology and feminist theory. In S.-E. Case (ed.), *Performing Feminisms: Feminist Critical Theory and Theatre*, 270–82. Baltimore, MD: Johns Hopkins University Press
Edgeworth, M. 2012. Follow the cut, follow the rhythm, follow the material. *Norwegian Archaeological Review* 45(1), 76–92
Fuchs, S. 2000. Beyond agency. *Sociological Theory* 19(1), 24–40
Gastaldi, M.R. 2010. Cultura material, construcción de identidades y transformaciones sociales en el Valle de Ambato durante el primer milenio d.C. Doctoral dissertation, Biblioteca Florentino Ameghino, Facultad de Ciencias Naturales y Museo, Universidad Nacional de La Plata. Available at http://sedici.unlp.edu.ar/handle/10915/5316
Gell, A. 1998. *Art and Agency: An Anthropological Theory*. Oxford: Oxford University Press
Gibson, J.J. 1971. More on affordances. In E.S. Reeds & R. Jones (eds.), *Reasons for Realism: Selected Essays of James J. Gibson*, 406–8. Hillsdale, NJ: Lawrence Erlbaum Associates Inc.
Gosden, C. & Marshall, Y. 1999. The cultural biography of objects. *World Archaeology* 31(2), 169–78
Gutiérrez, A. 2009. *Las Prácticas Sociales: Una Introducción a Pierre Bourdieu*. Buenos Aires, Arg.: Ediciones Tierra de Nadie
Henare, A., Holbraad, M. & Wastell, S. 2007. Introduction: thinking through things. In A. Henare, M. Holbraad & S. Wastell (eds.), *Thinking Through Things: Theorising Artefacts Ethnographically*, 1–31. New York: Routledge
Hitchings, R. 2003. At home with someone nonhuman. *Home Cultures* 1(2), 169–86

Hodder, I. 1982. *Symbols in Action: Ethnoarchaeological Studies of Material Culture.* Cambridge: Cambridge University Press

Hodder, I. 1994. *Interpretación en Arqueología. Corrientes Actuales.* Barcelona, Spain: Editorial Crítica

Hodder, I. 1997. Always momentary, fluid and flexible: towards a reflexive excavation methodology. *Antiquity* 71, 691–700

Hodder, I. 1999. *The Archaeological Process: An Introduction.* Oxford, UK: Blackwell

Hodder, I. 2000. Developing a reflexive method in archaeology. In I. Hodder (ed.), *Towards Reflexive Method in Archaeology: The Example at Çatalhöyük*, 3–15. Cambridge: McDonald Institute for Archaeological Research/British Institute of Archaeology at Ankara

Hodder, I. 2011. Human-thing entanglement: towards an integrated archaeological perspective. *Journal of the Royal Anthropological Institute* 17(1), 154–77

Hodder, I. & Berggren, A. 2003. *At the Trowel's Edge: An Introduction to Reflexive Field Practice in Archaeology.* Boulder, CO: Westview

Holbraad, M. 2007. The power of powder: multiplicity and motion in the divinatory cosmology of Cuban Ifá (or *mana*, again). In A. Henare, M. Holbraad & S. Wastell (eds.), *Thinking through Things: Theorising Artefacts Ethnographically*, 189–225. New York: Routledge

Laguens, A. 2006. Espacio social y recursos en la arqueología de la desigualdad social. In C. Gnecco & C.H. Langebaek (eds.), *Contra la Tiranía Tipológica en Arqueología: Una Visión desde Sudamérica*, 99–120. Bogotá, Col.: Universidad de los Andes, Facultad de Ciencias Sociales, CESO, Ediciones Uniandes

Laguens, A. 2007. Objetos en objetos: hacia un análisis relacional de lo estético en Arqueología. *Iconica Antiquitas*, 1–11.

Laguens, A. 2009. De la diáspora al laberinto: notas y reflexiones sobre la dinámica relacional del poblamiento humano en el centro-sur de Sudamérica. *Revista de Arqueología Suramericana* 5(1), 42–67

Laguens, A., Dantas, M., Figueroa, G., Gastaldi, M., Juez, M.S. & Pazzarelli, F. 2007. Vasijas + pucos con huesos + agua no son sólo sopa: la cerámica de uso doméstico en el siglo IX d. C. en el Valle de Ambato, Catamarca y sus relaciones con otros entramados sociales y materiales. *Pacarina Revista de Arqueología y Etnografía Americana*, número especial, 353–59

Laguens, A. & Gastaldi, M. 2008. Registro material, fisicalidad, interioridad, continuidad y discontinuidad: posiciones y oposiciones frente a la naturaleza y las cosas. In A. Troncoso, D. Salazar & D. Jackson (eds.), *Puentes Hacia el Pasado: Reflexiones Teóricas en Arqueología*, 169–89. Santiago, Chile: Serie Monográfica de la Sociedad Chilena de Antropología

Laguens, A. & Pazzarelli, F. 2011. ¿Manufactura, uso y descarte? O acerca del entramado social de los objetos cerámicos. *Revista del Museo de Antropología* 4, 113–26

Latour, B. 1990. Drawing things together. In M. Lynch & S. Woolgar (eds.), *Representation in Scientific Practice*, 19–67. Cambridge, MA: MIT Press

Latour, B. 1996a. On interobjectivity. *Mind, Culture and Activity* 3(4), 228–45

Latour, B. 1996b. On Actor-Network-Theory: a few clarifications. *Soziale Welt* 47, 369–81

Law, J. 1992. Notes on the Theory of the Actor Network: ordering, strategy and heterogeneity. Lancaster, UK: Centre for Science Studies, Lancaster University. At http://www.comp.lancs.ac.uk/sociology/papers/Law-Notes-on-ANT.pdf

Law, J. 2000. Objects, spaces and others. Lancaster, UK: Centre for Science Studies, Lancaster University. At http://www.lancs.ac.uk/fass/sociology/research/publications/papers/law-objects-spaces-others.pdf

Lemonnier, P. 1992. Elements for an anthropology of technology. *Anthropological Papers* 88, 1–24

Lucas, G. 2001. *Critical Approaches to Fieldwork: Contemporary and Historical Archaeological Practice*. London: Routledge

Lucas, G. 2012. *Understanding the Archaeological Record*. Cambridge: Cambridge University Press

Menacho, K.A. 2007. Etnoarqueología y estudios sobre funcionalidad cerámica: aportes a partir de un caso de estudio. *Intersecciones en Antropología* 8, 149–61

Normark, J. 2006. *The Roads In-Between: Causeways and Polyagentive Networks at Ichmul and Yo'okop, Cochuah Region, Mexico*. Göteborg, Swed.: GOTARC Serie B, Gothenburg Archaeological Theses 4, Göteborg University

Pazzarelli, F. 2010. La importancia de hervir la sopa: mujeres y técnicas culinarias en los andes. *Antípoda, Revista de Antropología y Arqueología* 10, 157–81

Pazzarelli, F. & Vargas, G. 2008. ¿Cómo hacer chicha en Córdoba? Reflexiones en torno a los aspectos políticos y materiales de la producción de chicha por inmigrantes bolivianos. *Revista del Museo de Antropología* 1(1), 29–40

Schiffer, M.B. 1972. Archaeological context and systemic context. *American Antiquity* 37(2), 156–65

Serrano, F.T. & Argemí, D.M. 2005. Asociaciones heterogéneas y actantes: el giro postsocial de la teoría del actor-red. *Revista de Antropología Iberoamericana*, *Edición Electrónica*, núm. especial, Noviembre-Diciembre, 1–26

Shanks, M. & Hodder, I. 1995. Processual, postprocessual and interpretative archaeologies. In I. Hodder, M. Shanks, A. Alexandri, V. Buchli, J. Carman, J. Last & G. Lucas (eds.), *Interpreting Archaeology: Finding Meaning in the Past*, 3–29. London: Routledge

Smith, R.G. 2003. World city topologies. *Progress in Human Geography* 27(5), 561–82

van Mensch, P. 1990. Methodological museology: or, towards a theory of museum practice. In S. Pearce (ed.), *Objects of Knowledge*, 141–57. London: Athlone Press

Yarrow, T. 2003. Artefactual persons: the relational capacities of persons and things in the practice of excavation. *Norwegian Archaeological Review* 36(1), 65–73

PART II
Working with Materials

Andrew Meirion Jones

Rethinking the nature of materials is a central aim of this book. In Euro-American culture matter is predominantly considered as passive and inert, and only set in motion by humans who utilize it as a means of survival, imposing meanings on it or using it as a medium of aesthetic expression. Similar approaches to matter can be observed in recent accounts concerned with materiality in archaeology. For example, recent arguments concerning the changing architecture of Stonehenge, Wiltshire from a timber- to stone-built monument suggest that wood was considered to be impermanent and subject to decay and therefore related to the human life cycle, whereas stone, as a more permanent hard-wearing material, was associated with the ancestors and the dead (Parker Pearson & Ramilisonina 1998; Parker Pearson 2012). Although this account provides an understanding of the changing use of materials in the architecture of this archetypal Neolithic monument, it nevertheless imposes singular meanings on the materials employed in that architecture; in fact, such perceptions of materials may have only occurred for a relatively brief period of time (Pollard 2009).

Even though the approaches to materials discussed above seems commonsense, in fact when we look closely at them, whether at the atomic level (Coole & Frost 2010, 11–15) or at the macro-scale (Ingold 2007), materials appear to be vibrant and changeable; it is possible to imagine matter as a lively materiality that is self-transformative (Bennett 2001, 2010) and already infused with the capacity for agency and significance that is typically accorded to humans in idealist and subjectivist accounts. We are able to consider how materials change and evolve, and think about the fecundity and dynamism of matter. In a sense, such attempts to understand matter differently underscore phenomenological accounts. Diana Coole (2010) notes that the aim of Merleau-Ponty's existential phenomenology was to counter the predominant philosophical accounts of Descartes, who argued for an ontological dualism between thinking substance (*res cogitans*) and extended substance (*res exstensa*), dividing the world between thinking human subjects and inert and quantifiable matter. Merleau-Ponty is concerned with understanding how matter and perception are irreducibly interwoven in the perceptual lifeworld. Phenomenological approaches have been discussed within archaeology. Curiously, by insisting on the significance of the interpreting subject, the versions of Heiddegger and Merleau-Ponty's work most influential in archaeology have preserved precisely those Cartesian distinctions that phenomenologists sought to overcome (see Olsen 2007, 2010).

However, archaeologists and anthropologists have begun to think differently about matter and materials (Ingold 2007, 2012). The most sophisticated recent analysis is the one offered by Chantal Conneller (2011). Conneller, in a wide-ranging study of Paleolithic and Mesolithic technology, discusses the analytical possibilities of materials by tracing the technologies in which matter both transforms and solidifies (ibid., 124); in that sense, the liveliness of materials is implicit to her account. Conneller highlights how the properties of materials arise through processes of technological interaction, rather than being imposed upon them by the human subject. A similar understanding of materials is discussed by anthropologists Amiria Henare, Martin Holbraad, and Sari Wastell (2007). They argue for collapsing the analytical distinction between thing and concept and for tracing the paths of things during fieldwork so that they "dictate the terms of their own analysis" (Henare et al. 2007, 4). Again, the vibrant, lively, and motivational character of materials and matter is emphasized.

The authors discussing materials in this section of the book closely follow the approach outlined above. **Chantal Conneller's** chapter examines skeuomorphism in Paleolithic Europe. She argues against prevailing assumptions of skeuomorphs as unfaithful copies made from one material medium into another, and instead emphasizes how the process of creating skeuomorphs draws out the equivalence between materials; the possession of a shared inner essence allows materials to share similar exterior forms. The subject of **Lesley McFadyen's** chapter is architecture. She examines the relationship between materials and form in architectural construction through an overview of the building practices on various British Neolithic sites, including long barrows and causewayed enclosures, and a case study relating architecture and material artifacts at the Chalcolithic site of Castelo Velho, Portugal. McFadyen emphasizes the timing and intercalation of materials and architecture in episodes of architectural construction at the site, and in doing so she highlights the dynamism of materials. The contribution by **Andrew Meirion Jones** and **Emilie Sibbesson** is concerned with questions of ontology related to the transitions between the Mesolithic and Neolithic periods in Britain. They argue that the transition is best understood as an ontological multiplicity, an ontologically ambiguous period with multiple facets, and suggest that various facets are drawn out by researchers with differing perspectives. As an alternative way of understanding the complexity and ambiguity of the period, they examine aspects of material change over the long term and look at how these materials interact in social practices during the transitions between these periods. Their chapter emphasizes less the materials of the prehistoric past and more the ontological character of approaches to the study of past material evidence.

In each contribution in this section materials are acknowledged as dynamic and vibrant in themselves, but it is through interaction that their properties arise, whether in the practices involved in achieving equivalent aesthetic effects as discussed by Conneller, in the working together of materials in architectural construction as discussed by McFadyen, or in the intellectual interaction between various archaeologists and the ontologically complex Mesolithic-Neolithic transitions as argued by Jones and Sibbesson. Each contribution traces the material relationships generated by these interactions.

REFERENCES

Bennett, J. 2001. *The Enchantment of Modern Life: Attachments, Crossings, Ethics.* Princeton, NJ: Princeton University Press

Bennett, J. 2010. *Vibrant Matter: A Political Ecology of Things.* Durham, NC: Duke University Press

Conneller, C. 2011. *An Archaeology of Materials: Substantial Transformations in Early Prehistoric Europe.* London: Routledge

Coole, D. 2010. The inertia of matter and the generativity of the flesh. In D. Coole & S. Frost (eds.), *New Materialisms: Ontology, Agency, and Politics*, 92–115. Durham, NC: Duke University Press

Coole, D. & Frost, S. 2010. Introducing the new materialisms. In D. Coole & S. Frost (eds.), *New Materialisms: Ontology, Agency, and Politics*, 1–43. Durham, NC: Duke University Press

Henare, A., Holbraad, M. & Wastell, S. 2007. Introduction: thinking through things. In A. Henare, M. Holbraad & S. Wastell (eds.), *Thinking Through Things: Theorising Artefacts Ethnographically*, 1–31. London: Routledge

Ingold, T. 2007. Materials against materiality. *Archaeological Dialogues* 14(1), 1–16

Ingold, T. 2012. Toward an ecology of materials. *Annual Review of Anthropology* 41, 427–42

Olsen, B. 2007. Keeping things at arms length: a genealogy of asymmetry. *World Archaeology* 39(4), 579–88

Olsen, B. 2010. *In Defense of Things*. New York: Kluwer/Plenum

Parker Pearson, M. 2012. *Stonehenge: Exploring the Greatest Stone Age Mystery*. New York: Simon and Schuster

Parker Pearson, M. & Ramilisonina 1998. Stonehenge for the ancestors: the stones pass on the message. *Antiquity* 72, 308–26

Pollard, J. 2009. The materialisation of religious structures in the time of Stonehenge. *Material Religion* 5, 332–53

CHAPTER SIX

Deception and (Mis)representation: Skeuomorphs, Materials, and Form

Chantal Conneller

Pliny the Elder recounts in his *Natural Histories* a contest between the painters Parrhasius and Zeuxis. Zeuxis revealed a painting of a bunch of grapes so realistic that birds flew down from the sky to peck at the fruit. Satisfied with the effect his contribution had produced, Zeuxis turned to Parrhasius and asked him to pull back the curtain that hid his picture. When he realized the curtain itself had been painted by Parrhasius, Zeuxis admitted defeat, saying that whereas he had deceived the birds, Parrhasius had deceived him, an artist.

As Newman (2004) points out, this story reflects a widespread ambivalence towards imitation in antiquity: the idea that the painter or sculptor by imitating nature was engaging in counterfeit. The most explicit attack on artistic mimesis came in Book X of the *Republic*, where Plato contrasted a carpenter with a painter. Both work by imitation, he suggested, the carpenter by mimicking the ideal form of a bed, the painter by copying what the carpenter has made. As a result, the painter is imitating an imitation and so is inferior to the carpenter, and both in turn are inferior to nature (which was considered the origin of the prototypes that human technical endeavors were imitating). The problem with artistic representations for the ancient Greeks is that they were just that, representations: they either reflected, or (in Plato's view) misrepresented reality.

In more recent times artists have tended to be thought of as primarily creative rather than deceptive, following Neoplatonic ideas that saw artists as perfecting or improving the material world. However, ideas of deception still persist and, in particular, are frequently associated

Archaeology after Interpretation: Returning Materials to Archaeological Theory, edited by Benjamin Alberti, Andrew Meirion Jones, and Joshua Pollard, 119–33. ©2013 Left Coast Press, Inc. All rights reserved.

with a particular class of material culture: skeuomorphs. Skeuomorphs are artifacts made from one material to imitate a form more usually made from another. The distrust accorded to skeumorphs can be seen in Childe's definition (1956, 13) of them as "objects, aping in one medium shapes proper to another."

The motivation behind skeuomorphic activity has commonly been interpreted in two different ways (Frieman 2010). The concept was initially used to refer to techniques or forms associated with a traditional technology, such as basketry, which were employed on a new material, such as metal, in order to make the new material acceptable to contemporary tastes (Wengrow 2001; Taylor 2006). Alternatively, skeuomorphism has been considered as a means of emulation whereby lower-class individuals would reproduce elite objects made of high-status materials, such as gold, in a cheaper or more accessible material (Sherratt & Taylor 1997; Vickers 1999). Though in the former interpretation the use of old forms could be seen to "trick" people into accepting new materials, it is this latter interpretation that carries more of the sense of the skeuomorph as deceptive.

The idea of skeuomorphs as deceptive lingers even in approaches inspired by recent material culture theory (Knappett 2002; Hurcombe 2007, 2008; Frieman 2010). Knappett (2002) has distinguished between "honest" and (by implication) "deceptive" skeuomorphs in his study of examples from the Minoan Middle Bronze Age. "Honest" skeuomorphs reveal their true material; Knappett offers the example of a pottery skeuomorph of a basket that does not erase or disguise the line of the mold into which the clay was placed. There is also an indexical relationship in this case between source and subject, in that the mold that produced the skeuomorph was itself created by being impressed onto a basket; thus a technological connection exists between the organic and the clay basket. "Deceptive" skeuomorphs, by contrast, are those that try to erase their origins in their imitation of a higher status object. Pottery drinking vessels were made to imitate metal cups through the addition of clay rivets, thin handles, and crinkled rims. These have an iconic relationship to the prototype. However, Knappett argues that this is not simply a passive representation; instead, drawing primarily on Gell's (1998) work, he suggests that these objects work in the same way as sympathetic magic, in that they create power over the thing emulated.

Although Knappett's account goes some way to circumventing the passivity of imitation and highlighting the connections forged between seemingly disparate materials through the technological process, the persistent idea that deception is an appropriate concept for understanding skeuomorphs is problematic. The idea of deception in skeuomorphs appears to be founded on two mainstays of Western ontology: an essentialist view of materials, whereby particular materials occupy discrete, immutable categories; and the privileging of form over material, or representation over reality.

AN ESSENTIALIST VIEW OF MATERIALS

The Western idea that materials have a series of essential properties that make them discrete substances has a long history. In Europe, classical and medieval thought on materials was based on the Aristotelian conceptualization of substances and the distinction between "substantial" and "accidental" form. The substance was considered the essential nature of a material or being; accidents, by contrast, were contingent and could change without fundamentally altering the nature of the thing (Ross 1964). Iron, for example, will be iron whether it is polished or dull, cool and solid or molten (Newman 2004). In this view, changes in appearances are deceptive, masking an inner reality that is constant; there is no possibility for transformation of substance. The current dominant Euro-American thinking on materials appears to retain this long-standing essentialist inheritance. In archaeology, for example, different specialists deal with stone, clay, or metals, and technical manuals describe the essential properties of each material.

The assumption that materials such as metal or stone are *per se* substantially different is the crux on which the idea of deception turns. However, recent cross-craft studies reveal that connections are forged between seemingly discrete materials through practice (Hurcombe 2007, 2008). Furthermore, ethnographic and ethnohistorical studies reveal alternative categorizations of materials. Saunders (1999), for example, reports Columbus's surprise that the Amerindian groups he encountered did not distinguish between gold and pyrites. In Columbus's view those people were confusing accidental similarities with substantial ones. To the Amerindians, gold and pyrites shared gleaming properties that revealed their being filled with sacred light. This shared inner light made them identical to all intents and purposes.

THE PRIVILEGING OF FORM OVER MATERIALS

The privileging of form over material, or mental representations over passive nature, is a longstanding trope in Western thinking, and one that has also played a part in contemporary views of skeuomorphs. Because of the contemporary value placed on form, it is presumed that mimicry of form was the main concern during skeuomorph production, the shape of the object being deemed sufficiently important to make up for the fact that it was not made of the original, desired material. However, as

Frieman (2010, 246) has argued, skeuomorphs are the result of a complex interplay between technology, material, form, and consumption. It is by tracing the interplay of these that factors, for example, that Knappett noted the close technological connection between the basket prototype and its clay skeuomorph, and thus concluded that not all skeuomorphs are deceptive.

BEYOND DECEPTION

In order to start thinking more productively about skeuomorphs, we can turn to look at another practice that has been considered deceptive, precisely because its purpose has also been to imitate or produce the effect of a higher status material: the transformation of a base metal into gold through alchemy. Debate raged in alchemical texts as to whether alchemists' attempts to turn base metals to gold produced true gold (reproducing its substantial form) or simply transformed the appearance of the base metal so that it looked like gold (transforming its accidental appearance). Ibn Sina (Avicenna), the tenth-century Persian philosopher and alchemist, for instance, denied that alchemists could ever make genuinely natural products (Newman 2004, 37). Similarly, St. Thomas Aquinas, who was opposed to alchemical practice, argued that only a natural agent could transform substances. Thus gold could not be produced by alchemical fire, because this differed from the heat of the sun, which was considered responsible for the generation of metals.

However, Thomas's work did raise the possibility that by using similar methods to nature alchemists might be able to effect a transmutation of substance. As a result, the thirteenth-century European alchemist Geber argued that alchemists *could* replicate the processes of nature and, as a result, produce true gold (Newman 2004). Geber differed from Thomas because he saw the equivalence of human technology and the working of natural processes. To Thomas the use of artificial heating produced very different effects than the sun; to Geber, by contrast, the heat of a furnace, being analogous to the sun's heat, could be used to produce real gold. Geber was not attempting to deceive through his practice; rather, he was drawing on his knowledge of both scholastic philosophy and the working of alchemical processes to replicate the natural processes that made gold. By taking seriously (Viveiros de Castro 1998) past people's understandings of materials and technology, we can see that to call Geber's work deceptive is not appropriate. Geber's writings assert the potential to make gold because his practice breaks down the boundaries between culture and nature, or between representation and reality.

The same concerns can be seen in a rather different case. The hyperreal ceramic representations of the French potter Bernard Palissy

(1510–1590) could be read in the same way as Zeuxis's painting—as mimicking nature through a formal, iconic representation. Palissy is known for his molding from life of plants, fish, amphibians, and reptiles (Amico 1996). These creatures were captured alive, immersed in urine or vinegar, coated in grease, and finally pressed into plaster (Shell 2004). The resulting mold was used to make a clay impression of the animal, which was then posed with other animals and plants in a naturalistic scene, usually on a large shallow dish known as a rustic platter (see Figure 6.1).

These creatures appear extremely realistic: the process of manufacture permits every scale of fish or snake to be recorded, and Palissy spent years perfecting the glazes that allowed replication of the color and sheen of the living animal. However, rather than considering his work as mere imitation or mimicry of these creatures, Palissy saw his ceramics as replicating natural processes of fossilization (Smith 2000; Newman 2004; Shell 2004). In his *Discours Admirables*, Palissy describes the power of "generative salt" and "congealative water," which provided the material substrate of the minerals (Shell 2004, 27). Minerals were seen as having a tendency to congeal within the earth, through the evaporation of "accidental water." If this happened in an enclosed space, the mineral would congeal in the shape of its container. Palissy considered this to be the method by which fossils were generated. As Newman (2004, 157) argues, Palissy considered natural processes and the potter's process of fabrication to be the same. His clay was also composed of congealing and generative material. He also made accidental water evaporate in his kiln, thus faithfully reproducing the process whereby

Figure 6.1   Rustic platter of Bernard Palissy

nature created fossils. Palissy's belief in the equivalence of clay animals and fossils is made evident in his catalogue of his "teaching exhibit," which he insisted visitors view after attending his lectures. These consisted of a series of fossils displayed alongside items of his own work. Both were used to illustrate the operation of natural processes (Shell 2004, 35–36).

These examples offer alternative ways of thinking through concepts of deception, imitation, and representation in the technical process. Rather than imitating a particular form in a new material, Geber sought to transform base materials to produce gold by faithfully reproducing the processes through which gold was generated in nature. This process questioned the essential nature of this metal by focusing on the contingent processes of its generation. Palissy's work could be described as deception or imitation; however, this would mean misreading his intention. The platters were not imitating the form of snakes or fish; instead, Palissy was producing fossils by reproducing the processes whereby fossils were generated. Palissy was one of the earliest writers on fossils, and the experimental processes he undertook in his pottery manufacture furthered his understanding of the natural world, which in turn influenced the direction of his own technological endeavors.

Two broader points can be taken from these examples. First, neither can be understood simply through a focus on the end product; instead, tracing in detail the technological process is paramount. This allows to question the essential nature of materials and break down the distinction between cultural and natural processes that has guided views on representation since classical times. Second, in both cases the manufacture of gold and pottery is caught up in broader medieval and early modern ontologies; however, technologies are not simply a product of these but are actively involved in producing understandings of the world (Conneller 2011). Geber's work grew from longstanding traditions of medieval scholasticism and alchemical practice, yet through his work he produced new practical understandings of the world; similarly, Palissy's experimental practices furthered his knowledge of fossils and guided the scientific thinking on fossils for some time.

Returning to skeuomorphs, then, perhaps we can look at these not simply through their final form, but through the processes of their generation; and we could think of them not so much in terms of what they represent, but in terms of what they do (Deleuze & Guattari 1999). We need to understand how particular articulations of materials, technology, and knowledge combine to actively produce broader ontologies. In the remainder of this chapter I will explore these issues through an example of skeuomorph production in Early Upper Paleolithic Europe.

SKEUOMORPHS IN THE EARLY UPPER PALEOLITHIC

Between 30,000 and 45,000 years ago, there was a significant change in the composition of the European archaeological record. The traditional material repertoire of stone and woodworking was augmented by new substances and by new technologies with which to work them: extensively carved antlers, bones, and mammoth ivory, numerous pierced shells, and a range of colorful stones such as amber and soapstone. These new substances were associated with new categories of material culture: the first human and animal figurines, the widespread manufacture of beads and pendants, and a new range of organic tools. These are taken to be the hallmarks of "the human revolution" of the Upper Paleolithic (Mellars & Stringer 1989), and evidence for what in the archaeological literature has been termed "behavioral modernity," a rather uncritical shorthand for a series of traits that are considered to be uniquely shared by all extant humans. This "symbolic explosion" (Mellars 1989, 361) has been associated with the migration of the first *Homo sapiens* groups into Europe and the extinction of the indigenous Neanderthals.

Beads are probably the most important of these new artifact types. They appeared with the earliest Upper Paleolithic assemblages and are often found in large numbers, suggesting that issues of identity and differentiation were important to the earliest *Homo sapiens* groups. A variety of materials were employed for the manufacture of Early Upper Paleolithic (Aurignacian) beads: shell, teeth, bone, antler, ivory, and stone. Considerable effort appears to have gone into the procurement of these materials and the manufacture of the beads. Shells were widely exchanged, often over distances of over 300 kilometers: Mediterranean shells are found on sites in Austria and southeastern France, and Atlantic shells are present in French Mediterranean sites (Vanhaeren & d'Errico 2006, 1118). Though shell and animal teeth simply needed perforation or grooving to turn them into beads, more effort was expended on carved beads. Experiments suggest that the process required between one and three hours per bead, depending on material, with ivory beads taking around three hours (White 1995, 2007).

Shell beads seem to have been part of a broad cultural repertoire carried by the first *Homo sapiens* groups to move into Europe, appearing intermittently in Africa and western Asia between 100,000 and 40,000 years ago. However, as groups moved into inland areas of Europe, away from coastal areas where shells were readily available, new materials appear to have been substituted for shells. From as early as 43,000 BP, teeth were used at Bacho Kiro Cave in Bulgaria. Teeth, like shells, have lustrous qualities, and it is probably for this reason that they have been viewed as adequate substitutes. As people moved into inland areas of central and western Europe, between 40,000 and 35,000 year ago, a broader range of lustrous materials such as soft stone, antler, and especially mammoth ivory gradually began to be used. Unlike shell and teeth, which needed no modification apart from perforation before being sewn onto clothing, these new materials had to be transformed from their original form in order to be made into beads.

This is the context in which the first skeuomorphs appear. Teeth and shells made from stone and animal materials, most commonly ivory, are found in the archaeological record (see Figure 6.2 and Table 6.1). Some of these are very elaborate: at La Souquette, Dordogne, six shell facsimiles in ivory have been recovered. They not only reproduce the form of the shell but also show meandering rows of punctuation that appear to mimic those on Atlantic seashells from the site (White 1989). White also suggests that stone and ivory basket-shaped beads, the most

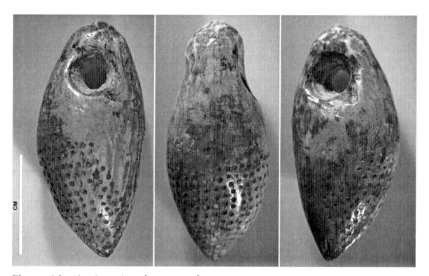

Figure 6.2   Aurignacian skeuomorphs

Table 6.1   Skeuomorphs on Aurignacian archaeological sites (not including basket-shaped beads)

	Ivory	Antler	Bone	Steatite	Limestone	Total
Red deer canine	5	1	4	1	2	13
Fox canine	1	–	–	–	–	1
Horse incisor	–	–	1	–	–	1
Shell	7	–	–	–	–	7
Total	13	1	5	1	2	22

common Aurignacian bead type form in southern France and found in their hundreds on some sites, were designed to mimic the Mediterranean seashell *Cyclope neritea* (White 2004).

Since shell appears to have been the original material desired for bead manufacture, and shells were exchanged several hundred kilometers into inland areas, these skeuomorphs could be read in a traditional way, as attempts to mimic a high-status object in a more readily available material. However, is this really the case? Though shells were a common subject for skeuomorphs, animal teeth were the most common imitated form, despite the fact that teeth were readily available as a by-product of hunting and trapping and would need minimal modification in comparison with the carving of material used to produce skeuomorphs. Furthermore, rather than being easy to acquire, as one might expect, the materials used to make the skeumorphs themselves often appear to have been transported long distances. Talc or steatite, which were used to make basket-shaped beads in the Dordogne, came from at least 100 kilometers away, from either the Massif Central or the Pyrenees (White 1989). Furthermore, White argues that mammoths were not present in southwest France during the Aurignacian (White 1997), and that mammoth tusks—the most common material from which skeuomorphs were made—were imported from other regions to be used as a raw material.

What, then, was the impetus for the appearance of skeuomorphs if they were not necessarily made of a more easily accessible material? The answer can be found through a broader examination of the relationship between the different materials, forms, and technologies employed in Aurignacian bead manufacture. Although the incorporation of new materials into the bead repertoire should be understood in the historical context of groups moving away from areas with ready supplies of shells, this cannot alone explain their adoption. By tracing the technical interactions involved in bead manufacture it becomes evident that these new materials cannot be seen as inferior replacements to an original desired material; furthermore, their adoption had unintended consequences for Aurigancian life.

MATERIALS AND TECHNOLOGY

White (1992, 1995, 2007) has highlighted that the materials selected for bead manufacture all share a common property, namely luster. Luster is an effect of the mother-of-pearl sheen of shells, the original material used in bead manufacture. It is shared by dental enamel, making teeth (both human and those of various animal species) the second major material to be taken up in the production of beads. The stones selected to make beads were often soft and brilliantly colored and included limestone, schist, chlorite, talc, calcite, steatite, hematite, amber, jet, pyrite, and lignite. These mimicked the luster or color of some shells, but also offered new possibilities in the range of colors and surface effects represented. Ivory could also be lustrous and was warm to the touch, which perhaps imbued this material with the feeling of animacy (White 1995). Soft stones and ivory needed polishing to produce luster, and considerable effort went into producing this effect; the beads were polished with hematite in order to achieve the desired sheen.

Tracing the process of bead manufacture reveals how technical practice created further similarities between the materials employed. The basket-shaped beads that White suggests are skeuomorphs of seashells are highly standardized and were made in the same way, despite differences in the properties of the various materials that were employed (White 2007). Pencil-shaped rods, either of ivory or soft stone, were created; these were grooved into segments 1–2 centimeters long and then snapped to create cylindrical blanks. These blanks were thinned at one end to form a stem; a perforation was gouged out, and the bead was finally polished to bring out its luster (see Figure 6.3). White (1997, 105) suggests that the production of long ivory rods, which appears to have been undertaken through splitting and wedging, is not naturally suggested by the structure of ivory itself (a very intractable material) and is in fact difficult to achieve. Working ivory in this way could only ever be a struggle against the material. White suggests that beads were

Figure 6.3   The *châine opératoire* of basket-shaped beads

manufactured in this counterintuitive way because people wanted to achieve standardization (White 1989). However, we might also see that, by treating materials with very different properties in the same way, the technological process worked to create equivalence between the different materials used in bead manufacture.

Tracing the processes behind the selection of materials and the manufacture of Aurignacian beads suggests a departure from the emulation model in our understanding of skeuomorphs. I would argue that the skeuomorphs were not made to replicate particular materials, but rather to reveal the equivalence between what today we would consider as discrete substances. The manufacture and display of skeuomorphs drew attention to and made explicit the relationship that already existed between the different materials used in Aurignacian bead manufacture. It is not that ivory could simply look like shell: the skeuomorphs revealed that ivory could actually *be* shell because shell and ivory share a common quality, that of luster.

TOWARDS A MATERIAL PERSPECTIVISM

Viveiros de Castro has described the concept of perspectivism as a "bomb" disrupting Western understandings (Latour 2009). This notion offers the potential to rethink the material/form relationship and is a point of departure for a more nuanced understanding of the relationship between the various materials used in Aurignacian bead manufacture and the focus on luster. The aim here is not to faithfully apply perspectivism to another context, but to see where some of the precepts of perspectivism will take us if we apply them to a very different historical situation.

Briefly, Viveiros de Castro argues that whereas Western ontologies are characterized by multiple cultures and a single nature, Amerindian groups posit a single culture and multiple natures. In contrast to Western groups, which differentiate between humans and animals based on the presence (or absence) of soul or mind, perspectivist groups in Amazonia view humans, animals, and certain things as sharing an identical internal component (a soul) but as being externally differentiated though their bodies, which are the source of their perspective. Whereas souls are identical and immutable, bodies, as assemblages of affects that compose a particular species' way of acting in the world, can be transformed. Therefore taking on a bear's body, for example, would entail taking on a bear's perspective, and thus would enable a person to function as a (and thus be a) bear.

Though Viveiros de Castro does not explicitly discuss material culture in perspectivist societies, what we might term a "material perspectivism" has considerable potential for thinking about material culture.

Conceptualizations of the relationship between body and soul on the one hand, and material and form on the other, have obvious parallels. Just as Aristotle could use the hylomorphic model to support a universal system of classification encompassing both inorganic and organic entities (Simondon 1964, 27), so perspectivism, though focused on the relationship between body and soul, has potential for rethinking material culture, in particular the relationship between material and form around which skeuomorphism revolves.

Taking a perspectival approach to Aurignacian skeuomorph manufacture and bead production more generally, we can perhaps understand the quality of a variety of materials to shine and gleam as their inner, identical essence—their shared, immutable quality or soul. By contrast, the external part of these materials, their form, appears mutable, since different lustrous materials were able to take on the appearance of shells or teeth of different animal species. The reasons these materials could take on the outer form of another material was that they shared this common inner essence.

These beads may thus work in similar ways to the masks described by Ingold in his analysis of animist ontologies. Masks representing animals are not worn to disguise the human wearer (Ingold 2000, 123; see also Conneller 2004), but rather to reveal the animal itself. Ingold argues that the reason for which these animal masks frequently do not look much like the animal they are said to depict is that each reveals the animal's true face, its inner essence or soul. Similarly, the production of beads may be not so much about imitation as about revelation, exposing the inner essence of the material, its eternal, gleaming quality. This act of revelation, embodying as it did the ability to recognize the inner essence of a material, may thus have shared some of the power and danger of shamanic acts of transformation.

The material/form relationship elucidated for the Aurignacian skeuomorphs shows considerable differences from the Western standard view. We can perhaps see these materials as having essential properties in their lustrous and gleaming qualities. However, the nature of these properties, and what they might effect, is rather unexpected. In Western societies, we are used to thinking of the essential properties of materials as functioning to differentiate substances from each other. In the Aurignacian case, by contrast, different materials share a single essence. Properties do not differentiate matter, as in Western culture, but in fact reveal their similarity.

A material perspectivism reverses many of the equations on which Western understandings of material and form are built. The Aurignacian example provides a rather different articulation to the Aristotelian conceptualization of substance and accidents. It has been argued here that luster in the Early Upper Paleolithic is the essence of the material; in the Aristotelian formation, shininess, as a contingent property that in the case of ivory and soft stones needs polishing to come out, would be viewed as an accident of the material. In a related fashion, the "standard view" (Ingold 2000, 341) of the relationship between material and form—which posits form as a product of culture existing in the human mind and then imposed on formless, malleable, natural materials—is reversed. Form, generally viewed as primary in the creation and fixing of an object, is in the Aurignacian case mutable; it is a particular material property, namely luster, that makes these objects what they are.

CONCLUSION

The idea that skeuomorphs are deceptive depends on Western ideas of the discrete separation of substances and the primacy of form over matter. In the case of the Aurignacian bead skeuomorphs, these concepts are not appropriate. Materials we might consider as entirely separate based on our ideas of substantial difference are made equivalent in the Aurignacian case, both through technological practices that treat materials identically and through the privileging of certain qualities that reveal a common inner essence that makes the materials interchangeable. The concept of form in the Aurignacian does have some importance, but the particular material/form relations revealed challenge our expectations. Here form cannot be equated with representation, as in Western contexts; rather, form reveals an essential truth of the nature of particular materials. It is the possession of a shared inner essence that allows certain materials to assume particular outer forms and become other things.

Although many of the insights in this study pertain to the case of Aurignacian skeuomorphs, some broader issues can be highlighted. Material perspectivism is a concept that may merit broader investigation in that it offers an alternative reconfiguration of the material/form relationship. The aim of such an endeavor would not be to seek to identify ancient cases of perspectival ontology, but rather to harness the disruption provided by the concept to work through alternative configurations of culture and nature in the past.

Finally, it is important to emphasize that all the examples drawn on in this study reveal the necessity of a close analysis that intimately traces the various human/material interactions whereby material culture is produced. These tracings reveal how materials and forms are processual, their specific properties emerging during particular kinds of interactions. Following the technological process also permits a glimpse into how materials, technology, forms, and knowledge combine to reveal broader ontological concerns. Rather than being a formless substrate or simply a constraint to human action, materials are more fundamental: tracing the processes by which the properties of past materials emerge reveals configurations of past worlds and particular articulations of the cultural, the natural, and the supernatural.

ACKNOWLEDGMENTS

Many thanks to Thomas Yarrow and Ben Alberti for providing detailed comments on this chapter and to all workshop participants whose input has enhanced the final version. Many thanks also to Randall White for kind permission to reproduce Figures 6.2 and 6.3.

REFERENCES

Amico, L.N. 1996. *Bernard Palissy: In Search of Earthly Paradise*. Paris: Flammarion

Aristotle. 1950. *Physics*. Oxford, UK: Clarendon Press

Bensaude-Vincent, B. 2001. The new science of materials: a composite field of research. In C. Reinhardt (ed.), *Chemical Sciences in the 20th Century: Bridging Boundaries*, 258–70. Weinheim, Germ.: Wiley-VCH

Childe, V.G. 1956. *Society and Knowledge*. New York: Harper

Conneller, C. 2004. Becoming deer: corporeal transformations at Star Carr. *Archaeological Dialogues* 11(1), 37–56

Conneller, C. 2011. *An Archaeology of Materials*. New York: Routledge

Deleuze, G. & Guattari, F. 1999. *A Thousand Plateaus: Capitalism and Schizophrenia*. London: Athlone

Frieman, C. 2010. *Skeuomorphs and Stone Working: Elaborate Lithics from the Early Metalworking Era in Coastal Northwest Europe*. Unpublished PhD thesis, Institute of Archaeology, University of Oxford

Gell, A. 1998. *Art and Agency: An Anthropological Theory*. Oxford, UK: Clarendon Press

Hurcombe, L. 2007. *Archaeological Artefacts as Material Culture*. London: Routledge

Hurcombe, L. 2008. Organics from inorganics: using experimental archaeology as a research tool for studying perishable material culture. *World Archaeology* 40(1), 83–115

Ingold, T. 2000. Totemism, animism and the depiction of animals. In T. Ingold (ed.), *The Perception of the Environment: Essays in Livelihood, Dwelling and Skill*, 111–31. London: Routledge

Knappett, C. 2002. Photographs, skeuomorphs and marionettes: some thoughts on mind, agency and object. *Journal of Material Culture* 7(1), 97–117

Latour, B. 2009. Perspectivism: "type" or "bomb." *Anthropology Today* 25(2), 1–2

Mellars, P. 1989. Technological changes in the Middle-Upper Palaeolithic transition: economic, social, and cognitive perspectives. In P. Mellars & C. Stringer (eds.), *The Human Revolution: Behavioural and Biological Perspectives on the Origins of Modern Humans*, 338–65. Edinburgh, UK: Edinburgh University Press

Mellars, P. & Stringer, C. (eds.), 1989. *The Human Revolution: Behavioural and Biological Perspectives on the Origins of Modern Humans*. Edinburgh, UK: Edinburgh University Press

Newman, W.R. 2004. *Promethean Ambitions: Alchemy and the Quest to Perfect Nature*. Chicago, IL: University of Chicago Press

Newman, W.R. 2006. *Atoms and Alchemy: Chemistry and the Experimental Origins of the Scientific Revolution*. Chicago, IL: Chicago University Press

Pliny 1952. *Natural History* XXXV (65–66), vol. ix, libri xxxiii–xxxv (trans. H. Rackham). Cambridge, MA: Harvard University Press

Ross, W.D. 1964. *Aristotle*. London: Methuen & Co.

Saunders, N.J. 1999. Biographies of brilliance: pearls, transformations of matter and being, c. AD 1492. *World Archaeology* 31(2), 243–57

Shell, H.R. 2004. Casting life, recasting experience: Bernard Palissy's occupation between maker and nature. *Configurations: A Journal of Literature, Science, and Technology* 12, 1–40

Sherratt, A. & Taylor, T. 1997. Metal vessels in Bronze Age Europe and the context of Vulchetrun. In A.G. Sherratt (Collected Papers), *Economy and Society in Prehistoric Europe*, 431–56. Edinburgh, UK: Edinburgh University Press

Simondon, G. 1964. *L'Individu et Sa Genése Physico-Biologique*. Paris: Presses Universitaires de France

Smith, P.H. 2000. Artists as scientists: nature and realism in early modern Europe. *Endeavor* 24, 13–21

Taylor, T. 2006. The human brain is a cultural artefact. In J. Brockman (ed.), *What is Your Dangerous Idea?* 258–62. London: Free Press

Vanhaeren, M. & d'Errico, F. 2006. Aurignacian ethno-linguistic geography of Europe revealed by personal ornaments. *Journal of Archaeological Science* 33, 1105–28

Vickers, M. 1999. *Skeuomorphismus, oder die Kunst aus wenig viel zu machen*. 16. Trierer Winckelmannsprogramm. Mainz, Germ.: Verlag Philipp von Zabern

Viveiros de Castro, E. 1998. Cosmological deixis and Amerindian perspectivism. *Journal of the Royal Anthropological Institute* 4(3), 469–88

Wengrow, D. 2001. The evolution of simplicity: aesthetic labour and social change in the Neolithic Near East. *World Archaeology* 33(2), 168–88

White, R. 1989. Production complexity and standardization in Early Aurignacian bead and pendant manufacture. In P. Mellars & C. Stringer (eds.), *The Human Revolution: Behavioural and Biological Perspectives on the Origins of Modern Humans*, 366–90. Edinburgh, UK: Edinburgh University Press

White, R. 1992. Beyond art: toward an understanding of the origins of material representation in Europe. *Annual Review of Anthropology* 21, 537–64

White, R. 1995. Ivory personal ornaments of Aurignacian age: technological, social and symbolic perspectives. In J. Hahn, M. Menu, Y. Taborin, P. Walter & F. Widemann (eds.), *Le Travail et l'Usage de l'Ivoire au Paléolithique Supérieur*, 29–62. Rome, It.: Instituto Poligrafico e Zecca dello Stato

White, R. 1997. Substantial acts: from materials to meaning in Upper Palaeolithic representations. In M. Conkey, O. Soffer, D. Stratmann & N. Jablonski (eds.), *Beyond Art: Pleistocene Image and Symbol*, 93–123. San Francisco: Californian Academy of Sciences

White, R. 2004. La parure en ivoire des homes de Cro-Magnon. *Pour la Science* 43, 98–103

White, R. 2007. Systems of personal ornamentation in the Early Upper Palaeolithic: methodological challenges and new observations. In P. Mellars, K. Boyle, O. Bar-Yosef & C. Stringer (ed.), *Rethinking the Human Revolution*, 287–302. Cambridge, UK: McDonald Institute

CHAPTER SEVEN

Designing with Living: A Contextual Archaeology of Dependent Architecture

Lesley McFadyen

This chapter begins with a series of generalizations. In archaeology we are very good at separating things out for study—to the extent that, it can be argued, we have the subdisciplines of landscape archaeology, architectural history, and material culture studies (McFadyen 2008a). Furthermore, we study these subdisciplines at different scales. And we also have a fraught relationship between theory and archaeological evidence to contend with. Of course, there have been, and there still are, many archaeologists who effectively negotiate these divisions, but the problem of their existence is still concrete. All of these categories, and the divides that have been created for them, relate to the research that I want to account for in this chapter. In order to get across a sense of the history and endurance of this problem, I am going to refer again to each of the parts in their chronological order—the sequence in which they appear in publication.

THEORY

I start with theory, and the edited volume *The Archaeology of Contextual Meanings* (Hodder 1987). This book is about the inference of symbolic meanings from material culture; it is about a symbolic archaeology, and in it Ian Hodder wrote that his aim was to set out a contextual approach that involved the notion of structure—"the structured 'text'" (ibid., viii, 1). The use of "context" to outline a theory is slightly confusing because "context" in archaeology is also the material, spatial, and temporal medium that we work with (the archaeological evidence) and as such

Archaeology after Interpretation: Returning Materials to Archaeological Theory, edited by Benjamin Alberti, Andrew Meirion Jones, and Joshua Pollard, 135–50.

it is more than material culture, and it is more than an understanding of the social dimensions within which material culture is situated. It is very difficult to find a discussion of context in Hodder's work; instead, he focuses on contextual meanings (Hodder 1987) or contextual interpretation (Hodder 2012).

The contextual approach as a theory, and the term "contextual archaeology," became associated with Hodder. I am not suggesting that it is a bad approach; what is important here is that we clearly understand that it is a symbolic and structural theory (Hodder 1982) that has to do with reading material culture as text (Shanks & Tilley 1987; Tilley 1990, and later commentary by Jones 2007; Hodder 2012, 21). My first key question is: should this be the archetypal "contextual archaeology"?

Another edited volume, titled *The Archaeology of Context in the Neolithic and Bronze Age: Recent Trends* (Barrett & Kinnes 1988), is a study of "context" (i.e., the medium we work with) and not the outline of an approach (see also discussion in Jones & Alberti, in this volume). More specifically, it explores the relational qualities and dimensions of the material, spatial, and temporal (conceptualized by the editors of this volume as material, traceable relationships). For example, it is in this publication that we read of Barrett's confidence in context and his assertion that archaeology is an engagement with the *material and historical conditions* of past people's lives (Barrett 1988; see also Barrett 1994). The divide that I have outlined between theory and archaeological evidence was uppermost in John Barrett's and Ian Kinnes's minds: "The consequence of this division of labor has been to foster a belief that knowledge about the past is initially gained in the realm of theory and that available archaeological data are simply a means to assess the validity of those theories. However, a disconformity exists between theoretical knowledge of the past which is generalizing and unspecific and a practical knowledge of present data which is particular and specific" (Barrett & Kinnes 1988, 1).

This point has always stayed with me, and it is going to look naïve in writing, but my understanding is that the nature of the archaeological evidence comes first and is what everything else is about. Of course, we have to engage with evidence on a critical and theoretical level, but the order in which that is done is crucially important. And there is a further phrase that Barrett and Kinnes use: "Our knowledge of the past derives from the evidence we have available" (ibid.).

Such an approach is not about looking elsewhere, perhaps supplementing understanding with an anthropological perspective, and it is not about wishing for a better kind of evidence. The evidence is what it is, and we learn something about past people and ourselves from those particular conditions. I have, therefore, always taken Barrett and Kinnes's book as an example of the practice of contextual archaeology: "The human past took place in the context of those material conditions we recover as fragmentary remains today. It follows that our knowledge of the past is itself context specific. The more detailed our understanding of those material contexts and of the way humans act in relation to their material world the better will be our understanding of the past" (Barrett & Kinnes 1988, 1). My second key question is: Have we forgotten this?

ARCHITECTURE

In Barrett & Kinnes's volume there is a chapter by Chris Evans in which he argues that causewayed enclosures should be understood as "acts of enclosure" (1988, 85). This is an original approach. Previously in archaeological accounts, architecture had been understood by conflating the idea of design in plan with the record of a surviving form. This perception of a built object collapsed the actions of architecture (with all of the complexity of their making) and the time-depth of archaeology into the one frozen register that took shape in the plan drawing. By contrast, Evans's emphasis on the project of construction opened up the conditions of context. He stated that "spatial qualities may have only been 'emergent' in the sequence of their construction" (ibid., 88). In other words, to understand architecture, archaeologists have to engage with the material conditions that were available in the past, and in the process of doing that, knowledge could change. If we examine, as Evans did, the segmented nature of ditches, we see that each segment was cut as a series of intercutting pits: the arena of action here was not at a monumental scale, but rather at the scale of a small group of people making a ditch together, with each of them cutting a pit at a time. Evans argues that even if all of the segments were cut at the same time, this would not change the conditions of action because it was impossible to move out of them: architecture could only take place, and come into being, at the scale of intercutting pits. He states: "This implies that a maximal labour force could have been employed along a ditch circuit with only a minimal level of team co-ordination and given these conditions divergence from 'Design' (circuit regularity) would not be unexpected" (ibid., 88).

For me, the beauty of this research is that knowledge of the past comes from a negotiation of the material and historical conditions that were also part of past people's lives. This study explored the nature of the archaeological evidence and took inspiration from that setting. I was less interested in the part of his research that emphasized "concentricity as an extraordinary spatial configuration" (ibid., 85), partly because I was not studying enclosure at the time and, in a more critical vein, because I felt here he had fallen back into the dominant perception of things as existing in the plan only, and not as latent in the material.

At the time I first read this, I was carrying out my first excavation work on a series of Neolithic tumuli in northern France. I was presented with a sophisticated and messy architecture that could not be easily picked apart, and which was in reality a tangled assemblage of materials and projects. I was hooked. And even more so when it came to researching and writing my undergraduate dissertation, because the accounts other archaeologists gave of these sites were of buildings and tombs that were planned in their execution and structurally sound—i.e., with a layout. I was fascinated by this contrast. Why did such a wide array of detail get trimmed and narrowed down in reports of construction? Why were some materials overlooked altogether, and why was architecture in these narratives so *perfect*? This was not simply a matter of editing. I understood that to write a monograph, a piece of work needed to be clearly laid out and have a structure. But why did the subject, the built world, have to follow this template? It was exactly at this point that I read the Evans's (1988) chapter, but most important of all, it was the nature of the available archaeological evidence that struck me. So much of it was there without being used.

ARCHITECTURE AS PRACTICE

What I want to focus on here is the nature of the archaeological evidence. It is true, and surely significant, that I was taught by John Barrett, that one of the excavations was codirected by Ian Kinnes, and that I went on to carry out excavations for the Cambridge Archaeological Unit, of which Chris Evans is the director (and, at that time, Ian Hodder was the executive director). But now that this is out of the way, and references to the ideas of those in the academy have been acknowledged, I want to turn to say something about the nature of the archaeological evidence itself (i.e., explore the relational qualities and dimensions of the material, spatial, and temporal context).

I examined the architectural materials and building techniques that were a part of several Neolithic long mound and long cairn sites in southern Britain. Often, in the early part of the building process (e.g., at Hazleton North [Saville 1990] and Ascott-under-Wychwood [Benson & Whittle 2006]), turfs had been used. They had been laid flat lengthways and then stacked on top of each other in such a way to make a solid structure. There was time with this kind of a build for a process to be thought through, which could have involved many or few builders since the architectural features were structural and stable—it was slow architecture (McFadyen 2006a, 2007; Bailey & McFadyen 2010).

Interestingly, when stone was used in construction (in particular at Ascott-under-Wychwood), it was in the upper part of the build; these were large thin stones that were held up vertically and on edge. These stones are outlined in ink in plan drawings, but they could not have acted as a physical template in designing the build because they came late in the practice, and because they were not structural elements but were instead precariously propped. By setting stones on edge, a need was created for future work; otherwise the building project would have collapsed. The stones required further materials dumped quickly on either side of them. I have argued that this building technique altered the qualities of the material from solid matter to *dependent* material, and that this had a direct effect on the builders and their experience and participation in the building process—it was quick architecture (McFadyen 2006a, 2007). This practice created demanding and direct articulations of how things and people were caught up with each other. It is important to stress here that in this research I did not try to picture construction, but to explore positionally the junctions between people and things and to think about the inter*dependency* and participation that this required (McFadyen 2007, 27).

So, starting from the nature of the archaeological evidence, I found myself reading and thinking theory in order to articulate a problem. I analyzed in particular the history of ideas between archaeology and architecture, and as a result of this research I have argued that prehistoric architecture is better understood as a practice (Hill 2003), because it is constructed through experience and involves different kinds of participation in building (Till 2005), and that it should be an account of actions that emerge in time. So design is not simply equated with innovation, but is a thinking-through-practice that actively engages with the changes, alterations, and uses that occur along the way and as part of the making process—and perhaps this happens at a deeper level than suggested by Evans (1988). The works of architectural historians such as Jonathan Hill (2003) and Jeremy Till (2005) have helped me find a way to articulate an archaeological problem. Furthermore, these works, through accounts of occupying architecture (Rendell, in Hill 1998) and creative users (Hill 2003), open up design and extend the design process into use.

MATERIAL CULTURE

I have talked above about an archaeological practice that attempts to works between different subdisciplinary scales (in terms of material crossovers between landscape, architecture, and material culture). The scale of this archaeology has been one of small things, using the material detail to undermine the larger scale issues of design and monumentality (i.e., it is practical knowledge that is particular and specific [Barrett & Kinnes 1988, 1]). However, my account so far has been about architecture—architecture as practice—without material culture.

I have found excavation to be the most dynamic point of contact with the context of prehistoric architecture. It is here that I have perceived archaeological evidence to be at its richest. If we return to the practice of pit-cutting in the Neolithic, but focus this time on long barrow ditches rather than causewayed enclosure segments, there is a point to note. During the excavation of the long barrow Gussage Cow Down 294, we encountered a shared practice between material culture and architecture, whereby flint was knapped at the point where pits were cut to intersect (McFadyen 2006b, 2008b). Material culture and architecture were joined through the practice of making, and they could not be explained as a deposition of the former into the latter. The same occurred at several other barrows, such as Thickthorn Down (Drew & Piggott 1936) and Horslip (Ashbee et al. 1979). At that point, I was interested in exploring and developing an approach that considered material culture as architecture, but I didn't know how to do that in terms of the evidence. What I mean by this is that in other parts of the ditches, and in other long barrows, there were broken pottery and animal bones (see Pollard 1993; Thomas 1999). These materials had not been made or broken when pits were cut. I realized that I would have to follow these materials in a different way than I had observed the knapped flint, and look at the other things that material culture holds to it, in order to get at an understanding of activities outside the arena of the pit/ditch and the excavation. For me, these deposited materials were still *latent* and carried within them time and space.

One further note on the timing of things: it is interesting that there is now a shared theoretical discourse between architecture and material culture studies in archaeology, whereby material culture is understood through practice (see Conneller 2011). Chantal Conneller (ibid., 1) even asks a very architectural question about material culture: "What is the relationship between materials and the forms of things that are made from them?" What is really important about this work is that Conneller has turned things around and is understanding practice starting from the material and not from the object. These relationships, and our knowledge of them, are *emergent* (see Evans 1988).

MATERIAL CULTURE AS ARCHITECTURE

How to develop the latent material in archaeological evidence? How to make material as important as form, or how to fit material culture into architecture? These questions stayed with me as I started to think about material culture as architecture, and I moved from working on the Neolithic in southern Britain to the Chalcolithic in northern Portugal. The case study that I want to present here is about getting at architectural history through material culture studies (see also McFadyen, in press).

Figure 7.1 shows the Chalcolithic walled enclosure of Castelo Velho in the Alto Douro, excavated by Susana Oliveira Jorge. The site dates from 3000 to 1300 BC and is comprised of a series of subcircular structures and wall footings made out of schist that once had clay superstructures. The main enclosure wall, with multiple entranceways, is elliptical in shape and contains an inner tower. This is a very simple and static description of a building project that consisted of a series of makings and unmakings, cuttings and blockings, with different durations and scales of change and alteration, over a period of 1700 years. The phased plan drawing conveys the impression of a sequence of clearly defined architectural objects, a series of "still frames"—this happened, then this, and then this—and therefore it does not get at the actions or movement of architecture.

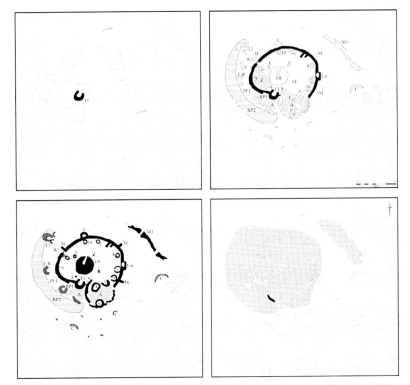

Figure 7.1 The sequence of phased plans of Castelo Velho, from top left to bottom right

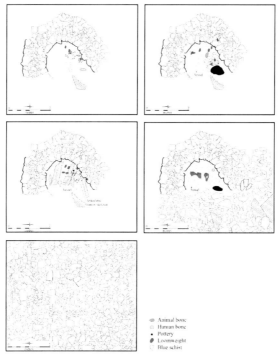

Figure 7.2 The sequence of phased plans of the C-shaped structure and the deposition of material culture from Castelo Velho, from top left to bottom left

In the archive of the site, there were several studies at the scale of materials that investigated the detail and dynamic of deposition in the past (see Figure 7.2) (Jorge et al. 1998–99). However, what interested me was that the material culture was kept to the time of the structure. In a sense this was still latent material that still had to be developed. I decided to study the fragmentation of the pottery and how this related to the excavated context in time. My aim was to get at the immediacy, or distance, between the breaking of a vessel and the deposition of its fragments, and to pinpoint the other practices that the sherds were caught up in (after Knight, in Garrow et al. 2005, and Brudenell, in Brudenell & Cooper 2008). I learned about the actions of architecture from this different point of contact.

Things happen to pots before and after they break; they do not remain frozen as perfect objects but rather have extended histories (see Figure 7.3). So focusing on the pre- and post-breakage histories of pots tells us something about what happened to the objects prior to deposition; it gets at other kinds of practice, other times, and it takes us into other spaces. This is a study of something before walls and before deposition. It is

Figure 7.3 From pot to sherd: a temporal trajectory

an interesting overlap, for in following the extended history of material culture, the broken pot takes us back to the construction of the stone structure. In architectural terms, this would be conceptually understood as the use that happens before design. In archaeological terms, this is a context that physically exists through a study of material culture.

Figure 7.4 is a photograph of the pottery that was recovered from the structure. An investigation of the overall percentage of small-, medium-, and large-sized sherds showed a clear prevalence of medium-sized sherds. The photograph shows the homogenous character of the pottery and the greater proportion of medium-sized sherds. It also portrays

Figure 7.4 The pottery assemblage from the C-shaped structure at Castelo Velho

to some extent the large number of refits, suggesting an immediacy to the deposition of the pots after breaking, but crucially not a direct relationship. Several refitting sherds were recovered from the outside of the stone structure, at the scale of the site. These connections across the site must have been made during the use of the object, because this was sealed with a stone capping soon after it had been used (see Figure 7.2 above).

Rather than thinking in traditional terms about architecture and its subsequent use, I used the work on the pottery to turn things around and think about building projects at Castelo Velho as a series of activities that emerge out of the rhythm and tempo of occupation (after Lefebvre & Régulier 2004). This is where the large proportion of medium-sized sherds and the incomplete nature of the vessels really come into play, because there is no evidence of a direct connection between breakage and deposition; there is also a crucial absence of large-sized pieces and near-complete refits. There is a substantial number of small sherds with weathered and abraded edges that are evidence of other post-breakage and pre-deposition practices, but they do not dominate the assemblage. Therefore, people were living around broken pots before they entered structures, prior to deposition, but this was not a simple matter of residuality: the relationship was more direct than that. Instead, it was the tempo of occupation, the daily practice of living with things (many in a broken state), that created the conditions for the structure.

I carried out a refitting program and studied the fragmentation of the pottery on a context-by-context basis throughout the site. The analysis of the patterns of fragmentation demonstrated that occupation, the playing out of time, was a part of the building project, and not something that happened afterwards. The following graph shows the same pattern of distribution repeated in several of the contexts studied (see Table 7.1). It is not simply the case that the study of material culture needs to be drawn into an understanding of the architectural history of the site; rather, an analysis of the patterns of fragmentation of pottery demonstrates that occupation, the playing out of time, was part of the building project. In a sense, the nature of these things *as they already were* (after Irwin, in Weschler 2008) was a part of the actions of architecture. To me, this is really important: architecture was as dependent on these conditions as it was on wall footings in stone.

INHABITED ARCHITECTURE

The interpretation I proposed above may seem a little strange compared to the way in which we normally conceptualize a building project and the design process. However, a precedent for this different take on the

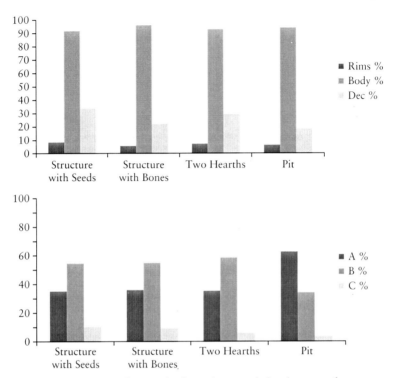

Table 7.1 Percentages of rim to body to decorated sherds across four contexts at Castelo Velho. Distribution of small, medium, and large sizes of sherds across the four contexts by percentage.

making of things can be seen in the "As Found" movement of the 1950s, which looked at inhabitation as a creative part of the design process itself; creativity had to do with an attentiveness and a concern for that which already exists. The architects Alison and Peter Smithson described their building projects as "the task of making something from something" (in Lichtenstein & Schregenberger 2001, 10). This movement showed an awareness of the importance of the *already there* in the creative practice of architecture. This seems to me to be very similar to the archaeological endeavor because it is a material practice, one that is all about the time of things and where inhabitation does not occur post-design but is a vital part of design practice.

The architect Jeremy Till has taken things a step further and argued that architecture is contingent as a discipline and as a practice—it depends on so many things. In his view a dependent architecture, and the contingent nature of architectural practice, should be seen as an opportunity for creativity and future work. He writes: "Architecture's *dependency* is finally seen as an opportunity and not a threat, with the architect working out from the contingencies of the given situation and using their embedded knowledge, skills, and imagination in an open and curious way in order to contribute to the making of new spatial possibilities" (Till 2009, 151, my emphasis).

In architectural history I have found what I would describe as an archaeological approach to architectural understanding. In drawing attention to these works, I am not implying that they exhibit the same dynamics that are latent in the Castelho Velho material, but rather that they are further examples that illustrate the relational qualities of things. Besides, Till's focus is spatial, and the Smithsons made new structures out of older buildings: the archaeology is also temporal in its focus, and material culture is the condition for future architecture. The use of things in the Chalcolithic was not something that came after design, but was instead *always there* as a precondition of creativity (see Figure 7.5). And this reverses the meaning of the concept of living with

Figure 7.5 Sherds from Castelo Velho laid out during a refitting exercise

design and delves a little deeper into the time it takes to make things. This is designing with living.

THE EVIDENCE WE HAVE AVAILABLE

This case study is an account of dealing with archive, not excavation, and with pottery rather than turf or stone. The excavation of Castelo Velho was completed in 2005 and I started my research in 2009; therefore, archive and pottery were the evidence that was available. These particular conditions taught me to understand the context of prehistoric architecture in a completely different way. There were other dimensions to context (other than the excavated deposit), and these existed in the assemblages of pottery; these other aspects of context were also defined by material, spatial, and temporal dimensions. My research with assemblages of pottery explored relations in other places and other times before those deposits had been created—what I call *latent material*.

And where does that leave theory? I hope I have demonstrated so far that theoretical insights are *indivisible* from an emphasis on the significance of materials and practice. This is a theory that is not generalizing or non-specific (see Barrett & Kinnes 1988, quoted above). But I hope that I have also demonstrated that material is intrinsically spatial-temporal. This is context as the medium we work with—assemblage and deposit.

In his latest book *Entangled*, Hodder (2012) makes the claim that there is a gap in studies on "the human dependence on things" (ibid., 17). This is an interesting and important book, containing several great pieces of writing on different forms and levels of dependence. However, I am not convinced by the argument of an existing gap in archaeological work in relation to the human dependence on things. In writing this chapter, I have been arguing that context will always bring to the fore the other times and spaces that materials hold to them—the dependent qualities of the material. For example, I have argued that architecture is dependent on the other times and spaces that material culture is caught up in, and that creativity and design have to do with an understanding of the *already there*. Hodder (ibid., 193) has a great way of describing the relational qualities between material culture and time: "Things have their own temporalities that stack up around the present." However, although he mentions the temporal and spatial presence of house architecture at Çatalhöyük, this dynamic is only about putting one wall on top of another (similar to the creative dynamic of the architects Alison and Peter Smithson); material culture does not seem to intervene (ibid.). There is no material crossover between architectural history and material culture studies. Moreover, Hodder limits his discussion of time to the "sequencing of entanglements" (2012, 192): material culture is a memory or marker in the creation of history, more specifically in the house's history, rather than being a precondition for the creativity of further architectural design. I see a distinction in these two kinds of dependency and in the possibilities that they offer: one is situated within the force and presence of past and history, and the other within the milieu of future and design. To entertain the force and presence of future and design does not mean to forego dependency or to privilege a human-centered account in archaeology, for material culture is always latent material. Therefore, it is always our task in archaeology to follow the other times and spaces material culture is caught up in, but without denying the creative potential of the already there in the making of future worlds. I argue that when assemblage and deposit are both considered as elements of context, the contingent nature of worlds is opened up to us *along with* the determination of future design. In our relational or entangled archaeologies, let us not forget the archaeology of context.

ACKNOWLEDGMENTS

I would like to thank Mark Knight, Jen Baird, and the editors and other contributors to this volume for reading and commenting on the text. I would also like to dedicate this work to Ian Kinnes, with all my love.

REFERENCES

Ashbee, P., Smith, I.F. & Evans, J.G. 1979. Excavation of three long barrows near Avebury, Wiltshire. *Proceedings of the Prehistoric Society* 45, 207–300
Bailey, D. & McFadyen, L. 2010. Built objects. In M.C. Beaudry & D. Hicks (eds.), *The Oxford Handbook of Material Culture Studies*, 562–87. Oxford: Oxford University Press
Barrett, J.C. 1988. The living, the dead and the ancestors: Neolithic and Early Bronze Age mortuary practices. In J. Barrett & I. Kinnes (eds.), *The Archaeology of Context in the Neolithic and Bronze Age: Recent Trends*, 30–41. Sheffield, UK: Department of Archaeology & Prehistory, University of Sheffield
Barrett, J.C. 1994. *Fragments from Antiquity: An Archaeology of Social Life in Britain 2900–1200 BC*. Oxford, UK: Blackwell
Barrett, J. & Kinnes, I. 1988. *The Archaeology of Context in the Neolithic and Bronze Age: Recent Trends*. Sheffield, UK: Department of Archaeology & Prehistory, University of Sheffield
Benson, D. & Whittle, A. (eds.) 2006. *Building Memories: The Neolithic Cotswold Long Barrow at Ascott-under-Wychwood, Oxfordshire*. Oxford, UK: Oxbow Books
Brudenell, M. & Cooper, A. 2008. Post-middenism: depositional histories on later Bronze Age settlements at Broom, Bedfordshire. *Oxford Journal of Archaeology* 27(1), 15–36

Conneller, C. 2011. *An Archaeology of Materials: Substantial Transformations in Early Prehistoric Europe*. London: Routledge

Drew, C.D. & Piggott, S. 1936. The excavation of long barrow 163a on Thickthorn Down, Dorset. *Proceedings of the Prehistoric Society* 2, 77–96

Evans, C. 1988. Acts of enclosure. In J. Barrett & I. Kinnes (eds.), *The Archaeology of Context in the Neolithic and Bronze Age: Recent Trends*, 85–96. Sheffield, UK: Department of Archaeology & Prehistory, University of Sheffield

Garrow, D., Beadsmoore, E. & Knight, M. 2005. Pit clusters and the temporality of occupation: an Earlier Neolithic Site at Kilverstone, Thetford, Norfolk. *Proceedings of the Prehistoric Society* 71, 139–57

Hill, J. (ed.) 1998. *Occupying Architecture: Between the Architect and the User*. London: Routledge

Hill, J. 2003. *Actions of Architecture: Architects and Creative Users*. London: Routledge

Hodder, I. (ed.) 1982. *Symbolic and Structural Archaeology*. Cambridge: Cambridge University Press

Hodder, I. (ed.) 1987. *The Archaeology of Contextual Meanings*. Cambridge: Cambridge University Press

Hodder, I. 2012. *Entangled: An Archaeology of the Relationships between Humans and Things*. Oxford, UK: Wiley-Blackwell

Jones, A. 2007. *Memory and Material Culture*. Cambridge: Cambridge University Press

Jorge, S.O., Oliveira, M.L., Nunes, S.A. & Gomes, S.R. 1998–99. Uma estrutura ritual com ossos humanos no sítio pré-histórico de Castelo Velho de Freixo de Numão (V.N. de Foz Côa). *Portugalia* (Nova Série) 19–20, 29–70

Lefebvre, H. & Régulier, C. 2004. The rhythmanalytical project. In H. Lefebvre, *Rhythmanalysis: Space, Time and Everyday Life*, 71–84. London: Continuum

Lichtenstein, C. & Schregenberger, T. (eds.) 2001. *As Found: The Discovery of the Ordinary*. Baden, Switz.: Lars Müller Publishers

McFadyen, L. 2006a. Building technologies, quick and slow architectures and Early Neolithic long barrow sites in southern Britain. *Archaeological Review from Cambridge* 21(1), 115–34

McFadyen, L. 2006b. Material culture as architecture: Neolithic long barrows in southern Britain. *Journal of Iberian Archaeology* 8, 91–102

McFadyen, L. 2007. Neolithic architecture and participation: practices of making at long barrow sites in southern Britain. In J. Last (ed.), *Beyond the Grave: New Perspectives on Barrows*, 22–29. Oxford, UK: Oxbow Books

McFadyen, L. 2008a. Building and architecture as landscape practice. In B. David & J. Thomas (eds.), *The Handbook of Landscape Archaeology*, 307–14. Walnut Creek, CA: Left Coast Press

McFadyen, L. 2008b. The long barrows and their regional setting. In C. French, H. Lewis, M. Allen, R. Scaife & M. Green (eds.), *The Changing Landscape of Cranbourne Chase: Wyke Down and Knowlton Environs*, 72–74. Cambridge, UK: McDonald Institute Monographs

McFadyen, L. In press. The time it takes to make: design and use in architecture and archaeology. In W. Gunn & J. Donovan (eds.), *Crafting Potentials: People as Skilled Innovators*. London: Ashgate Press

Pollard, J. 1993. *Traditions of Deposition in Neolithic Wessex*. Unpublished PhD thesis, University of Wales College Cardiff

Saville, A. 1990. *Hazleton North, Gloucestershire, 1979–82: The Excavation of a Neolithic Long Cairn of the Cotswold-Severn Group*. English Heritage Archaeological Report 13. London: English Heritage

Shanks, M. & Tilley, C. 1987. *Re-Constructing Archaeology: Theory and Practice.* Cambridge: Cambridge University Press

Thomas, J. 1999. *Understanding the Neolithic.* London: Routledge

Till, J. 2005. The negotiation of hope. In P. Blundell Jones, D. Petrescu & J. Till (eds.), *Architecture and Participation,* 23–42. London: Spon Press

Till, J. 2009. *Architecture Depends.* Cambridge, MA: MIT Press

Tilley, C. 1990. *Reading Material Culture: Structuralism, Hermeneutics and Post-Structuralism.* Oxford, UK: Blackwell

Weschler, L. 2008. *Seeing is Forgetting the Name of the Thing One Sees.* Berkeley: University of California Press

CHAPTER EIGHT

Archaeological Complexity: Materials, Multiplicity, and the Transitions to Agriculture in Britain

Andrew Meirion Jones and Emilie Sibbesson

The question of local versus exotic origins may be poorly posed, resting on the assumption that there is a Mesolithic way of life without domestication, and a Neolithic way of life with domestication, and that the transition from one to the other can only have occurred on one occasion and in one restricted region. Such an assumption, along with its requirement to identify the specific ingredient that sharply differentiates the one normative mode of production from the other, would seem increasingly to belong to a discredited theory of social evolution.

—Geoff Bailey (2008, 366)

In the final analysis, everything is suspended in movement.

—Tim Ingold (2000, 200)

INTRODUCTION

The discipline of archaeology aims to study long-term change, yet archaeologists adopt a very simplified model for understanding temporal change. This chapter will consider this problem in relation to one of the more dramatic changes in European prehistory, the transition to agriculture. Our focus will be on the debate around this transition in Britain, and specifically the suite of new scientific analytical techniques applied to this problem. Our argument will center on the topics of epistemology and ontology. We begin by considering the epistemological

Archaeology after Interpretation: Returning Materials to Archaeological Theory, edited by Benjamin Alberti, Andrew Meirion Jones, and Joshua Pollard, 151–72.

and ontological nature of scientific enquiry related to the problem of the Mesolithic–Neolithic transition. In addition, we question accepted views concerning causality and the role that ontological issues play in the transition. Most authors discussing the Mesolithic–Neolithic transition in Britain attempt to impose clarity on the subject, typically by arguing for the significance of one causal factor over others. By contrast our explicit intention is to argue for less mono-causal explanations and greater complexity when considering the transition.

THE MESOLITHIC–NEOLITHIC TRANSITION IN BRITAIN

Transitions from a way of life based on hunting and gathering to one based upon animal husbandry and cereal agriculture mark a significant change in European and world prehistory; the transition is a topic of continued discussion (Barker 2009). The debate regarding this issue in Britain is no less heated, and can be summarized by a series of recently discussed scenarios:

- Migration by Neolithic farmers from different parts of the Continent to western and eastern Britain: this view is associated with the work of Alison Sheridan and is centered upon the appearance of pottery and certain kinds of monumental architecture (e.g., Sheridan 2004, 2007, 2010);
- Migration by Neolithic farmers to southern England and southern Scotland: this view is associated with the work of Mark Collard and colleagues and is based on an increase in radiocarbon date densities on sites that postdate 4000 BC (Collard et al. 2010);
- Migration of Neolithic farmers of undisclosed origins into Britain around 4000 BC, resulting in major dietary change from wild to domestic food species: this view is associated with the work of Richard Schulting and Mike Richards and is based on variations in carbon and nitrogen stable isotope values of Mesolithic and Neolithic human skeletal remains (e.g., Schulting & Richards 2002a, 2002b; Richards 2003; Schulting 2004);
- Major influx of Neolithic farmers into all regions of Britain, resulting in dramatic upheaval of Mesolithic ways of life: this view is associated with the work of Peter Rowley-Conwy and draws on multiple lines of evidence (e.g., Rowley-Conwy 2004);
- Indigenous adoption of Neolithic traits by Mesolithic hunter-gatherers: this view is associated with the work of Julian Thomas and draws on multiple lines of evidence (e.g., Thomas 2008);
- In addition, some authors argue for a role for both indigenous adoption and incoming farmers, with beginnings in southeastern England: this view is associated with the work of Alasdair Whittle and colleagues (Whittle 2007; Whittle et al. 2011) and is primarily, but not exclusively, based on Bayesian statistical modeling of radiocarbon dates from Early Neolithic sites in southern Britain.

We may tease out several aspects on which these authors, and their datasets, would disagree with one another. However, the most contentious issues have to do with the tempo of the transition and the ancestry of its participants. In other words, the fundamental distinction is between authors who argue for a *rapid* transition from hunting and gathering to farming, typically driven by incoming Neolithic farmers, and authors who argue for the *gradual* adoption of agriculture, and other features of the Neolithic repertoire, by indigenous Mesolithic hunter-gatherers. It is also possible to distinguish between authors who rely predominantly on single lines of (scientific) evidence and those who engage with multiple lines of evidence. We do not intend to evaluate each scenario or the datasets that underpin them; yet, in order to characterize these more fundamental differences, it is worth considering a few of them in a little more detail.

Arguments for rapid change are supported by the appearance of distinctively Neolithic material culture. For example, Sheridan (2003) has drawn attention to stylistic similarities between Early Neolithic pottery in northern France (Late Castellic Ware) and pottery from Achnacreebeag, Argyll, western Scotland. She suggests that some of the Scottish ceramics predate pottery found in England. The earliest known pottery in southern Britain dates to c. 4000–3850 BC (Cleal 2004, 181).[1] Significant early assemblages of distinctive Carinated bowls have been found at the Sweet Track, Somerset, and the Coneybury Anomaly, Wiltshire (Cleal 2004). Sheridan argues that the pottery found at the chambered tomb of Achnacreebeag, Argyll, Scotland, is likely to have been brought from mainland Europe by a small group of agriculturalists. On the basis of the accomplished nature of early Carinated bowl pottery, Sheridan (2007) also argues for a rapid introduction of that ceramic style at an earlier stage.

In addition, carbon and nitrogen stable isotope values obtained from Mesolithic and Neolithic human skeletal remains have been presented in support of the hypothesis of a rapid dietary change (e.g., Richards & Hedges 1999; Schulting & Richards 2002a, 2002b; Richards & Schulting 2006). Individuals who predate 4000 BC tend to yield values consistent with significant consumption of marine foods, whereas those who date to later periods appear to have consumed more terrestrial plant and animal species. This pattern is interpreted as indicative of a wholesale and rapid dietary shift around 4000 BC.

A further example of new data that supports a scenario of rapid change and disruption is provided by recent work on radiocarbon date densities at Mesolithic and Neolithic sites, which are utilized as proxies for population size (Collard et al. 2010). The study rests on the premise that larger populations will enhance the number of site phases that are recovered archaeologically, and it indicates a sharp rise after 4000 BC. Collard et al. (2010, 867) argue that the documented surge in radiocarbon dates in southern England and Scotland was too rapid to represent the "learning curve" for the uptake of agriculture and subsequent population boom among indigenous hunter-gatherers.

Counter to these arguments, Julian Thomas (2004, 2008) has noted the peculiarity of the idea that groups of Neolithic farmers at a series of points around the near Continent simultaneously chose to introduce farming to Britain. He further notes dissimilarities between the pottery assemblages of the Belgian and Dutch Michelsberg, the nearest continental neighbors (Thomas 2008, 76), making the wholesale transportation of Neolithic artifacts from the continent to Britain unlikely. As Thomas (ibid., 65) notes, it is important to accept the possibility that "Mesolithic people had some role in the formation of the British Neolithic." To support this argument he points out the continuities in the use of places in the landscape during the Mesolithic and Neolithic and potential continuities in lithic technologies. Thomas is not alone in making this argument; indeed he concurs with several authors (e.g., Bradley 1993; Barrett 1994; Tilley 1994; Whittle 1996). The basis of the argument for a gradual cultural adoption lies in the concept of the Neolithic as a set of cultural approaches or ideas (e.g., Hodder 1990). We see this articulated at an early stage in Thomas's work: "These ambiguities in the evidence, it is argued, support an interpretation in which 'the Neolithic' is less a particular economy than a system of social reproduction, a set of structured social relationships which were organised about an interlocking series of binary oppositions" (Thomas 1991, 182).

EPISTEMOLOGIES AND SCIENTIFIC ANALYSIS

Curiously, despite their disagreements over the evidence, each of these sets of authors appears to agree on the epistemological nature of the evidence. Each author appears to assume the existence of a world distinct from scientific engagement that awaits discovery "out there." It is simply a case of finding the correct model to investigate this world that will ultimately reveal the truth. This is perhaps most starkly observed in Sheridan's (2004, 9) assertion, in relation to pottery, that "the earliest communities whom we identify as 'Neolithic' shared the same continental ancestry and so brought the same basic traditions to Britain and Ireland" despite the fact that there are no identical parallels for the Carinated bowls found in Britain and Ireland; the assumption here is that we simply haven't found them yet (Thomas 2008, 75–76). Thomas offers a more sophisticated theoretical approach in which indigenous Mesolithic hunter-gatherers act on or manipulate inert materials according to cultural attitudes; here again an ontological distinction is assumed to be at play between the inanimate world and animate subjects. Thomas deploys the same body of evidence as Sheridan (2004, 2007, 2010), Collard et al. (2010), and Schulting and Richards (2002a, 2002b), but argues for a quite different scenario. Each author therefore believes in the self-evident nature of the evidence, and each is attempting to assert his or her truth claims to this evidence.

In fact when we examine the works of these authors it becomes obvious that rather than passively observing, documenting, and commenting on aspects of this evidence, each of them, through argumentation and scientific documentation, is actively shaping the evidence. This much is obvious from early sociological studies of laboratory procedure and scientific practice. For example, in their early analysis of laboratory life Latour and Woolgar (1987) noted that scientific practices simultaneously produce statements about realities and the same realities that they describe. They also noted that in and through the routine application of methodological procedures, potential differences in perspective become invisible or less apparent, and realities are turned into the causes of statements. This is precisely what we see in the approaches of many of the authors discussed above. An example is Schulting and Richards's (2002a, 2002b) analysis of bone isotope data: bone samples are selected and the recorded changes in $\delta^{13}C$ and $\delta^{15}N$ values become the evidence by which rapid changes in diet are surmised, and the concept of a sharp distinction between the Mesolithic and Neolithic is produced afresh. The bone sample selection process fades into the background; what emerge instead are the results, which, unsurprisingly, confirm the expected distinction between Mesolithic and Neolithic periods. The same issue arises in Collard et al.'s (2010) analysis; here the selection of AMS radiocarbon dates and their statistical treatment are used to support evidence of a rapid shift from the Mesolithic to Neolithic. Again the selection of specific dates and the application of specific statistical procedures are left in the background and what emerges are a set of results that confirm the sharp shift to the Neolithic; here, too, the evidence is turned into the cause of statements.

ONTOLOGICAL MULTIPLICITIES

It is relatively easy to point out the fact that evidence is used to explain realities through scientific procedures and methods. More significant, argue sociologists of science Annemarie Mol (2002) and John Law (2005), is that scientific procedures and methods actively *produce* realities. In a detailed analysis of the medical treatment of atherosclerosis in hospitals in the Netherlands, Mol (2002) observed that medical opinions and treatments differed and provided quite different pictures of the disease; these differing views coexisted in the treatment of individual patients (see also Mol 2006). Rather than conceptually fragmenting the body of the patient and resulting in opposing forms of treatment, she observed that these opposing views of the disease were held together; the body of the patient was not then a singular body, but a *multiple* one. Scientific procedures and methods not only *construct* realities, as we discussed above, but they also *enact* them (Law 2005, 56). This analysis suggests that we have to think quite differently about the ontological nature of "evidence." Rather than imagining an epistemological distinction between observer and reality, in which we take up differing perspectives on an unchanging world that awaits discovery, we imagine realities to be enacted of multiple overlapping ontologies, or multiplicities.

Although this may seem a counterintuitive idea, we can illustrate it quite easily in terms of our case study. For example, even though the positions of Sheridan and Thomas appear distinct and polarized, in fact their deployment of evidence overlaps. Whereas Sheridan (2007) claims that the rapid introduction of Carinated bowls is due to wholesale movement by Neolithic settlers, Thomas (2008, 76) argues that the remarkably accomplished nature of this early pottery style is due to "the active selection of a very specific element from Continental assemblages, precisely because it was held in common by a range of diverse and geographically dispersed communities." Again, Schulting's (2000) discussion of rapid dietary change from the Mesolithic to the Neolithic is accommodated by Thomas (2003) in terms of cultural choice, as a result of the dietary avoidance of fish by the earliest Neolithic communities. Similarly, Whittle (2007; Whittle et al. 2011) is able to accommodate both the introduction of the Neolithic and its gradual adoption by indigenous hunter-gatherers. Archaeologists therefore enact a multiplicity when they discuss the Mesolithic–Neolithic transition for Britain, a multiplicity held together by differing perspectives on the same evidence and by the accommodation of opposing views.

We want to be quite clear about what we are proposing here. We are *not* arguing for a postmodern plurality of approaches, in which each person takes up a different stance on the same body of material. Instead we are arguing that evidence does not exist by itself; it is crafted, or assembled. Evidence is being enacted, sets of realities are made visible, and relations, processes, and contexts that are essential and necessary to the presence of this evidence are finessed in the background. We are not dealing with different and possibly flawed perspectives on the same evidence or object. Rather we are dealing with different objects or pieces of evidence produced by different methods, approaches, or outlooks; these different objects or pieces of evidence may overlap, but *they are not the same* (Law 2005, 55). The differing statements concerning the Mesolithic–Neolithic transition suggest that the authors are occupying different worlds, though these worlds overlap and coexist (Mol & Law 2006, 8).

We do not present the notion of multiplicity in the Mesolithic–Neolithic transition out of bloody-mindedness. Rather, we foreground the notion of ontological multiplicity because we feel that this is the best approach to the Mesolithic–Neolithic transition. Arguing from the standpoint of classic Euro-American epistemology, Collard et al. (2010, 866) bemoan the fact that "to date, none of the lines of evidence that has been brought to bear on this debate has proven capable of *unambiguously* refuting any of the hypotheses" (our emphasis). We would argue that this is because the Mesolithic–Neolithic transition *is* an ontological multiplicity: it is *characterized by ambiguity*.

Rather than thinking of ontological multiplicities as a problem, we wish instead to embrace the multiple nature of the Mesolithic–Neolithic transition and rethink it. Our aim here is not to "solve" the causes of the transition between foraging and farming, and thereby add an extra ontological dimension to the multiplicity. Instead, we aim to think multiply about transitions. As Mol and Law (2006, 8) note, "multiplicity is about coexistences at a single moment. To make sense of multiplicity, we need to think and write in topological ways, discovering methods for laying out a space, for laying out spaces, and for defining paths to walk through these." That is what we aim to do now.

LIVES IN TRANSIT

We began this chapter by remarking on the simplified nature of change in archaeologists' models, and we highlighted Geoff Bailey's quote arguing that looking for specific ingredients to sharply differentiate one mode of production from another is associated with an outmoded notion of social evolution. Why might social evolution be a problem? Why do archaeologists present a simplified approach when handling the topic of change? Part of the problem with our accounts of social change arises from the conceptual schemes that we have devised to define units of archaeological time. Though dividing periods of time according to technological or economic changes seems reasonable on the basis of the evidence, there is a sense that the conceptual schemas for defining "the Mesolithic" and "the Neolithic," rather than being conceptual tools of clarity and definition, have in fact become conceptual constraints; this point has been noted on several occasions in the past (Zvelebil 1996,

1998, 2008; Pluciennik 1998, 1999, 2005, 2008). One of the clear outcomes of this conceptualization is a sense of time being stopped in its tracks, of particular regions of time being compartmentalized and frozen (Lucas 2005, 15–24). This makes it very difficult to understand change, and indeed the topic of change, and of origins, necessarily arises from this compartmentalization of time; as soon as we define time as compartmentalized blocks, we are required to understand how we get from one compartmentalized block of time to another. In this sense, the topic of the Mesolithic–Neolithic transition is of our own making (Pluciennik 1998)—though this does not deny that the transition has an empirical basis.

The idea of dividing time in this way is quite artificial. When we stop to consider it, we rarely experience time as a series of jump cuts from one ontological state to another; instead, we tend to experience time as a duration or flow (Bergson 1911). What would our accounts of change look like if we adopted accounts of temporal flow and duration? With this in mind, we wish to step aside from the overarching period definitions and look at various aspects of changing practice from the tenth millennium to the third millennium BC, crossing the Mesolithic–Neolithic divide; in each case, we want to consider the tempo and direction of change in various aspects of life.

MATERIALS AND PRACTICES IN TRANSIT: A LONG VIEW

STONE AND BONE TOOLS

Let us begin by considering stone tool technologies. Lithic technologies obviously have gone through millennia of change and development prior to the tenth millennium BC, with little obvious change since the thirteenth millennium BC (Tolan-Smith 2008, 141). Microlithic technologies characterize the earliest lithics from the tenth millennium onward. Traditionally a distinction has been established between a broad blade technology in the earlier millennia, from c. 9600 BC to c. 8000 BC, and a narrow blade technology from c. 8000 to c. 4000 BC, although there is a clear blurring in these lithic technologies, with a greater proportion of broad blades at an earlier stage and of narrow blades at a later stage (Smith 1997, 5). Toward the end of the fifth millennium and the beginning of the fourth millennium we begin to observe new changes in lithic technologies with the appearance of leaf-shaped and, later, laurel arrowheads. In turn, these arrowhead forms are replaced by chisel and petit tranchet forms at the end of the fourth millennium and the beginning of the third millennium. Notably, Edmonds (1995, 37) points out that single platform flint cores characterize lithic technologies during the fifth–fourth millennia. If we consider larger stone tool technologies, axes of chipped flint or stone of tranchet type characterize the fifth millennium, and chipped flint axes continue to be produced into the fourth millennium. In addition we observe the rise of ground stone axes during the fourth and into the third millennium BC, alongside a notable increase in the scale of production activities typified by flint mines and axe production quarries (Bradley & Edmonds 1993; Barber et al. 1998). However, the specialist exploitation of stone resources is also evident at an early date, from the mid-eighth millennium BC, on Scottish islands such as Rhum, where bloodstone was extracted (Wickham-Jones 1990), and Arran, where pitchstone was extracted (Ballin 2009). Indeed, raw materials were exchanged around the northwestern coast of Scotland at an early date (Saville 2004), echoing the long-distant exchanges of raw materials into the fourth–third millennium BC (e.g., Bradley & Edmonds 1993).

Some stone tools are produced from found pebbles, such as the pebble mace-heads of the fifth millennium BC (Roe 1979); although there seems to have been little continued use for pebble forms during the fourth millennium, worked lumps of rock or large pebbles appeared as mace-head forms in the late fourth millennium–beginning of the third millennium BC. The deposition of artifacts in watery contexts in certain regions, such as the Thames Valley, potentially had an origin in the fifth millennium and continued through the third millennium (Bradley 1990; Lamdin-Whymark 2008; Hey et al. 2011).

Bone tools are also an important feature from the tenth–eighth millennia, with the emergence of uniserial barbed points on antler beam or split longbones, made using the "groove and splinter" technique. In addition we observe the appearance of elk antler mattocks. Bone technologies changed quite markedly after c. 8000 BC with the emergence of squatter and blunter uniserial and biserial points (Tolan-Smith 2008, 147); again in this later period we observe the use of antler mattocks and bone or antler bevel-ended tools. Bone tools of different forms appear in the fourth millennium, when cattle scapula and red deer antler tines were utilized as working tools, typically for the shifting of chalk and flint at flint mines and causewayed enclosures and, by the end of the fourth millennium, cursus monuments.

POTTERY

The picture for pottery technologies differs dramatically from the one just described. We observe no evidence of pottery in Britain prior to the close of the fifth millennium BC (Whittle et al. 2011, 755–62). Carinated bowls, appearing c. 4185–3975 BC, are likely to represent the earliest form of pottery, followed (but not replaced) by plain bowls around 3970–3715 BC (Whittle et al. 2011, 762). Around 3745–3690 BC (ibid., 763), a series of regional decorated pottery styles begin to emerge in southern England, again in addition to the existing repertoires. Elsewhere, other decorated regional forms, such as the Unstan Ware and Hebridean Ware of northern and western Scotland, are produced at a less certain date. During the mid-fourth millennium BC, c. 3400 BC, we again see the emergence of decorated pottery forms with a wider national currency, such as Impressed/Peterborough Ware, and at the beginning of the third-millennium Grooved Ware. At this stage we see a transformation in pottery from round-based to flat-based forms.

Subsistence

Evidence of dietary habits is variable. During the tenth–eighth millennium BC, evidence from sites on lake margins such as Star Carr, Yorkshire, and Thatcham, Berkshire, indicate the exploitation of terrestrial animal species such as aurochs, elk, and red and roe deer, with wild pigs and horses also evident at Thatcham. Evidence of coastal exploitation at this early stage is sparse, though signs of it can be found in northwestern Scotland among the "Obanian culture" sites of MacArthurs Cave and Druimvargie Rockshelter, as well as the offshore islands of Risga, Ulva Cave, and several sites on Oronsay. Obanian sites date from the eighth millennium to the fifth millennium BC, and the most plentiful evidence of the coastal exploitation of resources comes from five shell midden sites on Oronsay (Mellars 1987), where shells of a variety of marine mollusks, particularly limpets, are deposited. In addition, there is evidence of the remains of grey and common seals, dolphins, porpoises, and probable rorqual whales. The accumulation of shell and bone in these midden sites on Oronsay is probably indicative of a specialist hunting of seals and fishing of saithe (Tolan-Smith 2008, 154). By the beginning of the fourth millennium BC, we begin to see dramatic changes in the species utilized, with the appearance of domestic cattle, sheep/goats, and domestic pigs. In southern England there is a marked emphasis on the early exploitation of cattle, with a shift to the use of pigs during the third millennium BC. However, in regions such as northern Scotland the prominence of cattle continues throughout the fourth–third millennia. During this later period we also continue to see the exploitation of particular animal species. For instance, red and roe deer are found both in southern England and northern Scotland, whereas red deer are present throughout the fourth–third millennia in regions such as Orkney (Clutton-Brock 1979). Tools of red deer antler continue to be used throughout the fourth–third millennia, and are especially evident at sites in the southern areas of chalkland. Some animal species continue to be relevant throughout the period surveyed; for example, dogs are known from eighth-millennium sites such as Star Carr, and are evident at sites down to the third millennium BC. The nature of plant exploitation varies, with hazelnuts being ubiquitous on sites from at least the eighth millennium BC to the fifth millennium BC. Hazelnuts are also found in smaller quantities on sites dating to the fourth–third millennium BC. From the fourth millennium we begin to see evidence of cereal cultivation (Brown 2007; Jones & Rowley-Conwy 2007). There is circumstantial evidence of cereal-type pollen in the mid-fifth millennium BC from regions such as the Isle of Man, though its veracity is disputed (Whittle et al. 2011, 849). Domestic species were not alone on the menu; dental wear of individuals from fourth-millennium BC Whitwell Quarry, a long barrow in Derbyshire, indicates that diets included significant proportions of fibrous wild plants (Chamberlain & Witkin 2003, 55). The transition from the fifth to the fourth millennia has not been detected in dental wear studies so far, although this may be an underexplored line of evidence. Instead, dental wear evidence for the period under review differs from the evidence from the Bronze and Iron Ages, since diets of the later, fully agricultural communities appear to have been rougher, possibly due to higher frequencies of quern stone grit (Nyström & Cox 2003, 65).

In addition, stable isotope analysis of human bone has indicated differences in the $\delta^{13}C$ and $\delta^{15}N$ values of individuals of the sixth and fifth millennium compared to individuals of the fourth millennium BC. As described above, this variation is interpreted as a rapid shift from marine to terrestrial foods around 4000 BC (Richards & Hedges 1999; Schulting & Richards 2002a, 2002b; Richards 2003; Schulting 2004). We are not entirely convinced of the validity of this scenario, given the poorly defined chronological resolution of the data and the evidence of terrestrial game hunting in the fifth millennium and of continued exploitation of marine foods into the third millennium BC (Lidén et al. 2004; Milner et al. 2004; Milner 2006). Nonetheless, emerging from the stable isotope dataset is an indication that the diets became more homogenous after 4000 BC, probably as a consequence of the introduction of domestic food species (Milner 2006, 66; Richards & Schulting 2006, 448). Aspects of food consumption in the fourth and third millennia have been more closely addressed through lipid residue analysis of pottery by GC/MS and GC/C/IRMS (Dudd et al. 1999; Copley et al. 2005; Jones et al. 2005; Copley & Evershed 2006; Mukherjee et al. 2008). These datasets confirm the picture of extensive use of animal source foods derived primarily from the main domesticates and including both meat and dairy (Copley et al. 2005) along with increased consumption of cereals such as barley (Jones et al. 2005).

MONUMENTS AND MORTUARY PRACTICES

There are a few instances of monumentality from an earlier period, such as the eighth-millennium BC pine posts erected near Stonehenge, Wiltshire (Vatcher & Vatcher 1973; Lawson 2007), and the Mesolithic post-holes from Runnymede, Thames Valley (Hey et al. 2011, 215). In addition, other sites could be argued to be monumental in character, such as the shell middens of Oronsay. These sites were the result of gradual accretions over time and by the fifth millennium BC may have been impressive features in the landscape, though many of the midden sites were less impressively sited in caves (Chatterton 2005, 112–14). Notably, many fourth-millennium architectural constructions were built on, and from, places with earlier occupational histories in the fifth millennium or earlier. This is particularly the case of the constructions beneath the Cotswold-Severn long barrows, such as Hazelton North, Gloucestershire; Beckhampton Road, Wiltshire, England; and Gwernvale, Breconshire, Wales (Barrett 1988; Darvill 2004; McFadyen 2007). This is also the case for sites in the far north of Scotland, such as Camster, Caithness (Masters 1997).

Evidence of mortuary practices from the earlier millennia of the period under discussion is sparse, though we do have good early evidence of human burial, such as a child's skull dated to the ninth millennium BC that was found at Badger Hole, part of the cave complex at Wookey, Somerset. There are further burials into the ninth–eighth millennium BC at this site and other sites in southwest England, such as Gough's Cave, Somerset; Kent's Cavern, Devon; Greylake, Somerset (Brunning & Firth 2011); and Ogof-yr-Ychen and Daylight Rock, southwest Wales (see Conneller 2005 for details). The most spectacular of these are the circa fifty burials at Aveline's Hole, Somerset, dated to the ninth–eighth millennia BC. There appears to be a marked gap in the evidence of mortuary practice around the seventh and sixth millennia in these areas (Conneller 2005, 147), though fragments of human bone were deposited in caves at Pontnewydd and Paviland, Wales, dating to the sixth and fifth millennia BC. Again we find fragments of bone dating to the fifth millennium at Cnoc Coig, one of the Oronsay middens. Notably a number of these regions persist in their significance into the fourth millennia, with many caves in southwest Wales being utilized for human burial (Burrow 2006, 83), including Nanna's Cave, Priory Farm Cave, Red Fescue, and Ogof-yr-Benlog. Evidence of mortuary practices is particularly striking in the chambered tomb and earthen long barrows of the fourth millennium BC.

LANDSCAPES

One final factor to discuss is the changing nature of the environment and settlement. We do not consider the environment as a determining factor standing apart from humans; rather, with geographer Sarah Whatmore (2002), we find it more helpful to think of the environment as a component of a lively other-than-human world that humans come to know through active experience. Environmental forces therefore intersect with human lives, rather than simply determining them.

After the maximum extent of the ice sheets during the Dimlington Stadial at 19,500 BC, Britain was free of glaciers. By the mid-thirteenth millennium BC, and following a period of abandonment, Britain was resettled. Tolan-Smith (2008, 142) identifies several phases of settlement. The first phase, beginning c. 12,700 BC, saw people moving into Britain from adjoining areas of the north European Plain; this early phase is characterized by a lack of familiarity with local raw materials and the importation of nonlocal raw materials over distances greater than 160 kilometers. A secondary consolidation phase occurs from 10,950 to 8,250 BC; in this period human populations expand into unoccupied regions, such as northern England and Scotland, and human presence in southern Britain increases. Here we observe a greater interest in the availability and use of local raw materials. The migration of the Polar front northwards and the eustatic sea-level rise in the eighth millennium BC saw an effective reduction in the altitude of upland areas and a general amelioration in their conditions. Concomitantly, we observe a gradual movement of populations to the north and the increased use of upland environments. Finally, by c. 5000 BC, the rise in sea level effectively cut off Britain from Continental Europe by the English Channel. Climatic amelioration continued into the fifth–fourth millennium. By the fourth millennium BC, we again observe human population movement from northern France into southern Britain.

Settlement evidence is relatively sparse for the ninth–eighth millennia BC, and the most well-known sites, such as Star Carr, Deepcar, and Thatcham are located in lakeside environments; these locations appear to have been seasonally occupied, probably in the summer (Tolan-Smith 2008, 145). Upland hunting camps, such as Broom Hill, Broomhead Moor site 5, Dunford Bridge, March Hill, and White Gill, all located in the North York Moors, date from the eighth–fifth millennia BC. More permanent settlement is evident in northern England: the site of

Howick, Northumberland, features a circular timber-framed structure associated with pits dating to 7850 BC (Waddington 2007; Tolan-Smith 2008, 150). More specialized settlement associated with fishing and the exploitation of bivalve species is observed at the sixth-millennium BC site of Morton, Fife, on the east coast of Scotland. These early sites are characterized by a degree of occupational specialization. Settlement evidence is only marginally more evident in the fourth millennium BC, with the appearance of timber halls in regions such as central Scotland—e.g, Balbridie, Claish, and Crathes (see Barclay et al. 2002; Brophy 2007)—and the recently identified group of rectangular timber settlement structures in southern and central England, such as at Yarnton, Oxfordshire; Horton, Berkshire; and White Horse Hill, Kent (Hey et al. 2011). These sites are likely to date from c. 3800 BC (Whittle et al. 2011). Settlement is especially in evidence in northern Scotland: regions such as Orkney show evidence of continuous settlement from c. 3600 BC at sites such as Wideford and Knap of Howar, and well into the third millennium BC at sites including Pool, Rinyo, Skara Brae, Barnhouse, Crossiecrown, Links of Noltland, and Ness of Brodgar. With the possible exception of the timber halls of central Scotland, many of the settlement sites of the fourth to third millennia appear to suggest a wide spectrum of activities, and are much less specialized in character than earlier settlements.

INTERSECTING PRACTICES FROM THE TENTH TO THIRD MILLENNIUM BC

Our overview of a range of changing material practices has been necessarily brief. Our purpose in taking this long view of changing circumstances is to observe the flow, rhythm, and direction of changes that occur over extended periods of time. Let us review these now. Some material practices undergo long, slow, and gradual changes, such as those associated with lithic technologies; these appear to persist with minor variations from the tenth to the fifth millennia with the production of narrow blade and broad blade microliths: lithic armatures used in composite hunting tools and plant processing tools. These give way by the fourth millennium BC to a variety of lithic arrowheads, also parts of a composite hunting technology. More gradual are larger lithic technologies such as the tranchet axes of the fifth millennium, which are reproduced in the chipped flint and polished stone axes of the fourth millennium BC. Bone tools appear to undergo significant fluctuations, assuming different forms across three major periods—10,000–8000 BC, 8000–5000 BC, and 4000–3000 BC.

Mortuary practices offer a complex picture of change, with evidence of single and collective burials between the ninth and eighth millennia, and sparse or partial evidence of burials in the seventh and sixth millennia BC. Evidence of collective burial appears again in the fourth–third millennia BC, with the deliberate construction of earth- and stone-chambered tombs and long barrows to contain the dead. We appear to observe then an undulating rhythm of change from the ninth–eighth millennia to the fourth–third millennia, but also gradual changes in the persistent significance of some places, especially places of burial. Many of the sites of significance in the ninth–sixth millennia were of significance during the Upper Paleolithic period; and places of significance for settlement during the sixth–fifth millennium BC continued to be important in the fourth millennium BC as sites for the construction of mortuary monuments.

Other changes appear quite rapid and sudden. For example, ceramic artifacts appear quite markedly in the fourth millennium BC in Britain and are relatively rapidly produced in a series of regional styles by c. 3800 BC; these regional styles are then replaced by common styles by the end of the fourth/beginning of the third millennium BC. After its appearance, then, pottery underwent a series of developments over a short period of time.

Taking the evidence at face value, the isotopic analysis of human bone suggests that diet also underwent rapid changes after the fifth–fourth millennium BC, with a shift from marine to terrestrial, presumably domestic, sources. Again we do observe both change and continuity in the animals and plants exploited across this time period, with species such as elk being exploited during the ninth–eighth millennia and domestic animal species appearing by the fourth millennium; some species such as roe and red deer are exploited from the ninth through the third millennium.

The character of settlements appears to change markedly. Smaller shifting settlements characterized the period from the ninth to the fifth millennium BC; many of these are occupationally specialized, and we can observe a shift in settlement regions. The settlement of the fourth–third millennia BC is characterized by a broader spectrum of activities and greater duration of occupation, and we observe a weaker relationship between settlement and climatic change.

We can therefore think of change over the period we have discussed, from the tenth to the third millennia BC (conventionally termed the Early Mesolithic to the Middle Neolithic) as a multiplicity made up of a series of differing strands of changing technological practices and environments; each of these has differing tempos and durations. We argue that the whole should be considered as a complex field of interactions, and that change occurs where these strands of technological practice converge and intersect. For example, it appears evident that dietary change occurs around the beginning of the fourth millennium BC; it is also evident that ceramic technologies appear at around the same time. It seems reasonable to assume that the two strands of practice resonate together and are related. Note, however, that although there are changes in lithic technologies, there are also continuities. Similarly, we can observe continuities in the use of places and in the location of mortuary practices. Dietary changes have less impact on lithic technologies and mortuary practices than they do on ceramics. Interestingly, it seems clear that environmental change resonates with changing patterns of settlement in the ninth–fifth millennia; other than the dramatic infilling of the English Channel around 5000 BC (Waller & Long 2003), there seems little reason to relate environmental changes to other strands of practice around 4000 BC. Each aspect of the evidence therefore has differing durations and resonates differently with other practices. Such a perspective allows us to see that the transition is a multiplicity made up of differing practices; we are able to see that the much discussed dietary changes are simply one strand of practice (e.g., Schulting & Richards 2002a, 2002b), and more gradually unfolding developments, such as the persistent significance of place (e.g., Thomas 2008), are another; neither provides causal explanations for the transition in itself.

BEYOND THE NEOLITHIC PACKAGE

Having presented a picture of changing and intersecting strands of technological activity (see Figure 8.1), we now want to consider how this picture of change differs from conventional accounts, and how this alters our understanding of transitions.

The conventional methods of discussing time in archaeology treat each archaeological period as a bracketed and circumscribed period of time—e.g., "the Mesolithic," "the Neolithic." This has dramatic consequences when we wish to discuss the change from one period to another, and particularly when we observe sharp changes in material culture between periods, such as during the Mesolithic–Neolithic transition; there is a sense of one block of time simply being shifted out of the way and being replaced by another unit of time. This problem is exacerbated by the notion of the "Neolithic package," first used by Childe (1936) to denote a series of related practices occurring at the Neolithic transition. This suggests the emergence of a closed and packaged unit of time and set of practices that simply appear and replace the Mesolithic.

In another formulation, the arrival of the Neolithic appears to be conceptualized in terms of either a domino effect or a contagion, as if

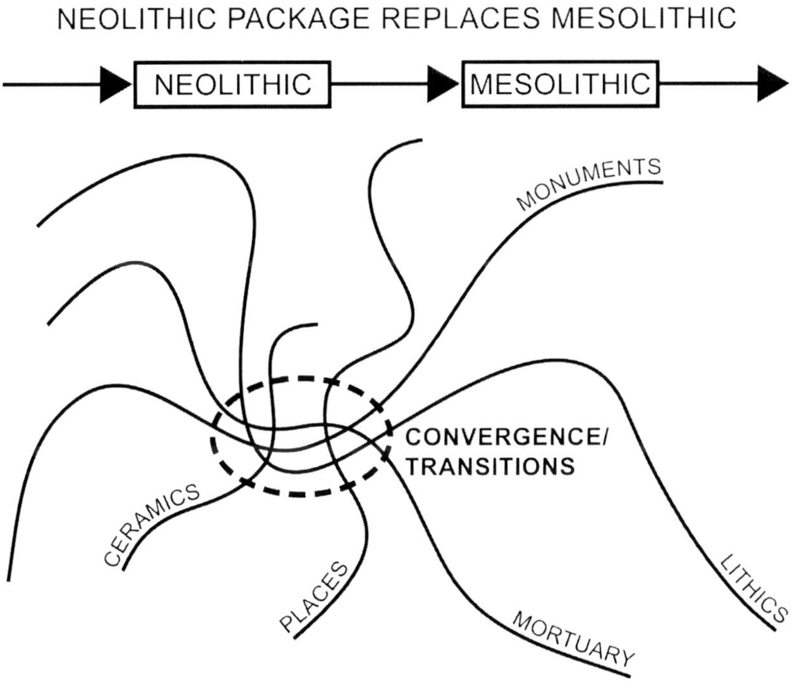

NEOLITHIC PACKAGE REPLACES MESOLITHIC

Figure 8.1   Two visualizations of the Mesolithic–Neolithic transition

the arrival of Neolithic people and the creation of Neolithic architecture, whether in western Scotland or southern England, had irrevocably rippled through the surrounding populations and made them Neolithic (Sheridan 2003; Rowley-Conwy 2004). In another variation of this idea, dietary change is considered to be sufficient to produce a change from Mesolithic to Neolithic (Schulting 2000).

Alternatively, the Neolithic is conceptualized as a set of ideas that are gradually adopted by forager populations. This concept drives a wedge between forager and farmer populations and we erect a distinction between populations who have Neolithic concepts and those who do not (Barnard 2007). However, presumably at some stage foragers became farmers: How did they create the concept of being Neolithic? Again we see a distinction between two ideal and contrasting states—being a "forager" and "farmer"—and little sense of how we get from one state to another; there is little sense of process.

We prefer not to think of the Neolithic as a sealed entity such as a "package," a contagion, or as a set of ideals, but instead as an assemblage, a group of entangled and intersecting activities. In emphasizing the Neolithic as an assemblage we want to remain deliberately open as to its form, "its durability, the types of relations and the human and non-human elements involved" (see Anderson & MacFarlane 2011, 124). Rather than thinking of the Mesolithic and Neolithic as states of *being*, in which prehistoric societies switch from one state to another, we argue that it is difficult to pinpoint when the Mesolithic ends and the Neolithic begins, because both are bound up in a process of *becoming*. In addition, if these periods are made up of multiple strands of practice we should take care in discussing "the Mesolithic" or "the Neolithic" as monolithic and singular entities; instead, we need to be open to the possibility of multiple Mesolithics leading to multiple Neolithics. The multiplicity of regional Neolithics is supported by the recent radiocarbon analysis by Whittle et al. (2011). In sum, what we are observing is not a single transition from the Mesolithic to Neolithic but rather a series of overlapping *transitions*.

NOTE

1. All dates are expressed as cal (calibrated) BC.

REFERENCES

Anderson, B. & MacFarlane, C. 2011. Assemblage and geography. *Area* 43(2), 124–27

Bailey, G. 2008. Mesolithic Europe: overview and new problems. In G. Bailey & P. Spikins (eds.), *Mesolithic Europe*, 357–72. Cambridge: Cambridge University Press

Ballin, T.B. 2009. *Archaeological Pitchstone in Northern Britain: Characterization and Interpretation of an Important Prehistoric Source*. Oxford: British Archaeological Reports, British Series 476

Barber, M., Field, D. & Topping, P. 1998. *The Neolithic Flint Mines of England*. Swindon, UK: English Heritage

Barclay, G.J., Brophy, K. & MacGregor, G. 2002. Claish, Stirling: an early Neolithic structure in its context. *Proceedings of the Society of Antiquaries of Scotland* 132, 65–137

Barker, G. 2009. *The Agricultural Revolution in Prehistory: Why Did Foragers Become Farmers?* Oxford: Oxford University Press

Barnard, A. 2007. From Mesolithic to Neolithic modes of thought. In A. Whittle & V. Cummings (eds.), *Going Over: The Mesolithic-Neolithic Transition in Northwest Europe*, 5–19. Proceedings of the British Academy 144. London: British Academy

Barrett, J.C. 1988. The living, the dead and the ancestors: Neolithic and early Bronze Age mortuary practices. In J.C. Barrett & I.A. Kinnes (eds.), *The Archaeology of Context in the Neolithic and Bronze Age: Recent Trends*, 30–41. Sheffield, UK: Department of Archaeology & Prehistory, Sheffield University

Barrett, J.C. 1994. *Fragments from Antiquity: An Archaeology of Social Life in Britain, 2900–1200 BC*. Oxford, UK: Blackwell

Bergson, H. 1911. *Matter and Memory*. New York: Zone Books

Bradley, R. 1990. *The Passage of Arms: An Archaeological Analysis of Prehistoric Hoards and Votive Deposits*. Cambridge: Cambridge University Press

Bradley, R. 1993. *Altering the Earth: The Origins of Monuments in Britain and Continental Europe*. Edinburgh: Society of Antiquaries of Scotland, Monograph Series 8

Bradley, R. & Edmonds, M. 1993. *Interpreting the Axe Trade: Production and Exchange in Neolithic Britain*. Cambridge: Cambridge University Press

Brophy, K. 2007. From big houses to cult houses: early Neolithic timber halls in Scotland. *Proceedings of the Prehistoric Society* 73, 75–96

Brown, A. 2007. Dating the onset of cereal cultivation in Britain and Ireland: the evidence from charred cereal grains. *Antiquity* 81, 1042–52

Brunning, R. & Firth, H. 2011. An Early Mesolithic cemetery at Greylake, Somerset, UK. *Past* 69, 6–8

Burrow, S. 2006. *The Tomb Builders in Wales, 4000–3000 BC*. Cardiff, UK: National Museum of Wales

Chamberlain, A. & Witkin, A. 2003. Early Neolithic diets: evidence from pathology and dental wear. In M. Parker Pearson (ed.), *Food, Culture, and Identity in the Neolithic and Early Bronze Age*, 53–58. Oxford: British Archaeological Reports

Chatterton, R. 2005. Ritual. In C. Conneller & G. Warren (eds.), *Mesolithic Britain and Ireland: New Approaches*, 101–20. Stroud, UK: Tempus

Childe, V.G. 1936. *Man Makes Himself*. Bradford-on-Avon, UK: Moonraker Press

Cleal, R. 2004. The dating and diversity of the earliest ceramics of Wessex and south-west England. In R. Cleal & J. Pollard (eds.), *Monuments and Material Culture: Papers in Honour of an Avebury Archaeologist, Isobel Smith*, 164–92. East Knoyle, UK: Hobnob Press

Clutton-Brock, J. 1979. Report of the mammalian remains other than rodents from Quanterness. In C. Renfrew (ed.), *Investigations in Orkney*, 112–34. London: The Society of Antiquaries

Collard, M., Edinborough, K., Shennan, S. & Thomas, M. 2010. Radiocarbon evidence indicates that migrants introduced farming to Britain. *Journal of Archaeological Science* 37, 866–70

Conneller, C. 2005. Death. In C. Conneller & G. Warren (eds.), *Mesolithic Britain and Ireland: New Approaches*, 139–64. Stroud, UK: Tempus

Copley, M.S., Berstan, R., Mukherjee, A.J., Dudd, S.N., Straker, V., Payne, S. & Evershed, R.P. 2005. Dairying in antiquity III: evidence from absorbed lipid residues dating to the British Neolithic. *Journal of Archaeological Science* 32, 523–46

Copley, M.S. & Evershed, R.P. 2006. Organic residue analysis. In D. Benson & A. Whittle (eds.), *Building Memories: The Neolithic Cotswold Long Barrow at Ascott-under-Wychwood, Oxfordshire*, 283–88. Oxford, UK: Oxbow Books

Darvill, T. 2004. *Long Barrows of the Cotswolds and Surrounding Areas*. Stroud, UK: Tempus

Dudd, S.N., Evershed, R.P. & Gibson, A.M. 1999. Evidence for varying patterns of exploitation of animal products in different prehistoric pottery traditions based on lipids preserved in surface and absorbed residues. *Journal of Archaeological Science* 26, 1473–82

Edmonds, M. 1995. *Stone Tools and Society*. London: Batsford

Hey, G., Garwood, P., Robinson, M., Barclay, A. & Bradley, P. 2011. Part 2: The Mesolithic, Neolithic and early Bronze Age and the establishment of permanent human occupation in the valley. In A. Dodd & C. Hayden (eds.), *Thames through Time. The Archaeology of the Gravel Terraces of the Upper and Middle Thames: Early Prehistory to 1500 BC*, 151–464. Oxford, UK: Oxford Archaeology

Hodder, I. 1990. *The Domestication of Europe*. Oxford, UK: Blackwell

Ingold, T. 2000. *The Perception of the Environment: Essays in Livelihood, Dwelling and Skill*. London: Routledge

Jones, A.M., Jones, R. & Cole, W.J. 2005. Organic residue analysis of Grooved Ware from Barnhouse. In C. Richards (ed.), *Dwelling among the Monuments: An Examination of the Neolithic Village of Barnhouse, Maeshowe Passage Grave and Surrounding*

Monuments at Stenness, Orkney, 283–89. Cambridge, UK: McDonald Institute Monograph Series

Jones, G. & Rowley-Conwy, P. 2007. On the importance of cereal cultivation in the British Neolithic. In S. Colledge & J. Conolly (eds.), *The Origins and Spread of Domestic Plants in Southwest Asia and Europe*, 391–419. Walnut Creek, CA: Left Coast Press

Lamdin-Whymark, H. 2008. *The Residue of Ritualised Action: Neolithic Deposition Practices in the Middle Thames Valley*. Oxford: British Archaeological Reports

Latour, B. & Woolgar, S. 1987. *Science in Action: How to Follow Scientists and Engineers through Society*. Cambridge, MA: Harvard University Press

Law, J. 2005. *After Method: Mess in Social Science Research*. London: Routledge

Lawson, A.J. 2007. *Chalkland: An Archaeology of Stonehenge and Its Region*. East Knoyle, UK: Hobnob Press

Lidén, K., Eriksson, G., Nordqvist, B., Götherström, A. & Bendixen, E. 2004. The wet and the wild followed by the dry and the tame—or did they occur at the same time? *Antiquity* 78, 39–48

Lucas, T. 2005. *The Archaeology of Time*. London: Routledge

Masters, L. 1997. The excavation and restoration of the Camster long chambered cairn, Caithness, Highland, 1967–80. *Proceedings of the Society of Antiquaries of Scotland* 127, 123–83

McFadyen, L. 2007. Neolithic architecture and participation: practices of making in early Neolithic Britain. In J. Last (ed.), *Beyond the Grave: New Perspectives on Barrows*, 22–29. Oxford, UK: Oxbow Books

Mellars, P. 1987. *Excavations on Oronsay: Prehistoric Human Ecology on a Small Island*. Edinburgh, UK: Edinburgh University Press

Milner, N. 2006. Subsistence. In C. Conneller & G. Warren (eds.), *Mesolithic Britain and Ireland: New Approaches*, 61–82. Stroud, UK: Tempus

Milner, N., Craig, O., Bailey, G. & Andersen, S. 2004. Something fishy in the Neolithic? An assessment of the use of stable isotopes in the reconstruction of subsistence. *Antiquity* 78, 19–38

Mol, A. 2002. *The Body Multiple: Ontology in Medical Practice*. Durham, NC: Duke University Press

Mol, A. 2006. Cutting surgeons, walking patients: some complexities involved in comparing. In J. Law & A. Mol (eds.), *Complexities: Social Studies of Knowledge Practices*, 218–57. Durham, NC: Duke University Press

Mol, A. & Law, J. 2006. Complexities: an introduction. In J. Law & A. Mol (eds.), *Complexities: Social Studies of Knowledge Practices*, 1–22. Durham, NC: Duke University Press

Mukherjee, A.J., Gibson, A.M. & Evershed, R.P. 2008. Trends in pig product processing at British Neolithic Grooved Ware sites traced through organic residues in potsherds. *Journal of Archaeological Science* 35, 2059–73

Nyström, P. & Cox, S. 2003. The use of dental microwear to infer diet and subsistence in past human populations: a preliminary study. In M. Parker Pearson (ed.), *Food, Culture, and Identity in the Neolithic and Early Bronze Age*, 59–67. Oxford: British Archaeological Reports

Pluciennik, M. 1998. Deconstructing "the Neolithic" in the Mesolithic-Neolithic transition. In C. Richards & M. Edmonds (eds.), *Understanding the Neolithic of Northwest Europe*, 61–83. Glasgow, UK: Cruithne Press

Pluciennik, M. 1999. Archaeological narratives and other ways of telling. *Current Anthropology* 40, 653–78

Pluciennik, M. 2005. *Social Evolution*. London: Duckworth

Pluciennik, M. 2008. Hunter-gatherers to farmers? In A. Jones (ed.), *Prehistoric Europe: Theory and Practice*, 16–34. Oxford, UK: Wiley-Blackwell

Richards, M.P. 2003. Explaining the dietary isotope evidence for the rapid adoption of the Neolithic in Britain. In M. Parker Pearson (ed.), *Food, Culture and Identity in the Neolithic and Early Bronze Age*, 31–36. Oxford: British Archaeological Reports

Richards, M.P. & Hedges, R.E.M. 1999. A Neolithic revolution? New evidence of diet in the British Neolithic. *Antiquity* 73, 891–97

Richards, M.P. & Schulting, R.J. 2006. Against the grain? A response to Milner et al. (2004). *Antiquity* 80, 444–56

Roe, F.E.S. 1979. The typology of implements with shaftholes. In W.A. Cummins (ed.), *Stone Axe Studies*, 23–48. London: Council for British Archaeology, Research Report 21

Rowley-Conwy, P. 2004. How the west was lost: a reconsideration of agricultural origins in Britain, Ireland, and Southern Scandinavia. *Current Anthropology* 45, 83–113

Saville, A. 2004. The material culture of Mesolithic Scotland. In A. Saville (ed.), *Mesolithic Scotland and its Neighbours: The Early Holocene Prehistory of Scotland in its British and Irish Context, and Some Northern European Perspectives*, 185–220. Edinburgh: Society of Antiquaries of Scotland

Schulting, R.J. 2000. New AMS dates from the Lambourn barrow and the question of the earliest Neolithic in southern England: repacking the Neolithic package? *Oxford Journal of Archaeology* 19, 25–35

Schulting, R.J. 2004. An Irish sea change: some implications for the Mesolithic-Neolithic transition. In V. Cummings & C. Fowler (eds.), *The Neolithic of the Irish Sea: Materiality and Traditions of Practice*, 22–28. Oxford, UK: Oxbow Books

Schulting, R.J. & Richards, M. 2002a. The wet, the wild and the domesticated: the Mesolithic-Neolithic transition on the west coast of Scotland. *European Journal of Archaeology* 5(2), 147–89

Schulting, R.J. & Richards, M. 2002b. Finding the coastal Mesolithic in southwest Britain: AMS dates and stable isotope results on human remains from Caldey Island, south Wales. *Antiquity* 76, 1011–25

Sheridan, A. 2003. French connections I. In I. Armit, E. Murphy, E. Nelis & D. Simpson (eds.), *Neolithic Settlement in Ireland and Western Britain*, 3–17. Oxford, UK: Oxbow Books

Sheridan, A. 2004. Neolithic connections along and across the Irish Sea. In V. Cummings & C. Fowler (eds.), *The Neolithic of the Irish Sea: Materiality and Traditions of Practice*, 9–21. Oxford, UK: Oxbow Books

Sheridan, A. 2007. From Picardie to Pickering and Pencraig Hill? New information on the "Carinated Bowl Neolithic" in northern Britain. In A. Whittle & V. Cummings (eds.), *Going Over: The Mesolithic–Neolithic Transition in Northwest Europe*, 441–92. Proceedings of the British Academy 144. London: British Academy

Sheridan, A. 2010. The Neolithisation of Britain and Ireland: the "big picture." In B. Finlayson & G. Warren (eds.), *Landscapes in Transition*, 89–105. Oxford: Oxbow Books/Council for British Research in the Levant, Supplementary Series 8

Smith, C. 1997. *The Late Stone Age Hunters of the British Isles*. London: Routledge

Thomas, J. 1991. *Rethinking the Neolithic*. Cambridge: Cambridge University Press

Thomas, J. 2003. Thoughts on the "repacked" Neolithic revolution. *Antiquity* 77, 67–74

Thomas, J. 2004. Current debates on the Mesolithic–Neolithic transition in Britain and Ireland. *Documenta Praehistorica* 31, 113–30

Thomas, J. 2008. The Mesolithic–Neolithic transition in Britain. In J. Pollard (ed.), *Prehistoric Britain*, 58–89. Oxford, UK: Wiley-Blackwell

Tilley, C.Y. 1994. *A Phenomenology of Landscape: Places, Paths, and Monuments*. Oxford, UK: Berg

Tolan-Smith, C. 2008. Mesolithic Britain. In G. Bailey & P. Spikins (eds.), *Mesolithic Europe*, 132–57. Cambridge: Cambridge University Press

Vatcher, F. de M. & Vatcher, H.L. 1973. Excavation of three post-holes in Stonehenge Carpark. *Wiltshire Archaeological & Natural History Magazine* 68, 57–63

Waddington, C. 2007. *Mesolithic Settlement in the North Sea Basin: A Case Study from Howick, North-East England*. Oxford, UK: Oxbow Books

Waller, M.P. & Long, A.J. 2003. Holocene coastal evolution and sea-level change on the southern coast of England: a review. *Journal of Quaternary Science* 18(3–4), 351–59

Whatmore, S. 2002. *Hybrid Geographies: Natures, Cultures, Spaces*. London: Sage

Whittle, A. 1996. *Europe in the Neolithic: The Creation of New Worlds*. Cambridge: Cambridge University Press

Whittle, A. 2007. The temporality of transformation: dating the early development of the southern British Neolithic. In A. Whittle & V. Cummings (eds.), *Going Over: The Mesolithic–Neolithic Transition in Northwest Europe*, 377–98. Proceedings of the British Academy 144. London: British Academy

Whittle, A., Healy, F. & Bayliss, A. 2011. *Gathering Time: Dating the Early Neolithic Enclosures of Southern Britain and Ireland*. Oxford, UK: Oxbow Books

Wickham-Jones, C. 1990. *Rhum: Mesolithic and Later Sites at Kinloch, Excavations 1984–86*. Edinburgh: Society of Antiquaries of Scotland

Zvelebil, M. 1996. Farmers our ancestors and the identity of Europe. In P.Graves-Brown, S. Jones & C. Gamble (eds.), *Cultural Identity and Archaeology: The Construction of European Communities*, 145–66. London: Routledge

Zvelebil, M. 1998. What's in a name? The Mesolithic, the Neolithic and social change at the Mesolithic–Neolithic transition. In C. Richards & M. Edmonds (eds.), *Understanding the Neolithic of Northwest Europe*, 1–36. Glasgow, UK: Cruithne Press

Zvelebil, M. 2008. Innovating hunter-gatherers: the Mesolithic in the Baltic. In G. Bailey & P. Spikins (eds.), *Mesolithic Europe*, 18–59. Cambridge: Cambridge University Press

PART III
Assembling the Social

Joshua Pollard

Forty years have passed since a social archaeology was proclaimed (Renfrew 1973), its express goal being "the reconstruction of past social systems and relations" (Renfrew 1982, 10). The relations talked of were of course those between people, which might be mediated through things, buildings, landscapes, and burial and ceremonial practices. The realization of the goal has not been as easy as early attempts implied. Within both processual and post-processual frameworks—which social archaeology has, in chameleon-like fashion, transcended—a race after the (past) "social" emerged in the wake of disciplines such as social/ cultural anthropology and sociology. Archaeology was always a little behind, always a little wanting, because it felt it lacked direct access to "the Indian behind the artifact," or to the system or *mentalité* behind the artifact (Lucas 2010; Thomas 2010). Absence was felt.

Greater maturity now reigns, brought about by the substantial recursive experience of working with the material traces of the past and the theories and philosophies with which we engage. There is recognition that archaeology is not simply a past tense of anthropology (see papers in Garrow & Yarrow 2010), but something different, even if the two disciplines may occasionally intersect. Social archaeologies (and the plural is key) remain alive and well, as demonstrated by the success of publications such as the *Journal of Social Archaeology*. However, the remit has shifted: from initial attempts to reconstruct past systems or entities, to a concern with the mapping out of the past practice of social relations (via the sociology of structure, agency, and identity), to a current position that is broadly interdisciplinary and much more present-focused, engaging with ethnography, heritage, politics, and ethical commitment (Meskell 2011).

To return to that original formulation of a social archaeology, where do the "social" and "society" lie now? The problem is revealed in language and concepts that refer to social entities—*social* relations, *social* practices, *social* life, etc.—presupposing both the existence of reified social forms and a distinction between the "social" and other things, people, processes, relations, etc. The resulting ontological separation of practices and of the material from the "social" cannot be sustained. What we observe in the world are not simply relations between people, held together by mental templates of order that float above everything else. As recent work under the banners of Actor-Network Theory (ANT), science and technology studies, relational ontology, and symmetrical archaeology has ably shown, the social needs to be relocated as emergent within networks/meshworks of interactions not just between humans, but within wider assemblages that take in other organisms, things, energies, performances, technologies, and so forth. A realist social ontology is one that is located within assemblage work (DeLanda 2006). This may mean decentering the human, or at least not automatically privileging humans as the principal actors or causative agents within the network. For a discipline like archaeology, the difficulty relates to what Lucas (2012, 259) describes as an "unease" with post-humanocentrism that might be felt by some; after all, archaeology is commonly conceived as being about humans and their past. Lucas suggests that the solution is to see humans as the "connective tissue" that defines the limits of what might be described as archaeological; here the human is the "one indispensable agent" but is closely shadowed by other things (ibid., 262). Influenced by the realist ontology of Manuel DeLanda, Lucas offers a description of a "new" social archaeology in which the social exists not as an entity or abstraction, but as "an immanent process of aggregation": "Societies are real, material assemblages composed of people, stones, plates, and horses" (ibid., 265).

The contributors in this section tackle these issues, exploring ways in which the social is put together and emergent in a post-humanocentric archaeology. If a theme (beyond a common philosophical/theoretical orientation) runs through these chapters, it is describing the world through its fluidity, movement, and process. The first chapter, by **Joshua Pollard**, describes some of the problems posed by explanations that account for the monumental architecture of Neolithic Britain primarily in terms of relations between human actors alone or of concerns to represent the world. By juxtaposing Neolithic architecture with another form of monumental architecture—the *marae* of Polynesia—Pollard shows how a relational and animist ontology allows us to destabilize the images we currently hold of monuments, forcing us to focus on assemblies, flows, and meshworks of materials, and on the emergence of different kinds of ontological condition through the process of building and beyond.

Sarah Baires, Amanda Butler, Jacob Skousen, and **Timothy Pauketat** offer subtle and persuasive insight into the trans-dimensional qualities of human and nonhuman movements within Hopewellian and Mississippian religious practices. They draw explicitly upon the animist ontology of Native American populations to describe the relational fields emergent within activities of community and world renewal: namely, the practices of pilgrimage, mound construction, and pipe smoking. They describe a world in which everything was alive and related; where movement was a condition of a life force that did not distinguish between objects, persons, places, times, or other dimensions. Critically, they argue that it is through the motion inherent in these relational fields that human history unfolds.

Ben Jervis asks, how stable is the social? Drawing explicitly on Actor-Network Theory, his study offers a detailed and innovative perspective on the agential role of medieval ceramics in the continuities and changes in life in Saxo-Norman Southampton. Jervis follows the interactions between people and objects, moving beyond an anthropocentric view of change. Whereas "Normanization" is normally seen as a top-down process, in his chapter Jervis highlights how assemblages of things, people, practices, and so on served to create a group of Normanized people. The social is formed through networks/connections and the actions that take place within them; and those actions result from the unfolding of the temporary and distributed agency present in the interactions of people and things. Jervis shows that the "social hierarchy" often evidenced in this period is not a reified entity, but something that was brought about and sustained through action.

Chris Fowler continues the theme of assemblage work, describing a personal intellectual journey that emerged from the study of Early Bronze Age mortuary practices in Northeast England. He describes his realization that understanding mortuary practice involved not just a relational study of personhood, but a relational study of everything else within the assemblage (things, theories, techniques, methodologies, histories, documentation, and so forth). Rejecting the "correspondence theory of truth"—the idea that interpretation proceeds from evidence by way of theory—Fowler offers insight into how archaeology might respond to the features and challenges of non-representational approaches. It is the struggle with the paradoxes presented by non-representational theory—especially with the fact that an assemblage can be both momentary and enduring—that, Fowler argues, offers new possibilities for thinking about time and materiality.

In the final chapter of this section **Marcus Brittain** provides an attentively crafted account of the topology of place as explored through narratives of assembly. As with other contributions, this account works through the complexity of life via routes that exceed the human, neatly circumscribing the relational quality of place. Working through the dimensions of two architectures—Welsh Early Bronze Age barrows and cairns and the *benna kulugto* of the Mursi lands of the Lower Omo Valley, Ethiopia—Brittain outlines how deeply embedded archaeology is in the processes of place-making and world-making, and how that entails an accountability that researchers should not neglect.

REFERENCES

DeLanda, M. 2006. *A New Philosophy of Society: Assemblage Theory and Social Complexity*. London: Continuum

Garrow, D. & Yarrow, T. (eds.) 2010. *Archaeology & Anthropology: Understanding Similarity, Exploring Difference*. Oxford, UK: Oxbow Books

Lucas, G. 2010. Triangulating absence: exploring the fault lines between archaeology and anthropology. In D. Garrow & T. Yarrow (eds.), *Archaeology & Anthropology: Understanding Similarity, Exploring Difference*, 28–39. Oxford, UK: Oxbow Books

Lucas, G. 2012. *Understanding the Archaeological Record*. Cambridge: Cambridge University Press

Meskell, L. 2011. Editorial. *Journal of Social Archaeology* 11(2), 127–29

Renfrew, C. 1973. *Social Archaeology: An Inaugural Lecture*. Lecture delivered at the University of Southampton, March 20. Southampton, UK: The Camelot Press

Renfrew, C. 1982. *Towards an Archaeology of Mind*. Cambridge: Cambridge University Press

Thomas, J. 2010. Commentary: walls and bridges. In D. Garrow & T. Yarrow (eds.), *Archaeology & Anthropology: Understanding Similarity, Exploring Difference*, 179–84. Oxford, UK: Oxbow Books

CHAPTER NINE

From *Ahu* to Avebury: Monumentality, the Social, and Relational Ontologies

Joshua Pollard

A particular set of conditions coalesced during the fifth–third millennia BC in Atlantic and northwestern Europe (Iberia, western France, Britain, Ireland, and southern Scandinavia) that resulted in the creation of monumental constructions of stone, earth, timber, and other media. Following the narrative of movements and interplays of matter and energy outlined by DeLanda (2000), we might describe those conditions as comprising a flux of biological agents (people, animals, plants, among others), energy flows, geological and vegetational affordances, religious convictions, and bonds and divisions of kinship and history. For the sake of historical order, archaeologists apply to these conditions the label "Neolithic" (see also Jones & Sibbeson, in this volume). The materialized outcome was a variety of constructed forms: wooden and stone boxes to contain human bodies and other materials; mounds; enclosures of timber, earth, and stone; and individual, paired, linear, circular, and other configurations of free-standing timbers and stones. United by the considerable energy and resources absorbed by their creation, and the lack of immediate connections to subsistence activities, these formations are grouped together by archaeologists as "monuments," and their study is often conducted as a specific line of investigation in itself (e.g., Bradley 1998; Scarre 2007; Midgley 2008).

So how, as archaeologists, have we come to understand these constructions? Vicki Cummings (2008) has usefully summarized the dominant interpretive themes that structure recent research on British Neolithic monuments and has classified them into the categories of "social relations," "process," "landscape," and "experience." These

Archaeology after Interpretation: Returning Materials to Archaeological Theory, edited by Benjamin Alberti, Andrew Meirion Jones, and Joshua Pollard, 177–96.

distinctions are worth reiterating briefly here. The first, explicit attempts to provide social frameworks for understanding the creation of monuments characterized certain processual approaches of the early 1970s, most notably Renfrew's classic 1973 essay on monumentality and social evolution in Neolithic Wessex, in which he used emerging monument scale as an index of the increasing labor mobilization afforded by the evolution of ever more centralized forms of authority (Renfrew 1973). Neo-Marxist-inspired approaches of the mid-1980s/early 1990s stressed the role of monuments and attendant ritual practices in processes of ideological control, as for example in Thorpe and Richards's (1984) application of the concept of "ritual authority structures" to the Late Neolithic of Yorkshire and Wessex, Shanks and Tilley's (1982) research on ideological manipulation and mystification in Swedish and British Neolithic mortuary practice, and Thomas's (1993) discussion of monumental architecture as a device to control access to esoteric knowledge. In reaction, other approaches have sought to stress not division and distinction, but rather social cohesion as a result of inclusion in monument building (e.g., Whittle 1997); and they have seen social formations as being as much the outcome as the precondition of monument building (Barrett 1994).

The second interpretive category, that of process, places a focus on construction itself. Some accounts highlight the possible relations between sequences of monument development and changing social circumstances (e.g., Bradley 1993); the connections engendered between people and materials through the act of building (e.g., McFadyen 2003); and the physical and social risks involved in participating in projects whose successful outcome could not always be assured (e.g., Richards 2004). The role of monuments as a feature of memory work, which actively creates images of the past or stands as testament to historical and mythic accounts, might be identified as another dimension to process (Bradley 2002). The third and forth categories of landscape and experience are often collapsed, especially within approaches inspired by the philosophy of phenomenology (e.g., Tilley 1994; Cummings 2009), which foregrounds the embodied experience of encountering and engaging with monumental spaces. Landscape as a frame of reference is explored in the work of Bradley, Cummings, Richards, and others: here attention is drawn to processes of mimicry and visual reference that link natural features and monumental architecture, and to the way that monumental form might provide a microcosm homology and representation of the wider world (Richards 1996; Bradley 2000; Cummings & Whittle 2004; Watson 2004). To this can be added a concern with materiality and with how the dimensional properties of substances such as timber, stone, earth, and water were called upon to signify the presence of elemental forces or different domains of being (Richards 1996; Parker Pearson & Ramilisonina 1998; Cummings 2009).

MOMENTS OF TENSION

There is no denying the energy and interpretive vibrancy that characterizes work on such monuments, but there are instances in which archaeology itself sits uncomfortably with these interpretive strands, calling into question explanations that account for this architecture primarily in terms of its involvement in social strategies (here defined as negotiated relations between human actors alone) or concerns to represent the world. The tension generated, I would like to argue, results from a failure to incorporate the full range of actors/actants (both human and nonhuman) into our understandings of these constructions, and from our tendency to present monuments as occupying *stable* ontological states. Two related instances are offered to illustrate this point.

Located on the chalk downland of north Wiltshire in southern England is a remarkable complex of monumental constructions belonging to the fourth and third millennia BC (Pollard & Reynolds 2002). At the center of this complex is a substantial earthwork enclosure—the Avebury henge—that contains within its perimeter massive megalithic settings of local sarsen stone (Smith 1965; Gillings & Pollard 2004). Leading from the southern and western entrances of the henge are two "avenues" of paired sarsen stones: the Beckhampton Avenue, which runs over a distance of c. 1.3 kilometers from the henge, terminating at a box-like setting of megaliths known as the Longstones Cove; and the longer West Kennet Avenue, which winds its way from the southern entrance of the henge and eventually connects with the timber and stone circles of the Sanctuary on Overton Hill (see Figure 9.1).

The intention behind the construction of these avenues is commonly conceived as the creation of sacred walkways along which participants would solemnly (or raucously) process to take part in ceremonies at the henge (Thomas 1993; Barrett 1994), the route being additionally designed to "frame" a landscape experience that brought in significant earlier constructions and natural features (Watson 2001). However, there is a problem. Although constructed after the earthwork of the Avebury henge, the course of the Beckhampton Avenue manages to miss the gap provided by the henge's western entrance, heading instead for the tail of its colossal bank (Gillings et al. 2008, 118). The West Kennet Avenue is likewise offset to the west of the southern henge entrance to which it first appears to be heading (Smith 1965). Any procession along these routes would have ended in celebrants scrambling over the banks of the earthwork and risking lethal falls into the enclosed 10-meter-deep

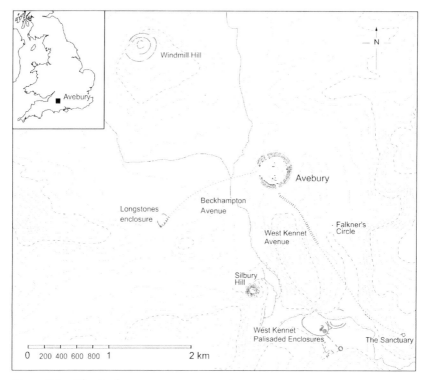

Figure 9.1 The Avebury monument complex

ditch (see Figure 9.2). A route outward along the West Kennet Avenue presents similar difficulties for our eager celebrants, since its connection to the Sanctuary runs off alignment to the entrance to the timber circles and is blocked by a large stone (Cunnington 1931). From the perspective of a human participant, these are not satisfactory arrangements.

Our conventional understanding of monuments sees them as ready-made spaces designed to facilitate social action within the context of ritual and ceremonial practice; and so features like the Avebury avenues take the form they do "because of the ways in which they were intended to be used and inhabited" (Thomas 2004, 101). Monumental architecture takes on the quality of theatre—of stage and screen (Bradley 2011)—and it is meant to assist in the ordering of performances that serve to reproduce and stabilize (human) social relations. Clearly this is not going to work well in the case of the Avebury avenues. It is difficult to see what kind of social relations or embodied experiences are being reproduced or engendered here. In fact, it is difficult to sustain any notion that the avenues were created with the idea that people, at least in their living, corporeal form, would ever process along them.

Figure 9.2 The Avebury henge ditch under excavation during the early twentieth century

A second "moment of tension" is provided by a monument that lies just to the south of Avebury, on low ground overlooking the headwaters of the River Kennet. Created a few generations after the Avebury earthwork had been raised, Silbury Hill is the largest artificial prehistoric mound in Europe (Whittle 1997; Leary & Field 2010). Academic and fringe interpretations of its function have ranged widely: from a monumental memorial to King Arthur's victory at Badon Hill (Fergusson 1872, 61–89), to the representation of an earth goddess (Dames 1977), to a component of a complex created around lunar-solar symbolism (Sims 2009), to a raised platform used in performances by an elite (Barrett 1994). In fact, the logic of single interpretation or function just does not work (see Whittle 1997), simply because it fails to account for how this mound came into being. Recent investigations by English Heritage have revealed an unexpected complexity to the process of its construction (see Leary 2010, from which this account is derived) (see Figure 9.3).

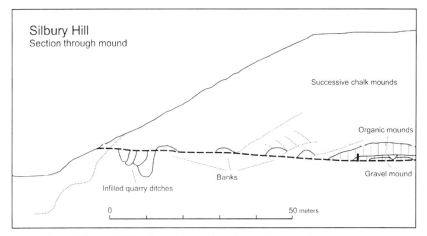

Figure 9.3   Silbury Hill: schematic section through mound

Silbury began with people bringing together clay, gravels, and other materials from adjacent riverbeds to form a low and unimpressive gravel mound (the Gravel Mound). This was enlarged (the Lower Organic Mound) by adding dumps of topsoil, subsoil, and turf to form a mound over 16 meters in diameter, the edge of which was demarcated with stakes. Close to this were created two much smaller mounds. Though situated in open grassland, one of the mini-mounds contained plant remains associated with woodland and scrub. Pits were then cut into the Lower Organic Mound, and worked flint and a little animal bone were placed within them. The next stage involved creating a much larger mound having a diameter of 35 meters (the Upper Organic Mound), still made of topsoil and subsoil. Incorporated into this were small and unmodified sarsen boulders, though these did not serve any structural purpose. At this stage the scale of construction work changed dramatically, as did the substance that was worked in. A large ditch over 6.5 meters deep was dug around the mound, leaving a considerable berm—in fact the emergent mound was enclosed within an earthwork c. 100 meters in diameter. Some of the chalk from that ditch was used to create an internal bank against the ditch; other chalk was piled up in a series of at least five banks against the base of the Upper Organic Mound. The banks were not simple mound enlargements, since they did not provide a capping; rather, they ringed and successively enclosed the central mound. The enclosure ditch was repeatedly backfilled then recut as the banks were created, in an unfolding process that must have appeared as demoralizing as it was back-breaking—and perhaps seemingly endless? The final acts of labor involved quarrying chalk on a massive scale from an encircling quarry ditch and sealing the embanked inner mound and its surrounding enclosure, resulting in a chalk mound over 150 meters in diameter and 40 meters high. Incorporated within the top of this were large fragments of shattered sarsen stone.

Until the creation of the final chalk mound, Silbury was never stable: its form and composition changed with each act of construction. While the process of building worked in social relationships via participation and coordination, the progressive unfolding of this creation prevented its reduction to a simple strategy or mode of representation. Creating Silbury was a process of working toward or in response to something, but perhaps through an emerging rather than established sense of what that goal may be.

MONUMENTS AND RELATIONAL ONTOLOGY

What I wish to argue is that the potential for understanding the events and intentions behind the creation of the Avebury henge, its avenues, and Silbury Hill—and their subsequent affects—is limited by the idea that the motivation for creating monuments lay primarily in the domain of social (that is human-to-human) relations; that stability in monumental form was necessary to facilitate this role; and that monuments somehow "represented" the world. Beginning with the first of these concerns, I do not deny that making monuments involved the articulation of relations between people (as mapped out through networks of debt, obligation, affinity, and a desire to partake "in history"), or that the building process was exploited by some in strategies of aggrandizement or power positioning. However, by privileging relations of this kind the participation of many other agents is sidelined. As other chapters in this volume illustrate, our understanding of how the world unfolds must be reconfigured in the light of relational perspectives that understand the constitution of process/action/event in terms of heterogeneous relationships that take in complex collectives of humans and nonhumans (be it things, places, animals, spirits, and so forth), knowledge, practices, etc. (e.g., Olsen 2003, 2011; Latour 2005; Webmoor 2007; Knappett & Malafouris 2008; Webmoor & Witmore 2008). This involves distributing agency, as in approaches inspired by the Actor-Network Theory (Latour 2005; Law & Mol 2006; Robb 2010); or, in the frame of relational or animist ontology, seeing life as emergent (Brown & Walker 2008; Alberti & Bray 2009; Ingold 2011). Power is therefore distributed across things, people, places, and cosmic forces. It comes into play when these strands mesh and cannot be located solely within the domain of an individual person or even a human-only "social" group. Describing relational fields of action within native North-American life, Pauketat (2013, 43–47) notes how constrained the opportunity for the exertion of personal political power might have been, because of the way human beings were enmeshed or "bundled" in arrays of elements and forces.

The virtue of such perspectives also lies in their capacity to destabilize essences and the notion that things (monuments included) might be conceived as occupying stable states (see Ingold 2011; Jones 2012); and this brings us back to the second concern that monumental architecture was, or needed to be, stable. Lesley McFadyen's work provides the clearest articulation of the emergent qualities of properties and people within the field of architectural practice. Inspired by the rhizomatic thinking of Deleuze and Guattari (2004), she describes the construction practices of Early Neolithic long barrows in southern England as heterogeneous and evolving assemblages (McFadyen 2003, 2006, 2007). McFadyen describes how mixes of soils, rock, timberwork, hurdles, turfs, antler, flints, animal bone, and people were caught up in construction practices; and how those practices changed the materials, sometimes making them less stable, sometimes creating new substances and material connections.

Of course, the very description of these constructions as "monuments" (though retained here by convention) provides little help, in that it projects a false image of their stability and fixed endurance over time. This is especially problematic in the case of Silbury Hill, since its very form altered through the process of construction and any sense of final "design" may only have emerged towards the end of the construction process. A stability perspective also presumes that on a micro-temporal scale the ontological status of monumental constructions was essentially unchanged; movements in status would only emerge through periodic acts of human modification (defined as "phases"), and through the monuments' constant incorporation into external social developments (i.e., a biographic perspective). Furthermore, once human interaction with monuments ceases, they are deemed "abandoned," and their ongoing presence within environments still active with life is often ignored (though see Lucas [2005] and Gosden & Lock [1998] for multi-temporal perspectives that seek to overcome this). Such views ignore the emergent properties and unfolding qualities of architectural constructions. Even the recent focus on materiality can leave the materials used to make the banks, palisades, and circles of standing stones or timbers of these monuments appear rather inert and lifeless (Ingold 2007), in that they are often conceived to *represent* rather than *hold* ontological qualities.

We do not know if the communities of Neolithic Britain possessed an animist ontology, though there are hints they may have done so (e.g., Jones et al. 2011). Based on their depositional practices, and the treatment of the human dead and the remains of animals (Thomas 1999, 2000; Pollard 2008; Fowler 2010), we can be more confident that they conceived of the world as consisting of a dynamic and vital matter that was in flux and required constant attending to, and out of which new configurations emerged. Most critically, we should not forget that part of that vitality would come through the intercession of spiritual agencies, whose copresence at certain times would radically alter the ontological status of matter, places, people, and the monuments themselves (see Pauketat 2013). To properly understand monuments is therefore to engage in a comprehension of their relational ontologies; to see them as meshworks that variously drew together flows of substances, cosmic power, people, histories, etc., into moments of creation and form; to understand them as in a constant state of coming into being; in effect, as being in motion, as being *alive*.

THE *MARAE* OF POLYNESIA

At this point I would like to take a detour away from the British Neolithic to enter the traditional worlds of island Polynesia and advance a consideration of other kinds of monumental construction. These are the range of enclosed spaces and platforms that served as communal and sacred architecture, which are described as *marae*, *ahu* (often referring to stone platforms), and, in Hawai'i, *heiau*. They are found across much of central and eastern Polynesia, where they developed as often elaborate architectures during the middle centuries of the second millennium AD (Kirch 2000).[1]

There has been a good body of archaeological research on marae/ahu structures, though most of it has been directed at understanding their morphology, chronology, and evolutionary development (Wallin & Solsvik 2010, 18–20). We are fortunate here in that the archaeological evidence can be supplemented by written observations of activities at marae made during the period of European contact, during the late eighteenth and early nineteenth centuries. Although that process of contact brought fundamental changes to Polynesian worlds, traditional religious practices were maintained for a period of time prior to missionary conversion. Contemporary accounts by Europeans and some remarkable exercises in historical anthropology (e.g., Sahlins 1985; Thomas 1991; Dening 1992; Salmond 2009, 2011) provide invaluable insight.

This is a world in which power can be present (if unevenly and variably distributed) in anything: in people, animals, structures, rocks, trees, and so forth. That power is normally conceived as *mana*, a kind of spiritual energy or efficacy that might be derived from ancestral lines or could be generated through achievement or contact with other powerful things or actions (Shore 1989). This power is often linked to authority (e.g., chiefs have *mana*); it is intensely fluid, can be lost and gained, and is made manifest through actions and events. Things, places, and people can achieve a state of extreme and potent sacredness, often through their mana, and become *tapu*. Being a state of contagious sacredness, tapu must be carefully managed through restrictions, prohibitions, and elaborate control measures that involve forms of segregation, containment, and binding (see Gell [1993] on the protective deployment of technologies of tattoo and wrapping, for instance). Life is therefore made up of the presence and management of flows of power that emanate from supernatural, human, and nonhuman achievement and genealogical statuses. This fluidity is also found in the presence of the divine, since gods can come or go according to season (Henry 1928) and be manifest in places and even people. Needless to say, their copresence must be carefully negotiated.

The seasonal round of festivals and ceremonies in traditional Polynesia was directed at ensuring reproduction of the world in its entirety (including the categories we might define as biological, social, and cosmic) and in a fashion that made time recursive, so that visions of the past became projections of the future (Strathern 1990). This is what Sahlins (1985) describes as mytho-praxis—the acting out of mythic reality. In this comingling of different times and different human, nonhuman, and divine agents, it is not surprising that marae could be built by gods (which of course might be materialized in substances or people). The role of gods was central, and they would return to dwell within the marae when summoned by priests, taking occupancy in images wrapped in long rolls of bark cloth and kept in wooden god houses located within the marae. In her magisterial narrative of late eighteenth-century events in Tahiti, Anne Salmond provides a compelling account of the marae of the Society Islands, particularly those linked with the 'Oro cult (Salmond 2009, 26–27). The most famous of these, the marae called at Taputapuatea at Cape Matahira-i-te-ra'i, in 'Opoa, Ra'iatea, was considered to be built by the trickster god Hiro. With the spread of the 'Oro cult, Taputapuatea was at the center, and stones and god images were carried from it to other distant islands where other marae called Taputapuatea were established.

Looked at in detail, marae were complex, heterogeneous assemblages; they were much more than just the stones that made up their structure. Marae were subjects—extended, distributed subjects—in every sense: they had names, biographies, and even a capacity to reproduce. It was they who made chiefs through investiture, and it was they who awakened the gods. They were often surrounded by sacred trees such as the *miro* and *aito* or casuarinas, and frequently located at the junction of land and water, and so at the interface between different realms.

Within them were placed animal and human sacrifices, burials, and stones from other lands. Around and on top were god houses and god images, acting as points of real, if fluctuating, presence of divine entities. Salmond notes that such was their sacredness that they could become terrifying to people. The high priests of Tahiti and Mo'orea described to the missionary John Orsmond how the marae was "a place of dread and of great silence," those of the royal line being even more "terrible" in their "stupendous silence" and awe-inspiring capacity to affect (quoted in Salmond 2009, 26–27). They were conduits of sorts: places where *Te Po* (the realm of darkness, death, and the gods) entered *Te Ao* (the world of light, life, and people):

> People spoke of these places as the jawbones of the gods, biting the spirits who passed into the dark underworld where they were consumed by the gods; while the stone uprights on their pavements were called their *niho* or teeth. Vai'otaha *marae* on Borabora, for instance, with its yellow feather girdle, was spoken of as the upper jawbone of the god; Mata'ire'a *marae* on Huahine with its black feather girdle was his lower jawbone; while Taputapuatea *marae* on Ra'iatea with its red feather girdle was his throat, swallowing spirits into the darkness. (Salmond 2009, 26)

Descriptions project marae as "hungry," as subject/architecture that would consume. Recent investigations of the marae on Huahine in the Society Islands showed the repeated presence of deposits of pig, dog, and human bone, much probably the residue of sacrifice (Wallin & Solsvik 2010). Those substances were literally worked—or consumed— into the stone structures of ahu as they were built and rebuilt, often being sandwiched between slabs of stone. At Mata'ire'a Rahi (a national marae), a human skull was crushed under a flat corner stone (Wallin & Solsvik 2010, 64). The process of weaving in and consuming materials also extended to elements of earlier marae/ahu structures, which were destroyed so that the constituents parts of coral and limestone slabs could be broken, crushed, and worked back in. In other instances (as at Haupoto) upright slabs were pushed/buried/consumed into the soil next to the ahu (Wallin & Solsvik 2010, 102). There was a constant movement and transformation of substances in place that served to renew the generative potency and cosmic sacrality of these constructions.

This accords well with Hamilton et al.'s (2011) description of Rapa Nui (Easter Island) ahu as structures that were unstable and animate (see Figure 9.4). The processes of rebuilding and the recycling of broken stones caused them to be "in a constant state of flux" (ibid., 184). Upon these were set the famous statues or *moai*. Whereas we might interpret these sculptural forms as representations of ancestors, perhaps deified ones, a more Polynesian take would be to regard them as forms of god

Figure 9.4   Toppled *moai* at Ahu Akahanga, Rapa Nui

houses that would facilitate the ongoing copresence of the ancestors themselves. Moai were periodically brought back to life, or ancestral spirits were enticed to become resident in them, through the insertion of white coral and obsidian eyes (Van Tilburg 1994, 147). Just as with the human subjects from which they descended, the embodied form of moai could be brought to an end and their transformed, broken remains "fed" back to the ahu. At Tongariki and other ahu, broken moai fragments have been found worked back into the stony structure of the constructions, intermingled with human bones, cremations, fragments of crushed stone, and other stuff of life (Hamilton et al. 2011).

A RETURN TO AVEBURY

Inspired by the ethno-historical record of Polynesia, how might we begin to think of the Avebury monuments through a relational ontology? We could take the deployment of stone in the creation of the avenues, circles, and other settings of stone at Avebury as one line in our meshwork. Mike Parker Pearson and Ramilisonina (1998) have made a compelling case for the identification of stone monuments like the Avebury avenues and circles with ancestral realms, an ontological relationship that holds well in the case of the nearby later Neolithic complex at Stonehenge

(Parker Pearson 2012). If there are problems with this argument, they lie in treating stone as a stable and enduring substance unaffected by its fluctuating relations with other things, and in allowing materials to *represent* rather than *be* particular states of being. What then if the stones of Avebury's henge and avenues were or had the capacity to periodically become ancestors, or even just living forms of their own right? Their procession into and away from the henge might mimic the movement of living humans, or journeys that only they could take. The danger of this interpretation, of course, is that we still fall into the logic of presuming a prior planned form that, once executed, allowed something to happen. Engaging with the emergent properties of the avenues might help us overcome this. First, it is clear through modern excavation and antiquarian observation that neither the West Kennet nor the Beckhampton Avenues are uniform along their length. There are gaps and stretches that become single lines of stone (Gillings et al. 2008), suggesting that the avenues' creation was more accretive and negotiated than it appears at first. Moving and erecting these stones created new configurations within a stony landscape—the gaps from where these stones came and the cleared trails along which they moved generated "negative" (stone-free) networks that incorporated other places. Along their sinuous course they also took in, or absorbed, elements of the landscape and older material traces, notably the seasonal stream of the Winterbourne west of Avebury and traces of earlier occupations on the side of Waden Hill and on Overton Hill (Pollard 2005). Other lines within the mesh were drawn in or "bundled" (Pauketat 2013), out of which the avenues drew life—the kinetic energy of gathered human labor, clay and smaller sarsen stones for support, and presumably real cosmic power. Even when the stones were gathered and set up, they continued to remain in motion. Stones would fall and might be reset. The performance of rites and the unfolding of calendrical events would create junctures in which supernatural/cosmic forces would be imminent, recreating the avenues as "charged" lines connecting the potent nodes represented by the Sanctuary, Avebury henge, and Longstones Cove. Other substances continued to be drawn in. Along both avenues are burials of the late third millennium BC, placed in pits often so close to individual stones that their digging risked destabilizing the stones (Smith 1965). Those "Beaker" burials were frequently positioned so that the heads of the dead individuals would be proximate to the stones, melding together the newly dead and the stones in a way that connected present and deep time and conveyed the transmutability of substance.

What of the Avebury henge itself? It is commonly presumed that the spaces created by henge (bank and ditch) earthworks served as arenas for periodic gatherings (Cummings 2008). It would be a mistake to accept such an interpretation as uncontentious. The act of enclosing with chalk and stone marked a significant ontological transformation of this place (indeed it defined it as a distinct place), separating it from the surrounding landscape and bringing together many potent substances, including the stones themselves. It is telling that despite quite extensive excavation of the interior, no trace of contemporary occupation or indeed human presence beyond that which was necessary in construction work and depositional acts has been found (Smith 1965). Perhaps through its creation and inhabitation by supernatural agencies, periodically or otherwise, Avebury became another of those silent, awe-inspiring, and terrifying places that could absorb and transform, and which lay at the interface of different cosmic realms. Warner (2000) and Gibson (2004) make the highly pertinent observation that the common "inverted" earthwork format of henge monuments such as Avebury (with a ditch inside a bank) was designed to keep spiritual agencies or other sacred forces inside, thus protecting the outside world: it was a technology of control. The decision to enclose a space with a henge earthwork could therefore reflect a change in the ontological status of that space and the traces it would contain, engaging with a newly enhanced potency or sacredness. The ditch at Avebury was excessively deep (up to 10 meters) and the bank excessively high. Rather than being intended to prevent "visual access" into the monument as part of a strategy to protect esoteric knowledge, the earthwork's scale may indicate a desire to control states of extreme sacredness and the power that went with them, as well as enhance that cosmic power through physical connections deep into the earth and high into the sky.

The weathering of the earthwork, the ongoing incorporation of deposits of human bone, antler, pottery, and stones within the fabric of the henge, and the periodic movement and resetting of certain stones (Gillings & Pollard 2004; Pollard & Cleal 2004) again endow the henge with a sense of movement, of animacy, of life. The incorporation of deposits of disarticulated human bone in the ditch provided a means by which ancestors were made present, capturing their efficacy but also turning the substance of the henge into something that had absorbed and was physically an extension of the communities of the dead and their descendants (Pollard & Reynolds 2002, 127–28). Paul Ashbee's (2004) highly pertinent observation that the deep ditch was dug with the knowledge that it would immediately begin to fill with silt and chalk rubble illustrates that naturally induced change was worked into the very fabric of the henge, and that stability of the earthwork was even negated (see Figure 9.2). The conserved and heritage-stabilized henge we encounter today perhaps offers little sense of the movements of substances, people, and, of course, immaterial agents that unfolded within this place during prehistory.

An analogous vision can help in understanding the colossal mound of Silbury Hill. Jim Leary and Andy Jones have rightly critiqued any attempt at seeing Silbury as a planned entity, constructed with a particular "function" in mind (Leary 2010; Jones 2012, 180–83). This was an emergent "monument," an assemblage, with a gathering logic of its own. The unfolding narrative of its creation could be read as one in which an entity, perhaps the primary Gravel Mound itself, was successively wrapped by "skins" of material. As with Avebury, that process might be one of controlling and containing the emerging potency, sacredness, or agency of the place. Leary is rightly keen to stress the siting of Silbury at the headwaters of the Kennet, a river that by virtue of the copresence of the Avebury complex was regarded as sacred in itself. The first mound was created from river materials, from the stuff out of which springs issued. Perhaps we could see those materials as considerably "charged" with the agentive power of the river source itself. This mound was then sealed with other substances from the landscape—soil, sarsen, turf, woodland vegetation, and finally chalk. The final acts of sealing involved violence, not to people (though this may have happened), but to sarsen stones, which were smashed and worked into the chalk cap of the mound as a kind of apotropaic lens. Much the same process of controlling emergent power and sacredness by "wrapping" successive layers of timber and stone could explain the overly "redundant" format of constructions like the nearby Sanctuary and main stone phase at Stonehenge (Colin Richards, pers. comm.). At the Durrington Walls Southern Circle, near Stonehenge, this very process can be seen in action through the sequence of intercutting postholes and post ramps (Wainwright & Longworth 1971; Thomas 2007): here a relatively simple timber structure became transformed through the accretion of a complex set of timber ring "layers." These were "monuments in motion" (Leary 2010).

To consider process and motion is also to consider history; in the case of Silbury, its creation/emergence must be located within a very particular set of conditions present during the third quarter of the third millennium BC. This was a time in which new networks/meshworks that involved exotic materials (copper, gold, Beaker ceramics, etc.), different configurations of the cosmos (the intervention of new spirits and gods, perhaps), and even "exotic" people had become present, even if fleetingly and from a distance at first (Needham 2005). Even without positing the unfolding of events and constructional activities at Silbury as a direct response to this, any understanding of its coming into being must be located within these flows of matter, ideas, people, and spiritual agencies. Perhaps its working out—an experimental engagement with the parameters, threats, and affordances of these flows—offers insight into the shifting form that Silbury was to take.

CONCLUSION

There exists enormous potential for thinking about what monument construction *did*, its affects, and the new meshworks of conditions, powers, and agencies it generated. Concepts of relational and animic ontology allow us to destabilize the images we currently hold of monuments, not least because they force us to focus on acts of assembly, flows, and meshworks of materials, and on the emergence of different kinds of ontological condition through (and beyond) the process of building. Creating these structures was always a complex process that involved intercession with other powers and conditions, both material and immaterial. With reference to both the marae/ahu of Polynesia and the diverse monumental forms of the British Late Neolithic, the ontological position of monumental constructions was often unstable and might constantly shift according to the copresence/absence of myriad agents—not least spiritual agencies that were evoked, enticed into "residence;" and dispelled through the unfolding of ritual cycles. Opening up involvement to other "things" or kinds of being, whether material or immaterial, could help us sidestep the problems of overly social and representational modes of thinking. To follow Ingold (2011), the challenge is to think through monuments as lines of life, movement, and growth.

ACKNOWLEDGMENTS

I would like to thank the participants at the seminar for their constructive feedback and for providing such a stimulating and collegial environment within which to explore the issues addressed by this volume. It's amazing what sofas, socks, and a good cup of coffee can do.

NOTE

1. I am not proposing this detour as a direct analogy between marae/ahu and British Neolithic monuments; more as a juxtaposed image that hopefully destabilizes some of the social- and representation-centered accounts that have dominated our comprehension of the latter. I do not wish to import analogy, being aware of the problematic position this might engender (Barrett & Fewster 1998). Yet, in much the same way that our adventures in theoretical literature embroil us in a mesh of cognitive possibilities from which it becomes impossible to extricate oneself, the influences brought about by the encounter with the archaeology and ethnography of other regions inevitably shape the conditions for our understanding of other archaeologies.

REFERENCES

Alberti, B. & Bray, T. 2009. Animating archaeology: of subjects, objects and alternative ontologies. *Cambridge Archaeological Journal* 19(3), 337–43

Ashbee, P. 2004. Early ditches: their forms and infills. In R. Cleal & J. Pollard (eds.), *Monuments and Material Culture. Papers in Honour of an Avebury Archaeologist: Isobel Smith*, 1–14. East Knoyle, UK: Hobnob Press

Barrett, J. 1994. *Fragments from Antiquity: An Archaeology of Social Life in Britain, 2900–1200 BC*. Oxford, UK: Blackwell

Barrett, J. & Fewster, K. 1998. Stonehenge: is the medium the message? *Antiquity* 72, 847–56

Bradley, R. 1993. *Altering the Earth: The Origins of Monuments in Britain and Continental Europe*. Edinburgh, UK: Society of Antiquaries of Scotland

Bradley, R. 1998. *The Significance of Monuments: On the Shaping of Human Experience in Neolithic and Bronze Age Europe*. London: Routledge

Bradley, R. 2000. *An Archaeology of Natural Places*. London: Routledge

Bradley, R. 2002. *The Past in Prehistoric Societies*. London: Routledge

Bradley, R. 2011. *Stages and Screens: An Investigation of Four Henge Monuments in Northern and North-Eastern Scotland*. Edinburgh: Society of Antiquaries of Scotland

Brown, L.A. & Walker, W.H. 2008. Prologue: archaeology, agency and non-human agents. *Journal of Archaeological Method and Theory* 15, 297–99

Cummings, V. 2008. The architecture of monuments. In J. Pollard (ed.), *Prehistoric Britain*, 135–59. Oxford, UK: Blackwell

Cummings, V. 2009. *A View from the West: The Neolithic of the Irish Sea Zone*. Oxford, UK: Oxbow Books

Cummings, V. & Whittle, A. 2004. *Places of Special Virtue: Megaliths in the Neolithic Landscapes of Wales*. Oxford, UK: Oxbow Books

Cunnington, M.E. 1931. The "Sanctuary" on Overton Hill, near Avebury. *Wiltshire Archaeological & Natural History Magazine* 45, 300–35

Dames, M. 1977. *The Avebury Cycle*. London: Thames & Hudson

DeLanda, M. 2000. *A Thousand Years of Nonlinear History*. New York: Swerve Editions

Deleuze, G. & Guattari, F. 2004. *A Thousand Plateaus: Capitalism and Schizophrenia*. London: Continuum

Dening, G. 1992. *Mr. Bligh's Bad Language: Passion, Power and Theatre on the Bounty*. Cambridge: Cambridge University Press

Fergusson, J. 1872. *Rude Stone Monuments in All Countries: Their Age and Uses*. London: Murray

Fowler, C. 2010. Pattern and diversity in the Early Neolithic mortuary practices of Britain and Ireland: contextualising the transformation of the dead. *Documenta Praehistorica* 37, 1–18

Gell, A. 1993. *Wrapping in Images: Tattooing in Polynesia*. Oxford, UK: Clarendon Press

Gibson, A. 2004. Round in circles. Timber circles, henges and stone circles: some possible relationships and transformations. In R. Cleal & J. Pollard (eds.), *Monuments and Material Culture. Papers in Honour of an Avebury Archaeologist: Isobel Smith*, 70–82. East Knoyle, UK: Hobnob Press

Gillings, M. & Pollard, J. 2004. *Avebury*. London: Duckworth

Gillings, M., Pollard, J., Wheatley, D. & Peterson, R. 2008. *Landscape of the Megaliths: Excavation and Fieldwork on the Avebury Monuments, 1997–2003*. Oxford, UK: Oxbow Books

Gosden, C. & Lock, G. 1998. Prehistoric histories. *World Archaeology* 30(1), 2–12

Hamilton, S., Seager Thomas, M. & Whitehouse, R. 2011 Say it with stone: constructing with stones on Easter Island. *World Archaeology* 43(2), 167–90

Henry, T. 1928. *Ancient Tahiti*. Honolulu, HI: Bishop Museum Bulletin 48

Ingold, T. 2007. Materials against materiality. *Archaeological Dialogues* 14(1), 1–16

Ingold, T. 2011. *Being Alive: Essays on Movement, Knowledge and Description*. London: Routledge

Jones, A.M. 2012. *Prehistoric Materialities: Becoming Material in Prehistoric Britain and Ireland*. Oxford: Oxford University Press

Jones, A.M., Freedman, D., O'Connor, B., Lamdin-Whymark, H., Tipping, R. & Watson, A. 2011. *An Animate Landscape: Rock Art and the Prehistory of Kilmartin, Argyll, Scotland*. Oxford, UK: Windgather Press

Kirch, P. 2000. *On the Road of the Winds: An Archaeological History of the Pacific Islands before European Contact*. Berkeley: University of California Press

Knappett, C. & Malafouris, L. (eds.) 2008. *Material Agency: Towards a Non-Anthropocentric Approach*. New York: Springer

Latour, B. 2005. *Reassembling the Social: An Introduction to Actor-Network Theory*. Oxford: Oxford University Press

Law, J. & Mol, A.-M. 2006. *Complexities: Social Studies of Knowledge Practices*. Durham, NC: Duke University Press

Leary, J. 2010. Silbury Hill: a monument in motion. In J. Leary, T. Darvill & D. Field (eds.), *Round Mounds and Monumentality in the British Neolithic and Beyond*, 139–52. Oxford, UK: Oxbow Books

Leary, J. & Field, D. 2010. *The Story of Silbury Hill*. London: English Heritage

Lucas, G. 2005. *The Archaeology of Time*. London: Routledge

Lucas, G. 2012. *Understanding the Archaeological Record*. Cambridge: Cambridge University Press

McFadyen, L. 2003. *A Revision of the Materiality of Architecture: The Significance of Neolithic Long Mound and Chambered Monument Building Practice, with Particular Reference to the Cotswold-Severn Group*. PhD dissertation, Department of Archaeology and Prehistory, University of Wales, Newport

McFadyen, L. 2006. Building technologies, quick and slow architectures and Early Neolithic long barrow sites in Southern Britain. *Archaeological Review from Cambridge* 21(1), 115–34

McFadyen, L. 2007. Neolithic architecture and participation: practices of making at long barrow sites in Southern Britain. In J. Last, (ed.), *Beyond the Grave: New Perspectives on Barrows*, 22–29. Oxford, UK: Oxbow Books

Midgley, M. 2008. *The Megaliths of Northern Europe*. London: Routledge

Needham, S. 2005. Transforming Beaker culture in north-west Europe: processes of fusion and fission. *Proceedings of the Prehistoric Society* 71, 171–217

Olsen, B. 2003. Material culture after text: re-membering things. *Norwegian Archaeological Review* 36(2), 87–104

Olsen, B. 2011. *In Defense of Things: Archaeology and the Ontology of Objects*. Lanham, MA: AltaMira Press

Parker Pearson, M. 2012. *Stonehenge: Exploring the Greatest Stone Age Mystery*. London: Simon & Schuster

Parker Pearson, M. & Ramilisonina. 1998. Stonehenge for the ancestors: the stones pass on the message. *Antiquity* 72, 308–26

Pauketat, T. 2013. *An Archaeology of the Cosmos: Rethinking Agency and Religion in Ancient America*. London: Routledge

Pollard, J. 2005. Memory, monuments and middens in the Neolithic landscape. In G. Brown, D. Field, & D. McOmish (eds.), *The Avebury Landscape: Aspects of the Field Archaeology of the Marlborough Downs*, 103–14. Oxford, UK: Oxbow Books

Pollard, J. 2008. Deposition and material agency in the Early Neolithic of southern Britain. In B.J. Mills & W.H. Walker (eds.), *Memory Work: Archaeologies of Material Practices*, 41–59. Santa Fe, NM: SAR Press

Pollard, J. & Cleal, R.M.J. 2004. Dating Avebury. In R. Cleal & J. Pollard (eds.), *Monuments and Material Culture. Papers in Honour of an Avebury Archaeologist: Isobel Smith*, 120–29. East Knoyle, UK: Hobnob Press

Pollard, J. & Reynolds, A. 2002. *Avebury: The Biography of a Landscape*. Stroud, UK: Tempus

Renfrew, C. 1973. Monuments, mobilisation and social organisation in Neolithic Wessex. In C. Renfrew (ed.), *The Explanation of Culture Change: Models in Prehistory*, 539–58. London: Duckworth

Richards, C. 1996. Monuments as landscape: creating the centre of the world in Late Neolithic Orkney. *World Archaeology* 28, 190–208

Richards, C. 2004. Labouring with monuments: constructing the dolmen at Carreg Samson, south-west Wales. In V. Cummings & C. Fowler (eds.), *The Neolithic of the Irish Sea: Materiality and Traditions of Practice*, 72–80. Oxford, UK: Oxbow Books

Robb, J. 2010. Beyond agency. *World Archaeology* 42(4), 493–520

Sahlins, M. 1985. *Islands of History*. Chicago, IL: University of Chicago Press

Salmond, A. 2009. *Aphrodite's Island: The European discovery of Tahiti*. Berkeley: University of California Press

Salmond, A. 2011. *Bligh: William Bligh in the South Seas*. Berkeley: University of California Press

Scarre, C. 2007. *The Megalithic Monuments of Britain and Ireland*. London: Thames & Hudson

Shanks, M. & Tilley, C. 1982. Ideology, symbolic power and ritual communication: a reinterpretation of Neolithic mortuary practices. In I. Hodder (ed.), *Symbolic and Structural Archaeology*, 129–54. Cambridge: Cambridge University Press

Shore, B. 1989. *Mana* and *tapu*. In A. Howard & R. Borofsky (eds.), *Developments in Polynesian Ethnography*, 137–73. Honolulu: University of Hawaii Press

Sims, L. 2009. Entering, and returning from, the underworld: reconstituting Silbury Hill by combining a quantified landscape phenomenology with archaeoastronomy. *Journal of the Royal Anthropological Institute* 15(2), 386–408

Smith, I.F. 1965. *Windmill Hill and Avebury: Excavations by Alexander Keiller, 1925–1939*. Oxford, UK: Clarendon Press

Strathern, M. 1990. Artefacts of history: events and the interpretation of images. In J. Siikala (ed.), *Culture and History in the Pacific*, 25–43. Helsinki: Finnish Anthropological Society

Thomas, J. 1993. The politics of vision and the archaeologies of landscape. In B. Bender (ed.), *Landscape: Politics and Perspectives*, 19–48. Oxford, UK: Berg

Thomas, J. 1999. *Understanding the Neolithic*. London: Routledge

Thomas, J. 2000. Death, identity and the body in Neolithic Britain. *Journal of the Royal Anthropological Institute* 6(3), 603–17

Thomas, J. 2004. The Late Neolithic architectural repertoire: the case of the Dunragit complex. In R. Cleal & J. Pollard (eds.), *Monuments and Material Culture. Papers in Honour of an Avebury Archaeologist: Isobel Smith*, 98–108. East Knoyle, UK: Hobnob Press

Thomas, J. 2007. The internal features at Durrington Walls: investigations in the Southern Circle and Western Enclosures, 2005–6. In M. Larsson & M. Parker Pearson (eds.), *From Stonehenge to the Baltic: Living with Cultural Diversity in the Third Millennium BC*, 145–57. Oxford: British Archaeological Reports International Series

Thomas, N. 1991. *Entangled Objects: Exchange, Material Culture and Colonialism in the Pacific*. Cambridge, MA: Harvard University Press

Thorpe, I.J. & Richards, C.C. 1984. The decline of ritual authority and the introduction of Beakers into Britain. In R. Bradley & J. Gardiner (eds.), *Neolithic Studies: A Review of Some Current Research*, 67–84. Oxford: British Archaeological Reports

Tilley, C. 1994. *A Phenomenology of Landscape: Places, Paths and Monuments*. Oxford, UK: Berg

Van Tilburg, J.A. 1994. *Easter Island: Archaeology, Ecology and Culture*. Washington, DC: Smithsonian Institution Press

Wainwright, G.J. & Longworth, I.H. 1971. *Durrington Walls: Excavations 1966–1968*. London: Society of Antiquaries of London

Wallin, P. & Solsvik, R. 2010. *Archaeological Investigation of* Marae *Structures in Huahine, Society Islands, French Polynesia*. Oxford: British Archaeological Reports International Series 2091

Warner, R. 2000. Keeping out the Otherworld: the internal ditch at Navan and other Iron Age "hengiform" enclosures. *Emania* 18, 39–44

Watson, A. 2001. Composing Avebury. *World Archaeology* 33(2), 296–314

Watson, A. 2004. Monuments that made the world: performing the henge. In R. Cleal & J. Pollard (eds.), *Monuments and Material Culture. Papers in Honour of an Avebury Archaeologist: Isobel Smith*, 83–97. East Knoyle, UK: Hobnob Press

Webmoor, T. 2007. What about "one more turn after the social" in archaeological reasoning? Taking things seriously. *World Archaeology* 39(4), 547–62

Webmoor, T. & Witmore, C.L. 2008. Things are us! A commentary on human/things relations under the banner of a "social" archaeology. *Norwegian Archaeological Review* 41(1), 53–70

Whittle, A. 1997. *Sacred Mound, Holy Rings. Silbury Hill and the West Kennet Palisade Enclosures: A Later Neolithic Complex in North Wiltshire*. Oxford, UK: Oxbow Books

CHAPTER TEN

Fields of Movement in the Ancient Woodlands of North America

Sarah E. Baires, Amanda J. Butler, B. Jacob Skousen, and Timothy R. Pauketat

The world is in motion. People, animals, organisms, materials, and phenomena of all kinds move around within larger fields of activity, coming into contact and becoming associated with each other (Ingold 2000, 63; 2007a, 2007b). Such motions are felt if not remembered by various beings, whose sensory perceptions and memory work might be considered as movements in and of themselves (following Gibson 1979). The results are entangled webs of relationships that define or mediate future movements in complicated ways (e.g., Alberti & Bray 2009; Jones & Boivin 2010; Hodder 2011). But *how* they do this bears further consideration, because certain mediations or mediators might enable more or less movement of one kind or another and, hence, affect history in different ways.

Non-anthropocentric, animist, phenomenological, neurophenomenological, and practice-based approaches in archaeology begin to address the question of *how* by giving explanatory priority to movements and relational fields (e.g., Webmoor 2007; Zedeño 2008, 2009; Alberti & Bray 2009; Baltus & Baires 2012; Pauketat 2013a). How entities come to be related or associated is the fundamental process in the larger set of causal relationships between people, places, things, and other entities or phenomena. Movement itself is the key phenomenon to be studied, since it defines whatever it is that we then call agents, human beings, cultures, and societies (following Latour 2005). Recognizing this is central to relational approaches that are alternatives to "representational" approaches, those

---

Archaeology after Interpretation: Returning Materials to Archaeological Theory, edited by Benjamin Alberti, Andrew Meirion Jones, and Joshua Pollard, 197–218.

timeworn materialist, structuralist, and post-structuralist archaeologies that tend to essentialize agency, humanity, culture, and society, among other things (Barrett 2000).

Our goal is to move beyond representational perspectives and to understand how webs mediate movements. We aim to illustrate how such movements connect very different phenomenal realms; they are not merely movements along lines or threads, but entanglements of experiences tied to past, present, and future realms. Our focus is on specific American Indian religious practices—pilgrimages, mound constructions, and pipe smoking—in the ancient Hopewellian and Cahokian pasts in the American Midwest (150 BCE–400 CE and 1050–1350 CE, respectively) (see Figure 10.1). The Cahokian case is particularly telling of the potential trans-dimensional qualities involved in movements and other mediating entanglements of moving bodies and beings, and powerful, animate substances. These qualities coupled together two or more dimensions of experience (spatial, temporal, material, visual, spiritual, emotional, etc.). They also juxtaposed entire fields of human and nonhuman relations in ways that produced significant long-term historical change. Here, we

Figure 10.1   Map of Eastern Woodlands

suggest that specific sorts of entanglements and juxtaposed movements entail a reconceptualization of fields.

ANIMISM, LIFEFORCE, AND DREAMS

We envision a relational field, much like a "landscape" or "cultural milieu," as being a web of associations brought about by movements (following Gell 1998; Ingold 2000). These movements include physical actions but also perceptions and sensory experiences that variously "position" certain people, places, things, and other seen and unseen phenomena with respect to each other (Pauketat 2013a). These associations and the positions upon which they are based in turn define and are defined by bodies, beings, objects, forces, and substances moving in space. The results are entanglements, interconnections, assemblages, bundles, convergences, or associations of experiences, actions, persons, objects, elements, spirits, etc. A relational field, in other words, is dynamic. The relationships and entanglements are never fixed, but are always becoming, made and remade contingent on movements and positions in space. A human being walks across terrain; a tree bends in the wind; two animals cross paths; a cloud sails across the sky (Ingold 2000). All such seemingly incidental, everyday happenings—including those involving nonhuman powers or animate forces—have the potential to reconfigure the field wherein humans experience the world. Such concepts are intrinsic to Native American creation histories and religions emphasizing the relatedness of beings (e.g., Deloria 2006).

We begin with some considerations on animism before turning to pilgrimage, mound building, and pipe smoking in the Hopewellian and Cahokian worlds. Traditionally, animism has been defined as a generalized belief in an "animating" spirit or soul, a way of experiencing the world alternate to Western notions of dualisms (Tylor 1873; Bird-David 1999; Harvey 2006). Irving Hallowell (1960, 48) argued that animism is the "entire psychological field in which they [Native persons] live and act . . . [and] by the sanctioned moral values which guide the relations of those persons." Following this, Vine Deloria Jr. (2006, 195) argues that in order to fully understand Native American experience, one must "examine substance, space, and time and try to understand people who lived and experienced life in a world in which everything was alive and related." This provides a mode of thinking that moves beyond dualisms and emphasizes the totality of existence, in which "the relational constitution of being consists of 'a field' of 'interwoven lines'—or a 'meshwork'" (Alberti & Marshall 2009, 348; Ingold 2006, 2007b). The emphasis is on the movements that constitute experience rather than on single persons, places, or things.

In Indigenous America, life force itself, variously called Wa-kan-da, Orenda, Waruksti, Manitou, etc., was the most mobile of living entities (see Hall 1977, 1997; Pauketat 2008, 2013a; Baltus & Baires 2012). Such powers among Siouan, Muskogean, Caddoan, and Algonquin speakers in the American Midwest, Plains, and South were distributed among human and other-than-human agents including animals, objects, places, and deities (e.g., Fletcher & La Flesche 1968; Powers 1977; Bailey 1995). "Through this mysterious life and power all things *are related to one another*, and to man, the seen to the unseen, the dead to the living, a fragment of anything in its entirety" (Fletcher & La Flesche 1968, 134, emphasis added). Importantly, this all-pervasive power did not distinguish between objects, persons, places, times, or other dimensions. It moved between the realms of the living and the dead, the sky and the ground, and the waking hours and dreamtimes of people.

American Indian dreams and visions situate experiences that transcend the material and provide context to the movements among such trans-dimensional realities. Black Elk's Great Vision, as recounted by Neihardt (1988), emphasizes the pervasiveness of the Great Spirit and the transcendental nature of the material and spiritual worlds. Black Elk says, "For I was seeing in a sacred manner the shapes of all things in the spirit, and the shape of all shapes as they must live together like one being" (as cited by Neihardt 1988, 43). The spiritual world and the natural world, for Black Elk, were the same (Deloria 2006, 201).

Such dreams and visions are themselves movements within relational fields of experience. Deloria (ibid., 20), expounding on Lame Deer's vision (a Brule Sioux medicine man), explains, "The physical world recedes into the background and the seeker is not concerned with the distractions that plague the everyday life," but focuses instead on the unity with all living beings that transcends time and space. The body and the mind of the person transcend the physical world, moving into a space that "reassembles" or reconstructs the spiritual and the material. The traces of the dreamer or the vision quester are visible not only as things, persons, or places, but as trans-dimensional "bundles" or associations in this new state of being (Pauketat 2013a; see Latour 2005, 7–8). In the following we choose to explore such "bundles" through movements of people, earth, and smoke.

PILGRIMAGE

Dreams and visions, of course, are kinds of journeys, or planned long-distance movements. So too are pilgrimages (Underhill 1938; Momaday 1968, 1969; Silko 1977; Hall 1997; Blaeser 2003; Oetelaar 2012).

In Indigenous America, individuals embarked on numerous journeys (including pilgrimages) throughout their lives that varied in duration, purpose, and practice (Blaeser 2003). Many of these were probably timed or oriented in ways that paralleled the paths of celestial entities (Pauketat 2013a).

Pilgrimages were a way of retracing such paths, reliving memories, and retelling histories of origins and ancestors (Blaeser 2003; Oetelaar 2012). Far from passive reenactments of past events or sacred ideals ingrained in memories and oral traditions, pilgrimages were transformative, life-altering movements necessary, meaningful, and continually undertaken (Underhill 1938; Momaday 1968, 1969; Silko 1977; Blaeser 2003). They might be cosmic in scale or association, enabling actual people to engage more directly with ancestors and deities as well as other human and nonhuman agents, places, and things in more than one dimension (see Momaday 1968, 1969; Hall 1997; Blaeser 2003). Each participant, while weaving his or her own associations into the experience, might also knot together the threads of other moving entities, altering the larger relational fabric. Indeed, the scale and trans-dimensional qualities of such movements would seem to give pilgrimage significant transformative potential, affecting how people, histories, practices, and destinies were intertwined in the future, in this world as well as in others (Blaeser 2003; Oetelaar 2012). Evidence for such sacred pilgrimages are known from the Hopewell and Cahokian periods and the extent to which they entangled cosmic realms may be the degree to which the journey was sacred (Pauketat 2013a).

Between 150 BCE and 400 CE, in central Ohio, the great Hopewell culture earthworks were at the heart of such entanglements. Among the greatest of the 900 or so monumental geometric embankments were complexes around the contemporary cities of Newark and Chillecothe, Ohio (see Figure 10.2). The largest of these enclosed as much as 20 hectares, had earthen walls several meters high, and were associated with great embanked avenues and other earthen mounds (Squier & Davis 1998; Romain 2000, 2009; Carr & Case 2005; Charles & Buikstra 2006). The terrain surrounding such places seems to have been home mostly to scattered inhabitants, living in dispersed settlements consisting of clusters of small single-family houses (Prufer 1961; Dancey & Pacheco 1997; Lepper & Yerkes 1997; Lepper 2010).

Several scholars have argued that these were destinations for locals if not distant pilgrims. Certainly, they were large enough to contain great periodic gatherings in which people might congregate, build earthen monuments, bury their dead, participate in religious processions and ceremonies, and watch celestial bodies advance through the sky (Lepper & Yerkes 1997; Romain 2000, 2009; Byers 2011).

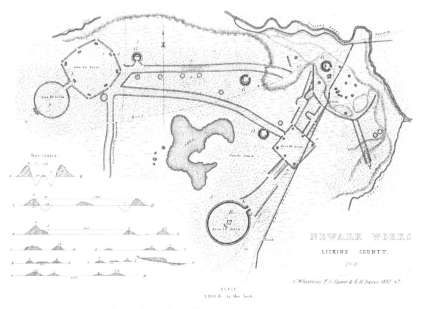

Figure 10.2   Newark earthworks, Ohio

The convergence of such a diversity of people, things, monuments, and movements was undoubtedly a multilayered, sensuous experience with profound impacts on the participants. They were "engaged and entangled as aspects of larger social fields (or networks of agents) in ways that reconfigure those fields" (Pauketat 2013a, 5). Perhaps most importantly, the great earthworks at Newark, if not most of the other 900 or so embanked spaces of the Ohio Hopewell, had to be navigated and experienced in a way that merged otherworldly dimensions with the physicality of bodily motions. Pilgrims who arrived at Newark via a long processional avenue found themselves directly in front of the Observatory Circle and Octagon, where, upon entering, they might commune with the sky and align themselves with rare lunar events (Hively & Horn 2010). Other visitors traveled to Newark by stream and entered the earthworks at the water's edge, passing through these portals as if leaving the watery realm and entering the new world of earth, bodies, and sky (Romain 2000).

These experiences were multifaceted. Earthworks, pathways, and journeys constituted entanglements of lines within an even larger bundle of persons, places, and things. The experience of traveling on foot to these Hopewell earthworks was a trans-dimensional one that included not only immediate physical surroundings, but also broader temporal and spiritual realms.

Similar convergences also occurred around 1050 CE, when a large-scale influx of immigrants and pilgrims from across the American mid-continent traveled to and settled in the greater Cahokia region (Alt 2001, 2002, 2012; Pauketat 2003). Many of these visitors and relocated residents moved to Cahokia, a newly founded and monumental American Indian city (Pauketat 2004, 2007, 2009) (see Figure 10.3). This singular place was located opposite of modern-day St. Louis, Missouri, in the heart of a much larger trans-regional domain. By itself, Cahokia was the largest pre-Columbian settlement in North America and, likely, the center of a "revitalized religion" or politico-religious movement (in the spirit of Wallace 1956). Besides its sheer scale and population (ca. 10,000 at Cahokia alone), this pre-Columbian phenomenon featured new iconography, pottery types, household construction

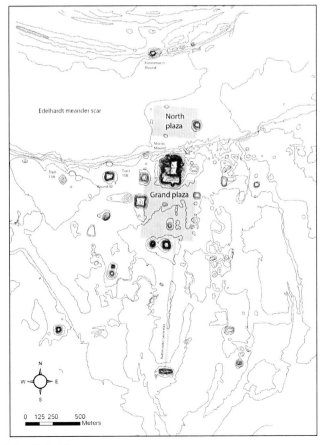

Figure 10.3   Cahokia

methods, architectural orientations, and mortuary practices that might have included burial processions and pilgrimages (Pauketat & Emerson 1991; Emerson 1997a, 1997b, 1997c, 2002; Emerson et al. 2003; Alt & Pauketat 2007; Emerson & Pauketat 2008; Pauketat 2008, 2010, 2013a).

Specifically, the bodies of the deceased were apparently carried in from afar on stretchers and in bundles and were interred in mounds during elaborate mortuary ceremonies (Rose 1999; see also Fowler et al. 1999; Goldstein 2000; Porubcan 2000; Ambrose et al. 2003). These ceremonies may have been similar to the Spirit Release and Feasts of the Dead recorded by early Europeans; Native groups traveled to a central location, releasing spirits from wrapped and bundled remains so that they could continue their journey to the afterworld (Hall 1997, 24–31, 35–36; see also Fletcher 1883; Brown 1953). Family members were also interred in communal graves as part of this process (Hickerson 1960).

In some cases, these mortuary mounds might have marked the outer limits of the ordered space of Cahokia; at least one of them was connected to the inner sanctum of the city via an approximately 18-meter-wide earthen causeway. Presumably, bodies and living persons moved to and from these outer realms along constructed earthen embankments, engaging both the afterworld and the world of the living in the process (Baires 2012). A roadway ran eastward from the city center to the Emerald site, a lunar shrine and possible pilgrimage center (Pauketat 2013a). Presumably, both causeway and roadway were formal avenues that served as pathways for spirits traveling to the other world or as links between the two worlds that humans and nonhumans alike might visit and experience (see Hall 1997; Lankford 2007). In short, pilgrims, bodies, pathways, spirits, and worlds converged and assembled at Cahokia, and, like the periodic gatherings in the Hopewell world, fashioned experiences that ultimately transformed the history of North America. Integral to that fashioning was the construction of earthen monuments where such journeys seemingly culminated.

MOUND CONSTRUCTION

The construction of earthen monuments in the pre-Columbian Southeast was a pervasive process, which incorporated massive quantities of prepared sediments, laborers, and planning (see Pauketat 1993, 2004; Fowler 1997). During the Hopewell period, mound construction took the form of conical burial mounds, flat-topped platform mounds, geometrically shaped earthen enclosures, and, occasionally, effigy mounds (Van Nest 2006). Cahokian earthen mounds took on the shapes of platforms (both rectangular and circular in plan) and ridgetops (see Fowler 1997 for a review); these mounds were usually situated around a constructed plaza or, in a couple of instances, were united by raised earthen embankments (Fowler 1997; Demel & Hall 1998; Dalan et al. 2003) (see Figure 10.4).

Wherever mounds were constructed, they seem to have embodied socially and experientially dynamic places that in various ways aligned with what analysts have summarized as an underworld, a lived-in world, and an upper world (see Knight 1986; Brown 1997; Hall 1997; Emerson et al. 2008). Building and subsequently visiting these monuments potentially transported people if not other beings from one dimension (the living, visible, earthly) to another (the dead, invisible, otherworldly). Movement in the context of mounds traversed the lived-in-world, the past, and the ancestral world. Mounds were, in short, portals between worlds (see also Knight 1989). They became, through construction, multidimensional places.

Robert Hall (1977, 1997) emphasized the importance of these locations as references to the historic earth-diver myth, according to which the earth was constructed by bringing up black mucky dirt from the bottom of a body of water and placing it on the back of a floating turtle. The choice to construct mounds near floodplains or on islands surrounded

Figure 10.4   Monks Mound at Cahokia, view of the spring equinox

by water not only referenced this origin history but also recreated it, in a sense reanimating the world with each movement of earth needed to construct the mounds (see Hall 1977, 1997; Emerson et al. 2008; Brown 2010; see also Knight 1989). In this sense, the construction of a mound physically instantiated the cosmos: the mound *was* the origin of the world retold with each reconstruction and reuse (Hall 1977, 1997; Brown 2010; see also Baires 2011).

The construction of these monuments entailed a physical gathering and moving of specially selected soils borrowed from discrete locals; for both Hopewellian and Cahokian earthen mounds, fills were selected, prepared, placed, and sometimes packed intentionally (Holley et al. 1993; Pauketat 1993, 2004; Sullivan & Pauketat 2007) (see Figure 10.5). This method of construction was planned and coordinated, consisting of fill types unique to a specific purpose.

In their recent analysis of mound construction in the Mississippian period, Sherwood and Kidder (2011) identify five types of fills: sod

Figure 10.5 Profile of a Mississippian mound

blocks, soil blocks, fills (i.e., basket loading), zoned fill, and prepared veneers. Sod blocks and soil blocks consist of intact soils cut from the ground, with or without removal of the surface organic material. The remaining three fill types are characterized by the preparation and purification of selected soils used to construct the mound in particular ways. For example, basket-loaded fills "represent visible single dumping events that are amassed to construct one fill event" (Sherwood & Kidder 2011, 77). Identified in many of the Cahokia site's pyramids, these fill zones are composed of "organically enriched clays" from the old Mississippi River channel immediately north of the mound (ibid.). This type of construction is also seen at the recently excavated Rattlesnake Mound at Cahokia (Baires 2011), where light- and dark-colored silty clay fills are placed one atop the other making the mound profile look like a patchwork of yellow and black (see also Moorehead 2000). Presumably, soil color and texture were chosen not only for their physical properties but also as references to past experience (e.g., the earth-diver creation history). This is seen in the choice of alternating colors, textures, and patterns of fill types, which if read correctly seem to tell their own story of creation.

Acts of mound construction and use constituted the social, historical, and experiential world; mound building, as the physical movement of human beings, the transport of sediments, and the retelling of creation narratives not only constituted the relational field but also engaged the senses. Each person, clod of dirt, and construction episode became enmeshed in a broader bundle of experiences (Pauketat 2013a). Therefore, mound construction (like pilgrimage) afforded particular trans-dimensional movements that continuously recreated the social world; a world not limited to sentient beings but including deities and ancestors—an enmeshment of persons, places, and things—and having its own temporality.

PIPE SMOKING

Such movements may be better exemplified by pipe smoking. In Indigenous North America, the pipe was almost universally understood to be sacred (Brown 1953; Paper 1988; Hall 1997). Moreover, pipe smoking entailed a number of practices: the growing of tobacco, the procurement of raw materials, the assembling of the pipe, the packing of the bowl, and the dynamic act of inhaling and exhaling smoke, the latter ascending from the realm of the visible on earth to the invisible in the sky.

As understood in more recent times, the pipe consists of two parts: a pipe bowl (female) and the pipe stem (male), kept apart and protectively stored in bundles (Brown 1953; Paper 1988; Hall 1997). As historically known, once the stem and bowl were joined in an act of creation, the pipe was filled with four pinches of tobacco, one for each of the sacred directions, and lit (Brown 1953; Neihardt 1988; Paper 1988). Subsequent actions ensured the proper centering of the smokers and the various practices associated with the pipe relative to one another and to the broader cosmos, making the pipes mediators of social life. These pipes' most powerful responsibility was to forge, maintain, or fracture relationships with all persons, including nonhumans (Thwaites 1900; Paper 1988; Hall 1997). Also crucial was a pipe's ability to anchor and recenter the participants and their relationships. In other words, the pipes themselves were active participants in the creation of community and the mediation of the cosmos. The act of smoking was thus a religious experience (Thwaites 1900; Neihardt 1988; Paper 1988; Hall 1997):

> As the pipe is passed around the circle, so the center passes with it. The pipe is always at the center of the cosmos. The smoke is offered in all directions radiating outward from the pipe. In communal smoking, the ritual also indicates the cosmos of social relationships. At the center is the self, the one holding the pipe. Next come the circles of human relationships: family, clan, and "nation." Further outward is the sphere of animal relations: those who walk on the earth in the four directions, those who fly in the sky above, and those who crawl through the earth below or swim in the sea. Finally there is the sphere of the most powerful spirits: the four directions/winds, the sky and the earth/sea. Together these spheres of beings form "all my relations." (Paper 1988, 643–44)

The domestication and use of tobacco in North America dates to the Early Woodland period (c. 300 BCE), and the cosmological dimension associated with the practice is evident during the Middle Woodland or Hopewell periods (150 BCE to 400 CE) in the Eastern Woodlands of North America (von Gernet 1995; Hall 1997; Winter 2000; Rafferty 2006; see also Paper 1988, 2007). Two of the most well-known Hopewell discoveries include the cache of about 200 broken and burned pipes at Mound City in Ross County, Ohio, and 136 burned and broken pipes recovered from the Tremper Mound in Scioto County, Ohio (Mills 1916; Squier & Davis 1998).

Hopewell platform pipes, like the ones recovered from Tremper Mound and Mound City, are reddish in color and exhibit bird, bear, and frog effigies among other animal forms (see Figure 10.6). The animal effigy faces the smoker, and the bowl is located on the animal's back (see Mills 1922). The presence of such large quantities of pipes carved to embody powers harnessed by the smokers, and in association with burials, may point to their use and disposal as a means of situating a

Figure 10.6   Hopewell platform pipe with frog effigy

person in relation to the lived-in-world and the spiritual realm; the use and disposal of such pipes may also allude to the creating and severing of connections between persons, places, situations, or ancestors (Paper 1988; Butler 2011).

Cahokian pipes have been discovered at multiple archaeological sites across the Midwest and South, and are made from a distinctive material, Missouri flint clay, quarried near Cahokia (Emerson et al. 2003). Emerson et al. (2003) argue that the male warrior and shaman pipes were originally cast as figurines and transformed into pipes through use, since the bowl is intrusive to the original design. These pipes were carried from Cahokia to surrounding Mississippian peoples between the years of 1100–1400 CE, with their relationships changing as they were moved.

As an important part of Cahokia's new religion, pipe smoking probably enabled a new kind of community if not also a new spirituality (consider the "magico-ritual" practices discussed in Emerson [1989]). The recovery of large quantities of tobacco within one feasting pit at Cahokia (Pauketat et al. 2002) and of special male-figurine pipes from mound sites outside Cahokia (Emerson et al. 2003) underscores the importance of communication and connections through time and realms. As in Black Elk's accounts, the "sacredness of relationship is one of the most important aspects of . . . culture; for since the whole of creation is essentially One, all parts within the whole are related" (Brown 1953, 15).

The Hopewell and Cahokia-Mississippian periods illustrate similarities in the practices of community and world renewal through mound construction, pilgrimage, and pipe smoking. Yet pipe smoking visibly transmogrified substances—the stone of the bowl and the tobacco inside it—in ways that must have had immediate effects on people. The immediate, visible results were smoke and ash, two substances viewed by many later American Indians as powerful in their own right. Undoubtedly this is because of the multiple transformational associations: pipe smoking merged stones from the earth with the tobacco plants, the smoke that rose into the sky, and the ashes returned to the earth (Pauketat 2008; Baltus & Baires 2012). The smoke itself created a pathway to the above world, a means to engage ancestors and life forces, not unlike mound construction and pilgrimage. Pipes and the act of smoking epitomized relations that spanned the worlds of the tangible and intangible, earth and sky, and human and nonhuman.

DISCUSSION

In these three brief examples we presented different experiences that emphasize the movement of beings and the sensory perceptions and associations generated by such movements (the path of travel, the transference of materials, and the transcendence of spirit). In an earlier work, Tim Ingold (2000) included perceptual movements among those that might produce "couplings" or associations (following Gibson 1979). These couplings link strands "in a tissue of trails that together make up the texture of the lifeworld. That texture is what I mean when I speak of organisms being constituted within a relational field. It is a field not of interconnected points but of interwoven lines, not a network but a *meshwork*" (Ingold 2006, 13). In a later work, Ingold (2007b) focuses more on the wayfaring movements of bodies. He imagines such moving bodies to produce meshworks of lines, thread-like connections, and traces that look something like fungal mycelium or rhizomes (following Deleuze & Guattari 1987).

In elevating the lines of movements rather than the movers or agents as such, Ingold (2007b) seeks to avoid essentializing and hence giving explanatory preference to specific beings, places, or nodes as fixed agents in fields of relations. Such preferential treatment would be an aspect, he argues, of other modes of thinking about networks, including the Actor-Network Theory (see Latour 2005). The notion of networks found in those theories, Ingold (2007b, 75) believes, is a modernist fragmentation of the lines of movement that define human experience. This fragmentation has, among other things, "transformed our understanding of place: once a knot tied from multiple and interlaced strands of movement and growth" into "a node in a static network of connectors" (ibid.).

In considering wayfaring, Ingold (2007b, 87–88; citing 2000, 227) considers perception but de-emphasizes it as movement:

> Proceeding on our way things fall into and out of sight, as new vistas open up and others are closed off. By way of these modulations in the array of reflected light reaching the eyes, the structure of our environment is progressively disclosed. It is no different, in principle, with the sense of touch and hearing, for together with vision these are but aspects of the total system of bodily orientation. Thus the knowledge we have of our

surroundings is forged in the very course of our moving through them, in the passage from place to place and the changing horizons along the way.

This kind of experience he calls "the integration of knowledge *along a path of travel*" (Ingold 2007b, 88, emphasis original).

As it turns out, this sense that movement through space entails perceptual or sensual reconfigurations of knowledge (which we might define as sets of associations) was also described by Bruno Latour (2005), albeit using different terminology. Following Latour, the movements of anything through space afford connections that change with each step or turn, the result being not simply a line but a pathway tethered, if only momentarily, to a series of connections, couplings, or intersections with other moving phenomena (Pauketat 2013a). A person attempting to make sense of a novel experience or a foreign object might begin, for instance, by comparing it to known relationships, proceeding to craft a set of associations by altering the form or position of the experience or object. We might also call this process "mimesis" (Taussig 1993) or "citation" (Butler 1993), since one is a copy of the other, or a gathering of associations (see also Hastorf 2003; Joyce 2004; Jones 2007). From such points of view, the close associations made by Native Americans between pilgrimage and celestial movements, earth and regeneration, or pipesmoking, gender, and the skyworld are not difficult to understand. These are elemental associations closely linked to sensory experience and fundamental perceptions.

Is it useful to consider these associations as parts of meshworks produced principally through wayfaring movements? Or is there something more to the entanglements (a.k.a. intersections, couplings, or bundles) wherein the associations are produced? For example, perception, citations, and memory work generally involve more direct and linear movements of sensory organs, which are then associated through combinations of qualities, materials, and emotions. These are more than "wayfaring" or "transportational" movements (Ingold 2007b). One might feel good about pottery production, flint knapping, weaving, or any number of activities, for instance, if a pleasant or meaningful story, song, location, or memory is associated with them. Thus, if pots, flint tools, or woven fabrics embody one's identity, community, or cosmology, then practice is actually a series of movements that connect the human being who makes or engages the object with another realm. Of course such connections, as movements, are integrated along a path of travel, in Ingold's terms (2007b). But these movements—he might call them "threads" or lines of transport—are at least as significant as other physical acts he analyzes, such as wayfaring, gesturing, writing, or recounting a storyline.

All relationships reviewed here—pilgrimage, mound construction, and pipe smoking—go beyond the wayfaring of beings to the sensuous associations and entanglements of moving beings, phenomena, and substances. First, pilgrimage was not only a physical event, but also a spiritual journey made via one's dreams, visions, and afterlife experiences. These journeys sometimes paralleled the movements of celestial bodies, as if the nonhuman luminaries were making their own sacred journeys (Pauketat 2013a). Second, mound construction was a physical convergence between the lived-in and ancestor worlds. The excavation, transport, and preparation of colored earthen fills, the rapid constructions, and the prolonged experience of these monuments forged relations not limited to the physical realm. Third, pipe smoking articulated the relations of the earth with those of the sky. The physical effects of nicotine ingestion on the human body were of course palpable, emphasizing that these were not abstract and disembodied but tangible experiences.

Such experiences, and the attendant associations and entanglements, *crossed boundaries* between the elements of the earth and the sky, the past and the present, and the dead and the living. It is in this transgressing of boundaries that relational fields become entanglements of experiences that move beyond human-to-human and human-to-object relations (see Gosden 2005, 209). Mircea Eliade (1987) would have called some of them "hierophanies," which is to say the presencing of supernatural powers among people (Pauketat 2013a). The casting of a moon shadow across an earthen embankment, the alignment of one's body with that shadow or embankment during a great gathering, procession, or dance, and at the same time the inhalation of nicotine-laced tobacco smoke (then exhaled into the air) would couple in powerful ways, if only momentarily, the seen and unseen dimensions of the cosmos (see also Ashmore 2007). The intersections of such sensual-citational movements would produce such thick trans-dimensional bundles and assemblages as to make the individual phenomena inseparable (see also MacGregor 2008).

Elsewhere, Pauketat (2013a) has argued that the resulting web or meshwork, combining the twists and turns of one sort of movement with the direct linear references of citations, associations, and perceptual links, might look like lines with distributed asterisks, "with a center surrounded by many radiating lines with all sorts of tiny conduits leading to and fro" (Latour 2005, 177). Each asterisk is a moment of mediation, in Latour's (2005) terms, where one thing, quality, being, or moving phenomenon is simultaneously perceived, cited, or in some way associated with another. These mediating sites are continuously expanding and contracting as the locations, sizes, and densities of entangled connections are in flux, generating trans-dimensional relational matrices that change as they fold into or transcend other relational webs.

This way of conceptualizing a relational field—as temporary, modulating, and expanding and contracting webs—parallels the description of a rhizome (a.k.a. "multiplicity") by Gilles Deleuze and Felix Guattari (1987, 21): "Unlike a structure, which is defined by a set of points and positions . . . the rhizome is made only of lines: lines of segmentarity and stratifications as its dimensions, and the line of flight or deterritorialization as the maximum dimension after which the multiplicity undergoes metamorphosis, changes in nature." Like Ingold, Deleuze and Guattari (ibid., 8) maintain that there are "no points or positions in a rhizome. . . . There are only lines." But, for our purposes, it is critical to consider *how* such lines are articulated with the perceptual movements and the mediating and radiating asterisks or bundles of citations. Because it is there, where dimensions are transgressed and entire relational fields articulate, that great causal power to alter the course of history resides.

The intersections, convergences, bundles, or entanglements that we analyze are not merely engagements between individual bodies, beings, or entities, but the interpenetration of entire fields absorbing and rearranging each other, transforming particular experiences, objects, places, and persons along the way. These movements, as we have discussed them, transgress the boundaries between substances, places, bodies, and things in dimensional terms. Any one movement is potentially an engagement with multiple points of articulation in multiple dimensions. Unraveling one entanglement means unraveling an entire tapestry, the latter woven with meandering and citational strands of life and death, sky and earth, day and night, and smoke and ash.

ACKNOWLEDGMENTS

Thanks to the editors and to the other participants for their comments on an earlier draft of this chapter. Also, thank you to the editors for inviting us to participate in a workshop where we benefited from fantastic scholarly discussion on earlier versions of our chapter. Thanks also to Kenneth Farnsworth for graciously allowing the use of his Hopewell pipe images.

REFERENCES

Alberti, B. & Bray, T.L. 2009. Animating archaeology: of subjects, objects, and alternative ontologies. *Cambridge Archaeological Journal* 19(3), 337–43
Alberti, B. & Marshall, Y. 2009. Animating archaeology: local theories and conceptually open-ended methodologies. *Cambridge Archaeological Journal* 19(3), 344–56
Alt, S.M. 2001. Cahokian change and the authority of tradition. In T.R. Pauketat (ed.), *The Archaeology of Traditions: Agency and History before and after Columbus*, 141–56. Gainesville: University of Florida Press

Alt, S.M. 2002. Identities, traditions, and diversity in Cahokia's Uplands. *Midcontinental Journal of Archaeology* 27, 217–36

Alt, S.M. 2012. Making Mississippian at Cahokia. In T.R. Pauketat (ed.), *The Oxford Handbook of North American Archaeology*, 497–508. New York: Oxford University Press

Alt, S.M. & Pauketat, T.R. 2007. Sex and the Southern Cult. In A. King (ed.), *The Southeastern Ceremonial Complex*, 232–50. Tuscaloosa: University of Alabama Press

Ambrose, S.H., Buikstra, J. & Krueger, H.W. 2003. Status and gender differences in diet at Mound 72, Cahokia, revealed by isotopic analysis of bone. *Journal of Anthropological Archaeology* 22(3), 217–26

Ashmore, W. 2007. Building social history at Pueblo Bonito: footnotes to a biography of place. In S.H. Lekson (ed.), *The Architecture of Chaco Canyon, New Mexico*, 179–98. Salt Lake City: University of Utah Press

Bailey, G.A. (ed.). 1995. *The Osage and the Invisible World: From the Works of Francis La Flesche*. Norman: University of Oklahoma Press

Baires, S.E. 2011. Ridge-top mortuaries and the experience of death at Cahokia. Paper presented at the 68th annual Southeastern Archaeology Conference, Jacksonville, Florida

Baires, S.E. 2012. Cahokia's causeway: myth or reality? Paper presented at the Mississippian Conference at Cahokia Mounds, Collinsville, Illinois

Baltus, M.R. & Baires, S.E. 2012. Elements of power in the Cahokian world. *Journal of Social Archaeology* 12, 167–92

Barrett, J.C. 2000. A thesis on agency. In M. Dobres & J. Robb (eds.), *Agency in Archaeology*, 61–68. London: Routledge

Bird-David, N. 1999. "Animism" revisited: personhood, environment, and relational epistemology. *Current Anthropology* 40 (supplement), 67–91

Blaeser, K.M. 2003. Sacred journey cycles: pilgrimage as re-turning and re-telling in American indigenous literatures. *Religion and Literature* 35, 83–104

Brown, J. 1997. The archaeology of ancient religion in the Eastern Woodlands. *Annual Review of Anthropology* 26, 465–85

Brown, J. 2010. Cosmological layouts of secondary burials as political instruments. In L.P. Sullivan & R.C. Mainfort (eds.), *Mississippian Mortuary Practices: Beyond Hierarchy and the Representationalist Perspective*, 30–52. Gainesville: University of Florida Press

Brown, J.E. 1953. *The Sacred Pipe: Black Elk's Account of the Seven Rites of the Oglala Sioux*. Norman: University of Oklahoma Press

Butler, A. 2011. Playing detective with Mississippian period axe-heads: detailing the results of a provenance study using portable X-ray Fluorescence. Paper presented at the 57th Annual Midwest Archaeological Conference, La Crosse, Wisconsin

Butler, J. 1993. *Bodies That Matter: On the Discursive Limits of "Sex."* New York: Routledge

Byers, M.A. 2011. *Sacred Games, Death, and Renewal in the Ancient Eastern Woodlands: The Ohio Hopewell System of Cult Sodality Heterarchies*. Lanham, MD: AltaMira Press

Carr, C. & Case, D.T. (eds.) 2005. *Gathering Hopewell: Society, Ritual, and Ritual Interaction*. New York: Kluwer Academic/Plenum

Charles, D. & Buikstra, J. (eds.) 2006. *Recreating Hopewell*. Gainesville: University of Florida Press

Dalan, R.A., Holley, G.R., Woods, W.I., Watters, Jr., H.W. & Koepke, J.A. 2003. *Envisioning Cahokia: A Landscape Perspective*. DeKalb: Northern Illinois University Press

Dancey, W.S. & Pacheco, P.J. 1997. A community model of Ohio Hopewell settlement. In W.S. Dancey & P.J. Pacheco (eds.), *Ohio Hopewell Community Organization*, 3–40. Kent, OH: Kent State University Press

Deleuze, G. & Guattari, F. 1987. *A Thousand Plateaus: Capitalism and Schizophrenia*. Translated by B. Massumi. Minneapolis: University of Minnesota Press

Deloria, V., Jr. 2006. *The World We Used to Live In: Remembering the Powers of the Medicine Men*. Golden, CO: Fulcrum Publishing

Demel, S.J. & Hall, R.L. 1998. The Mississippian town plan and cultural landscape of Cahokia, Illinois. In R.B. Lewis & C. Stout (eds.), *Mississippian Towns and Sacred Spaces: Searching for an Architectural Grammar*, 200–26. Tuscaloosa: University of Alabama Press

Eliade, M. 1987. *The Sacred and the Profane: The Nature of Religion*. Orlando, FL: Harcourt

Emerson, T.E. 1989. Water, serpents, and the underworld: an exploration into Cahokia symbolism. In P. Galloway (ed.), *The Southeastern Ceremonial Complex: Artifacts and Analysis*, 45–92. Lincoln: University of Nebraska Press

Emerson, T.E. 1997a. *Cahokia and the Archaeology of Power*. Tuscaloosa: University of Alabama Press

Emerson, T.E. 1997b. Cahokian elite ideology and the Mississippian cosmos. In T.R. Pauketat & T.E. Emerson (eds.), *Cahokia: Domination and Ideology in the Mississippian World*, 190–228. Lincoln: University of Nebraska Press

Emerson, T.E. 1997c. Reflections from the countryside on Cahokian hegemony. In T.R. Pauketat & T.E. Emerson (eds.), *Cahokia: Domination and Ideology in the Mississippian World*, 167–89. Lincoln: University of Nebraska Press

Emerson, T.E. 2002. An introduction to Cahokia 2002: diversity, complexity, and history. *Midcontinental Journal of Archaeology* 27(2), 127–48

Emerson, T.E., Alt, S.M. & Pauketat, T.R. 2008. Locating American Indian religion at Cahokia and beyond. In L. Fogelin (ed.), *Religion, Archaeology, and the Material World*, 216–36. Carbondale: Southern Illinois University, Center for Archaeological Investigations, Occasional Paper 36

Emerson, T.E., Hargrave, E. & Hedman, K. 2003. Death and ritual in early rural Cahokia. In R.J. Jeske (ed.), *Theory, Method, and Technique in Modern Archaeology*, 163–81. Westport, CT: Bergin and Garvey

Emerson, T.E., Hughes, R.E., Hynes, M.R. & Wisseman, S.U. 2003. The sourcing and interpretation of Cahokia-style figurines in the Trans-Mississippi South and Southeast. *American Antiquity* 68(2), 287–313

Emerson, T.E. & Pauketat, T.R. 2008. Historical-processual archaeology and culture making: unpacking the Southern Cult and Mississippian religion. In D.S. Whitley & K. Hays-Gilpin (eds.), *Belief in the Past: Theoretical Approaches to the Archaeology of Religion*, 167–88. Walnut Creek, CA: Left Coast Press

Fletcher, A.C. 1883. The Shadow or Ghost Lodge. In *Reports of the Peabody Museum of American Archaeology and Ethnology of Harvard University* 3, 296–307

Fletcher, A.C., & La Flesche, F. 1968 [1911]. The Omaha Tribe. *27th Annual Report of the Bureau of American Ethnology*. Lincoln: University of Nebraska Press

Fowler, M.L. 1997. *The Cahokia Atlas: A Historical Atlas of Cahokia Archaeology*. Urbana: University of Illinois/Illinois Transportation Archaeological Research Program, Studies in Archaeology 2

Fowler, M.L., Rose, J., Vander Leest, B. & Ahler, S.A. 1999. *The Mound 72 Area: Dedicated and Sacred Space in Early Cahokia*. Springfield: Illinois State Museum, Reports of Investigations 54

Gell, A. 1998. *Art and Agency: An Anthropological Theory*. Oxford: Oxford University Press

Gibson, J.J. 1979. *The Ecological Approach to Visual Perception*. Boston, MA: Houghton Mifflin

Goldstein, L. 2000. Mississippian ritual as viewed through the practice of secondary disposal of the dead. In S.R. Ahler (ed.), *Mounds, Modoc, and Mesoamerica: Papers in Honor of Melvin L. Fowler*, 193–206. Springfield: Illinois State Museum Scientific Papers 28

Gosden, C. 2005. What do objects want? *Journal of Archaeological Method and Theory* 12(3), 193–211

Hall, R.L. 1977. An anthropocentric perspective for Eastern United States prehistory. *American Antiquity* 42, 499–518

Hall, R.L. 1997. *An Archaeology of the Soul: North American Indian Belief and Ritual.* Urbana: University of Illinois Press

Hallowell, A.I. 1960. Ojibwa ontology, behavior, and world view. In S. Diamond (ed.), *Culture in History: Essays in Honor of Paul Radin*, 19–52. New York: Columbia University Press

Harvey, G. 2006. *Animism: Respecting the Living World.* New York: Columbia University Press

Hastorf, C.A. 2003. Community with the ancestors: ceremonies and social memory in the Middle Formative at Chiripa, Bolivia. *Journal of Anthropological Archaeology* 22, 305–32

Hickerson, H. 1960. The feast of the dead among the seventeenth century Algonkians of the Upper Great Lakes. *American Anthropologist* 62, 81–107

Hively, R. & Horn, R. 2010. Hopewell cosmography at Newark and Chillecothe, Ohio. In A.M. Byers & D. Wymer (eds.), *Hopewell Settlement Patterns, Subsistence, and Symbolic Landscapes*, 128–64. Gainesville: University of Florida Press

Hodder, I. 2011. *Entangled: An Archaeology of the Relationships between Humans and Things.* Oxford, UK: Wiley-Blackwell

Holley, G.R., Dalan, R. & Smith, P.A. 1993. Investigations in the Cahokia Site Grand Plaza. *American Antiquity* 58, 306–19

Ingold, T. 2000. *The Perception of the Environment: Essays in Livelihood, Dwelling and Skill.* London: Routledge

Ingold, T. 2006. Rethinking the animate, re-animating thought. *Ethnos* 71(1), 9–20

Ingold, T. 2007a. Earth, sky, wind, and weather. *Journal of the Royal Anthropological Institute* 13(S1), S19–S38

Ingold, T. 2007b. *Lines: A Brief History.* London: Routledge

Jones, A.M. 2007. *Memory and Material Culture.* Cambridge: Cambridge University Press

Jones, A.M. & Boivin, N. 2010. The malice of inanimate objects: material agency. In D. Hicks & M.C. Beaudry (eds.), *The Oxford Handbook of Material Culture Studies*, 333–51. Oxford: Oxford University Press

Joyce, R.A. 2004. Embodied subjectivity: gender, femininity, masculinity, sexuality. In L. Meskell & R.W. Preucel (eds.), *A Companion to Social Archaeology*, 82–95. Malden, MA: Blackwell

Knight, J.V. 1986. The institutional organization of Mississippian religion. *American Antiquity* 51(4), 675–87

Knight, J.V. 1989. Symbolism of Mississippian mounds. In P.H. Wood, G.A. Waselkov, & M.T. Hatley (eds.), *Powhatan's Mantle: Indians in the Colonial Southeast*, 279–91. Lincoln: University of Nebraska Press

Lankford, G.E. 2007. *Reachable Stars: Patterns in the Ethnoastronomy of Eastern North America.* Tuscaloosa: The University of Alabama Press

Latour, B. 2005. *Reassembling the Social: An Introduction to Actor-Network Theory.* Oxford: Oxford University Press

Lepper, B.T. 1995. Tracking Ohio's Great Hopewell road. *Archaeology* 48, 52–56

Lepper, B.T. 2010. The ceremonial landscape of the Newark earthworks and the Raccoon Creek Valley. In A.M. Byers & D. Wymer (eds.), *Hopewell Settlement*

Patterns, Subsistence, and Symbolic Landscapes, 97–164. Gainesville: University of Florida Press

Lepper, B.T. & Yerkes, R.W. 1997. Hopewellian occupations at the northern periphery of the Newark earthworks: the Newark Expressway sites revisited. In W.S. Dancey & P.J. Pacheco (eds.), *Ohio Hopewell Community Organization*, 175–206. Kent, OH: Kent State University Press

MacGregor, G. 2008. Elemental bodies: the nature of transformative practices during the late third and second millennium BC in Scotland. *World Archaeology* 40(2), 268–80

Mills, W.C. 1916. Exploration of the Tremper Mound in Scioto County. *Ohio Archaeological and Historical Society Publications* 30, 91–160

Mills, W.C. 1922. Exploration of the Mound City Group. *Ohio Archaeological and Historical Society Publications* 31, 423–584

Momaday, N.S. 1968. *House Made of Dawn*. New York: Harper & Row

Momaday, N.S. 1969. *The Way to Rainy Mountain*. Albuquerque: University of New Mexico Press

Moorehead, W.K. 2000. *The Cahokia Mounds*. Tuscaloosa: University of Alabama Press

Neihardt, J.G. 1988 [1932]. *Black Elk Speaks: Being the Life Story of a Holy Man of the Oglala Sioux*. New York: Morrow

Oetelaar, G.A. 2012. The archaeological imprint of oral traditions on the landscape of Northern Plains hunter-gatherers. In T.R. Pauketat (ed.), *The Oxford Handbook of North American Archaeology*, 336–46. New York: Oxford University Press

Paper, J. 1988. *Offering Smoke: The Sacred Pipe and Native American Religion*. Caldwell, ID: Caxton Press

Paper, J. 2007. *Native American Religious Traditions: Dancing for Life*. Westport, CT: Praeger Publishing

Pauketat, T.R. 1993. *Temples for Cahokia Lords: Preston Holder's 1955–1956 Excavations of Kunnemann Mound*. Ann Arbor: Memoirs of the University of Michigan Museum of Anthropology, Number 26

Pauketat, T.R. 2003. Resettled farmers and the making of a Mississippian polity. *American Antiquity* 68, 39–66

Pauketat, T.R. 2004. *Ancient Cahokia and the Mississippians*. Cambridge: Cambridge University Press

Pauketat, T.R. 2007. *Chiefdoms and Other Archaeological Delusions*. Walnut Creek, CA: AltaMira

Pauketat, T.R. 2008. Founders' cults and the archaeology of *Wa-kan-da*. In B. Mills & W.H. Walker (eds.), *Memory Work: Archaeologies of Material Practices*, 61–79. Santa Fe, NM: School for Advanced Research Press

Pauketat, T.R. 2009. *Cahokia: Ancient America's Great City on the Mississippi*. New York: Viking-Penguin Press

Pauketat, T.R. 2010. The missing persons in Mississippian mortuaries. In L.P. Sullivan & R.C. Mainfort (eds.), *Mississippian Mortuary Practices: Beyond Hierarchy and the Representationist Perspective*, 14–29. Gainesville: University of Florida Press

Pauketat, T.R. 2013a. *An Archaeology of the Cosmos: Rethinking Agency and Religion in Ancient America*. London: Routledge

Pauketat, T.R. 2013b. Bundles in/of/as time. In J. Robb & T.R. Pauketat (eds.), *Big Histories, Human Lives: Tackling Problems of Scale in Archaeology* 35–56. Santa Fe, NM: School for Advanced Research Press

Pauketat, T.R. & Emerson, T.E. 1991. The ideology of authority and the power of the pot. *American Anthropologist* 93(4), 919–41

Pauketat, T.R., Kelly, L.S., Fritz, G.J., Lopinot, N.H., Elias, S. & Hargrave, E. 2002. The residues of feasting and public ritual at early Cahokia. *American Antiquity* 67(2), 257–79

Porubcan, P. J. 2000. Human and Non-Human Surplus Display at Mound 72, Cahokia. In S.R. Ahler (ed.), *Mounds, Modoc, and Mesoamerica: Papers in Honor of Melvin L. Fowler*, 207–25. Springfield: Illinois State Museum Scientific Papers 28

Powers, W.K. 1977. *Oglala Religion*. Lincoln: University of Nebraska Press

Prufer, O.H. 1961. *The Hopewell Complex in Ohio*. Unpublished PhD dissertation, Peabody Museum, Harvard University

Rafferty, S.M. 2006. Evidence of early tobacco in northeastern North America? *Journal of Archaeological Science* 33(4), 453–58

Romain, W.F. 2000. *Mysteries of the Hopewell: Astronomers, Geometers, and Magicians of the Eastern Woodlands*. Akron, OH: University of Akron Press

Romain, W.F. 2009. *Shamans of the Lost World: A Cognitive Approach to the Prehistoric Religion of the Ohio Hopewell*. Lanham, MD: AltaMira Press

Rose, J.C. 1999. Mortuary data and analysis. In M.L. Fowler, J.C. Rose, B. Vander Leest & S.R. Ahler (eds.), *The Mound 72 Area: Dedicated and Sacred Space in Early Cahokia*, 63–82. Springfield: Illinois State Museum, Reports of Investigations 54

Sherwood, S.C. & Kidder, T.R. 2011. The DaVincis of dirt: geoarchaeological perspectives on Native American mound building in the Mississippi River Basin. *Journal of Anthropological Archaeology* 30, 69–87

Silko, L.M. 1977. *Ceremony*. New York: Signet

Snyder, J.F. 1909. Prehistoric Illinois: certain Indian mounds technically considered. Part third: temple or domicilary mounds. *Journal of the Illinois State Historical Society* 2(2), 71–92

Squier, E.G. & Davis, E.G. 1998 [1848]. *Ancient Monuments of the Mississippi Valley*. Washington, DC: Smithsonian Institution Contributions to Knowledge 1

Sullivan, L.P. & Pauketat, T.R. 2007. Cahokia's Mound 31: a short-term occupation at a long-term site. *Southeastern Archaeology* 26(1), 12–31

Taussig, M. 1993. *Mimesis and Alterity: A Particular History of the Senses*. New York: Routledge

Thwaites, R.G. (ed.) 1900. *The Jesuit Relations and Allied Documents: Travels and Explorations of the Jesuit Missionaries in New France, 1610–1791*. Volume 65. Cleveland, OH: The Burrows Company & The Imperial Press

Tylor, E.B. 1873. *Religion in Primitive Culture*. New York: Harper

Tylor, E.B. 1993 [1871]. *Primitive Culture: Researches into the Development of Mythology, Philosophy, Religion, Art, and Custom*. London: J. Murray

Underhill, R.M. 1938. *Singing for Power: The Song Magic of the Papago Indians of Southern Arizona*. Berkeley: University of California Press

Van Nest, J. 2006. Rediscovering this earth: some ethnogeological aspects of the Illinois Valley Hopewell mounds. In D.K. Charles & J.E. Buikstra (eds.), *Recreating Hopewell*, 402–26. Gainesville: University of Florida Press

von Gernet, A. 1995. Nicotine dreams: the prehistory and early history of tobacco in Eastern North America. In J. Goodman, P.E. Lovejoy & A. Sherratt (eds.), *Consuming Habits: Drugs in History and Anthropology*, 67–87. New York: Routledge

Wallace, A.F.C. 1956. Revitalization movements. *American Anthropologist* 58(2), 264–81

Webmoor, T. 2007. What about "one more turn after the social" in archaeological reasoning? Taking things seriously. *World Archaeology* 39(4), 563–78

Winter, J.C. 2000. From Earth Mother to Snake Woman: the role of tobacco in the evolution of Native American religious organization. In J.C. Winter (ed.), *Tobacco Use by Native North Americans: Sacred Smoke and Silent Killer*, 265–304. Norman: University of Oklahoma Press

Zedeño, M.N. 2008. Bundled worlds: the roles and interactions of complex objects from the North American Plains. *Journal of Archaeological Method and Theory* 15, 362–78

Zedeño, M.N. 2009. Animating by association: index objects and relational taxonomies. *Cambridge Archaeological Journal* 19(3), 407–17

CHAPTER ELEVEN

Objects and Social Change: A Case Study from Saxo-Norman Southampton

Ben Jervis

Within medieval archaeology objects are used as indicators of social change, be this in the form of pottery typologies that reflect changing influences, technologies, or patterns of use (e.g., Vince & Jenner 1991) or of metalwork styles that reflect changing tastes and cultural affiliations (Webster 2011). Medieval archaeologists have begun to consider the active role of objects, for example in the creation of identities (e.g., Smith 2009), but artifacts are typically seen as reflecting, rather than participating in, long-term processes of continuity and change. Ceramics in particular provide a valuable but underutilized resource for understanding these processes. The bulk of work on medieval ceramics has focused on characterization; however, studies are increasingly examining the role of ceramics either as reflections of identity or as having a role in its formation (e.g., Blinkhorn 1997; Gutierrez 2000). Ceramics are generally relegated to a secondary role however, being tools used by (rather than acting on) people in the process of identity formation. This chapter presents a fresh perspective, which deviates from conventional approaches by considering the range of interactions between people and objects and exploring how multiple forms of agency emerge through them. By following the relationships formed with ceramic vessels, this chapter will move beyond an anthropocentric view of change to explore how objects were enrolled in processes of continuity and change surrounding the Norman Conquest of England.

Although a major watershed in English history, the Norman Conquest of England in 1066 has not been the focus of sustained archaeological study. Research has typically focused on assessing the visibility of the

Archaeology after Interpretation: Returning Materials to Archaeological Theory, edited by Benjamin Alberti, Andrew Meirion Jones, and Joshua Pollard, 219–34. ©2013 Left Coast Press, Inc. All rights reserved.

Conquest (e.g., Sykes 2007) and exploring the directional movement of influences (Impey 2000; Sykes 2007) within a framework concerned primarily with a top-down process of "Normanization." Because of the absence of clear "Norman" material culture in many areas of Britain, the Norman Conquest has not been studied from a ceramic perspective.[1] Within these approaches concepts of change are largely anthropocentric. Yet we can consider that early medieval England was experienced in a multitude of connected but individual ways, determined not just by human intentionality but also by the ways in which people were drawn into a variety of associations with objects, with multiple effects. The approach taken here, grounded in Actor-Network Theory, follows these connections, allowing us to explore the social assemblage of Anglo-Norman Southampton not as a stage in which powerful actors managed change, but (to use an appropriate metaphor) more as a tapestry of tangled strands of action in which the agency for continuity and change was woven and distributed through interactions between humans and the material world. Such an approach is valuable in introducing multi-vocality into an archaeological interpretation of Normanization and in acknowledging that "the social" of Anglo-Norman England was achieved and maintained through a tangle of courses of action, of which both humans and nonhumans were part.

THE ROLE OF OBJECTS

In order to consider the role of objects in this process we need to define three core concepts:

- Objects are mediators, participating in, rather than reflecting processes of continuity or change;
- Agency is both distributed and temporary;
- "The social" does not guide action but is formed through it; therefore, hierarchical society is brought about by and sustained through action.

Social contexts are sets of associations between human and nonhuman actors, formed and maintained by action (Gregson & Rose 2000, 441); the agency to assemble and make durable a social assemblage (a collection of human and nonhuman "actors") is distributed and formed through these associations (Latour 2005, 65; Knappett & Malafouris 2008, xi). Within this framework, change can be seen in simple terms as a remapping of these associations (Witmore 2007, 555). The traditional approaches alluded to in the introduction of this chapter see objects as intermediaries in this process (Latour 2005, 39); they act as a medium for messages to be transmitted. I wish instead to consider objects as mediators, their meaning not being inherent in them or stable, but instead emerging, changing, and dissolving as they are enrolled in action (ibid.); they do not only reflect processes of continuity and change but are part of them. Furthermore, by considering "the social" as formed by connections, and therefore always in flux, we must consider that rather than being inherently structured and hierarchical, medieval society was achieved through action. Social hierarchy was undoubtedly a feature of the medieval "social," but it was achieved and maintained through action rather than being intrinsic to people. Therefore, we must consider the role of the material world in mediating status relationships and in creating and maintaining social status.

The concept of agency is of importance to us in considering continuity and change. In defining the "performance characteristics" of objects, Schiffer (1999) essentially equates the properties of objects with their agency. He specifies, however, that these characteristics are defined relationally and emerge through action (see also Conneller 2011). Although objects have a material durability that allows them to mediate continuity, this is only brought about if the connections made with them are maintained (Law & Mol 1995, 279). Conversely, human intentionality cannot be directly equated to agency, as it amounts to nothing if humans do not have the materials required to put their intentions into practice (Knappett & Malafouris 2008, ix). We can argue therefore that agency is not inherent in people or objects, but rather is temporary and spun through action (Whatmore 1999). Agency can be defined as distributed through an assemblage, with the process of assembly creating the possibility for a particular effect (or effects) to occur. The associations that construct "the social" at any one moment in time are fragile and fleeting (Latour 2005, 66). A social assemblage is therefore made durable by the maintenance of the associations between humans and nonhumans. Change can be conceptualized as the remapping of associations between human and nonhuman actors, the dissolution of once durable associations and the formation of new ones. The agency for change is therefore formed through a process of assembly; it is created by its initial formation and maintained through the constant remaking of the associations that hold it together. The remainder of this chapter is concerned with employing these ideas to consider the role of objects in the process of Normanization.

A CASE STUDY: POTTERY IN SAXO-NORMAN SOUTHAMPTON

The Norman Conquest is typically analyzed through a study of landscapes, be it changes to town plans (e.g., Palliser et al. 2000), the imposition of castles (Creighton 2002), or the reorganization of rural landscapes

(Sawyer 1985). Naomi Sykes's (2007) study of the zooarchaeology of the Norman Conquest has added a new perspective, demonstrating that the Conquest had variable impacts upon people's everyday lives. The relational approach outlined above can allow us to explore further this plurality of experiences of the Conquest. I will focus here on a specific case study, that of Saxo-Norman Southampton.

Late Saxon (c. AD 900–1066) Southampton was a new settlement that replaced the earlier *wic* trading site of Hamwic (see Figure 11.1). Excavations have revealed a dispersed settlement layout with a mixed economy based on trade and craft production (Platt 1973, 6), with some evidence of cultivation within the settlement (Jervis 2011b, 232–33). The town continued to develop after 1066. Domesday Book of 1086 records 96 newcomers in Southampton, the majority of whom were French (Golding 1994, 78). A castle was constructed in the northwest corner of the town, and it is in the western half of the settlement that the impact of the Conquest can be most obviously seen, with a "French quarter" emerging around the waterfront (Brown & Hardy 2011). This appears to have been built upon an existing immigrant community in

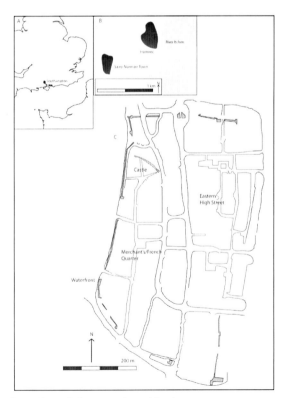

Figure 11.1   Location of sites mentioned in the text

Southampton, and cross-channel contact is clearly demonstrated within the ceramic assemblage (Brown 1994).

I will seek to explore the effect of the interactions between people and pottery in early medieval Southampton. These interactions will first be outlined against the backdrop of Southampton; in the following section, I will consider their role in the emergence of Anglo-Norman Southampton as a social assemblage. In particular, I will focus upon three key areas: exchange, use, and deposition.

Exchange

Analysis of distribution patterns within Southampton and its region has revealed that several exchange mechanisms were in place. Most of Southampton's late Saxon pottery is locally produced Flint-tempered Ware (Brown 1994) (see Figure 11.2). It is probable that several producers were in operation, distributing their wares across Southampton. Regional products were also marketed in Southampton. Michelmersh-type Wares

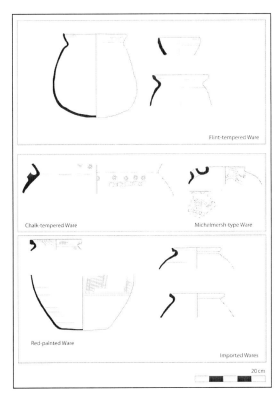

Figure 11.2 Examples of late Saxon pottery from Southampton (redrawn from Brown 1994)

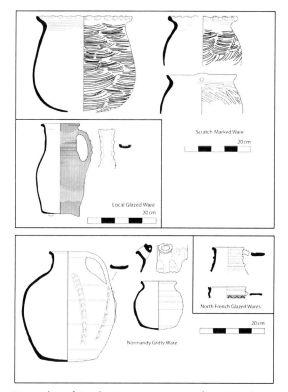

Figure 11.3 Examples of Anglo-Norman pottery from Southampton (redrawn from Brown 2002)

produced to the north of Southampton and Chalk-tempered Wares produced around Winchester were marketed widely. A market for imported (primarily French) wares also existed in Southampton. The most common wares are similar to those used in Hamwic (Timby 1988; Brown 1994); newer types, particularly north French Red-painted Wares have a more limited distribution, tending to be recovered from excavations around the waterfront.

The Anglo-Norman period sees the development of Scratch Marked Wares, similar in fabric and form to earlier local wares, but generally larger and characterized by the presence of scratch marking (see Figure 11.3). These were probably produced outside of the town and, although found across Southampton, are particularly abundant in the western, "French," part of the settlement (see Figure 11.4).

In the east, the supply of late Saxon-type Flint-tempered Wares persists, at least in the years immediately following the Conquest, based on the composition of assemblages from post-Conquest features (Jervis 2011b, 113). The east shows some continuity in supply patterns, and a

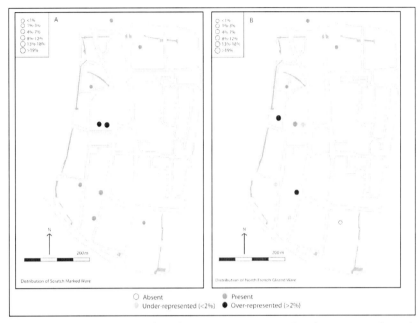

Figure 11.4 Distribution of Anglo-Norman pottery in Southampton: a) Scratch Marked Ware; b) North French Glazed Ware

market developed to supply the French quarter with a particular type of pottery. A market for regionally produced and imported pottery also continued to expand. The primary imported ware was Normandy Gritty Ware, a development of the typical late Saxon imported wares that was exchanged and used widely across Southampton. Locally produced glazed wares were exchanged in Southampton and filled a gap in the market for serving vessels, not catered for by the local industries (Brown 2002, 10–11). Other imports, particularly glazed wares from northern France, are rare outside of the French quarter; they appear to signal an ongoing importation of goods not available on the open market for the benefit of particular members of Southampton's population (Figure 11.4b).

USE

A program of use-wear analysis (the study of sooting patterns and indicators of physical and chemical attrition; see Skibo 1992) has further added to this picture of continuity and change (Jervis 2013). An analysis of cooking practices, based on sooting patterns, reveals major differences between the English and French quarters of Southampton (see Figure 11.5).

Figure 11.5   a) Black carbonized sooting on a late Saxon vessel; b) Glossy black sooting on a Scratch Marked Ware vessel

In the late Saxon period thick, carbonized sooty deposits are common, indicating that vessels were placed in, or close to, the fire. A similar cooking method was also common in the later phases of occupation at Hamwic (Jervis 2011a, 252). A small number of vessels recovered from the waterfront area, however, have a different sooting pattern. These are characterized by the presence of thinner, glossy sooty deposits, which suggest that the vessels were suspended over the fire. Among the Anglo-Norman Scratch Marked Ware this sooting pattern dominates. It appears that immigrants living around the waterfront used local cooking pots in a distinct way, favoring slower cooking, which would perhaps result in more tender meat. Contemporary north French vessels often have suspension holes built into them, suggesting that they were designed for suspension (e.g., Routier 2006), and a small number of Scratch Marked Ware vessels have been recovered with similar suspension holes (see Figure 11.3).

Storage vessels are present in both phases but increase in size following the Conquest, perhaps due to an increase in household size or to a changing relationship with the hinterland, which meant that more foodstuffs were available for storage in towns. A final function of pottery to be considered is serving. Late Saxon serving vessels are present in Southampton, but their provision increases during the Anglo-Norman period. These newer types were most commonly used around the French quarter (Jervis 2011b, 213).

DEPOSITION

The late Saxon period sees continuity in depositional practice from Hamwic, with waste typically building up onto middens before redeposition. A key difference however is the undertaking of horticulture within the settlement, which leads to a more dispersed settlement layout (Platt 1973, 6; Jervis 2011b, 232–36). This period also sees an increase in secondary deposition into disused pits, which increases further in the Anglo-Norman period, particularly in the French quarter (Jervis 2011b, 223–26). These changes can be closely related to issues of class structure and urban topography (see below), and are perhaps amongst the clearest ways in which objects can be shown to be agents of change.

CONSIDERING CONTINUITY AND CHANGE

So far I have mapped the associations between people and pottery in early medieval Southampton. We must now follow the courses of action formed by these associations, to explore how pottery came to be engaged in the processes through which the social assemblage of early medieval Southampton was shaped and maintained. In order to do so, we need to discuss two related themes: maintaining the social and building identities.

MAINTAINING THE SOCIAL

Towns can be considered as social assemblages, formed and constantly remade by the continued assembly of actors (Thrift 2008, 201). Pottery was one such actor, and continued engagements with it both brought continuity to Saxo-Norman Southampton, as well as mediating change. Objects act in two key ways to build durability into a social assemblage. Rather than being a property of an object, the agency to build durability emerges through action and therefore it can reform through repeated engagements with the same object or a string of similar objects (Jones 2007, 79). This agency is very much spun in the moment, the object fleetingly becoming a mediator before retiring, perhaps only temporarily, to an intermediary role. The second way in which objects build durability relies upon the ever-present material permanence of objects, which can continue to act for long periods even though the nature of this action may change over time (Law & Mol 1995, 279). In the case of pottery, a durable but portable artifact, this variation in the nature of agency is a matter of biography, with some engagements being short-lived and leading to the creation of fleeting agency, whereas the constant repetition of action with the same or similar vessels caused this agency to be constantly reformed and therefore to persist. Importantly, the agency to create multiple effects can be distributed through a given object at any one time, meaning that a pot can act in multiple and unpredictable ways depending upon the web of associations that have been formed with it.

Exchange activity is one set of associations through which towns were formed and maintained as social assemblages, with pottery playing a clear role in mediating change in, but also ensuring the durability of, the associations formed through this activity. The agency for Southampton to function as a port was (and still is) distributed through a number of nonhuman actors: its strategic location, maritime technology, legislation, and the objects of trade. Therefore pottery, as part of this trade, played a role in making the market in late Saxon Southampton durable. Pottery did not possess the agency to remake Southampton. This emerged through the relationships formed with pottery as it was transported to the market and entered into exchange. Just as this agency emerged through exchange, so it disappeared following the transaction, being lost until it was formed again, with a new vessel, in the next moment of exchange. Exchange must be conceptualized as a process of assembly, the coming together of human intentionality and objects which is neither human- or object-led and which has implications for the durability of the place (or social assemblage) in which it occurs. A vessel only plays an intermediary role after the exchange, except perhaps in the case of a prototype that influences future exchanges or if the object breaks, forcing a new exchange to occur. The market's durability came to be mediated through multiple exchange events in which the agency for continuity and change was repeatedly spun. For example, at the beginning of the period the continued exchange of locally produced pottery had the effect of translating exchange mechanisms from Hamwic into the new town, remaking ties and translating elements of Hamwic's sociality into a new physical environment. A similar process was at work in relation to the market for imported pottery. Again, there appears to be a near direct translation of the port role from Hamwic to Southampton, although the intensity of trade was probably lower (Hall 2000). International trade was seasonal, but repeated trade and memory of this trade, cued by continued engagements with imported products, maintained Southampton's role as a port.

The exchange of local and imported products created continuity after the Norman Conquest. However, as new sources of pottery emerged, these ties slowly began to break. The formation of relationships with these products through exchange contributed to the emergence of a process of change that altered the economic landscape of Southampton, distributing the reach and certain functions of the town into the wider hinterland. Associations had always existed between Southampton and its hinterland, as proven by the exchange of Michelmersh-type and Chalk-tempered Wares in the late Saxon period, but as Scratch Marked Ware gained currency, associations between consumers and producers were remapped. Ties with local producers were cut and tighter bonds with the hinterland were formed, perhaps in part due to the reallocation of rural estates following the Conquest (Golding 1994, 68). It was here, then, that we can locate some agency for change—in the flashes of action that constitute the exchange of these regional products.

A changing relationship with the hinterland, relating to the increased burden placed by landlords on rural producers, the growth of urban markets, and the strengthening of tenurial links (Golding 1994, 180; Dyer 2002, 74, 99; Sykes 2007, 37), can also be observed in the increased number of storage vessels present in Southampton. At a basic level, the material properties of pottery as containers allowed to distribute the agency for processes of exchange and storage; these processes could not be achieved by humans alone. The mediatory role of these vessels is more profound, since by acting as containers they permitted the reproduction of a provisioning system, or the formation and reformation of particular relationships (see also Knappett 2011, 87), which in turn engaged these vessels in the process of change. This is an important subtlety that demonstrates the varying nature of agency as the material durability of these vessels comes into play. Placing these observations into a wider context, we can begin to see how the agency for changing relationships between town and country in the post-Conquest period was not purely the possession of elites. Instead, it was formed in the assembly of a cast of actors, a process that formed and sustained the associations that not only comprised the provisioning systems but also allowed wealth and power to be generated and sustained.

Changing relationships between Southampton and its hinterland can also be explored through a study of waste disposal. In late Saxon Southampton, waste simultaneously acted to mediate continuity and change; the building up of middens directly cited and reproduced engagements with waste in Hamwic, whereas its redeposition onto garden plots introduced a major difference. This change in practice suggests a change in the mechanism of food supply, although the degree to which a tributary system was in place to supply urban populations remains unclear (Dyer 2002, 51; Astill 2006, 250). In the late Saxon period, waste, along with processing vessels,[2] came to be one of a number of material actors through which the agency for this changing relationship with the hinterland was located, as the settlement seemingly became more self-sufficient. Waste is an interesting actor. On the one hand, sensory experiences of waste mediated continuity, with the smell in particular likely cuing memory and familiarity. On the other, waste came to be a mediator of significant changes in the economy of the town, as it was drawn into a process of changing associations between townspeople, their rural counterparts, and their produce.

Further shifts in this relationship are demonstrated by the increase in secondary waste disposal in certain areas of the town around the Norman Conquest. Here waste did not afford production and was instead disposed of, as these households were drawn into tighter provisioning relationships with Southampton's hinterland. Interactions with waste mediated status relationships, forming contrasts between groups who needed to practice horticulture and those who did not. The agency of waste emerged through interactions with it at the household scale, leading to the emergence of multiple conceptualizations of waste and engaging it in multiple trajectories of continuity and change.[3] A number of agents, including pottery, came together to cause change to flow through provisioning mechanisms. These changes overflowed (Callon 1999, 188), creating wealth in the town and causing changes in the treatment of waste, which in turn acted on the urban landscape and the townspeople, introducing difference and stimulating physical changes to the townscape.

From a ceramic perspective the period is notable for the emergence of jugs and tripod pitchers, used as serving and transport vessels. These vessels can be considered a product of the emergence of the Anglo-Norman household, which was in turn reproduced through their use. The post-Conquest period saw an increased division of the territory, which implied that the associations that supported the presence of large late Saxon pitcher forms (e.g., Jervis 2009, 69) dissolved and were replaced by a need for portable vessels. The agency for the emergence of these forms was distributed through the context of use, and continued engagements with these vessels made these new contexts durable. A new household network was created, the result of overflowing associations that created wealth and power and resulted in the formation of a distinctly urban Anglo-Norman social structure, formed as old associations dissolved and new ones emerged. Not only were these vessels the result of these processes, but they also contributed to the formation and maintenance of hierarchical relationships, creating a medium through which social relationships could be negotiated at the table. For example, within the context of Southampton Castle these vessels were likely used only on specific occasions, such as royal visits (Platt 1973, 13), when a series of actors were assembled who used these vessels to reinforce hierarchy through the order in which drinks were taken and the formation of relationships between servants and their masters. The agency to reinforce hierarchical relationships was not inherent in people but was distributed, emerging in the act of serving and in the interaction between humans, wine, and the physical context of the formal dining hall. For a fleeting moment the actors required for this process were assembled by the physical act of serving; jugs became involved in this process, their agency emerging and dissolving in an instant. Jugs therefore do not reflect high-status households but were rather involved, through temporary but repeated serving activities, in a process of social distinction. Distinction was also introduced through the exclusion of the majority of the population from these events.

A focus on a single class of object restricts the scope of any discussion. We can begin to show, however, that the changes observed in the ceramic record are not the result of a newly imposed social order. Instead, engagements with pottery worked to bring about both continuity and change. They created the agency through which associations with the hinterland were renegotiated and power and wealth could be created and flow. Therefore, throughout their usage life (and beyond), ceramic vessels had a direct impact on the materialization of the social assemblage of Southampton's urban landscape.

CREATING IDENTITIES

We have already considered how engagements with pottery were bound up in processes of identity creation in relation to status. A key area for investigation must also be the role of pottery in the creation of new identities, defined as the way in which people relate themselves to their surroundings. No single concept of a "Norman" identity existed (Johnson 2005, 86); we should think instead in terms of a "Normanized" identity, whereby people came to feel in some way aligned with a conceptualized Norman identity. Ceramic use, like exchange, happens in a fleeting moment; however, cooking practices in particular are commonly repeated, meaning that the associations built in the kitchen constantly contributed to the creation and maintenance of identities.

The continuity in cooking practices from Hamwic to late Saxon Southampton suggests that the repetition of domestic practices, particularly the recreation of sensory experiences, mediated continuity despite the settlement's shifting location. The practicing of different techniques around the waterfront, as well as a greater use of imported pottery, suggests that for some individuals (probably immigrants) the use of locally produced vessels mediated continuity by creating durable identities in a foreign location. Cooking was more than a mode of identity expression. The familiarity bred through the replication of experience is central to the maintenance of a sense of self (Sutton 2001, 74) and a sense of home, which emerged through engagements with utensils, foodstuffs, and spaces in the house.

In eastern Southampton this process of continuity appears to have extended into the earlier part of the post-Conquest period, with vessels perhaps facilitating an element of resistance, as well as continuity. Noticeably the vessels used are still closely related to late Saxon types, suggesting a tension between households in relation to the role of these vessels in generating feelings of familiarity and difference: on the one hand French households brought continuity through practice, and on the other English households mediated continuity through the use of familiar vessels. Processes of adaptation and adoption led to the emergence of hybrid Anglo-Norman identities through domestic practice in Southampton, as engagements with ceramics mediated experiences of both continuity and change, which varied in relation to an individual's background (see Jervis 2013 for a more detailed analysis).[4]

When coupled with the changes discussed above, we can see that associations both within Southampton and between Southampton and its hinterland led to the formation of new structures of power and wealth materialized through differences in the topography of the town (including those related to waste disposal). Through the remapping of these associations, English practices and thus English identities came to be marginalized (see also Lilley 2009, 147). The agency for this marginalization was not possessed by inherently powerful individuals, but rather emerged through interactions between people and the material world, including the humble cooking pot.

CONCLUSION: THE NATURE OF CHANGE

This analysis has demonstrated that objects do more than reflect continuity and change; they are active in these processes. I have only scratched the surface in demonstrating the complexity of these processes, and further work, focusing on a broader range of actors, is clearly required. Close study can also inform us about the nature of change. Change is not a uniform phenomenon; it occurs at different rates and generates multiple narratives. In relation to Saxo-Norman Southampton, for example, engagements with cooking vessels led to varying responses to the Norman Conquest, causing Anglo-Norman identities to develop at different rates. Similarly, changes to the market were the result of a slow remapping of associations rather than a fracturing of the existing "social." Objects contributed something distinct to the agency for change: on the one hand they were fleeting actors, causing change to occur in a single moment or contributing to a more gradual development; on the other, their durability gave them a special role in mediating changing relationships between Southampton and its hinterland throughout the early medieval period, as we have seen in relation to waste and storage vessels. Only by considering how the agency for change emerges through relationships between humans and nonhumans, rather than residing within individuals, can we begin to understand this process rather than simply acknowledge it.

NOTES

1. See Kyle (2012), however, on the Anglo-Norman Conquest of Ireland.
2. Use-wear analysis has identified distinct groups of late Saxon processing vessels. Similar vessels are not present in the Anglo-Norman assemblage (Jervis 2011b, 206).

3. Treatment of waste in this way can also be related to the expansion of the town, since waste needed to be treated in a way that was spatially efficient.
4. Contemporary historical sources confirm a level of interaction between English and French households and a relatively rapid process of assimilation (Golding 1994, 182).

REFERENCES

Astill, G. 2006. Community, identity and the later Anglo-Saxon town: the case of southern England. In W. Davies, G. Halsall & A. Reynolds (eds.), *People and Space in the Middle Ages, 300–1300*, 233–54. Turnhout, Belg.: Brepols

Blinkhorn, P. 1997. Habitus, social identity and Anglo-Saxon pottery. In P. Blinkhorn & C. Cumberpatch (eds.), *Not So Much a Pot, More a Way of Life*, 113–24. Oxford, UK: Oxbow Books

Brown, D. 1994. Pottery and Late Saxon Southampton. *Proceedings of the Hampshire Field Club & Archaeological Society* 50, 127–52

Brown, D. 2002. *Pottery in Medieval Southampton c. 1066–1510*. York, UK: CBA Research Report 133

Brown, R. & Hardy, A. 2011. *Trade and Prosperity, War and Poverty: An Archaeological and Historical Investigation into Southampton's French Quarter*. Oxford: Oxford Archaeology Monograph 15

Callon, M. 1999. Actor-network theory—the market test. In J. Law & J. Hassard (eds.), *Actor Network Theory and After*, 181–95. Oxford, UK: Blackwell/The Sociological Review

Conneller, C. 2011. *An Archaeology of Materials: Substantial Transformations in Early Prehistoric Europe*. London: Routledge

Creighton, O. 2002. *Castles and Landscapes: Power, Community and Fortification in Medieval England*. London: Equinox

Dyer, C. 2002. *Making a Living in the Middle Ages*. New Haven, CT: Yale University Press

Golding, B. 1994. *Conquest and Colonisation: The Normans in Britain, 1066–1100*. Basingstoke, UK: Macmillan

Gregson, N. & Rose, G. 2000. Taking Butler elsewhere: performativities, spatialities and subjectivities. *Environment and Planning D: Society and Space* 18, 433–52

Gutierrez, A. 2000. *Mediterranean Pottery in Wessex Households (13th–17th Centuries)*. Oxford: British Archaeological Reports, British Series 306

Hall, R. 2000. The decline of the Wic? In T. Slater (ed.), *Towns in Decline AD100–1600*, 120–36. Aldershot, UK: Ashgate

Impey, E. 2000. The Siegneurial residence in Normandy, 1125–1225: an Anglo-Norman tradition? *Medieval Archaeology* 43, 45–73

Jervis, B. 2009. Pottery from Late Saxon Chichester: a reassessment of the evidence. *Sussex Archaeological Collections* 147, 61–76

Jervis, B. 2011a. A patchwork of people, pots and places: material engagements and the construction of "the social" in Hamwic (Anglo-Saxon Southampton), UK. *Journal of Social Archaeology* 11(3), 239–65

Jervis, B. 2011b. *Placing pots: an actor-led approach to the use and perception of medieval pottery in Southampton and its region c. AD 700–1400*. Unpublished PhD thesis, Department of Archaeology, University of Southampton

Jervis, B. 2013. Conquest, ceramics, continuity and change: beyond representational approaches to continuity and change in Early Medieval England. A case study from Anglo-Norman Southampton. *Early Medieval Europe* 21(4), 455–87

Johnson, E. 2005. Normandy and Norman identity in Southern Italian chronicles. *Anglo-Norman Studies* 27, 85–100

Jones, A. 2007. *Memory and Material Culture*. Cambridge: Cambridge University Press

Knappett, C. 2011. *An Archaeology of Interaction: Network Perspectives on Material Culture and Society*. Oxford: Oxford University Press

Knappett, C. & Malafouris, L. 2008. Material and nonhuman agency: an introduction. In C. Knappett & L. Malafouris (eds.), *Material Agency: Towards a Non-Anthropocentric Approach*, ix–xix. New York: Springer

Kyle, A. 2012. More than just a quick fix? Repair holes on early medieval Souterrain Ware. In B. Jervis & A. Kyle (eds.), *Make-do and Mend: Archaeologies of Compromise, Repair and Re-use*, 93–112. Oxford: British Archaeological Reports, International Series 2408

Latour, B. 2005. *Reassembling the Social: An Introduction to Actor-Network Theory*. Oxford: Oxford University Press

Law, J. & Mol, A. 1995. Notes on materiality and sociality. *The Sociological Review* 43(2), 274–94

Lilley, K. 2009. *City and Cosmos: The Medieval World in Urban Form*. London: Reaktion Books

Palliser, D., Slater, T. & Dennison, E. 2000. The topography of towns 600–1300. In D. Palliser (ed.), *The Cambridge Urban History of Britain*, Vol. 1, 153–86. Cambridge: Cambridge University Press

Platt, C. 1973. *Medieval Southampton: The Port and Trading Community, AD 1000–1600*. London: Routledge

Routier, J.C. 2006. Céramiques médiévales de Xᵉ et XIᵉ siécles en Flandre et sur le littoral du Nord-Pas-de-Calais. In V. Hincker & P. Hussi (eds.), *La Céramique du Haut Moyen Âge dans le Nord-Ouest de l'Europe Vᵉ–Xᵉ Siècles. Actes du Colloque de Caen, 2004*. Condé-sur-Noireau, Fr.: Éditions NEA

Sawyer, P. 1985. The Anglo-Norman village. In D. Hooke (ed.), *Medieval Villages*, 3–6. Oxford: Oxford University Press

Schiffer, M. 1999. *The Material Life of Human Beings*. London: Routledge

Skibo, J. 1992. *Pottery Function: A Use Alteration Perspective*. New York: Plenum Press

Smith, S. 2009. Materializing resistant identities among the medieval peasantry: an examination of dress accessories from English rural sites. *Journal of Material Culture* 14(3), 309–32

Sutton, D. 2001. *Remembrance of Repasts: An Anthropology of Food and Memory*. Oxford, UK: Berg

Sykes, N. 2007. *The Norman Conquest: A Zooarchaeological Perspective*. Oxford: British Archaeological Reports, International Series 1656

Thrift, N. 2008. *Non-Representational Theory: Space, Politics and Affect*. London: Routledge

Timby, J. 1988. The Middle Saxon pottery. In P. Andrews (ed.), *The Coins and Pottery from Hamwic*, 73–122. Southampton, UK: Southampton City Museums

Vince, A. & Jenner, A. 1991. The Saxon and Early Medieval pottery of London. In A. Vince (ed.), *Aspects of Saxo-Norman London: II, Finds and Environmental Evidence*, 19–119. London: LAMAS Special Paper 12

Webster, L. 2011. Style: influences, chronology and meaning. In H. Hamerow, D. Hinton & S. Crawford (eds.), *The Oxford Handbook of Anglo-Saxon Archaeology*, 460–501. Oxford: Oxford University Press

Whatmore, S. 1999. Hybrid geographies: rethinking the "human" in human geography. In D. Massey, J. Allen & P. Sarre (eds.), *Human Geography Today*, 22–39. London: Polity Press

Witmore, C. 2007. Symmetrical archaeology: excerpts of a manifesto. *World Archaeology* 39(4), 546–62

CHAPTER TWELVE

Dynamic Assemblages, or the Past Is What Endures: Change and the Duration of Relations

Chris Fowler

To say that we draw an "interpretation" from "evidence" by way of "theory" would be an inaccurate description of what archaeologists actually do, and yet this effective fiction has an impact on archaeology since its antiquarian inception. In this fiction, or *factish*[1] (Latour 1999, 16, 272–80), accurate interpretations correspond with a "reality" that is independent of those interpretations. Non-representational theories are diverse, but reject this kind of "correspondence theory of truth" on which classical positivism is founded. Non-representationalists point out that this position requires us to separate reality from ideas and yet know when ideas do in fact correspond with this ring-fenced reality. Instead, non-representationalists propose that theories, scholars, techniques, technologies, materials, and methodologies all interact with one another through research practices. Since all of this apparatus is equally real, copresent and entangled, it is impossible to separate reality from theory or interpretation and test one against the other. Theories are embedded in configurations of things, materials, and techniques, and vice versa. Thus, our apparatus, the object we study, ourselves, our ideas, and our theories are all part of a real, specific, historical, and local assemblage. Theories operate in reconfiguring the assemblage and thus in altering reality, bit by bit. It falls to us to understand the composition of the assemblage and the particular shape and nature of the phenomena that emerge temporarily while that assemblage endures. In this chapter I will develop my thinking on the relational nature of reality by focusing on the issue of change and persistence. I will argue that in rejecting a correspondence theory of truth, a host of different avenues for

Archaeology after Interpretation: Returning Materials to Archaeological Theory, edited by Benjamin Alberti, Andrew Meirion Jones, and Joshua Pollard, 235–56.

understanding time and archaeological research open up. I will argue that these avenues are fraught with paradoxes, but those paradoxes are productive and archaeologists are already adept at dealing with some of them because of our engagement within constantly changing assemblages of past material.

The focus of this chapter is an exploration of how we as archaeologists can make use of, and respond to the challenges of, some features that stem from recent non-representational theories. The position I have set out in this chapter is part of what I call a relational realism, and it summarizes (and also goes beyond) the argument I have developed in a recent book that explores a relational realist approach to Early Bronze Age mortuary practices in Northeast England (Fowler 2013). Relational realism adopts the view that relationality does not stem from human subjectivity, but is integral to reality. Relationality is a feature of ontology: it is deeply embedded in how the universe works.

Before I outline the key concepts of my approach, I want to briefly introduce the other members of the assemblage in which I have been involved and that have been instrumental in arriving at this position. Besides the concepts distilled from non-representational theories, my assemblage is composed of 355 mortuary deposits from 151 different locations in Northumberland, Tyne and Wear, and County Durham, excavated at various times from 1810 to 2009. But it is also composed of the written and visual accounts of the excavations of these deposits, the material remains recovered, archive information, osteological analyses, radiocarbon determinations, maps generated using GIS (and all the centuries of information, effort, and technology that lie behind the production of such maps), chronologies and typologies produced by comparison with similar objects, and past interpretations of the wider types of such burials across the British Isles and beyond. Thus, producing an archaeological synthesis of this assemblage (and writing an interpretation of changing Early Bronze Age mortuary practices) involved exploring non-representational theory, examining the different ideas, events, histories, techniques, materials, and practices that have given rise to the assemblage as I found it, and analyzing the material composition of the assemblage today (from human remains to pots, to the fills of cists, to the location of mortuary deposition). And of course, we ourselves are within the assemblage, part of the object, a feature of the phenomenon.

On the one hand any assemblage such as "Early Bronze Age mortuary practices in Northeast England" is a unique event, consisting of a specific set of interactions among the various participants (pots, photographs of pots, Greenwell's 1877 *British Barrows*, publications of excavations from the 1860s, 1920s, 1980s, and so on, the Great North

Museum archives, concepts such as elites, human remains, maps, GIS, myself, etc.). Each engagement revises an existing assemblage so that it becomes something new. How, then, do we reconcile the idea that each assemblage is a specific instantiation with the idea that assemblages (such as barrows or pots) are extended across time? Are we dealing with many different assemblages successively appearing, disappearing, and replacing one another, with one enduring assemblage "left" by past activity, or with something else? I will suggest that many of the components endure and can remain engaged with one another in successive revisions to the assemblage: certain regions of an assemblage, themselves smaller assemblages, may persist to some extent even when other elements diminish or dissipate. But given non-representational rejections of any essential features to phenomena, what is it exactly that endures? This is, I think, a key issue evident in several post-humanist and non-representational approaches (e.g., Latour 1999; Barad 2007; see Harman 2009; Fowler & Harris, under review) that is of particular interest for archaeologists, because it has profound implications for how we understand, treat, and transform our objects of study. It also has implications for the vital question of how interpretations are evaluated once a correspondence theory of truth has been rejected. This necessitates careful consideration of the way assemblages accrete and change, the duration of an assemblage, and the extent to which one assemblage or phenomenon enfolds or encompasses others. In this chapter I will work a path through the problem of the duration and extent of relations by reflecting on my engagement with Early Bronze Age mortuary practices in Northeast England, though there is insufficient space to present an interpretation of such evidence here (for that see Fowler 2013).

INSTANTIATIONS: ASSEMBLAGES, NETWORKS, MESHWORKS, PHENOMENA, ENTANGLEMENTS

Many non-representational theories revolve around a core metaphor or image, and I start with the proposition that these are to some extent similar. Influential examples include assemblage (e.g., Deleuze & Guattari 2004; Bennett 2005, 2010; Conneller 2011; Harris 2012; Lucas 2012), network (e.g., Latour 1999, 2005; Knappett 2011), meshwork (DeLanda 1997; Ingold 2011; Knappett 2011), phenomenon (Barad 2003, 2007), diffraction (Barad 2007), and entanglement (Barad 2003, 2007; Hodder 2011, 2012). Each of these images has a different focus and is shaped to deal with specific issues, and each has been very effective in that regard. Thus, for instance, Latour's network helped him to explain modern scientific research and technologies, and Barad's phenomena and entanglements explored the rapid occurrences of quantum physics. There are some significant differences between these various figurings of a relational reality—for instance, different authors use the concept of agency in different ways (e.g., Barad and Hodder)—but also key similarities and, in some cases, common roots (for a detailed comparative analysis see Fowler 2013, chapter 2).

I am not suggesting that all of these conceptual configurations are the same, but that they have been, and can be, used to similar effects. They describe what we could call *instantiations*: specific iterations that are not predetermined by any single preexisting model, form, or principle (see Marshall & Alberti 2013). Such an instantiation is composed of activity, of "intra-actions" (the term is Barad's) among its constituent elements. Such entities are unstable and changing, in the process of becoming or unfolding along paths that cannot be predicted in advance. The properties or qualities of an instantiation are a matter of its precise current configuration, and entities are inseparable from events, interactions, and instances: entities *are* events, as Lucas (2012, 208) has recently argued for archaeological remains. Throughout this text I treat each assemblage, each artifact, and each category as such an instantiation, resisting the urge to debate whether it is best described as a network or a meshwork or any other single metaphor. First and foremost, an instantiation has to be understood in itself, at the moment of encounter and based on the relations that comprise it at that time: a Food Vessel, a jet necklace, a deposit of some of the cremated bones of a man and a child. Yet my point is that these instantiations unfold over a long time and are part of other instantiations at a large scale, such as the corpus of short cists across Britain, or the Beaker burials, or round mounds, or histories of archaeological research, for instance. Archaeologists often perceive patterns in the shape of larger-scale instantiations, such as distributions, and sometimes posit that dominant structuring principles underlie these patterns. However, even for patterns at the very grand scale, such as the fractal patterning of coastlines, the scale and frequency of earthquakes, or stock market activity, the pattern is the outcome of a myriad of tiny interactions that are unique, historical, and unpredictable in scale, kind, and effect (Buchanan 2001). This is not to deny that some forces may pervade different assemblages and affect many of them in similar ways, but to stress that each instantiation has multiple points of origin and cannot be reduced to any single cause, no matter how clearly it may be patterned. For instance, a Food Vessel is what it is partly because of activity that happened thousands of years ago, and partly because of the actions of antiquarians and archaeologists. Instantiations are historical, they rely on enduring, persistent relations, and their history is not derived from a single origin. The question that concerns me here is how such instantiations unfold and the tension between momentary interactions and enduring assemblages.

TIME, CHANGE, AND THE CIRCULATING REFERENCE

Non-representational understandings of instantiations raise a provocative paradox in how we think about time and change, especially for archaeologists whose assemblages are of very long duration (see Witmore 2007a; Olivier 2011; Lucas 2012). Non-representational approaches involve specific understandings of time and change that do not divorce the past from the present. Latour's concept of the "circulating reference" provides an example. Latour examines how the object of a scientist's study is translated as it moves through successive interactions with apparatuses, ideas, and scientists. The reference in question could be anything, an idea, a person, an artifact, a category, a disease, or a storm. Let us say it is a set of jet beads from a cist that also contained a bowl Food Vessel, discovered on June 9, 1927 at Kyloe, in Northumberland. As the reference circulates it intersects with other actants,[2] and each is affected in some way by the interaction.[3] Each intersection, each translation, amplifies some aspects of the reference and reduces others. The Kyloe cist was discovered during preparations for blasting at a quarry, and the beads from the necklace were distributed among some of those present. It is unclear exactly who the workmen were who made the discovery in this rural Northumbrian quarry, or exactly who removed the cover slab and got among the contents. We are told that a Colonel Leather collected "most of the contents of the cist," and that in the evening he took photographs of the empty cist, one of which was published in the article describing the discovery (Brewis 1927, 26). The contents included "portions of a broken food-vessel [sic] and of a jet necklace" (ibid.). These were donated to the Society of Antiquaries of Newcastle upon Tyne and kept at their museum, first at the Black Gate in Newcastle, then at the University of Newcastle upon Tyne and, from 2010, at the Great North Museum. No bones are mentioned, but bones are not recovered from all cists in the region because some local soils are not generally conducive to their survival.

The cist and the necklace would have been attributed to the Bronze Age because antiquarians like Canon William Greenwell (1820–1918), who published reports of excavation of many Northumbrian Early Bronze Age mortuary sites in *British Barrows* (1877), had identified Food Vessel pottery and jet necklaces as accompaniments to single crouched inhumations in short cists, a number of which Greenwell had also associated with bronze implements. At Kyloe quarry, Colonel

Leather recorded what was left of the burial site, collected the broken remains of a Food Vessel from the cist, and recovered as many beads as possible "from various people" (Spain 1928, 145). It was clear that the necklace was incomplete, but at the museum Brewis (1927) attempted to reconstruct it by restringing the surviving fifty-three beads, as though only a few beads had been missing. A black and white photograph translated this reconstruction, allowing it to circulate well beyond the jet beads themselves (see Figure 12.1). This translation amplified the visual features of the beads that could be captured in two dimensions and in black and white, but it left out other features, say, the chemical composition of the jet (see Jones 2002). It also excluded other beads that were now missing from the assemblage. In 1976, following comparison with jet necklaces from other sites in northern Britain (such as Poltollach: see Craw 1929), Newman (1976) provided a drawing reconstructing the necklace differently and suggesting that many beads were missing (see Figure 12.1). This reconstruction has been used as the basis for the recreation of the necklace in the form of the replica on display at the Great North Museum today (the third image in Figure 12.1): it still leaves out some features of the necklace, but it extends others features beyond the "original" jet beads.

The idea of the circulating reference demonstrates that our connection is not between past and present or between evidence and interpretation, but conjoins jet, Early Bronze Age tools for working jet, people giving and receiving necklaces, mortuary practices, taphonomic processes, early twentieth-century demand for sandstone, gunpowder, quarrymen, the Society of Antiquaries of Newcastle upon Tyne, Colonel Leather, Parker Brewis, photography, printing presses, scholarly journals, Tim Newman, necklaces found in Scotland, archaeological typologies, the

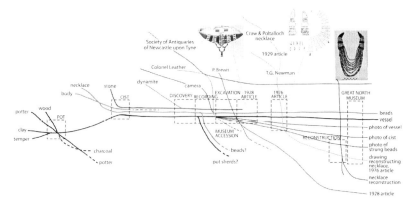

Figure 12.1   Some intra-actions translating the assemblage comprising the Kyloe cist, vessel, and necklace

Great North Museum, and so on. As the necklace circulates among these participants, so many of its constituent relations change; paradoxically, the various translations attempt to temporarily stabilize the necklace as one thing or another, yet also transform it and become drawn into the assemblage comprising it.

The Kyloe necklace was interacting, translating, and transforming relations long before 1927, though not, of course, as the Kyloe necklace as it is now. In the Early Bronze Age, I argue, the Kyloe necklace was itself a translator in relations between other entities *and resulted from* a translation of relationships in the first place—some of which extended back into the Carboniferous period, when plant resins became transformed into jet. The necklace is an enduring yet changing and proliferating assemblage of past relations, and at various moments becomes what it is inextricably from the other assemblages with which it conjoins or to which it jointly gives rise (e.g., certain bodies or certain archaeological typologies). It does not change all at once, but incrementally; not all of the relations constituting an assemblage or phenomenon change at the same time, even though the assemblage as a whole does change. Furthermore, the Kyloe necklace gathers a past as it circulates: the circulation is crucial to its persistence in this particular, historical form. As the assemblage we now know as "the Kyloe necklace" circulated over time (indeed, circulated in *producing* time) in both the distant and recent past, it was translated from one form to another, brought into relation with further entities, and through the mediation of these, spawned yet further assemblages through which some aspects of it became extended (e.g., drawings, photographs, texts). Taking a non-representational stance I would dismiss the view that these are simply "representations" of the "real" necklace. But are these photographs, texts, and reconstructions part of the Kyloe necklace, or are they distinct entities, actants, assemblages, references? Is an assemblage one object or many, instantaneous or enduring?

THE EXTENDED OBJECT, ASSEMBLAGE, OR PHENOMENON

My short answer to each of the questions above is, both. In order to explain this I would like to briefly explore a core paradox in non-representational approaches with reference to critical engagements with Latour's concept of network. Ingold (2011) argues that Latour's network starts with monadic entities and that relationships then happen "between" them: the network model therefore fails to prioritize relationships as fundamental to reality. I think this objection is easily answered: the "dots" that Ingold thinks Latour connects with lines are actually lines (forces, practices, entities, relations) heading in other directions in the multidimensional network. We are seeing these lines head on. They consist of many interwoven relations, temporarily "black-boxed"[4] or temporarily forming what Ingold calls "inversions" of relations in which intersecting relationships are seen as distinct entities (e.g., Ingold 2011, 152). Ingold is objecting that Latour's networks seem to retain some essential identity for each entity in the network, and he infers that in Latour's model entities cannot change, only their relations. By contrast, to Harman (2009), Latour's network suggests that any entity is *fundamentally* changed every time it enters a new relationship. We can see his point: any change in the composition of an assemblage does produce a new assemblage. Harman's objection is that Latour's network is unrealistically relational: things do not change in their entirety because one or two relationships in which they are engaged change. A necklace does not cease to be a necklace if we take it off. But, Harman argues, there are some things that are not changed by the new relationships, the new configuration, and that must be *essential* to the network for us to recognize it as the same entity. At odds with Harman, I do not think these are essential to the assemblage: rather, their continued existence suggests the continuation of certain past relationships. Taking off the necklace changes its position in relation to the body, but does not alter many of the other relationships that continue to make it a necklace, such as the way the beads are connected to one another. Stripping away all the relations leaves us with nothing, rather than an essence (see Fowler & Harris, under review); stripping away some relations and leaving others illustrates only how we have transformed the assemblage.

This problem of how an instantiation relates to change and continuity is evident in all the various non-representational theories I have encountered so far. Each time we instantiate a network, assemblage, or phenomenon, it is different: a unique configuration. Yet, I would argue, many of the components, actants, intra-actions, and so on do endure in similar ways from one instantiation to the next. One assemblage bleeds into others. These "new" assemblages are not exactly the same as the previous instantiations, but *some* of their properties seem to endure from one set of relations to another. Yet, as Conneller (2011) has convincingly argued, the properties of things—of materials, even—are relative to a given interactive assemblage, and not essential to a specific substance (see Barad 2003, 2007). Indeed, a material becomes something different when the relations producing and permeating it change. Given that properties are not inherent in materials, things, ideas, etc., how can properties endure in things? I think that some relationships persist within fundamentally *dynamic assemblages* in a diachronic world. Some of the properties that emerge from an assemblage can endure when the assemblage changes if the *relationships* giving rise to those properties extend with those properties through the change (Fowler 2013, chapter 2).

Conventionally put, relationships exist in space and time. From a relational realist position, they produce space and time. But some relationships persist for longer than others and are more pervasive: for instance, the gravity of the earth or strong nuclear force. These forces and their effects are not the same everywhere, but they participate in a great many assemblages and are instantiated in similar ways in radically different configurations of materials, things, people, ideas, and so on. They may bind together many connected assemblages and keep an assemblage coherent. Forces are relational; they are influences that effect change in other parties, and to that extent they rely on the existence of such other entities. Forces are always instantiated locally: the wind on your face as you queue for the bus, the precise gravitational relationship between a falling snowflake and the ground, or the role of gravity in mathematical equations when translated as a formulated constant in physics. Some forces have a dramatic effect on the rest of the assemblage within which they emerge; others have very little effect. Yet forces can also act to keep things as they are, binding atoms together, for instance. Matter does not endure simply because it is kept "quarantined" from forces that may disrupt its form (compare with Lucas 2012, 214), though some relations may be avoided by such quarantining, but it persists precisely because of the forceful relationships between, say, atoms (and other entities) that are continually keeping it how it is. The continued existence of an assemblage stems from the repeated iteration of *some* of the relationships that pervade it even as others wane and vanish.

An alternative, and complementary, way to put this is that the continued existence of an assemblage *once any single relationship has changed* relies on the *enduring effects of past relationships* within it. These enduring effects are themselves kinds of relationships, and they set the ground for further possible relations. The Kyloe necklace stems from other assemblages, such as the people who quarried the jet, those who shaped and bored the beads, the jet, the quarry, the tools, beliefs about the efficacy of jet, the intended destination for the necklace, and so on. That assemblage changes, for example, once the necklace is given to a certain person. But the enduring effect of a past assemblage extends some aspects of it into others because of the relationships that are repeatedly iterated. The pasts of each assemblage collide and combine. The necklace perpetuates some of the relationships that comprised it, such as the friction between the tool boring the hole in the bead and the bead itself, or the relationship between jet, color, and daylight. Such daylight comes and goes, but it repeatedly interacts with the jet necklace in a similar way. The tooling marks left on the bead endure as the relationships foundational to the edge of the holes continue even after the drilling ceases: "physical" and "chemical" relations keep the edges where they are and how they are (and, of course, "social" and "cultural" relations may do so too if, for instance, the artifact is curated in a museum). Recent approaches that stress how things are materials in a process of change are vitally important (e.g., Ingold 2007), but these processes are not simply a tendency towards an inevitable and continuous entropy: they are the result of the changing relations permeating material things. The necklace is at once an effect of past assemblages, a part of past assemblages, and an extension of some features of those assemblages into many other new assemblages. Assemblages are not only relational, then. They are historical; they grow. For instance, my project involves the reanalysis of human remains, the radiocarbon dating of some of them, and the typological synthesis of the Beaker pottery from the burials. All of these elements seem necessary as part of an attempt to come to terms with the real relationships that extend throughout the phenomenon—yet paradoxically each activity makes the phenomenon larger, creating more references, more things, and more past (see Olsen 2011, 126–28; Lucas 2012, 263–64). Assemblages grow, age, stretch, and overlap.

Lucas (2012) has developed an extremely sophisticated and inspiring approach to archaeological assemblages, founded on DeLanda's non-representational approach (stemming in turn from a reading of Deleuze and Guattari). Lucas argues that archaeological assemblages are continually susceptible to materializing and dematerializing forces: they can cohere through territorialization in a specific place and through coding into a certain form, and can dissipate when they become "exposed" and lose their coherence in place or their form is "dispersed." He argues that "fleeting" assemblages including human beings produce "residue" assemblages that can be preserved or erased (e.g., in palimpsests and in stratigraphy) over time, through the action of other fleeting assemblages. The distinction between "fleeting" or "momentary" assemblages and enduring "residue" assemblages is both useful and problematic. As Olsen (2011, 108) puts it, "things are not just traces or residues of absent presents";[5] but Lucas (2012, 210–11) uses the term residue advisedly, with residues "possessing a memory of the [fleeting] assemblage itself," and each residue being the remainder of "various assemblages." Nonetheless, to say that what endures is a residue may underestimate the history, ongoing vibrancy, and efficacy of this "residue" assemblage. Furthermore, just as things endure, so do memories and ideas, though Lucas does not perceive these as residues (however, his framing of the material remains of the past as a kind of memory, following Olivier, is fertile and important). A hypothetical historical hedgerow provides an opportunity for further reflection. This hedgerow was first shaped in the medieval period and has remained in more or less the same location ever since—but it has been comprised over time of thousands of different organisms and substances, and the mix of species and the composition of the feature has changed (over) time as the hedge matured and land uses, climate, and so on changed over the centuries. Why separate the foundation of the hedgerow as an "archaeological residue" from the plants in the hedge, when the assemblage of the hedgerow as it is now has unfolded from the hedgerow as it was? The archaeological "residue" has continued to act in this assemblage, even as it is and has been changed by it. Equally, although each act in the existence of the hedgerow is fleeting, human and nonhuman involvement with it is not—it is repeated, recurrent, and recursive. The hedgerow is as much a seething mass of fleeting assemblages as it is a residue, and it becomes difficult to see where the fleeting ends and the residue begins. The hedgerow is ongoing, and as some aspects of it emerge later than others in its existence, its origins are multiple: if it is a residue, then it is the residue of many events and is continually acting. Perhaps this residual aspect could then be described as relations that persist in cohering. If our hedgerow is in part an archaeological entity, that is not all that it is: it is, as Bennett (2010) puts it, "vibrant matter," and it has affected the development of the landscape and of history. This is not to deny that some assemblages endure longer than others—the farmers who built the bank, who planted and tended the hedgerow, were outlived by it—but to point out that what is materialized repeatedly and changingly is not simply a residue of a fleeting human involvement. As a result, I will work from the position that assemblages are events, that time and assemblage are inextricable, and that assemblages bleed into one another so frequently and so finely that it is not possible to discern where one assemblage ends and another begins, nor to distinguish what is fleeting and what is residual. Instead, whereas the present is fleeting, *the past is what endures*: fleeting moments are entangled within an unfolding past.

John Robb (2004) has proposed that we understand a thing as an "extended object" composed of material characteristics and the meanings, feelings, etc., that become associated with it. Robb's extended object has a material core, a "naked skeleton, the thing itself" (ibid., 133), and its extension is "social," "emotional," and so on. Given that an assemblage (at least in a world, such as the one we know, in which human beings exist) consists of ideas, emotions, meanings, etc., what endures cannot be reduced to matter alone. Emotions, ideas, and so on may persist too. But I would go further than Robb and avoid a qualitative distinction between the material and immaterial features of an assemblage. I have adopted the concept of the extended assemblage but developed it by arguing that such an extended object does not have a material core (Fowler 2013, 57). An assemblage such as our Kyloe necklace is, or can be, extended through texts, photographs, typologies of Early Bronze Age objects, ideas about dress, theories about power and prestige, and so on. Indeed, an extended object or assemblage need not be an artifact in the classic sense: it could be an idea, a technique, a word, or a belief. We could study the relational emergence, composition, and extension of the idea of Early Bronze Age elites, for instance (ibid., 75–95). Any such entity is multiply constituted and embedded in its relations with other entities. All its features emerge and depart through chains of relations as it circulates, including its (conventionally described) "more material" aspects and including various meanings and translations, which by their nature affect the extended object in some way. In this, I suspect, my relational realist approach differs from Lucas's (2012), from symmetrical archaeologies (e.g., Shanks 2007; Webmoor 2007; Witmore 2007a, 2007b; Webmoor & Witmore 2008; Olsen 2012), and from the perspective advocating a return to "things" (e.g., Olsen 2003, 2010).

Thus, just as the actions of prehistoric people, the effects of prehistoric relationships and the legacy of prehistoric practices and technologies extended the phenomenon of the Kyloe necklace by making a cist and putting the necklace, a body (probably), and a pot within it; just as the relations that keep jet being jet are going on all the time, so our actions, technologies, ideas, and practices in the present further extend the necklace in different directions. *Any object, any assemblage, is extended by our interactions with it, just as it has been extended by past interactions.* Although we could say that these extending interactions "distribute" the object through time, space, and experience, more precisely *they shape particular configurations of time, space, and experience* (see Barad 2007, 315–16). And we ourselves, as with past people, change the object, since it is an assemblage of relational properties. When we are interacting with it, the assemblage includes us. *As a whole, and in parts, the assemblage acts by drawing yet more assemblages into itself.*[6] In interacting with it we change the phenomenon as a whole, since a change to part of it brings about a change to the whole, but such change does not extend equally and identically across the entire assemblage. We could describe assemblages as having regions, each of which is an assemblage at another scale. Assemblages and regions have no predefined boundaries: the limits of an assemblage at any moment depend on the intra-actions within it at that time. When we discover something new through engaging with an assemblage, we change the past as it exists now, but we do not change the past when it was the present. Too much of that present has become absent, too much of that region of the assemblage has been relocated, reconfigured, or ceased to be.[7] We could say that some of the present becomes absent while the past is what endures (as memories, ideas, configurations of materials, buildings, etc.). So, changing the assemblage now does not mean that the past changes in the region of the assemblage occupied by the people who lived and died around 2100 BC. In an important way, many of the relations comprising those people have left the assemblage: their present is absent and cannot be changed. But what the past is now is changed. Indeed, the past is always changing and expanding. The key point is that whereas some of the origins of the assemblage lie in things that happened over 4000 years ago, other origins lie in the nineteenth century, in 1927, and in 2011. This is one reason the narrative of discovery has such potency: the past can be changed dramatically by interventions in the present because the past is ongoing, and the present can be changed dramatically at the same time as the past unfolds in a new way.

This returns to the paradoxical issue of how an assemblage can be at once one and many. There is only "one" jet necklace that was deposited in that cist at Kyloe, Northumberland thousands of years ago, but amplified and/or reduced aspects of it can be extended through translations (e.g., photographs, drawings, and texts) to times and places in which it would otherwise be absent. Furthermore, the different configurations in which the necklace participates means that it cannot be reduced to a singular, monadic entity. It is an extended entity: many-in-one and one-in-many.[8] All of the extensions to the assemblage change it. The object, the necklace, the burial, each is a *changing* assemblage of relational properties. What does the necklace retain that allows us to identify it as a particular assemblage if it changes all the time? What it retains are many, but not all, of the relationships that comprised it five minutes, five years, five centuries, four millennia ago—millions of years ago in the case of the jet used to make the necklace. These relations are both past and ongoing. There is no essential core, but neither is an assemblage a fleeting, momentary instantiation that vanishes as soon as one relation changes. Assemblages are sticky, entangling many of the other assemblages they come into contact with. But this entanglement is variable, and assemblages can disintegrate or be torn apart. The question is, if it is possible to extend assemblages in various directions, in what ways does and should archaeological research extend assemblages?

EXTENDING ASSEMBLAGES

In my study of Early Bronze Age mortuary practices in Northeast England, I was engaged in many different assemblages. Some of them contained others, some affected others massively, some had been articulated with others for centuries or millennia, and others were only now becoming part of the assemblage. Thus, an analysis of "Early Bronze Age mortuary practices in Northeast England" becomes a study of Beaker burials, the Kirkhaugh burial, a specific radiocarbon from a certain bone, radiocarbon dating, the conceptualization of exotic objects as denoting prestige, ideas about cosmology, and so on. The assemblage can be studied at various scales, from anthropological and archaeological engagement with mortuary practices, to the influence of structural Marxist anthropology, to the precise location of a certain artifact in a grave or cist. There are no natural and preexisting limits on a phenomenon, because as we investigate where those limits may be, we extend the phenomenon further in that direction. For instance, in attempting to understand the burial at Kyloe we may draw in other cists, other vessels, and other necklaces from the local region and well beyond, bringing in the work of many other archaeologists, many other techniques and tools of discovery, recovery, curation, and analysis. Each interaction with an assemblage immediately becomes an intra-action within it, extending it in a new direction and absorbing a new participant. What makes my work different from previous work in this assemblage is simply that I am attempting to take stock of it, to configure it, in a way that has not been formulated before. Nobody has yet attempted to draw this corpus of deposits together, nor combined them with recently refined typological schemes and radiocarbon dates, nor employed ideas about relational personhood or emergent causality, nor critically assessed the specific problems with various archaeological models that have been applied to similar mortuary evidence. This does not simply involve a change in perspective or a new idea: it is work, it involves actively doing things that reconfigure the material world. It is the network that acts, that works. It involves visiting archives, examining objects and bones, sending material for specialist analysis, reading books and journal articles, and all the other things that archaeologists do in conducting research. Work is instrumental in how the net*work*, mesh*work*, or however else we frame this relationality is changed in each intra-action. That work is changeable and ongoing, and the participants involved in it have changed throughout its sporadic course. Archaeologists are drawn into relation with the assemblage through the successive ways in which it works, has worked, and can be made to work further as it is rearticulated. We can work more effectively with it in some ways than others.

This emphasis on the archaeologist and archaeological ideas and apparatuses brings us back to the old yet vital debate about subjectivity, perspective, and meaning that was such an important feature of early post-processual archaeology. How do we decide between competing interpretations? These are not just different views, I would argue, but different realities, formulating the world differently from one another.

Thus, for instance, cultural difference is a real difference, not just in beliefs, but in the way the world is configured, in the things, practices, substances and persons, and ideas and experiences in that world (see Alberti et al. 2011). In effect, to talk about cultural difference is to talk about different assemblages. But just as there good arguments for removing qualifiers like "social" and "material" (Webmoor 2007; Webmoor & Witmore 2008), so we could remove "cultural." Rather, there is difference on a local level. From this point of view I very much appreciate the position on "relational ontologies" and multiple ontologies put forwards by Ben Alberti, Yvonne Marshall, and others: there are local realities (Alberti & Marshall 2009; Alberti et al. 2011; Harris & Robb 2012). Each reality can be different: in some intra-actions, say among certain Amazonian communities, humans can be jaguars; in others they cannot. Both understandings are correct. What I would add, though, is that many features of these local worlds are shared with many other local worlds, and that assemblages change. When watched by a skeptical Western anthropologist, an Amazonian shaman does still become a jaguar, but perhaps not in the region of the assemblage occupied by the anthropologist. This is not the same thing as saying that he does not become a jaguar "to" or "for" the westerner. Reality is uneven. Thus, the statements I make here about time, the past, and relations hold from where I am situated in various assemblages (especially those concerned with archaeological engagements with the past), but cannot be taken to describe all articulations in all assemblages. We can study the different ways that time and the past were configured and reconfigured by prehistoric communities, for instance, appreciating various ways in which time, the past, and relations may operate.

But if realities are continually reconfigured and changed through research, in what directions "should" assemblages be extended by the archaeologists working with them? If the work we do changes reality locally, rather than representing it in accurate or inaccurate ways, then how do we decide which interpretations, which transformations of reality, to produce? One component to an answer is to point out that the entanglements in each assemblage have momentum, and that the historical emergence of the techniques, theories, and approaches available to us play a large part in this decision (Fowler 2013, 261). Another is to anticipate the impact, the effect of a given approach—though such effects can be very unpredictable. But non-representational approaches also provide another answer. In Latour's terms, a proposition[9] may be well articulated with respect to other aspects of the assemblage and other assemblages, or it may not. In Ingold's (2011, 162) terms, better-related stories rely on those who can "tell" them well. And in Barad's (2007, 119–20, 339) terms (following early twentieth-century physicist

Neils Bohr), our work involves "accounting for" the "marks" produced on "bodies," bodies such as the apparatus involved in specific scientific entanglements. Barad (ibid., 340) argues that "objectivity is a matter of accountability to marks on bodies. Objectivity is based not on an inherent ontological separability, a relation of absolute exteriority . . . but on an intra-actively enacted agential separability, a relation of exteriority within phenomena." In other words, we as archaeologists are within our phenomena, but we also make ourselves distinct from what we study as we engage with it, and we seek to explain the "marks" produced on the "bodies," the things we study, through our intra-actions among those things and in respect to other entities and forces in the intra-action. And this articulation, telling, or accounting requires a good description of the intra-action and its many participants; as Barad (ibid.) has it, it requires "an accounting of the apparatuses that enact determinate causal structures, boundaries, properties and meanings. Crucially, the objective referent of measured values is phenomena, not (some abstract notion of) objects."

Of course, some intra-actions are less well articulated, less effective, or less enduring than others and may leave less of a mark: all intra-actions have some effect of a distinctive kind and result in some kind of a new assemblage, but those assemblages are not equally effective everywhere. Thus, some articulations I make may change the assemblage in a convincing way in regions occupied by other Early Bronze Age specialists, but not those inhabited by some druids, say. Perhaps my account fails to take account of too many of the components of the assemblage as it is configured by and around such druids. So the assemblage is again multidimensional, extending unevenly in different directions. There are locally different ontologies at work. This is not a surrender to an extreme relativism. It matters exactly how the assemblage is configured, and my analysis requires that I pull apart some weak articulations and make strong ones that will adhere to the assemblage for some time to come. These articulations need to be *archaeologically* effective, and that requires them to have affective properties that were not there before and that can bring about changes in other assemblages.

This brings me to the value of archaeological apparatuses for engaging with entities, such as typology. Ingold (2011) is particularly concerned that we should be wary of "inversions," those presentations of intersecting relationships as reified entities. I understand why, but I think archaeologists have to work (carefully) with inversions like vessel types for several reasons. For one thing, if our accounts are to be effective they have to articulate well with inversions such as typologies given the force these have in the ongoing past of archaeological practice and discourse. For another, many inversions are "black-boxed" assemblages that share a number of relationships with other inversions of the same kind. For instance, types of Beaker pottery are inversions, such as Short-Necked Beakers or Long-Necked Beakers. As such, they take something that was contingent, unfolding, and changing—each example of which (each vessel) was a unique assemblage—and reify it as a specific category of object. This is problematic but productive. These categories have very specific temporal frames and relate closely to other features of their assemblage, such as particular modes by which the dead were buried: they articulate well with these other participants in the assemblage. Thus my analysis makes significant use of inversions whereby burials are accorded to a certain type of funerary practice, and mortuary features and monumental architecture are identified as constituting certain types at certain times in specific sequences (Fowler 2013, chapters 4–6). The goal is to examine the relations that persisted and changed as these types arose, changed, and diminished, as one type gave way to another, for instance. Typologies have survived precisely because they articulate well with other features of the past, and they are dynamic: thus Beaker typologies have been successively revised during the twentieth and early twenty-first centuries (e.g., Abercromby 1912; Clarke 1970; Lanting & van der Waals 1976; Needham 2005), repeatedly reconfiguring the relationships between one pot and others, one burial and others. Through comparison of the relations between as well as within categories of pot—and particular vessels—it is possible to suggest periods when clear, restrictive categories of practice including such vessels emerged and other times when one type of vessel was involved in a fluid and changing range of practices and categories (Fowler 2013, chapter 6). We can work with these inversions, then, but we need to appreciate their dynamic nature and look at the historical relations comprising them in doing so (as I have had to do for, say, the concepts of prestige goods or hierarchy).

THE PAST IS WHAT ENDURES

The realization that time and scale, causality, property, and effect all emerge from intra-actions within phenomena, from our engagement with past relations and their effects alongside other entities and forces, presents us with a different position with respect to the past. It does not seem right to simply say that the past exists in the present or that we write the past in the present. Rather, perhaps we live in the past, in the unfolding relations that have persisted and mutated, giving rise to us among other entities; and this past is ever-changing as we work among its other participants, continually extending and expanding the features of past assemblages that remain the most effective. New assemblages emerge and proliferate because of the efficacy and fertility of past ones, and because they produce yet more instabilities, uncertainties, and possibilities for future relations. Archaeological remains are not a distinct category of residue entities, but are entangled with the other features of the world with which they are coterminous and contemporary. The regions of the past that are "gone" do not change, but much of the past is enduring and ongoing. "The past, unfolding" seems like a good description of assemblages—archaeological assemblages, at least. Exploring and participating in such unfolding pasts offer new presents, as pasts merge and intra-act. The rearticulation of assemblages continually produces momentary presents out of these pasts; but such rearticulations do not change everything at once, and so the past endures as many of its constituent relations and their effects persist. Thus, I think that one way that non-representational approaches may be useful is in realizing that though archaeologists do study the past, we do not really study "the past in the present," nor a series of snapshot pasts layered one after the other with many "gaps" where activity was not recorded; rather, we study the past as it is unfolding through the myriad of interactions that are going on all the time, and we involve ourselves in those interactions.

While a non-representational archaeology is in some ways radical, it need not throw the baby out with the bath water. Indeed, much of what I have been describing is what we already do and extends from the foundations of post-processual archaeology: as Thrift (2008, 20) puts it, "non-representational theory is genuinely intended to be a modest supplement." If a push "after interpretation" is required, then perhaps it is because we have sometimes not been sufficiently explicit in showing the articulations involved in our work and have focused instead on the resulting narrative interpretation. Again, this is a case of showing how the assemblage is being dynamically extended, or of describing its changing relations "well" or as effectively as possible (see Borić & Strathern 2010). I am not attempting to solve the productive paradoxes I think lie within non-representational theories: I am an archaeologist and I want an approach that allows me to make sense of the past, time, change, and material media as I appreciate them from within my phenomena. I have tried to learn from non-representational theorists in doing this. But from engaging with the assemblage "Early Bronze Age mortuary practices in Northeast England" I have also learnt that engagements with the prehistoric past raise different problems and opportunities for attending to these issues than the disciplinary encounters of Latour, Barad, or Ingold. I hope that the result can offer new methodological and theoretical possibilities for archaeologists engaging with other assemblages. Indeed, attending to our archaeological assemblages takes us to places that we might not expect. When I first started studying the prehistoric burials from Northeast England, I was looking for a good case study to explore differing ways that personhood might be relational. But as I learnt more and more about the assemblage, and as I started to follow or push it off in many different directions through different techniques and studies of different objects, I realized there was more to the assemblage than that, and that in fact to focus on any one factor like personhood was to overlook some of the strongest forces in the assemblage. Since it was not only personhood that was relational, but everything else besides, I needed to extend the study of relationality across the entire endeavor. Through conversations with colleagues and students, I became inspired to read non-representational and post-humanist theory, to consider how and why it was emerging in recent archaeological publications, and to explore how it related to relational approaches with which I was already familiar, which draw on some of the same metaphors, and which I have long found inspiring (e.g., Strathern 1988; Thomas 1996). I noticed that period- and region-based synthesis, the kind of interpretation so readily adopted in post-processual archaeology, was not being subjected to the same level of methodological scrutiny as field projects or scientific analyses (Lucas 2001, 2012; Jones 2002), and that none of the archaeological approaches inspired by non-representational theories had yet published such syntheses. In the end, the book I wrote was partly a study of the process and methods of archaeological synthesis, partly a synthesis of Early Bronze Age mortuary archaeology in Northeast England, and partly an exploration of a particular theoretical approach.

I would end by reflecting that non-representational theories clearly struggle with paradoxes and contradictions just as representational theories do—it is simply that the paradoxes are different. Thus, the paradox of how an assemblage can be at once momentary and also enduring offers new possibilities for thinking about time and materiality, and particularly how archaeological remains are ongoing participants, inseparable from other assemblages in a real, relational, historical world. We need to consider the implications and effects of these contradictions and paradoxes as we feel our way along with these approaches. Personally, I think they will be productive ones, and I look forward to finding out where they can take us.

ACKNOWLEDGMENTS

Numerous conversations have contributed to the assemblage of ideas related in this chapter, and I am particularly grateful to all the participants to the "Archaeology after Interpretation" workshop and to Oscar Aldred, Rachel Crellin, Ollie Harris, Yvonne Marshall, Sophie Moore,

Louise Tolson, and Elizabeth Kramer Fowler for our discussions. I am especially grateful to Sam Turner for discussions about relational approaches to historical landscapes and the hypothetical hedgerow.

NOTES

1. A *factish* is a fabrication, but this does not make it untrue or invalid: factishes can be well made and enduring, can come apart, and can have various kinds of effects.
2. An actant is any entity or force capable of affecting any other entity or force with which it interacts. The term is Latour's (e.g., Latour 1999).
3. And again this is an *intra-action*, in that it takes place within the phenomenon of the circulating reference as it extends (through) time. Please take it as read that whenever I say interaction I mean intra-action.
4. Black-boxing refers to an inversion whereby many of the relations that comprise a phenomenon are ignored in order to appreciate a specific relationship that is fundamental to that phenomenon. I "black-box" everything going on inside my computer when I type this text. The term is Latour's (1999).
5. Olsen (2011, 108) goes on to say, in agreement with Olivier, that things "are effectively engaged in assembling and hybridizing periods and epochs." My position is at odds with the idea of different times coexisting in the present or in the same place, though I am at heart in alignment with much of the spirit of what Lucas, Olsen, Olivier, and Witmore argue about the complex relatedness of time, the past, and matter. It seems to me rather that any single relationship draws together different assemblages in the course of the past becoming. Rather than seeing pasts as percolating, or measuring pasts topologically (Witmore 2007a), I think there are different regions of an unfolding past, an unfolding, unpredictable, and open-ended assemblage in which different fleeting presents bubble away. Some of what occurs in the present reshapes some of the ongoing past, some has so little impact it effectively becomes absent, and some transform certain features of the past so utterly that these become, in effect, absent or erased.
6. At the same time assemblages proliferate, producing new assemblages, but they remain intertwined with those to some extent, at least initially.
7. But even though, say, Early Bronze Age living human beings are now missing from this assemblage, they have had an enduring impact on it, and on that basis they are not entirely absent. Their present is absent, but the legacies of their actions may endure as the past.
8. I discuss the differences between this perspective and Harman's understanding of "essence" as plurality in unity elsewhere (Fowler 2013, chapter 2).
9. A proposition is the opportunity for interaction that one actant offers to others (Latour 1999, 288). When archaeologists make an interpretation, they offer a proposition that may change reality in particular ways if it articulates effectively with other actants.

REFERENCES

Abercromby, J. 1912. *A Study of the Bronze Age Pottery of Great Britain and Ireland and Its Associated Grave Goods.* Oxford, UK: Clarendon Press
Alberti, B., Fowles, S., Holbraad, M., Marshall, Y. & Witmore, C. 2011. "Worlds otherwise": archaeology, anthropology, and ontological difference. *Current Anthropology* 52(6), 896–912
Alberti, B. & Marshall, Y. 2009. Animating archaeology: local theories and conceptually open-ended methodologies. *Cambridge Archaeological Journal* 19(3), 344–56

Barad, K. 2003. Posthumanist performativity: how matter comes to matter. *Signs: Journal of Women in Culture and Society* 28(3), 801–31

Barad, K. 2007. *Meeting the Universe Halfway: Quantum Physics and the Entanglement of Matter and Meaning*. Durham, NC: Duke University Press

Bennett, J. 2005. The agency of assemblages and the North American blackout. *Public Culture* 17(3), 445–66

Bennett, J. 2010. *Vibrant Matter: A Political Ecology of Things*. Durham, NC: Duke University Press

Borić, D. & Strathern, M. 2010. Arriving at a good description: interview with Professor Dame Marilyn Strathern. *Journal of Social Archaeology* 10, 280–96

Brewis, P. 1927. A Bronze Age cist at Kyloe, Northumberland. *Archaeologia Aeliana* (4th series) 5, 26–29

Buchanan, M. 2001. *Ubiquity: The Science of History, or Why the World Is Simpler than We Think*. London: Phoenix

Clarke, D.L. 1970. *Beaker Pottery of Great Britain and Ireland*. Cambridge: Cambridge University Press

Conneller, C. 2011. *An Archaeology of Materials: Substantial Transformations in Early Prehistoric Europe*. London: Routledge

Craw, J.H. 1929. On a jet necklace from a cist at Poltalloch, Argyll. *Proceedings of the Society of Antiquaries of Scotland* 63, 154–89

DeLanda, M. 1997. *A Thousand Years of Non-Linear History*. New York: Zone

Deleuze, G. & Guattari, F. 2004 [1980]. *A Thousand Plateaus: Capitalism and Schizophrenia*. London: Continuum

Fowler, C. 2013. *The Emergent Past: A Relational Realist Archaeology of Early Bronze Age Mortuary Practices*. Oxford: Oxford University Press

Fowler, C. & Harris, O. Under review. Enduring relations and particularisation: an archaeological engagement with relationality and materiality. *Journal of Material Culture*

Greenwell, W. 1877. *British Barrows: A Record of the Examination of Sepulchral Mounds in Various Parts of England*. Oxford, UK: Clarendon Press

Harman, G. 2009. *Prince of Networks: Bruno Latour and Metaphysics*. Melbourne, AU: Re.press

Harris, O. 2012. (Re)assembling communities. *Journal of Archaeological Method and Theory*. DOI 10.1007/s10816-012-9138-3

Harris, O. & Robb, J. 2012. Multiple ontologies and the problem of the body in history. *American Anthropologist* 114(4), 668–79

Hodder, I. 2011. Human-thing entanglement: towards an integrated archaeological perspective. *Journal of the Royal Anthropological Institute* 17, 154–77

Hodder, I. 2012. *Entangled: An Archaeology of the Relationships between Humans and Things*. Oxford, UK: Wiley-Blackwell

Ingold, T. 2007. Materials against materiality. *Archaeological Dialogues* 14(1), 1–16

Ingold, T. 2011. *Being Alive: Essays on Movement, Knowledge and Description*. London: Routledge

Jones, A.M. 2002. *Archaeological Theory and Scientific Practice*. Cambridge: Cambridge University Press

Knappett, C. 2011. *An Archaeology of Interaction: Network Perspectives on Material Culture and Society*. Oxford: Oxford University Press

Lanting, J.N. & van der Waals, J.D. 1976. Beaker culture relations in the Lower Rhine basin. In J.N. Lanting & J.D. van der Waals (eds.), *Glockenbecher Symposium. Oberried 1974*, 2–80. Haarlem, NL: Fibula-Van Dishoeck

Latour, B. 1999. *Pandora's Hope: Essays on the Reality of Science Studies*. Harvard: Harvard University Press

Latour, B. 2005. *Reassembling the Social: An Introduction to Actor-Network Theory.* Oxford: Oxford University Press

Lucas, G. 2001. *Critical Approaches to Fieldwork: Contemporary and Historical Archaeological Practice.* London: Routledge

Lucas, G. 2012. *Understanding the Archaeological Record.* Cambridge: Cambridge University Press

Marshall, Y. & Alberti, B. 2013. A matter of difference: Karen Barad, ontology and archaeological bodies. *Cambridge Archaeological Journal* 23 (forthcoming)

Needham, S. 2005. Transforming Beaker culture in north-west Europe: processes of fission and fusion. *Proceedings of the Prehistoric Society* 71, 171–217

Newman, T.G. 1976. The jet necklace from Kyloe. *Archaeologia Aeliana* (5th series) 4, 177–82

Olivier, L. 2011. *The Dark Abyss of Time: Archaeology and Memory.* Lanham, CA: AltaMira Press

Olsen, B. 2003. Material culture after text: re-membering things. *Norwegian Archaeological Review* 36(2), 87–104

Olsen, B. 2011. *In Defense of Things: Archaeology and the Ontology of Objects.* Lanham, CA: AltaMira Press

Olsen, B. 2012. Symmetrical archaeology. In I. Hodder (ed.), *Archaeological Theory Today*, 208–28. 2nd edition. Oxford, UK: Polity

Robb, J. 2004. The extended artefact and the monumental economy: a methodology for material agency. In E. DeMarrais, C. Gosden & C. Renfrew (eds.), *Rethinking Materiality: The Engagement of Mind with the Material World*, 131–39. Cambridge, UK: McDonald Institute for Archaeology

Shanks, M. 2007. Symmetrical archaeology. *World Archaeology* 39, 589–96

Spain, G. 1928. Curator's report, 1927. *Proceedings of the Society of Antiquaries of Newcastle Upon Tyne* (4th series) 3, 145

Strathern, M. 1988. *The Gender of the Gift.* Berkeley: University of California Press

Thomas, J. 1996. *Time, Culture and Identity: An Interpretive Archaeology.* London: Routledge

Thrift, N. 2008. *Non-Representational Theory: Space, Politics, Affect.* London: Routledge

Webmoor, T. 2007. What about "one more turn after the social" in archaeological reasoning? Taking things seriously. *World Archaeology* 39(4), 547–62

Webmoor, T. & Witmore, C.L. 2008. Things are us! A commentary on human/things relations under the banner of a "social" archaeology. *Norwegian Archaeological Review* 41(1), 53–70

Witmore, C. 2007a. Landscape, time, topology: an archaeological account of the Southern Argolid, Greece. In D. Hicks, L. McAtackney & G. Fairclough (eds.), *Envisioning Landscape: Situations and Standpoints in Archaeology and Heritage*, 194–225. Walnut Creek, CA: Left Coast Press

Witmore, C. 2007b. Symmetrical archaeology: excerpts from a manifesto. *World Archaeology* 39(4), 546–62

CHAPTER THIRTEEN

Assembling Bodies, Making Worlds:
An Archaeological Topology of Place

Marcus W.R. Brittain

The seeds that have instigated the course of the ideas explored in this contribution have no doubt been sown by many hands; but in reflecting upon this development there appear to be particular, or at least memorable, points of convergence. The overriding concern has been the diversity of what it means to be human, explored not from the privileged standpoint of the human as a—or "the"—knowledgeable subject, but through accounts of the complexity of life via routes that exceed the human. What has developed is not so much a compass prescribing a particular methodology, but rather an orientation intended to be equally ludic and mathetic, advocating learning through experimentation and participation without deterring from analytical precision.

What follows focuses in particular on the following proposition: the boundaries and properties of object systems essential to legitimate archaeological knowledge are mutually emergent in practices configured by material surroundings. More broadly, this questions the legitimacy of images of human knowledge as pre-given representations of life or as interventions between knowers and their world. The premise here is that multiple perspectives observe a world that is not unitary or preordained, but becomes manifest through regular intelligible patterns that emerge not through the recognition and representation of such regularities, but through repeatable circumstances of material arrangement. The aim is to understand the active connections through which objects and concepts become recognized as such and are therefore fueled with generative potency. This includes systems of knowledge through which we identify with the human and the nonhuman, animate subjects and inanimate

Archaeology after Interpretation: Returning Materials to Archaeological Theory, edited by Benjamin Alberti, Andrew Meirion Jones, and Joshua Pollard, 257–76.

objects, and so on. Materialized patterns of human causality are not disclosed independent from discursive spaces; and in turn, these are not open fields of possibilities separable from the material surroundings that, through differing arrangements of "bodies," variously determine the conceptual boundaries through which the world is experienced. Therefore, my focus here is on the integration of human practices within larger material arrangements.

Underlying these statements is the need to take ontological questions seriously, to explore new ways to appropriately articulate a "lifeworld" that is imminent and entangled. This is accomplished in the examples explored here through what I call an archaeological topology of place. Place is becoming increasingly recognized as a central philosophical theme for an understanding of the nature of being. Although "an opaque and evanescent concept" (Malpas 2012, 43), place may be experienced with apparent clarity. This juxtaposition leaves place vulnerable to articulation independent from the nature of being, and yet each emerges in conjunction with the other; only shadowless bodies are devoid of place. A topological approach to place steers towards this connectedness, advancing a concern with place as a simultaneous concern with the issues at stake, as a topic (*topos*) of discussion, and as a critical engagement with the commonplace (*topoi*) of norms. Moreover, topology may be a study of connectedness in space; in mathematics this may concern properties that are preserved under conditions of continuous deformation caused by stretching and bending. The significance of these themes to archaeology will hopefully become apparent through examples drawn from ongoing research into preliterate notions of and engagements with place and architecture in both Ethiopia and Wales. Here attention is paid to assemblies of diverse "bodies" into novel spatial arrangements that constitute a "cut" between the known world and knowledgeable subjects, whereby the boundaries of normative concepts may be affirmed or realigned. Whereas on the surface these may appear as incomparable data sets, the binding attention to place and architecture, and at times the simultaneous engagement with both contexts, has led to an intersection of methodological and interpretative strategies and thereby their coevolution. Moreover, as Souvatzi (2012) has recently suggested, the combination of archaeological, ethnographic, and historiographic analyses is beneficial to studies into place, architecture, and space.

The ways in which we think and write about systems of knowledge has lasting effect upon the ways in which we live with one another and tend to the world. I argue here that a topology of place contributes toward a form of archaeology that accepts responsibility for the consequences of what is said and done, whether foreseen or unintended, for which we must be held to account (Brittain 2008). Henceforth, in taking these statements seriously, this contribution considers the possibilities of a narrative emerging from an accountable or standpoint archaeology that is practice-centered and attuned to an understanding that is equally situated and emergent.

THE ARCHAEOLOGY OF PLACE

Attention to "place" as a growing tradition within archaeological discourse has become increasingly recognized since Lewis Binford (1982) first approached place as a neutral space activated by cultural forces into archaeological material data. With insights from humanist geography, this was elaborated into an acknowledgment of place as socially meaningful, whereby spaces could become "colonized" by human values (Evans 1985; Chapman 1988, 1997, 1998). Importantly, this perspective highlights the imbalances of social hierarchies and tensions of power embedded within places (Thomas 1993a; Tringham 1994), thereby identifying the latter as dynamic and changeable systems. However, as Julian Thomas (1993b, 1996) has argued with regards to broader notions of landscape, if this implies a form of locality production, it is one that is envisaged as a one-way social construct actively imposed upon landscape while disconnecting landscape from experience. The cause of this, Thomas has argued, lies within underlying dualities, particularly the ones separating the mind from the body and the subject from its object, which lead to a conception of an exterior reality that is presented to human beings as an image or representation via the medium of the human body. Similar concerns have been raised about the ways in which place is conceived in understandings of the past as well as in contemporary policy-making affecting the social values inscribed upon particular heritage sites or landscapes (Shackel & Chambers 2004; Agha 2008; Ruberton 2008; Schofield & Szymanski 2010).

The archaeology of place is a diverse field, but there are commonalities in what is otherwise a varied debate. First, places are regarded as significant, and as loci in which not only events occur, but in which memories are also formed or reawakened, and experiences unfold and correspond between participants, simultaneously binding and parting bodies. Second, places are increasingly recognized for their multisensory qualities (Cummings 2002; Mills 2005; Scarre 2006; Boivin et al. 2007; Hamilakis 2011; Tringham 2012), evoking a field of emotional response (Harris 2009). Third, "self" and place are considered to be bound together through spatiotemporal pathways comprising the course of individual lives, memories of other places, and the presence or absence of multiple past, present, and future interpretive trajectories (Barrett 1994, 74–76). And whereas the interactive locality of place is dynamic and mobile, places are situated against the background of a meaningful landscape that in turn is composed of a topography of other significant places that are equally relational and entwined (Tilley 1994, 1999; Thomas 2001, 2008). Therefore, and this is the fourth point of commonality, landscape and place are indelibly connected, and any change in the landscape institutes a fundamental change in the way that places present themselves as meaningful. And so, by implication, landscapes are reconfigured upon each encounter of place.

Each of these four common viewpoints, though often pertaining to a broader landscape perspective, provides an important footing upon which to build nuanced understandings of the past and present values adhered to particular places and the affects that these return upon individual and group experience. However, these notions also present a considerable challenge concerning scales of analysis, particularly arising from the inter-relational connectivity of places to broader landscapes and the issues that this entails for reconciling the local and the global. There is a propensity, for example, to reduce smaller units of analysis such as architecture into a node within a landscape (McFadyen 2008), a local "arena" through which the "global" may be momentarily represented, but with little effectual impact otherwise. This argument may be applied to an even finer scale of analysis: for example, the bodies of substances that comprise the matrix of architectural form. These are the elements of physical structure utilized in the production of architecture, but more importantly they also provide a complex framework for place-making through the entangled processes and chains of social networks that enable their assembly. Whereas viewing landscape as composed of a topography of places enables a view into the pathways through which they are conjoined, a topology of place visualizes the assembly points at which pathways and bodies meet.

ASSEMBLIES

The architectures explored here are primarily composed of stone, although the traces of numerous other less durable materials suggest a complexity of mixing that may be difficult to reconstruct today. Nonetheless, the character of these locations and a consideration of the ways in which traditional schemes of analysis might be used to understand them is instructive for a broader discussion of a topology of place.

FORM AND FORMATION

To begin with, consider the form and material structure of the following sites. The first one is an Early Bronze Age (c. 2000–1500 BC) earthen barrow excavated in the first half of the twentieth century at Crick in

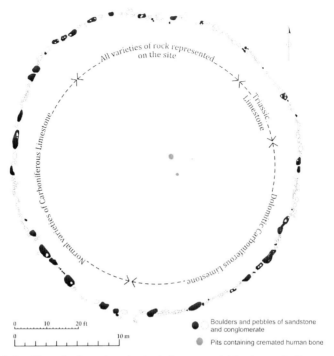

Figure 13.1 Plan of selected geological elements within the encircling stone ring of Crick barrow

Monmouthshire (Savory 1940). This was encircled by an arrangement of stones either positioned upright within tightly cut sockets or laid somewhat disorderly upon the ground surface (see Figure 13.1). Of these stones, nine different geological types were identified as originating from four separate sources, and their positioning around the barrow appeared to broadly correspond with the direction of those locations, effectively creating an axial geological "map" of the nearby landscape (North 1940). Similar observations could be made for a stone cairn at Simondston, near Bridgend, in which local sandstone was used for the majority of the cairn's body, but four additional geological types were also selected from a river tributary several miles away (ibid.).

Compare these with the stone platforms found in the Mursi lands of the Lower Omo Valley, in southwest Ethiopia (see Figure 13.2). The twenty-five platforms, named *benna kulugto* by local Mursi inhabitants, are distributed around an elevated volcanic spur leading from the Arichukgirong ridge, which dominates an otherwise flat valley cut by small and seasonally watered streambeds. Provisionally dated to the first half of the eighteenth century AD, excavation has shown the benna kulugto to be visually enigmatic and unique in form, ranging in diameter

Figure 13.2 Plan and photograph of an exposed and half-cleaned *benna kulugto* platform at Dirikoro

from 2 to 25 meters, and composed of a concentric arrangement of stones on the ground surface interrupted by a "gulley" (either left open or filled with a line of stones), consistently oriented to the northwest from the center of each platform (Clack & Brittain 2010). The size, shape, color, and geology of the stones vary within each platform, with occasional groupings of stone types along individual concentric alignments. As with the examples from Wales, the location of the originating stone sources from the benna kulugto is also diverse.

There is a growing literature revealing detailed knowledge of mineral properties throughout past societies, in which attention to qualities such as texture, color, or place of origin may have been significant (e.g., Owoc 2001, 2005; Boivin & Owoc 2004; O'Connor et al. 2009; Scarre et al. 2011). For example, in Early Bronze Age Wales there are a number of instances in which the placement of earth and stone burial mounds may correspond to particular soil or geological types not necessarily favored for their resource potential (Grimes 1945). These "subterranean landscapes" (Owoc 2000, 129) may be observed at Letterston in Pembrokeshire, where an earthen barrow was located directly above the underlying convergence of yellow and blue clays (Savory 1949, 69). Similarly, Twyn Bryn Glas cairn in Breconshire was situated upon a geological junction between Carboniferous Limestone and Old Red Sandstone (Webley 1960, 56), and Marlborough Grange barrow rested above a distinct geological fault (Savory 1969). Elsewhere the A/B horizons beneath these burial mounds have been stripped to reveal the subterranean landscape, or various imported clays have been laid upon the ground surface, effectively transporting a subterranean landscape into a new location.

Complex knowledge of geology is evident in a different form at Crick and Simondston barrows, where in addition to the selected stone for the encircling ring, other "bodies" were incorporated in varying ways, including, among other things, imported soils and clays, crafted items, and human and animal skeletal remains, much of which had been transported over considerable distances and often with expansive life histories of their own (Brittain 2006, 2007). The selected inclusion of differing clays and soils is also a characteristic of the benna kulugto in the Lower Omo Valley, along with animal bones, often of lower limbs with notable signs of fire damage, clay and stone crafted items, and high phosphate signatures perhaps indicative of the spreading of bodily fluids such as the blood or stomach contents of sacrificed livestock (Clack & Brittain 2011a).

In each of these examples, the included substances are not integral to the architectural structure, and along with their diverse depositional repertoire they are not easily accommodated into analytical categories, particularly as many do not fall into the traditional frame of material culture. It is possible that these inclusions may be explained as symbolic referents or metaphors for drawing upon absent presences within the performative activities carried out in these locations. A number of interesting narratives may be explored by these means, but such narratives need not begin with these premises, even if the outcome errs into this frame of analysis. For example, recent discussions concerning European prehistoric architecture have foregrounded the building process rather than the product of its constituent parts, providing an entry into alternative ways of conceiving of differing or even competing social elements that are manifest in engagements with architecture and place (e.g., Evans 1988a, 1988b; Turnbull 1993, 2002; Brittain 2002, 2004; Richards 2004; Watson 2004; McFadyen 2006, 2007, 2008; Bender et al. 2007). These highlight the complex networks of labor and materials that are coordinated in the processes of construction and argue that rigid classificatory schemes are often inadequate for documenting the heterogeneous forms and practices that emerge over time. In some cases the causality of authorship and design is altogether rejected in favor of ongoing "projects." Importantly, three main themes may be drawn from these approaches. First, architectures are formed by combinations of materials and networks of practice. Second, construction is a dynamic process of formation. The artist Paul Klee (1961, 169) neatly expressed this sense of emergence when he stated that "formation determines form. . . . Thus form may never be regarded as solution, result, end, but should be regarded as genesis, growth, essence." Third, practice is not something that takes place only when architecture is complete, for architecture is not a container or a surface within or upon which bodies perform social strategies; practice is ongoing before, during, and after the rhythms of construction, whereas architecture is momentary and fluid.

An important framework from which a topology of place may be more fully explored can be found in a merger of these three points within the notion of *assembly*. Recently, various geographies of translocal spaces have turned to "assemblage" as a node for examining heterogeneity (Whatmore 2002; Marcus & Saka 2006; McFarlane 2009). For the purposes of the examples outlined above, the use of assembly seems an appropriate starting point given the variety and combination of what may be referred to henceforth as "bodies." The use of this term for what has hitherto been labeled here as substances is an important departure from an otherwise preordained definition of what constitutes an object and a predetermined distinction between objects and between an object and its surroundings. Here I am drawing in particular from the work of Joseph Rouse (2002, 235–49), who states that bodies are not simply objects but are "patterns in the world," made intelligible through their practical capacities to coordinate an appropriate response to their material surroundings. Self and surroundings therefore do not have preformed rigid boundaries, but rather boundaries that are emergent and open to shifts and realignments. Bodies and surroundings are mutually constituted within what Rouse refers to as "intra-actions."[1] Perspectives of these boundaries that arise from intra-actions are marks of "an active interplay between the exploratory capacities of a habituated body and the surroundings that solicit, accommodate, and resist its explorations" (ibid., 253). Perspectives are therefore dynamic "practical configurations of the surrounding world as fields of significant possible activity," rather than inherent properties belonging to bodies or subjects (ibid., 254). Different bodies therefore are an outcome of differing "configurations of their surroundings as a field of possible activity" rather than detached sovereign perspectives (ibid., 253). Assemblies of diverse bodies within a single location alter the surroundings and enable the possibility for a powerful generative potency. Human practices are of course integral to this generative potency, but only inasmuch as they are situated within larger material arrangements. Indeed, who or what is an agent is dependent upon the emergence of a body as responsive to the locally situated possibilities for intra-acting with a surrounding environment. Rouse (2004, 146) refers to this intra-active totality as a phenomenon that can be simply defined as "a reproducible local material arrangement." This is an important term for expressing the interconnectedness of different phenomena between places, and I will explore it further below. What is important here, as Bruno Latour (2005) acknowledges, is that within the assembling of bodies into material arrangements, and through the emergence of perspectives on the world within localized surroundings, social norms are at stake as a common issue held by all participants irrespective of their differing perspectives. Assemblies are therefore implemented and sustained only through practical and hermeneutic labor.

PARTICIPANT SPACES

A return once again to the Lower Omo Valley provides a context through which the practical and hermeneutic labor invested into assemblies may be observed. The focus here is on the land of the Bodi (Fukui 2001), another agripastoral group and the tribal neighbors of the Mursi, where a rich tradition of past and present stone platform construction that is in many ways similar to the benna kulugto is steadily coming into light (see Clack & Brittain 2011a). Today, various enclosed Bodi settlements contain a stone platform, named *kôroch*, beneath a sacred tree inside a compound. Each kôroch is directly connected with an individual priest (*komorut*), who may activate the kôroch when acting in combination with other community members under particular circumstances to generate a beneficial outcome important to individual and group well-being. At any other time the kôroch is actively avoided, and the vegetation is allowed to overgrow until its use is once again required, at which point it is cleared and exposed. The activation of the kôroch necessitates a complex blend of practices and the assembly of bodies unique to the circumstances and persons for which the ceremony has been initiated. These are often chosen from a vast range of soils, clays, stones, milk, blood, and ivory and cowskin objects. Briefly summarized, the komorut requests that participants bring to the kôroch three or more stones of precise color, shape, and size, and perhaps from a specific source or type of location. The appropriateness of these stones and other bodies is carefully adjudged, often requiring numerous additional sourcing attempts and interpretation by the participants. Once stones meeting the required standards have been presented to the komorut, they are added to the kôroch platform alongside the stones that had been placed for the administering of previous ceremonies, thereby adding to the shape and size of the platform. At different stages of the ceremony particular cows are selected for either private or public sacrifice, again meeting the requirements of appropriate color, shape, and size. Once the final public sacrifice has been administered, stomach contents and blood are smeared over the stones of the kôroch and the bare flesh of the komorut, and the cow's head is set within the branches of the sacred tree alongside the severed heads of previously sacrificed cows (see Figure 13.3).

The success of the ceremony is contingent upon the assembly into a single location of bodies appropriate to the requirements of the desired outcome. In a traditional narrative these could be regarded as an aggregation of symbolic devices in which, for example, color provides a register of one's position in the ceremony and the broader community (Fukui 1977), and presents an additional mediation between the world and the cosmos. This remains a valid narrative, but only to the degree that color is a part, for instance, of cattle classificatory systems, and that its appropriateness to a specific issue at stake is contingent upon

Figure 13.3   Severed cow heads set within a sacred tree next to a Bodi *kôroch* platform

a local material arrangement. In other words, the assembly deemed appropriate for the success of the ceremony is negotiated on account of the surroundings against which bodies are to be assembled *as well as* the availability of material signifiers. Likewise, bodies only display object properties and boundaries within the surroundings of the assembly, and these properties and boundaries are only defined "by the marks they can make upon another component of a phenomenon" (Rouse 2002, 275). But it is the totality of intra-action that both constitutes and is constituted by the situated character of the participants as either interior or exterior to certain aspects or the entirety of the ceremonial practice (see Barad 2007, 181). Arguably, therefore, participants are never truly absent from phenomena, but only differentially situated with respect to them (Rouse 2009, 205).

A further point of clarity is necessary here: the ceremony, or any other event, is not a phenomenon. Rather, the Bodi ceremony, as enabled by the local specificities of the material arrangement, embodies an open-ended pattern of actual and possible events or outcomes that constitute a phenomenon. This means that the limits of a phenomenon—of an intra-action constituting a reproducible local material arrangement—is not set within the limits of the ceremony, but is mobile and effectual upon other phenomena. For example, the scale and form of the kôroch grows as novel assemblies are manifested over time, and these material arrangements have an impact on the possibilities for future assemblies. Moreover, individual kôroch are generative only during the life of the komorut priest, upon whose death their potency and uses dissipate. Nonetheless, the physical and conceptual outcomes of the ceremonies, combined with the passing of the komorut into oral traditions, all contribute towards the reconfiguration of normative practical engagement with the world. Place-making is indeed world-making.

GENERATIVE LOCALES

The crux of each of the three examples presented here is that a place, when viewed topologically as an assembly point or *contact zone*, is relational and dynamic in its own right, not "merely" through the result of implemented and strategic discourse (Rouse 2002, 271–93; 2004, 2009; Barad 2007; Woodward 2010; Woodward et al. 2010). The example of the kôroch is instructive, not only because it provides a useful nearby comparison for the older, and perhaps precursor benna kulugto platforms within the region, but also because it illustrates the relational properties of place as an assemblage undergoing an episodic process of physical and conceptual emergence. Ultimately, what the assembly of diverse bodies into a single location enables is the manifestation of novel and potent phenomena. Although the outcome may be the endorsement of a world that is known and familiar, this is nonetheless the ontological product of a subtle realignment, mixing, and adjustment—a complex social consensus.

The impact of these local assemblies and intra-actions stretches beyond the locality of place, outlining the dynamism of place into which different scales of practice are brought together (Amin 2004; Whitridge 2004). An example of this may again be found in the benna kulugto and their positioning within contemporary Mursi place-making. Mursi communities live through agripastoral subsistence strategies, with an inherent mobility across seasonal landscape resources. Traditionally the Mursi sense of place, David Turton (2005) has argued, is that of a moving frontier that is continuous and never complete—what Mursi refer to as "always in search of a cool place." This moveable frontier entered an area called Dirikoro in which the benna kulugto have been investigated. Oral tradition claims that Bodi communities once inhabited this landscape until several hundred years ago, when the Mursi entered and drove them away to northerly lands (Clack & Brittain 2010). The excavation of benna kulugto platforms within this area has raised a number of issues for the local Mursi communities; of particular interest here is what may be regarded as a merger of assemblies old and new.

The name *Dirikoro* refers to the distinct black alluvial soil that characterizes this small location, and which is locally significant for its qualities of strength and spiritual potency that may be activated through the guidance of a priest (*komoro*) in the appropriate assembly with other bodies. As has been outlined elsewhere (Clack & Brittain 2011b), Dirikoro is deeply embedded within the oral traditions of local Mursi occupants. A particular tree (*ragai*) valued as sacred for its protective shade may be found throughout the Mursi territory, but in Dirikoro one ragai tree is of particular importance to oral traditions as the only tree found in the landscape upon the arrival of the first Mursi settlers. The tree is a facilitator of history and origins, and continues to be used today for public meetings, initiations, and sacrifices. Its location among the primary cluster of buried benna kulugto is perhaps no coincidence (see Figure 13.4), although the number and nature of the benna kulugto in this area of Dirikoro was unknown to local Mursi. Nonetheless, upon the first exposures of the benna kulugto during the first season of fieldwork explanation of their concentric form, the interrupting gulley, the assemblies of deposited material culture, and their past use were ably configured within the preexisting oral narrative: benna kulugto were Bodi house units raised from the ground during a period of wet climate, and for which the gulley "drains" were also required.

Figure 13.4 A *benna kulugto* platform at Dirikoro in the foreground of the Mursi sacred *ragai* tree

However, one year later the narrative had begun to change, and new questions were increasingly raised as additional benna kulugto were exposed: Could these now be open-air "sleeping platforms," again protecting the occupant from wet ground? More recently, the discovery of a huge platform in excess of 25 meters of diameter has further problematized the alignment of benna kulugto into Mursi oral traditions. Social consensus has begun to sway, but the idea persists that for considerable time Dirikoro has in some way remained special and unique, and is one of only a few places that provide recognized, tangible links between the past and the present.

There are two important points that arise from this exposition. First, the Mursi sense of place forms an essential part of what it means *to be* Mursi. At present this aspect is being increasingly challenged by competing notions of place through the development projects and conservationist outlook espoused by two national parks adjacent to and partly within Mursi territory (Turton 2011). Likewise, encroachment of multinational corporate industry along with ethno- and eco-tourism, underscored by erroneous notions of primitive wilderness, provide additional surroundings with which the Mursi sense of place must engage. Increasing understanding of the benna kulugto provides a legitimate counterargument to notions of wilderness via both Mursi and archaeological perspectives (Brittain & Clack 2012). Significantly, differing senses of place have arisen from specific and historically situated phenomena that by and large maintain their properties in spite of concerted stretching and bending through intra-action. These are not measurable properties: the limits of place are indefinable since phenomena make an impact on other phenomena across time and space. It is not place as such that is mobile, but rather the phenomena in which the potency of place is generated, and this mobility may be more suitably expressed as a vibration (Deleuze 1993, 86–94) that is generated through intra-actions.

This leads to the second point I'd like to stress: archaeology is also inseparable from the intra-action of "place-making" and the mobility of phenomena. The final section briefly outlines this connectivity and the situated foundation of archaeological practice within the assembling of bodies and the mobility of phenomena.

PROPINQUITY OF PLACE

As assembly points, the benna kulugto bring together bodies that both configure and are configured by their surroundings. Different knowledge systems pertaining to objects are configured by the local arrangement of these bodies and are emergent as situated perspectives within intra-action. The platforms effectively present a common issue through which differing Mursi and archaeological knowledge systems meet, positioning perspectives in the company of one another, thereby shaping fields of possible action (Clack & Brittain 2011b; Brittain & Clack 2012). It is an obvious point therefore, and yet one that often passes unacknowledged, that archaeology engages in processes of place-making. Acceptance that phenomena vibrate through other phenomena reveals place as the point at which "the global is constituted, invented, co-ordinated, produced" (Massey 2004, 11). Place-making may therefore be considered also as world-making, and this is a powerful responsibility archaeology must be held accountable for.

The apparatus through which narratives of the past unfold are implicated within the process of place-making. For example, during the 1970s and 1980s new typological schemes devised for Bronze Age funerary monuments in Wales enabled rescue and conservation programs to document and subsequently mitigate the threats posed to archaeological sites by natural and human agencies (see Figure 13.5). Field survey benefited from an object system that provided balance to established artifact typologies. Integral to a sense of intellectual order, these also provided the basis for the identification and presentation of a distinct Welsh heritage and character, against which claims for the significance of individual places could be legitimized (Brittain 2007; 2008, 210–15).

Classificatory schemes continue to serve as a representation of regularities in the patterns generated by social behavior that are attributable

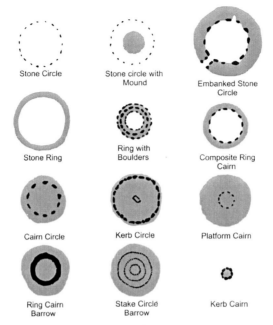

Figure 13.5 A typology of Bronze Age funerary monuments in Wales

to particular type forms. Without denying the value of ordering devices in archaeology, this chapter has raised the concern that their foundations are promissory of conceptual norms and are therefore problematic for understanding the ontological basis and the generative potency of object representations. A brief consideration of the way in which regularities are disclosed through analytical practice may serve to elucidate the connectivity of archaeology with place-making.

Archaeological ordering devices presuppose that their objects have definite and preformed boundaries. In a textual narrative these might be thought of as representations of patterns of meaningful activity, open to interpretative possibilities that are accountable to sovereign standards of measurement. But the reality is that discursive space is not an open field of possibilities and does not lie independent from materialized patterns of dialogue. Instead, the interpretation of regular patterns of material arrangement may be understood as a measurement enabled and constrained by its relation to the surroundings. Objects within these patterns therefore show up as bounded and with determinate capacities because of the marks that they are able to trace upon other bodies assembled within their locality. Measurement is therefore a materially configured intra-action, and the patterns identifiable by measurement are themselves within the intra-action, not external to it through the descriptive representation of a regularity (Rouse 2002, 280). For example, there is clear and consistent repetition in the form of benna kulugto at Dirikoro, in spite of their differing locations or varying sizes. But as the example of the Bodi kôroch has illustrated, form is emergent through the process of assembly that is contingent upon a given necessary outcome. On this basis, a topological narrative is accountable not to the repetition of patterns, but to the objects' capacity for repeatability that is embedded within the circumstances of the intra-action and the issues at stake.

CONCLUSION

In its various articulations, place is gradually becoming a central concept within archaeology. This is a welcome development: notions of place are integral to the complex diversity of life, and archaeology is deeply embedded within processes of place-making and, by virtue of the connectedness of places, world-making. Such responsibility demands that as archaeologists we are held to account for the consequences of our statements that may have real, even if not imminent, cost. This requires a serious consideration of the ontological basis of object systems in general, which, in the context of place, has benefited from the language of assembly and the intra-action of bodies within material surroundings. This chapter has attempted to illustrate the value of such a language for the articulation of an archaeological topology of place that is concerned with the connectivity of intelligible material patterns, the emergent and mobile nature of conceptual boundaries in conjunction with a normative understanding of the world, and the issue of who or what is an "agent" within situated practices. Ultimately, explanation of the world emerges in the form of a situated commentary seemingly unscathed through participative engagement with a material world.

ACKNOWLEDGMENTS

Many thanks are offered to Andy, Ben, and Josh for their invitation to contribute to the "After Interpretation" workshop and subsequent volume, and their forbearance during the completion of this article is gratefully acknowledged. Many of the ideas presented here concerning place and accountability in archaeology, particularly in relation to the examples drawn from Wales, were developed during Master's and PhD research at the University of Manchester, under the financial support of the Arts and Humanities Research Council. Ongoing fieldwork in the Lower Omo Valley is carried out in collaboration with Timothy Clack of St. Peter's College, Oxford: our countless long and fruitful discussions concerning Mursi and Bodi place-making have undoubtedly fertilized a number of the issues explored here. The project has benefited from grants from Oxford and Cambridge Universities, the British Academy, the British Institute in East Africa, and the Christensen Fund. Any oversights or errors of fact are the author's own.

NOTE

1. Rouse admits to a heavy reliance here upon the work of Karen Barad, and a parallel reading of Barad (2007) and Rouse (2002, 2004) is recommended.

REFERENCES

Agha, A. 2008. Place, place-making, and African-American archaeology: considerations for future work. *South Carolina Antiquities* 38(1–2), 53–66

Amin, A. 2004. Regions unbound: towards a new politics of place. *Geografiska Annaler* 86B(1), 33–44

Barad, K. 2007. *Meeting the Universe Halfway: Quantum Physics and the Entanglement of Matter and Meaning.* Durham, NC: Duke University Press

Barrett, J. 1994. *Fragments from Antiquity: An Archaeology of Social Life in Britain, 2900–1200 BC.* Oxford, UK: Blackwell

Bender, B., Hamilton, S. & Tilley, C. 2007. *Stone Worlds: Narrative and Reflexivity in Landscape Archaeology.* Walnut Creek, CA: Left Coast Press

Binford, L. 1982. The archaeology of place. *Journal of Anthropological Archaeology* 1, 5–31

Boivin, N., Brumm, A., Lewis, H., Robinson, D. & Korisettar, R. 2007. Sensual, material, and technological understanding: exploring prehistoric soundscapes in south India. *Journal of the Royal Anthropological Institute* 13(2), 267–94

Boivin, N. & Owoc, M. (eds.) 2004. *Soils, Stones and Symbols: Cultural Perceptions of the Mineral World.* London: UCL Press

Brittain, M. 2002. Traditions of substance: form versus formation in the monumentality of Early Bronze Age Wales. At http://humanitieslab.stanford.edu/ArchaeologyPerformance/19

Brittain, M. 2004. Layers of life and death: aspects of monumentality in the Early Bronze Age of Wales. In V. Cummings & C. Fowler (eds.), *The Neolithic of the Irish Sea: Materiality and Traditions of Practice*, 224–32. Oxford, UK: Oxbow Books

Brittain, M. 2006. Technologies of disclosure: posthuman practices and cremation in Neolithic and Early Bronze Age Wales. *Archaeological Review from Cambridge* 21(1), 76–97

Brittain, M. 2007. Do barrows matter? Politics and production of the Early Bronze Age in Wales. In J. Last (ed.), *Beyond the Grave: New Perspectives on Barrows*, 140–55. Oxford, UK: Oxbow Books

Brittain, M. 2008. *Accountability and Sociopolitics of Prehistoric Wales: With a Focus on Bronze Age Monumentality.* Unpublished PhD thesis, Department of Art, History and Archaeology, University of Manchester

Brittain, M. & Clack, T. 2012. Pristine wilderness, participatory archaeology, and the custodianship of heritage in Mursiland. In L. Mol & T. Sternberg (eds.), *Changing Deserts: Integrating People and Their Environment*, 192–212. Cambridge, UK: The White Horse Press

Chapman, J. 1988. From "space" to "place": a model of dispersed settlement and Neolithic society. In C. Burgess, P. Topping & D. Mordant (eds.), *Enclosures and Defences in the Neolithic of Western Europe*, 21–46. Oxford: British Archaeological Reports, International Series 403

Chapman, J. 1997. Places as timemarks: the social construction of prehistoric landscapes in Eastern Hungary. In J. Chapman & P. Dolukhanov (eds.), *Landscapes in Flux: Central and Eastern Europe in Antiquity*, 137–61. Oxford, UK: Oxbow Books

Chapman, J. 1998. Objectification, embodiment and the value of places and things. In D. Bailey & S. Mills (eds.), *The Archaeology of Value: Essays on Prestige and the Process of Valuation*, 106–30. Oxford: British Archaeological Reports, International Series 730

Clack, T. & Brittain, M. 2010. Excavations and surveys in Mursiland, S.W. Ethiopia, May–July 2009: a preliminary fieldwork report. *Nyame Akuma* 73, 65–76

Clack, T. & Brittain, M. 2011a. When climate changes: megaliths, migrations, and medicines in Mursiland. *Current World Archaeology* 46, 32–39

Clack, T. & Brittain, M. 2011b. Place-making, participative archaeologies and Mursi megaliths: some implications for aspects of pre- and proto-history in the Horn of Africa. *Journal of East African Studies* 5(1), 85–107

Cummings, V. 2002. Experiencing texture and transformation in the British Neolithic. *Oxford Journal of Archaeology* 21(3), 249–61

Deleuze, G. 1993. *The Fold: Leibniz and the Baroque*. Translated by T. Conley. London: The Athlone Press

Evans, C. 1985. Tradition and the cultural landscape: an archaeology of place. *Archaeological Review from Cambridge* 4(1), 80–94

Evans, C. 1988a. Monuments and analogy: the interpretation of causewayed enclosures. In C. Burgess & P. Topping (eds.), *Enclosures and Defences in the Neolithic of Western Europe*, 47–73. Oxford: British Archaeological Reports, International Series 403

Evans, C. 1988b. Acts of enclosure: a consideration of concentrically-organised causewayed enclosures. In J. Barrett & I. Kinnes (eds.), *The Archaeology of Context in the Neolithic and Bronze Age: Recent Trends*, 85–96. Sheffield, UK: University of Sheffield

Fukui, K. 1977. Cattle colour symbolism and inter-tribal homicide among the Bodi. In K. Fukui & D. Turton (eds.), *Warfare among East African Herders*, 147–78. Osaka, JP: National Museum of Ethnology, Senri Ethnological Studies 3

Fukui, K. 2001. Socio-political characteristics of pastoral nomadism: flexibility among the Bodi (Mela-Me'en) in Southwest Ethiopia. *Nilo-Ethiopian Studies* 7, 1–21

Grimes, W.F. 1945. Early man and the soils of Anglesey. *Antiquity* 19, 169–74

Hamilakis, Y. 2011. Archaeologies of the senses. In T. Insoll (ed.), *The Oxford Handbook of the Archaeology of Ritual and Religion*, 208–25. Oxford: Oxford University Press

Harris, O. 2009. Making places matter in Early Neolithic Dorset. *Oxford Journal of Archaeology* 28(2), 111–23

Klee, P. 1961. *The Thinking Eye*. Edited by J. Spiller, translated by R. Manheim. New York: George Wittenborn Inc.

Latour, B. 2005. From realpolitik to dingpolitik: or how to make things public. In B. Latour & P. Weibel (eds.), *Making Things Public: Atmospheres of Democracy*, 14–41. Cambridge, MA & London: MIT Press

Malpas, J. 2012. *Heidegger and the Thinking of Place: Explorations in the Topology of Being*. Cambridge, MA & London: MIT Press

Marcus, G. & Saka, E. 2006. Assemblage. *Theory, Culture & Society* 23, 101–9

Massey, D. 2004. Geographies of responsibility. *Geografiska Annaler* 86B, 5–18

McFadyen, L. 2006. Building technologies, quick and slow architectures and Early Neolithic long barrow sites in Southern Britain. *Archaeological Review from Cambridge* 21(1), 115–34

McFadyen, L. 2007. Neolithic architecture and participation: practices of making at long barrow sites in Southern Britain. In J. Last (ed.), *Beyond the Grave: New Perspectives on Barrows*, 22–29. Oxford, UK: Oxbow Books

McFadyen, L. 2008. Building and architecture as landscape practice. In B. David & J. Thomas (eds.), *Handbook of Landscape Archaeology*, 308–14. Walnut Creek, CA: Left Coast Press

McFarlane, C. 2009. Translocal assemblages: space, power and social movements. *Geoforum* 40, 561–67

Mills, S. 2005. Sensing the place: sounds and landscape. In D. Bailey, A. Whittle & V. Cummings (eds.), *(Un)settling the Neolithic*, 79–89. Oxford, UK: Oxbow Books

North, F. 1940. A geologist amongst the cairns. *Antiquity* 14, 377–94

O'Connor, B., Cooney, G. & Chapman, J. (eds.) 2009. *Materialitas: Working Stone, Carving Identity*. Oxford, UK: Oxbow Books

Owoc, M. 2000. *Aspects of Ceremonial Burial in the Bronze Age of Southwest Britain*. Unpublished PhD thesis, Department of Archaeology and Prehistory, University of Sheffield

Owoc, M. 2001. The times they are a changin': experiencing continuity and development in the Early Bronze Age funerary rituals of southwestern Britain. In J. Brück (ed.), *Bronze Age Landscapes: Tradition and Transformation*, 193–206. Oxford, UK: Oxbow Books

Owoc, M. 2005. From the ground up: agency, practice, and community in the southwestern British Bronze Age. *Journal of Archaeological Method and Theory* 12(4), 257–81

Richards, C. 2004. A choreography of construction: Monuments, mobilization and social organization in Neolithic Orkney. In J. Cherry, C. Scarre & S. Shennan (eds.), *Explaining Social Change: Studies in Honour of Colin Renfrew*, 103–13. Cambridge, UK: McDonald Institute for Archaeological Research

Rouse, J. 2002. *How Scientific Practices Matter: Reclaiming Philosophical Naturalism*. Chicago, IL & London: University of Chicago Press

Rouse, J. 2004. Barad's feminist naturalism. *Hypatia* 19(1), 142–61

Rouse, J. 2009. Standpoint theories reconsidered. *Hypatia* 24(4), 200–9

Ruberton, P. (ed.) 2008. *Archaeologies of Placemaking: Monuments, Memories, and Engagement in Native North America*. Walnut Creek, CA: Left Coast Press

Savory, H. 1940. A Middle Bronze Age barrow at Crick, Monmouthshire. *Archaeologia Cambrensis* 95, 169–91

Savory, H. 1949. Two Middle Bronze Age palisade barrows at Letterston, Pembrokeshire. *Archaeologia Cambrensis* 100, 67–86

Savory, H. 1969. The excavation of the Marlborough Grange barrow, Llanblethian (Glam.), 1967. *Archaeologia Cambrensis* 118, 48–69

Scarre, C. 2006. Sound, place, and space: towards an archaeology of acoustics. In C. Scarre & G. Lawson (eds.), *Archaeoacoustics*, 1–10. Cambridge, UK: McDonald Institute for Archaeological Research

Scarre, C., García Sanjuán, L. & Wheatley, D. (eds.) 2011. Exploring time and matter in prehistoric monuments: absolute chronology and rare rocks in European megaliths. *Menga: Journal of Andalusian Prehistory*, monographic issue. Junta de Andalucía: Andalusian Regional Government Ministry of Culture

Schofield, J. & Szymanski, R. (eds.) 2010. *Local Heritage, Global Contexts: Cultural Perspectives on Sense of Place*. Farnham, UK: Ashgate

Shackel, P. & Chambers, E. (eds.) 2004. *Places in Mind: Public Archaeology as Applied Anthropology*. London: Routledge

Souvatzi, S. 2012. Space, place, and architecture: a major meeting point between social archaeology and anthropology? In D. Shankland (ed.), *Archaeology and Anthropology: Past, Present and Future*, 173–76. London & New York: Berg

Thomas, J. 1993a. The hermeneutics of megalithic space. In C. Tilley (ed.), *Interpretative Archaeology*, 73–97. Oxford, UK: Berg

Thomas, J. 1993b. The politics of vision and archaeologies of landscape. In B. Bender (ed.), *Landscape: Politics and Perspectives*, 19–48. Oxford, UK: Berg

Thomas, J. 1996. *Time, Culture and Identity: An Interpretative Archaeology*. London: Routledge

Thomas, J. 2001. Archaeologies of place and landscape. In I. Hodder (ed.), *Archaeological Theory Today*, 165–86. Oxford, UK: Blackwell

Thomas, J. 2008. Archaeology, landscape, and dwelling. In B. David & J. Thomas (eds.), *Handbook of Landscape Archaeology*, 300–6. Walnut Creek, CA: Left Coast Press

Tilley, C. 1994. *A Phenomenology of Landscape*. Oxford, UK: Berg

Tilley, C. 1999. *Metaphor and Material Culture*. Oxford, UK: Blackwell

Tringham, R. 1994. Engendered places in prehistory. *Gender, Place & Culture: A Journal of Feminist Geography* 1(2), 169–203

Tringham, R. 2012. Sensing the place of Çatalhöyük and Building 3: the rhythms of daily life. In R. Tringham & M. Stevanovic (eds.), *House Lives: Building, Inhabiting, Excavating a House at Çatalhöyük, Turkey. Reports from the Bach Area, Çatalhöyük, 1997–2003*. Los Angeles: Cotsen Institute of Archaeology Publications, UCLA

Turnbull, D. 1993. The ad hoc collective work of building gothic cathedrals with templates, string, and geometry. *Science, Technology, & Human Values* 18(3), 315–40

Turnbull, D. 2002. Performance and narrative, bodies and movement in the construction of places and objects, spaces and knowledges: the case of the Maltese megaliths. *Theory, Culture & Society* 19(5–6), 125–43

Turton, D. 2005. The meaning of place in a world of movement: lessons from long-term field research in Southern Ethiopia. *Journal of Refugee Studies* 18(3), 258–80

Turton, D. 2011. Wilderness, wasteland or home? Three ways of imagining the Lower Omo Valley. *Journal of Eastern African Studies* 5(1), 158–76

Watson, A. 2004. Monuments that made the world: performing the henge. In R. Cleal & J. Pollard (eds.), *Monuments and Material Culture. Papers in Honour of an Avebury Archaeologist: Isobel Smith*, 83–97. Salisbury, UK: Hobnob Press

Webley, D. 1960. Twyn Bryn Glas: the excavation of a round cairn at Cwm Cadlan, Breconshire. *Bulletin of the Board of Celtic Studies* 19, 56–71

Whatmore, S. 2002. *Hybrid Geographies*. London: Sage

Whitridge, P. 2004. Landscapes, houses, bodies, things: "place" and the archaeology of Inuit imaginaries. *Journal of Archaeological Method and Theory* 11(2), 213–50

Woodward, K. 2010. Events, spontaneity, and abrupt conditions. In B. Anderson & P. Harrison (eds.), *Taking Place: Non-Representational Theories and Geography*, 321–40. Farnham, UK: Ashgate

Woodward, K., Jones III, J. & Marston, S. 2010. Of eagles and flies: orientations toward the site. *Area* 42(3), 271–80

PART IV
Beyond Representation

Andrew Meirion Jones

Archaeology is a discipline with a strong visual and material focus (Cochrane & Russell 2007). One of the defining features of archaeological enquiry is the need and desire to interpret the remains of the past. Whatever our theoretical dispositions, we are taught to treat the materials that we excavate as a variety of clues to past behavior. In a more specialized sense, since the early 1980s we have also learnt that materials can signify; they may carry representational or significatory loads.

This perspective has presented a number of problems. If we are to understand images and materials as signifying something else (i.e., images-as-signs or materials-as signs), how are we to understand the image-as-image or the material-as-material? Are we in danger of losing sight of the very materials and images we are interested in studying? Andrew Cochrane (2012) makes a useful point in his discussion of the disturbing art of the Chapman Brothers, two British artists. He notes that "their works are not analogies of something else—they are perfect models of themselves" (ibid., 181). This is a useful imperative for our position on representation. Rather than focusing immediately on the power of materials to signify, thereby overlooking their qualities and properties, the preliminary focus must be on materials. We must grasp that these materials are real entities, rather than representations. Our focus then shifts on the properties and qualities of these materials, in an effort to understand how these might have been employed to achieve certain visual effects in past human activities.

Presented thus, our position sounds very much in the great traditions of empiricist archaeology, with its concern with ancient technologies and economies (e.g., Hawkes 1954; Clark 1989). We do not intend to do away with the analysis of representation (that would be counterproductive: see Jones 2012), but to begin from a different starting point. Rather than assuming that all materials and images represent something, our aim is to analyze materials to consider how their properties and qualities of materials are utilized in making representations (see also Back Danielsson et al. 2012). Here, following the art theorist Nicolas Bourriaud (2002), we place the emphasis on materials as partners in the process of making representations.

The study of visual representation in archaeology is in its relative infancy (Moser 2012a), and researchers have largely adopted constructivist and semiotic approaches to the analysis of past images or representations of the past in museums or other public contexts. The work of Stephanie Moser has been key in developing this tradition of analysis. Curiously, Moser's work could be characterized as being firmly situated in a constructivist tradition, based on her detailed analyses of specific materials in the construction of our Paleolithic past (Moser 1998), the construction of otherness in the display of Egypt in the British Museum (Moser 2006), or the display of ancient cultures at the Great Exhibition of 1851 and its reconstruction in 1854 at the Crystal Palace in London (Moser 2012b). However, in each case study Moser carefully discusses how images are materially deployed to achieve their effect in differing contexts. In that sense her work acts as an exemplar of the kind of approach we wish to promote here. Echoing the development of a nonrepresentational theory in geography (e.g., Anderson & Harrison 2010), our concern is with how "representations enact worlds" (ibid., 25): How are materials utilized in projects of representation, and how do these effect and enact social life?

This close analysis of how representations enact worlds returns us to the key question of ontology, one of the major themes of this book. Cochrane and Jones (2012, 11) have argued, in the context of Neolithic imagery, that prehistoric images are less representational than they are related to a process of engagement with mutable materials in the environment, part of an unfolding process of creating fresh ontological relationships.

The contributors in this section take the ontological nature of representations seriously. In the opening chapter, **Sara Perry** provides a superb overview of the field of visual archaeology and offers a historical case study of the development of visual literacy in archaeology through an analysis of the use of images (mainly models and photography) in the Institute of Archaeology at University College London, one of the earliest teaching departments of archaeology in Britain. Perry's analysis pays close attention to the curious ontological character of these images as they were simultaneously deployed as pedagogical aids and as generators of revenue (as museum dioramas) for the department. Imagery, she argues, played a critical role in the growth of the department and in the sedimentation of crucial skills and forms of observational literacy among students of the new discipline of archaeology.

Ing-Marie Back Danielsson analyses the gold-foil figures of the Scandinavian Late Iron Age. She highlights the importance of examining practice in the production and destruction of these images; rather than being simple representations, the images are situated in an ongoing process of making and unmaking. Images are not only generated by the relations within which they are situated, but they are also generative: they produce affects.

This theme is also explored in **Fredrik Fahlander's** contribution, which discusses the Bronze Age rock art of southern Scandinavia. Fahlander argues that the images carved in stone are not so much representations as "material articulations." Images articulate a complex set of relations, and in a close analysis of the carving of images at a single site in Uppland, Sweden, he demonstrates how the scale of the images and their composition contribute to such articulation. Images are not solely the result of social circumstances, but they also help to generate, integrate, and reproduce social relations.

The final contribution in this section by **Andrew Cochrane** examines the imagery associated with the Neolithic passage tomb of Fourknocks, Ireland. Cochrane examines the variety of representational approaches that have been applied to this enigmatic and abstract imagery. Though he does not wish to reject representational approaches out of hand, he argues that we need to begin from a different starting point. Rather than assuming that images represent, we need to demonstrate how images represent in differing material contexts and conditions. His careful analysis of the relationship between images, architecture, and depositional practices at the tomb indicates how closely these components are interwoven in practices of building and remodeling at the site. Images are less associated with representation and are more closely related to the marking of architectural changes in the building.

Each contribution then underlines the complex ontological character of images as both composed and composing, generated and generative, whether the images are used in contemporary pedagogic practice as in Perry's example, composed from finely made gold and eventually crushed and destroyed as in Back Danielsson's example, carved on rocks in the landscape and related to previous carvings as in Fahlander's example, or involved in processes of architectural construction as in Cochrane's example. Images are only partly representational; being bound up in social practices and articulating social relations, they are also integrative, generative, and affective.

REFERENCES

Anderson, B. & Harrison, P. 2010. The promise of non-representational theories. In B. Anderson & P. Harrison (eds.), *Taking Place: Non-Representational Theories and Geography*, 1–36. Farnham, UK: Ashgate

Back Danielsson, I-M., Fahlander, F. & Sjöstrand, Y. 2012. Imagery beyond representation. In I-M. Back Danielsson, F. Fahlander & Y. Sjöstrand (eds.), *Encountering Imagery: Materials, Perceptions, Relations*, 1–12. Stockholm, Swed.: Department of Classical Studies & Archaeology Monograph

Bourriaud, N. 2002. *Relational Aesthetics*. Paris: Les Presses du Réel

Clark, G. 1989. *Economic Prehistory*. Cambridge: Cambridge University Press

Cochrane, A. 2012. Composing the Neolithic at Knockroe. In A. Cochrane & A.M. Jones (eds.), *Visualising the Neolithic: Abstraction, Figuration, Performance, Representation*, 179–97. Oxford, UK: Oxbow Books

Cochrane, A. & Jones, A.M. 2012. Visualising the Neolithic: an introduction. In A. Cochrane & A.M. Jones (eds.), *Visualising the Neolithic: Abstraction, Figuration, Performance, Representation*, 1–11. Oxford, UK: Oxbow Books

Cochrane, A. & Russell, I. 2007. Visualising archaeologies: a manifesto. *Cambridge Archaeological Journal* 17(1), 3–19

Hawkes, C. 1954. Archaeological theory and method: some suggestions from the Old World. *American Anthropologist* 56, 155–68

Jones, A.M. 2012. *Prehistoric Materialities: Becoming Material in Prehistoric Britain and Ireland*. Oxford: Oxford University Press

Moser, S. 1998. *Ancestral Images: The Iconography of Human Antiquity*. Ithaca, NY: Cornell University Press

Moser, S. 2006. *Wondrous Curiosities: Ancient Egypt at the British Museum*. Chicago, IL: Chicago University Press

Moser, S. 2012a. Archaeological visualization. In I. Hodder (ed.), *Archaeological Theory Today*, 292–322. 2nd edition. Cambridge, UK: Polity

Moser, S. 2012b. *Designing Antiquity: Owen Jones, Ancient Egypt and the Crystal Palace*. New Haven, NJ: Yale University Press

CHAPTER FOURTEEN

Archaeological Visualization and the Manifestation of the Discipline: Model-Making at the Institute of Archaeology, London

Sara Perry

Archaeological visual media (illustrations, drawings, maps, photos, models, videos, exhibitions, and related two- and three-dimensional analogue and digital graphic productions) have a crucial—but, until now, often unspoken—relationship to disciplinary theory. Arguably, practitioners' negotiations with such media presage larger archaeological philosophical trends, and in so doing, they provide an important mechanism for gauging nascent intellectual approaches. Since at least the late 1970s, archaeologists have often applied a distinctly semiotic methodology to their engagements with images, deconstructing visual content while questioning the epistemological foundations of the pictorial. Recently, an ontologically sensitive lens has been turned toward archaeological visualization, as a handful of practitioners have begun to trace its material impacts on past and present worlds. Running alongside these tendencies has been a far more pervasive and long-lasting inclination to ignore, disparage, or otherwise forget both the epistemological and the ontological implications of the discipline's visual methods and outputs. Critically, as archaeological theory slowly pushes away from preexisting interpretative paradigms—and as practitioners are increasingly confronted with the inescapability of visualization to the everyday doing of archaeology—we find ourselves again at a point where attention to the visual might anticipate broader cognitive and methodological shifts.

Archaeology after Interpretation: Returning Materials to Archaeological Theory, edited by Benjamin Alberti, Andrew Meirion Jones, and Joshua Pollard, 281–303.

I seek here to speak to such changes through a case study centered on the role of visual media—in particular, three-dimensional physical models of archaeological and paleontological subjects—in establishing one of the earliest academic departments of archaeology in Britain: the University College London's Institute of Archaeology (IoA). Tracking the development and growth of the IoA's pioneering Repair Laboratory—a conservation, artifact restoration, model production, and teaching unit—exposes both the path by which visualization has come to be theorized (or un-/undertheorized) by archaeologists, and also the productivity of applying an ontological approach to untangling and anticipating disciplinary traditions. This chapter aims at once, then, to tease out what visualization can tell us about the state of archaeological theory; to discuss how new approaches to visual studies in archaeology may provide an opportunity to close some of the deep-rooted conceptual gaps between archaeologists; and to suggest that a materially and relationally acute engagement with visual media has the potential to build capital (intellectual, social, and financial), and in so doing, tangibly transform our field of practice.

THEORIZING ARCHAEOLOGICAL VISUALIZATION

Skilled methods of seeing and representing information have long been pivotal to the solidification of archaeology as an expert pursuit. The honing of means of visualization was implicated in the demarcation of seventeenth-century antiquarian study itself (Moser 2012, in press); it proved fundamental to the birth of chronological sequencing (i.e., the Three-Age System) and the notion of a "scientific" archaeology (Eskildsen 2012); it featured prominently in both the earliest archaeological textbooks (e.g., Petrie 1904) and the earliest professional training programs (e.g., Perry 2011); and it is embedded in our very ways of thinking and working stratigraphically (Bradley 1997). Following broader trends in the sciences and social sciences (e.g., Rudwick 1976; Fyfe & Law 1988; Lynch & Woolgar 1990; Baigrie 1996), the past fifty years have seen a consolidation of enquiry into the role of the visual in defining the discipline. Such consolidation is perhaps best encapsulated in a buildup of edited scholarly volumes (e.g., Molyneaux 1997; Smiles & Moser 2005; Bonde & Houston 2011) and academic conferences,[1] which together testify to a broad-based critical philosophical engagement with matters of archaeological imaging. The nature of such engagement has generally paralleled theoretical movements in cognate fields, beginning with deconstructive interrogations of the epistemological foundations of (visual) representative approaches (most developed in the work of Moser [e.g., 1992, 1998, 2001, 2003], but arguably originating in Piggott's [1965, 1978] critical explorations of the history of archaeological illustration). In this way, it coincides with—or links to—the "interpretative turn" in the humanities (see Perry 2011 for a full review). Most recently, in line with the so-called "material turn," this philosophical engagement has manifested itself in ontologically sensitive analyses of the productivities of the archaeological visual object itself and its indivisibility from people (e.g., see Witmore 2004; Webmoor 2005; Cox 2010; Perry 2011). Simultaneously, and in step with broader inclinations, there survives a persistent tendency to produce purely descriptive and unpenetrative accounts of archaeological visualization, wherein visual practice and outputs come across as essentially atheoretical (e.g., see Llobera's 2011 discussion of virtual reality imaging). In all cases, though, visual theory in archaeology coincides with general disciplinary intellectual trends.

Given these philosophical alignments, one might assume that issues of visualization would have clear visibility in archaeology's key theory textbooks and review documents. However, although such issues do have a place in major disciplinary theoretical overviews, it is not unusual for them to be relegated to the last chapter of such volumes (e.g., Hodder 2012, chapter 14), to a single sentence (e.g., Johnson 2010, 263), or to a discussion that generally gravitates around popular culture alone (e.g., Bentley et al. 2008, chapter 23). In so doing, these texts miss the point that visual media are oftentimes the bridge not simply between academic and non-academic audiences, but also between academic audiences themselves—facilitating and perpetuating practice, and indeed, standing as the means by which archaeologists are inspired to take up archaeology in the first instance. Moreover, many of the foremost theoreticians in the field arguably come to articulate their broader archaeological philosophical stances precisely via grappling on-the-ground with forms of and exercises in visualization and seeing (e.g., see Leone 1981; Shanks & Tilley 1987; Thomas 1993). It is not uncommon, then, for the visual to be the impetus for larger conceptual changes in archaeology.

This presence of vision in the ongoing development of the discipline speaks to its potential not just as a barometer of intellectual climate, but also as an instrument for ground-level capacity building and remodeling of the field of practice. Such is the advantage of a materially and relationally oriented perspective on visual media, since it provides the infrastructure for tracing the tangible effects of these media on the world. Therein theory is not reduced to some elusive quest for the underlying meaning behind archaeological pictures, but instead becomes a resource for probing the enabling capacities of our disciplinary tools—their reverberating and accumulative impacts on people, ideas, other objects, and human/nonhuman networks. Such an approach can thus offer a mechanism for anticipating archaeological currents as well as exposing how seemingly "atheoretical" practical behaviors connect directly to epistemic and socioeconomic changes. In particular, it can allow us to understand how visualization might act at once as a transformative force and a reflection of the mundane.

MODEL-MAKING AT THE INSTITUTE OF ARCHAEOLOGY, C. 1936–1950

The establishment of the Institute of Archaeology at London University in the mid-twentieth century (later incorporated into University College London) provides an opportunity to test the efficacy of an ontological standpoint for mapping out the role of visual representation in disciplinary development. The IoA's history, beginning with its official launch in 1937, has been perfunctorily discussed by others (e.g., Evans 1975, 1987) but deserves more acute interrogation, not only because the organization is among the first university departments of archaeology in Britain, but because it was the only department that styled itself as a methodological laboratory, teaching students the practicalities of field excavation, recording, analysis, and conservation. Even before its 1937 inauguration, the IoA formed a series of visual production units—including a Photographic Laboratory, an illustrative department, and a Repair Laboratory (concerned with manufacturing three-dimensional models and mending and reconstructing archaeological artifacts)—which became literal industries for the institution. As highlighted in depth elsewhere (Perry 2011), such industries proved imperative both financially (in terms of generating an income for an organization that was otherwise economically unviable) and intellectually. In other words (following Wylie 2010), their visual outputs had epistemic weight: they were critical knowledge-making devices whose articulation directly affected scientific practice.

The IoA's reconstruction models (defined here as three-dimensional representations of human and nonhuman entities, oftentimes incorporated into full scenic dioramas) are especially significant in that, though seemingly trivial, they are well remembered by Institute alumni; they represented a lucrative component of the Institute's visual portfolio; and in the past they also functioned as key cognitive aids for archaeology's then-emerging subspecialties. Produced in the Repair Laboratory (later called the Technical Department) under the direction of Frederick Zeuner, the Institute's models seem to stand, in particular, as iconic materializations of the nascent field of geochronology (latterly known as environmental archaeology). The IoA tends to take credit for the initiation of this field, suggesting that Zeuner has in fact been largely responsible for its establishment as an integrated branch of archaeology, though the importance of its elements, geology, palaeontology, palaeobotany, climatology and kindred subjects, to archaeology has long been appreciated. The University, by its appointment of Dr. Zeuner as Honorary Lecturer in Geochronology at the Institute in 1936, was the first body in this country to give academic recognition to the integrated science, and has since led the way in its development.[2]

Although such claims might be questioned, given that Grahame Clark lectured on "Geochronology and Climactic History" at Cambridge as early as 1935,[3] and key organizations linked to the development of geochronological thinking had surfaced prior to that (e.g., the Fenland Research Committee at Cambridge in 1932; see Smith 2009), Zeuner was the first in Britain to hold a dedicated lectureship—and the first to run a full department—on the subject. Indeed, one year after its launch, the IoA solicited financial investment by parading its geochronology department (under Zeuner's direction) as a model of innovation: "Dr. Zeuner's work is essentially a pioneer-attempt in this country to correlate a number of different branches of science in relation to the study of Man, and its importance, both actual and potential, would be difficult to overestimate" (IoA 1939, 7).

What was critical about Zeuner and his department was their concern not just for conceptual associations between climate, plant life, fauna, soil, landscape, dating, and human history, but also for academic and generally accessible visual presentations of these associations. Zeuner observed an inseparable link between theory and its visible, physical exhibition, which he championed both in the classroom and in public spaces.[4] When his job came up for review in the late 1940s, Zeuner was clear to describe this link as something that could not be properly taught "by lecturing alone," but instead required that:

> all courses [be] given in the form of demonstrations at which specimens from teaching collections are provided to the students and methods of investigation shown. At the moment two courses are given per week, which means that the preparation of the material, apparatus, etc. and its subsequent removal, including the courses themselves require about two half days weekly. . . . Work on the teaching collection, *models for demonstration, etc. which is* [sic] *essential if the quality of the teaching provided is to be maintained*, takes another four half days.[5]

Moreover, he was conscious of the fact that employment at museological institutions across Britain's colonies was a likely outcome of his training program.[6] Thus it is not surprising that the Institute, via its Repair Lab, should become its own industry of graphic production. As Childe (1950, 58) encapsulates it,

> An important by-product of this [the Environmental—formerly Geochronology] Department's teaching and research has been the construction of scientifically accurate scale models of extinct Pleistocene mammals (giant Irish deer, woolly rhinoceros, mammoth, etc.) and the preparation of dioramas illustrating the lands in which Palaeolithic men encountered these beasts. Prepared originally for use in conjunction with the Diploma courses, copies of the models can be and have been supplied to museums and educational institutions.

Such models are major outputs of the IoA that quickly embed themselves in the intellectual and entrepreneurial mission of the technical departments. Although the Institute's first apparent Prospectus (for 1936–37) did not even acknowledge these outputs, its earliest annual report (for 1937) noted that the Repair Lab yielded "scale-models . . . of subjects ranging from sections of ditches and Iron Age pits at Maiden Castle, to Roman shops at Housesteads" (IoA 1938, 21). By its second annual report, for the academic year 1937–38, the IoA made explicit that its model-making activities were a purposeful and bankable institutional function:

> The technical staffs of most museums are so fully occupied with work on their own material that their services are not available to outside bodies. The need for some institution ready to undertake work of this sort has long been felt, and it is the aim of the Institute to fill the need. The greatest amount of work done has been in the Repair Laboratory. . . . The making of archaeological models is a side of the work which has been considerably extended this year. Work carried out included models illustrating dwellings and activities of man from prehistoric to mediaeval times, which were prepared to the order of a provincial museum for use in schools. (IoA 1939, 10–11)

Indeed, when the Institute appealed to the University Senate in 1938 for £2500, equipment for the Repair Lab was cited among the top four priorities to which the funding would be applied, owing to the lab's "prime importance to the work of the Institute."[7] The following academic year, the IoA seemed to begin to plan for the production of casts (which were arguably more economical and quick to manufacture), and by 1939–40, alongside pottery reconstruction and cleaning, the Institute's Prospectus characterized the Repair Lab as a site where "models can be made of buildings, earthworks, etc., and also of objects of archaeological or historical interest. Casts of scale models of a number of prehistoric animals are available. Estimates may be obtained from the Secretary."

When the IoA returned to full operations after World War II, its 1946–47 annual report indicated that these "accurately painted casts" were sold at £3–£5 each, alongside models and dioramas. Moreover, in the same report the Institute's photography lab suggested that requests for its services had increased, owing in part to demand for slides of the dioramas being prepared by the environmental archaeology department (IoA 1948a).

Besides the evident market value of these outputs, what is crucial is that a not insignificant body of evidence attests to the actual response of viewers to them. These viewers comprise specialist and nonspecialist audiences, including BBC producers (who seemingly commissioned the first full-length archaeological television show in 1937 as a partial consequence of having seen one of the Institute's models on display in the IoA's headquarters [Perry 2011]). As Zeuner wrote to one such producer, "I shall be pleased to show you and Miss Power the reconstructions of prehistoric animals which we have been making and also the small scale dioramas illustrating the environment in which man was living in the distant past. . . . *I feel sure that you will like our system of visual aid in the teaching of a difficult subject.*"[8]

That producer ultimately visited the Institute in the autumn of 1950, and her reaction to witnessing the Repair Lab's work betrays the typical seduction experienced by viewers: "I should like to tell you how much I enjoyed my visit to the Institute of Archaeology, and especially how much I liked your lovely little dioramas."[9]

Importantly, the emotional allure of reconstruction modeling has been linked to a fundamental human pleasure derived from mastering delicate, complex, hands-on technical tasks, and to modeling's tendency to expose that which is normally hidden (Jordanova 2004, 448–49). Such a perspective resonates with the one advanced by Mack (2007, 47, 75), who suggests that not only do "small things" test our assumptions about human capacity—stimulating feelings of wonderment in response—but their size also manifests a kind of fragile vulnerability which, in turn, forces upon us sensations of clumsiness. Evans (2008, 156) speaks of the model as a bridge between play and education, attributing part of its attractiveness to a "miniaturist phenomenology." In the context of archaeology, Jones (2012) links miniaturization to the concentration and articulation of experience and physical and geographical scale. Stewart (1993, 38–39) notes the natural relationship of miniatures to craft and discipline, given that the labor involved in creating such artifacts increases just as their physical presence decreases. What seems particularly critical for archaeologists (or specialists like Zeuner), to borrow from Mack (2007, 72), is that the model allows the "ruin" (e.g., the paleontological/archaeological find) to survive while also allowing "the possibility of reconstructing in miniature all the bits that human intervention and the vagaries of weather, earthquake or other natural forces have separated from the original. It represents the possibility of replacing what the passage of time has removed."

The Institute's models perhaps attract people owing to various aesthetic and embodied charms, but for my purposes I see them as epistemologically important to the IoA (and particularly to Zeuner's program of study) for precisely the reason that Zeuner explained to the BBC: geochronology is a difficult subject. In other words, geochronology pulls together multiple and diverse disciplines into contextualized statements about long-term human and environmental evolution; and in the mid-twentieth century, it still represented a novel science. Indeed, until it was established as a department at the Institute (and taught simultaneously at Cambridge), it had little institutional presence in the UK.[10] Zeuner (1945, 1946) published some of the first major texts on the subject matter, and Sidell (2000, 284) cites Zeuner's appointment at the IoA as the moment at which environmental archaeology was born as a conventional form of archaeological practice in Britain (see also Wilkinson & Stevens 2003, 18). The Institute's models and dioramas are arguably principal players in such conventionalization, making the science tangible in a way not necessarily possible in other respects. That is, these media actualize an often microscopic, fragmentary, and excessively multistranded pursuit, giving authenticity to emerging sciences (archaeology included) that might otherwise be characterized by their ephemerality. The IoA's dioramas became contextualized enactments of the archaeological and paleontological records (see Figure 14.1)—perhaps the only visible access to these records—and it is no surprise, then, that archaeologists like Mortimer Wheeler and Cyril Fox could be found "pleading" for their wider use, particularly in museum environments (Museums Journal 1937, 223; 1938, 235).[11, 12]

But these reconstructions have significance outside of the museum, standing as far more than tools of popular geochronological exposition alone. They are, indeed, prime movers of research, a point which, as de Chadarevian & Hopwood (2004, 3) note, tends to be eclipsed by perceptions of their exclusively pedagogical or popularizing purpose. In the case of the Institute of Archaeology, models in fact become the source of academic scholarship. Recounting its activities in 1939, prior to the outbreak of war, researchers at the IoA's Geochronology Department wrote that, with Ione Gedye's assistance, the department had initiated production of a suite of prehistoric animal reconstructions:

The following species have been completed: Woolly Rhinoceros, Merck's Rhinoceros, Mammoth, Straight-tusked Elephant, Bison priscus, Aurox,

A. Environment of Middle Acheulian and Clactonian Man. Scene on the banks of the Thames near Swanscombe in Great Inter-glacial times, with Merck's Rhinoceros and Swanscombe Fallow Deer

B. Environment of Gravettian and Magdalenian Man. Winter scene of the Last Glaciation, in the eastern Carpathians near Starunia, where bodies of the Woolly Rhinoceros (shown in the diorama) were found preserved with skin

Figure 14.1 Model/diorama reproduced in the IoA's fifth annual report and exhibited at the 1948 International Geological Congress

the Ice-age Elk (Alces latifrons) and Pleistocene wild horse. A series of 1/2 inch to the foot models was made first, but a new set of 1 inch to the foot models is now being constructed. These models are intended as a teaching collection for the course on the Environment of Early Man, and several of them will be incorporated in small dioramas which are being prepared. (IoA 1947, 21)

The same report went on to specify that "research on Pleistocene Mammalia—the big game of Palaeolithic man—has been carried out at intervals throughout the period [i.e., wartime], *in connection with the construction of the small-scale models*. Miss Ione Gedye has been most helpful on the technical side of this work, on which three papers have so far been published" (IoA 1947, 24; my emphasis).

The Institute's models became the focus of multiple scholarly articles (e.g., Zeuner 1942–43, 1943–44, 1944) and oral presentations to various scientific audiences, including natural historians at the British Museum on July 17, 1943 (Oakley & Zeuner 1944; Zeuner 1944) and members of the Linnean and Zoological Societies of London on June 8, 1944 (see Figures 14.2 and 14.3).

Figure 14.2   The IoA's model of *Elephas antiquus* exhibited at a talk to the British Museum on July 17, 1943

Figure 14.3   The IoA's models of the Woolly Rhinoceros and Merck's Rhinoceros exhibited at a talk to the Linnean and Zoological Societies of London on June 8, 1944

Zeuner's academic diaries contain assemblages of photos of, and notations on, the construction of the models, which appear to be the same (or near-identical) photos and notations that populate Zeuner's publications (see Figures 14.4 and 14.5; compare Figures 14.2 and 14.5).[13] In fact,

Figure 14.4 Photographs and notes on the construction of the IoA's *Elephas primigenius* model in Zeuner's diary for July 3, 1943

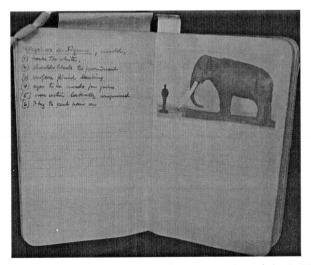

Figure 14.5 Photographs and notes on the construction of the IoA's *Elephas antiquus* model in Zeuner's diary for July 3, 1943

they also seem to be the same models that came to be displayed in the British Museum's Geological section (Zeuner 1942–43, 245) and in the IoA itself (see Figure 14.6).

In this way, Zeuner's models are at once a method, a theory, and a material output of the Institute, and Zeuner was clear to situate them within an established scientific genealogy. That is, his talks/ articles meticulously cited the existing international literature on two- and three-dimensional prehistoric mammalian reconstruction, as well as osteological, archaeological, and related evidence upon which his/ Gedye's finished products were premised (e.g., Zeuner 1942–43, 1943– 44). Indeed, his articles proceed from body part to body part—tusks, skull, hair, back, feet, etc.—tracing the evidential underpinning of each section of each model. For example, the head of the IoA's *Elephas antiquus* (Figures 14.2 and 14.5) takes into account reconstructions by Breuil, Osborn/Buba, and Berckhemer/Böck of prehistoric drawings from Spain and Algeria, as well as skeletal material from Germany and Italy (Zeuner 1942–43, 250–51).

In standard academic fashion, then, Zeuner was overt—and, of interest, critically reflective—about the legacy of scholarship behind his

Figure 14.6 The IoA's mammoth (*Elephas primigenius*) on display in the IoA's foyer

modeling practices, and hence the accumulative nature of the science. In contextualizing the Institute's *Elephas primigenius* model, he noted that "excellent reconstructions have been made in recent years. . . . After several early attempts by various authors, which were not successful and are chiefly of historical interest . . . O. Abel succeeded in producing a *satisfactory* reconstruction (Abel, 1912) *which has become the prototype of most later representations*" (1942–43, 246; my emphasis). Moreover, Zeuner's judgment of Abel's visualization as "satisfactory" implies the presence of an evaluative system of professional quality control to guide the production of reconstruction models. Indeed, validation based on academic peer review seems to be at the core of Zeuner's practice. Describing the intellectual background of the IoA's rhinoceros models (see Figure 14.3), he stated: "Of the numerous reconstructions of the Woolly Rhinoceros, only a few have been executed with sufficient care to face scientific criticism" (Zeuner 1943–44, 183). Moreover, Zeuner's original notes (subsequently crossed out) on his July 17, 1943 demonstration at the British Museum specify that "The ~~specimens~~ models as exhibited have not yet ~~received~~ been given their final finish, since it was thought admirable to invite the criticism of experts before doing so" (strikethroughs in original).[14]

What is significant here is the (visual) scrutiny to which these media were exposed. They were rigorous results of scientific activity and, as such, were subject—like most other results of science—to scholarly refereeing. Zeuner worked to make very explicit the conceptual integrity and genealogy of the Institute's reconstructions, with the consequence that in successfully establishing their credibility, he simultaneously validated the knowledge that originated from them. Indeed, what is special about these models is their ability to articulate new interpretations of the paleontological record. They are epistemological tools—actual sources of intelligence—whereby their physical construction reveals new information about the behavior, form, and habitat of prehistoric species. Such is apparent in Zeuner's (1943–44, 194) rhinoceros analyses, whose two- and three-dimensional reconstructions enable deductions both about the fauna themselves (i.e., that Woolly Rhinoceros' skulls evolved to permit "severe stretching of the neck") and their Paleolithic environment (i.e., that their "food must have been very low-growing").

The effect of these kinds of conclusions on the IoA was patent, as both students and staff came to appreciate its models as critical revelatory devices. Diploma student John Lewis (who attended the Institute in the early 1950s) hints at their potency in characterizing them as unprecedented creations "aiming at a new accuracy"—at a reality never seen before (in the sense that the models exposed extinct scenes and lifeways) and in a corporeal medium hardly used before (one which operated through vivid and three-dimensional, rather than flat, rendering).[15] In comparable language, Joan Sheldon, a student and later lecturer at the Institute, speaks of the models' ability to provide unparalleled access to species that were previously only known through skeletal remains (Sheldon 2001–2). So effective is their realism that the Institute itself recognizes them as an exploitable commodity, citing them in yet another appeal to the University of London for funding/personnel in the IoA's development plan for the 1952–57 quinquennium:

> The Technical Department [previously referred to as the Repair Lab] has been preparing models designed primarily to supplement oral instruction and specimens in . . . several courses. *But the scientific accuracy of these reconstructions*, together with their value in visual education, has led to the demand for copies from museums and educational institutions outside the University. To enable this demand to be satisfactorily met and further models produced a specially qualified artist is needed.[16]

However, it is worth emphasizing again that such models have relevance beyond simple pedagogy. This is critical because, in archaeology, only a handful of scholars have considered the actual disciplinary impacts of the historical practice of analogue modeling, whose verisimilitude, for instance, has sometimes been so exact as to point to as-yet-unexcavated earthworks (e.g., Evans 2008).[17] In terms of the IoA, its entire Technical Department—including both its model-making unit and its pottery and artifactual restoration divisions—is in fact both an educational and a research pursuit, not to mention a commercial enterprise. This multipurpose function is made clear, for instance, in the Institute's ongoing negotiations with the University for further infrastructural support: "As was anticipated, experience has proved that expert technical treatment of archaeological relics is vital both to their preservation as specimens in the University's essential teaching collections and also for their correct interpretation as primary documents for archaeological research."[18] And as described elsewhere:

> The Technical Department is no less vital to the research functions of the Institute. Staff members and research students are constantly making use of the Department. Indeed, its services are invoked by research workers outside London and have materially enhanced the prestige which the Institute has won throughout the British Isles and abroad, and constitute an important item in the contribution the Institute has made and is making in the advancement of knowledge. The preparation of reliable and accurate reconstructions by the Technical Department has not only been found of great value in teaching, but may also be regarded as a substantial contribution to knowledge.[19]

These visual reconstructions (be they literal reconstructions of artifacts or figurative reconstructions of archaeological fauna and landscapes) thus were not mere didactic aids, but theoretical implements with an epistemic pertinence that extended beyond the Institute itself. Just as the IoA produced them for its own research purposes, it also sold them to other institutions and expeditions for their own research activities.

Such an imbricated strategy of visual production and deployment is what I see as essential to the IoA's success. Under Zeuner's direction, the Repair Lab/Technical Department crafted a suite of visual media (literal and figurative reconstructions) that were indispensably entangled in all aspects of the archaeological endeavor: research, teaching, public engagement, and private industry. In particular, its models were sold to the academic community (through presentations and publications) as means for rethinking the paleontological record; these same (and other) models were sold to public museums and research institutions (including some of the same institutions to which Zeuner delivered scholarly presentations) for instructional purposes and further study; and they were sold to the Institute's own students as interpretive aids for the new field of geochronology.

This was, in fact, a literal profit-making endeavor for the IoA, for its reconstructions allowed it to persevere in times of need and provided leverage in repeated appeals to the university for financial investment. The Repair Lab earned £214 for its work in 1938–39, which, when added to the £57 derived from fees charged to its own students, amounted to more than 10 percent of the Institute's total income for the year.[20] Following the war, the Lab (now alternately called the Technical Department or Repair Department)[21] saw an income of £178 (plus £70 in compensation for war damages), £190, and £107 for the academic years 1945–46, 1946–47, and 1947–48, respectively.[22] Indeed, in 1947–48 it reported the production of scale models of Bos and rhinoceros species and four dioramas (e.g., Figure 14.1), as well as sales of casts to the British Museum, the Manchester Art Gallery, and the Rhodes-Livingstone Museum in Northern Rhodesia. Some of this material, including the dioramas, then went on display in an exhibition hosted by the IoA in conjunction with the 18th International Geological Congress, from August 26 to September 3, 1948 (IoA 1948b; again see Figure 14.1). Zeuner (IoA 1949, 17) noted that 15 percent of the Congress actually toured the displays, which likely amounted to at least 260 viewers.[23] Around this time, the same visual exhibit was also circulated to the Prehistoric Society, the Geologists' Association, the Richmond Scientific Society, and student audiences at Birkbeck College and University College, bringing the total viewership to an apparent 900 people (IoA 1949, 17). Zeuner indicated that its preparation consumed most of the spring and summer of 1948, and it is note-worthy that, simultaneous with its production, the Institute's technical students were also preparing their own exhibition for presentation at the Prehistoric Society conference.[24] Although only a single sentence in the Institute's annual report seemed to attest to the latter exhibit, it appears that the display entailed a showcase of the restoration skills of the Technical Department's pupils. As per the report, following the conference this showcase was kept on display for the summer, prov-ing useful in "impressing museum curators with the high standard of training provided at the Institute, but also in revealing to excavators how much can be done in the way of restoring unpromising looking specimens provided sufficient care is bestowed upon their extraction and conservation in the field" (IoA 1949, 9).

Such a statement points exactly to the cultural capital that I think the IoA's corpus of visual media is intended to wield. To display these arti-factual restorations is not to blandly illustrate some mundane methodology in the corridor of a conference venue, but to extend an active invitation to prospective employers (museum curators) to recognize the hireable potential of its graduates; to tout the legitimacy of the Institute as an expert training body for aspiring students; to alter the very nature of archaeological practice itself by promoting awareness of extraction and conservation techniques and their epistemological promise; and perhaps also to secure jobs from employers who could then recognize the technical services and skill the IoA could offer. The latter is not a negligible enterprise, as proven by the fact that between the Institute's opening in 1937 and mid-May 1944, the Repair Lab carried out work (restorations and model-making) for twenty-six expeditions (as well as eleven museums and twenty individuals).[25] Such expeditions often rented rooms at the IoA—another dimension to its business strategy—and then invested in the amenities of the technical departments.[26] Indeed, in its first full year back in operation after the war (1945–46), the Repair Lab was employed by five excavation committees/expeditions, two muse-ums, and seven individuals (IoA 1947). By 1947–48 it was apparent, as per above, that the Lab was producing commissions for international establishments (e.g., the Rhodes-Livingstone Museum), which arguably enabled the Institute to extend its visibility even further. That same year, the Lab itself stood as a hub of internationalism, with a near majority of foreign students (from India, Siam, Egypt, Transjordan, Canada, and Ireland) populating its technical program (IoA 1949, 18). This means that the Institute was promulgating a particular mentality and skillset for archaeological reconstructive method not only among a local audience, but also among a multinational audience that had the potential to influence (visual) practice globally.

THE PROMISE OF THE VISUAL

As I see it, the visual products of the Repair Lab—both the models/ restorations themselves and the actual student body whose archaeo-logical eyes were honed to reproduce such outputs for others—are ver-satile and tactical tools for the Institute. They bear witness and add intellectual weight to the science of archaeology and complementary disciplines (e.g., geochronology), to the expert skill of practitioners, and to the Institute as a pivotal learned organization—and they are purposefully fed to a diverse and substantial viewership of thousands of people via public and scholarly exhibitions. What thus seems to be operative here is a kind of a self-propelling feedback system, wherein the returns on one type of (visual) investment by the IoA fuel further returns in the form of employment, publicity, student enrollment, addi-tional graphic production, etc.

At the same time, however, these visual media become more and more normalized, blending innocuously into the disciplinary background—so much so that today the Woolly Rhinoceros of Figure 14.1 stands on display in the Institute as little more than decoration—with virtually no contextualization, as part of the IoA's 75th anniversary exhibitions. It is in tracing the development of such resources that we can tease out where theory and practice begin to splinter, as the IoA's models move from novel mechanisms of knowledge-making to ordinary and ubiquitous representations of rote forms of archaeological labor. Once at the apparent cutting-edge of the discipline, their entrenchment into everyday practice (through teaching, research, and commercialization) at the same time built capital and, ironically, rendered them essentially invisible—a generic output of the field. In this instance, then, an ontological approach offers an opportunity to untangle precisely where and how disciplinary traditions and tensions might manifest themselves and play out. More importantly, though, such a perspective exposes just how transformative our engagements with archaeological visualization can be. Visual representations are at once tools for thinking and means for reproducing that thinking. As such, experimenting with their dimensions (in the vein of the IoA's Repair Department) can enable disciplinary change, both in terms of our interpretations of the past and in terms of restructuring the very nature of our field of practice.

There is an advantage, then, to investing in visual studies. Its agents (who variously include art historians, anthropologists, cultural theorists, sociologists, geographers, philosophers, etc.) have been grap-pling with non-representational approaches for more than a quarter-century longer than archaeologists themselves (e.g., see Sontag's 1966 landmark *Against Interpretation* volume). They anticipated concepts intrinsic to materialist thinking before such thinking gained substantial intellectual ground in the last decade (e.g., Poole's 1997 notion of "visual economy," which was built out of a study of the circulation of images in the Peruvian Andes). And they have been identified as pioneering participants not only in the initial turn towards materialist perspectives in the second half of the twentieth century (see discussion in Edwards & Hart 2004), but also in critiquing the subsequent move away from representational theory prompted by the endorsement of those perspectives (e.g., compare Wolff 1981 and Wolff 2012). It is significant too that archaeological materials have played a role in helping such researchers to actually constitute aspects of non-representational theory. Indeed, both Goodwin (1994) and Latour (1995)—the former in the context of archaeology, the latter in the context of pedology—have drawn on Munsell color charts to trace the configuration and spread of expertise, and the implication of these inscription devices in the cocreation of the world (Grasseni 2011).

Arguably, it is visual thinking, visual practices, and the interrogation of visual regimes that facilitated the cultural critiques of the late 1970s–80s (e.g., see discussion in Edwards 2011) from which the so-called material turn then surfaced. As Edwards (2012, 222) notes elsewhere, "it is no coincidence that the rise of a newly figured and newly theorized, Marxist-derived material culture studies . . . emerged at the same time as the increasing recognition of the work of photographs." It is beyond the scope of this chapter to delve into such issues further; however, the number of social theorists who have articulated watershed intellectual frameworks by grappling with modes and means of seeing, displaying, surveying, and witnessing is not insignificant (e.g., Foucault, Benjamin, Barthes, Bourdieu, Latour). Archaeologists are among those whose whole disciplinary architecture has been affected not just by these ways of thinking, but also by the full "complex" (after Hevia's [2009] "photography complex") of making, taking, circulating, storing, embedding, replicating, exhibiting, observing, and critiquing visualizations (for a review of vision's place in the development of anthropology, see Grimshaw 2001).

More importantly, archaeologists have a deep legacy of material engagements that have informed both cultural theory and visual theory (as in the research of Goodwin [1994, 2001]). In general, archaeology and visual studies today attend to a comparable subject matter, namely the multi-layered, blurred, iterative relations between people and things. A dedicated effort to interlace these fields of practice promises, as in the case of the IoA, to meaningfully contribute to a historical understanding of the production of our disciplinary fabric. But so too does it promise an opportunity to fuel the fundamental future intellectual (and material) movements that will come to shape the wider world around us.

NOTES

1. For example, "Seeing the Past," Archaeology Center, Stanford University, Stanford, USA, February 4–6, 2005; "Past Presented: A Symposium on the History of Archaeological Illustration," Dumbarton Oaks, Washington, DC, October 9–10, 2009; "Visualisation in Archaeology," University of Southampton, Southampton, UK, April 18–19, 2011 (at www.viarch.org.uk).

2. IoA Mgm Committee Report to the Senate, 1945; UCL Senate House Files, Box 4; see also Harris (2009, 130). The Institute's Development Policy for the 1952–57 quinquennium specifically attributes the birth of environmental archaeology departments at European universities such as Bonn and Freiburg to their admiration of the IoA's department (UCL Senate House Files, Box 4).

3. Indeed, Cambridge's faculty minutes indicate that, in July 1935, Clark was approved to give eight lectures on geochronology. The following June 1936, these lectures factored (among others) into the Faculty Board's recommendation to promote Clark to Faculty Assistant Lecturer at a salary of £150 (Cambridge Faculty Board of Archaeology and Anthropology Minutes, July 19, 1935 and June 8, 1936.)

4. In terms of the latter, as Charles Thomas puts it, Zeuner like others from the IoA was "keen on museums" (personal correspondence with Charles Thomas, March 25, 2010).

5. IoA Mgm Committee minutes, October 29, 1947: Memo on the Teaching Requirements of the Department of Environmental Archaeology (my emphasis).

6. "I have been asked repeatedly whether students were available to fill Museum posts in the Empire. One of our former students has recently accepted a post in Rhodesia" (IoA Mgm Committee minutes, October 29, 1947: Memo on the Teaching Requirements of the Department of Environmental Archaeology).

7. UoL Court Minute #341, January 12, 1938.

8. Zeuner to Elwell, June 22, 1950 (my emphasis); BBC Archives, RCONTI, Zeuner, Talks, File 1, 1946–52.

9. Elwell to Zeuner, October 11, 1950; BBC Archives, RCONTI, Zeuner, Talks, File 1, 1946–52.

10. Although, again, groups such as the Cambridge-based Fenland Research Committee (whose first meeting was convened on June 7, 1932) attended to geochronological issues in their engagements.

11. Indeed, in the case of Fox, he implied that dioramas (among certain other visual displays) were a necessary in situ-style explication of the archaeological record, and that it was primarily only through direct participation in fieldwork that one might articulate such a "competent exhibition technique" (Museums Journal 1938, 235).

12. Margot Eates, while employed at the London Museum under Wheeler's direction, was actually charged with giving public lectures on the Museum's models. These included, on November 22, 1937, a talk on "Models of Old London in the Museum," and on November 29, 1937, a talk on "Historical Dioramas in the Museum" (MoL Archives, DC4).

13. These books are held in UCL's Special Collections: Zeuner, Box 6, especially Diary #7. Zeuner's notes in Diary #7, on July 3, 1943, pp. 74–76, are very similar to the first few pages of text in Zeuner 1942–43.

14. UCL Special Collections, Zeuner, Box 6, Diary #7, p. 74. See also see Oakley and Zeuner (1944), Zeuner (1944).

15. Interview with John Lewis, March 25, 2010.

16. IoA Statement of Development Policy for the Next Quinquennium, Second Draft, December 5, 1950 (my emphasis); UCL IoA Senate House Files, Financial, 2.

17. Digital modeling has similar epistemic ramifications for archaeological enquiry and has been the subject of more concerted study (e.g., Earl 2007; Earl and Wheatley 2002).

18. IoA Statement of Development Policy for the Next Quinquennium, Second Draft, December 5, 1950 (my emphasis); UCL IoA Senate House Files, Financial, 2.
19. n.d., "Appendix A"; UCL Senate House Files, Box 4.
20. UoL Court Minute #571, May 24, 1944: APPENDIX A, Review of the Past Work of the IoA.
21. As the IoA (1949, 18) reports, "The work of the [Repair] Department now having progressed far beyond the mere repair of pottery, it was thought proper that it should have a new title. 'Technical' suggested itself as a more comprehensive term, including all the new activities."
22. UoL Court Minutes, UoL Audited Accounts for the Years 1945–46, 1946–47, 1947–48; UCL IoA Senate House Files, Financial, 2: Estimates.
23. Oakley (1949, 56) reports a total membership at the conference of 1760 people from 76 countries.
24. The proceedings of the Prehistoric Society for 1948 mention its London Conference, April 16–18, 1948, held in conjunction with the IoA at St. John's Lodge on the theme of "Problems of the Late Bronze and Early Iron Ages" (Prehistoric Society 1948, 240). However, there is no acknowledgement herein of the technical students' exhibition.
25. UoL Court Minute #571, May 24, 1944: APPENDIX A, Review of the Past Work of the IoA.
26. In 1938–39 alone, the IoA listed the Wellcome-Marston Expedition and the Mond Expedition of the Egypt Exploration Society, along with excavations at Maiden Castle, Brittany, Charlbury, Poundbury, Leicester, Wroxeter, Silchester, Angmering, Transjordan, Gurnard's Head, and Saunderton, as occupying space at its headquarters in St. John's Lodge (UoL Court Minute #63, Appendix 15, December 4, 1940: Report for the Session 1938–39 for Circulation to Members).

REFERENCES

Baigrie, B.S. (ed.) 1996. *Picturing Knowledge: Historical and Philosophical Problems Concerning the Use of Art in Science*. Toronto: University of Toronto Press
Bentley, R.A., Maschner, H.D.G. & Chippindale, C. (eds.) 2008. *Handbook of Archaeological Theories*. Lanham, MD: AltaMira Press
Bonde, S. & Houston, S. (eds.) 2011. *Re-Presenting the Past: Archaeology through Image and Text*. Oxford, UK: Joukowsky Institute Publications/Oxbow
Bradley, R. 1997. "To see is to have seen": craft traditions in British field archaeology. In B.L. Molyneaux (ed.), *The Cultural Life of Images: Visual Representation in Archaeology*, 62–72. London: Routledge
Childe, G. 1950. University of London Institute of Archaeology. *The Archaeological News Letter* 3(4), 57–60
Cox, A. 2010. *Framing Machu Picchu: Science, Photography and the Making of Heritage*. Unpublished PhD thesis, Department of Anthropology, University of Florida
de Chadarevian, S. & Hopwood, N. (eds.) 2004. *Models: The Third Dimension of Science*. Stanford: Stanford University Press
Earl, G. 2007. De/construction sites: Romans and the digital playground. In J. Bowen, S. Keene & L. MacDonald (eds.), *Proceedings of the Electronic Visualisation and the Arts London 2007 Conference held at the London College of Communication, University of the Arts London 1–13 July 2007*, 1–11. London: London College of Communication University of the Arts Hampton Hill, UK, EVA Conferences International
Earl, G. & Wheatley, D. 2002. Virtual reconstruction and the interpretative process: a case-study from Avebury. In D.W. Wheatley, G.P. Earl & S. Poppy (eds.), *Contemporary Themes in Archaeological Computing*, 5–15. Oxford, UK: Oxbow

Edwards, E. 2011. Tracing photography. In M. Banks & J. Ruby (eds.), *Made to Be Seen: Perspectives on the History of Visual Anthropology*, 159–89. Chicago, IL: Chicago University Press

Edwards, E. 2012. Objects of affect: photography beyond the image. *Annual Review of Anthropology* 41, 221–34

Edwards, E. & Hart, J. 2004. Introduction. In E. Edwards & J. Hart (eds.), *Photographs Objects Histories: On the Materiality of Images*, 1–15. London: Routledge

Eskildsen, K.R. 2012. The language of objects: Christian Jürgensen Thomsen's science of the past. *Isis* 103(1), 24–53

Evans, C. 2008. Model excavations: "performance" and the three-dimensional display of knowledge. In N. Schlanger & J. Nordbladh (eds.), *Archives, Ancestors, Practices: Archaeology in the Light of its History*, 147–61. New York: Berghahn Books

Evans, J.D. 1975. Archaeology as education and profession. *Bulletin of the Institute of Archaeology* 12, 1–12

Evans, J.D. 1987. The first half-century—and after. *Institute of Archaeology Bulletin* 24, 1–25

Fyfe, G. & Law, J. (eds.) 1988. *Picturing Power: Visual Depiction and Social Relations*. London: Routledge

Goodwin, C. 1994. Professional vision. *American Anthropologist* 96(3), 606–33

Goodwin, C. 2001. Practices of seeing visual analysis: an ethnomethodological approach. In T. van Leeuwen & C. Jewitt (eds.), *Handbook of Visual Analysis*, 157–82. London: Sage

Grasseni, C. 2011. Skilled visions: toward an ecology of visual inscriptions. In M. Banks & J. Ruby (eds.), *Made to Be Seen: Perspectives on the History of Visual Anthropology*, 19–44. Chicago, IL: Chicago University Press

Grimshaw, A. 2001. *The Ethnographer's Eye: Ways of Seeing in Modern Anthropology*. Cambridge: Cambridge University Press

Harris, O. 2009. Making places matter in Early Neolithic Dorset. *Oxford Journal of Archaeology* 28(2), 111–23

Hevia, J.L. 2009. The photography complex: exposing Boxer-Era China 1900–1. In R. Morris (ed.), *Photographies East: The Camera and its Histories in East and Southeast Asia*, 79–99. Durham, NC: Duke University Press

Hodder, I. (ed.) 2012. *Archaeological Theory Today*. 2nd edition. Cambridge, UK: Polity Press

IoA. 1938. *University of London Institute of Archaeology First Annual Report, 1937*. London: University of London, Institute of Archaeology

IoA. 1939. *University of London Institute of Archaeology Second Annual Report, 1937–38*. London: University of London, Institute of Archaeology

IoA. 1947. *University of London Institute of Archaeology Third Annual Report, 1946*. London: University of London, Institute of Archaeology

IoA. 1948a. *University of London Institute of Archaeology Fourth Annual Report, 1946–47*. London: University of London, Institute of Archaeology

IoA. 1948b. *The Exhibition of Stone Age and Pleistocene Geology from the Cape to Britain*. Held on the Occasion of the XVIII International Geological Congress, August 26 to September 3, 1948. London: University of London, Institute of Archaeology

IoA. 1949. *University of London Institute of Archaeology Fifth Annual Report, 1947–48*. London: University of London, Institute of Archaeology

Johnson, M. 2010. *Archaeological Theory: An Introduction*. 2nd edition. Malden, MA: Wiley-Blackwell

Jones, A. 2012. *Prehistoric Materialities*. Oxford: Oxford University Press

Jordanova, L. 2004. Material models as visual culture. In S. de Chadarevian & N. Hopwood (eds.), *Models: The Third Dimension of Science*, 443–51. Stanford: Stanford University Press

Latour, B. 1995. The "pedofil" of Boa Vista: a photo-philosophical montage. *Common Knowledge* 4(1), 144–87

Leone, M. 1981. The relationship between artifacts and the public in outdoor history museums. *Annals of the New York Academy of Sciences* 376, 301–13

Llobera, M. 2011. Archaeological visualization: towards an archaeological information science (AISc). *Journal of Archaeological Method and Theory* 18(3), 193–223

Lynch, M. & Woolgar, S. (eds.) 1990. *Representation in Scientific Practice*. Cambridge, MA: MIT Press

Mack, J. 2007. *The Art of Small Things*. London: British Museum Press

Molyneaux, B.L. (ed.) 1997. *The Cultural Life of Images: Visual Representation in Archaeology*. London: Routledge

Moser, S. 1992. The visual language of archaeology: a case-study of the Neanderthals. *Antiquity* 66 (253), 831–44

Moser, S. 1998. *Ancestral Images: The Iconography of Human Origins*. Ithaca, NY: Cornell University Press

Moser, S. 2001. Archaeological representation: the visual conventions for constructing knowledge about the past. In I. Hodder (ed.), *Archaeological Theory Today*, 262–83. 1st edition. Cambridge, UK: Polity Press

Moser, S. 2003. Representing archaeological knowledge in museums: exhibiting human origins and strategies for change. *Public Archaeology* 3(1), 3–20

Moser, S. 2012. Archaeological visualisation: early artefact illustration and the creation of the archaeological image. In I. Hodder (ed.), *Archaeological Theory Today*, 2nd edition, 292–322. Cambridge, UK: Polity Press

Moser, S. In press. Making expert knowledge through the image: connections between antiquarian and early modern scientific illustration. *Isis*

Museums Journal. 1937. The Museums Association conference at Newcastle upon Tyne: the archaeologist and museums. *Museums Journal* 37(5), 223

Museums Journal. 1938. Belfast Conference report: museums and field archaeology. *Museums Journal* 38(5), 235–37

Oakley, K.P. 1949. International Geological Congress, 1948. *Man* 49, 56

Oakley, K.P. & Zeuner, F.E. 1944. New exhibits in the Geology Galleries at the British Museum (Natural History), London: report of demonstrations held on July 17, 1943. *Proceedings of the Geologists' Association* 55(2), 115

Perry, S.E. 2011. *The Archaeological Eye: Visualisation and the Institutionalisation of Academic Archaeology in London*. Unpublished PhD thesis, Department of Archaeology, University of Southampton

Petrie, W.M.F. 1904. *Methods and Aims in Archaeology*. London: Macmillan and Co.

Piggott, S. 1965. Archaeological draughtsmanship: principles and practice, Part I: principles and retrospect. *Antiquity* 39, 165–76

Piggott, S. 1978. *Antiquity Depicted: Aspects of Archaeological Illustration*. London: Thames and Hudson

Poole, D. 1997. *Vision, Race, and Modernity: A Visual Economy of the Andean Image World*. Princeton: Princeton University Press

Prehistoric Society. 1948. London conference: April 16th–18th, 1948. *Proceedings of the Prehistoric Society* 14, 240

Rudwick, M.J.S. 1976. The emergence of a visual language for geological science, 1760–1840. *History of Science* 14(25), 149–95

Shanks, M. & Tilley, C. 1987. *Re-Constructing Archaeology: Theory and Practice*. Cambridge: Cambridge University Press

Sheldon, J. 2001–2. Environmental archaeology at the Institute: the early years. *Archaeology International* 5, 9–11

Sidell, J. 2000. Twenty-five years of environmental archaeology in London. In I. Haynes, H. Sheldon & L. Hannigan (eds.), *London under Ground: The Archaeology of a City*, 284–94. Oxford, UK: Oxbow

Smiles, S. & Moser, S. (eds.) 2005. *Envisioning the Past: Archaeology and the Image*. Malden, MA: Blackwell

Smith, P.J. 2009. *A "Splendid Idiosyncrasy": Prehistory at Cambridge 1915–50*. Oxford: BAR British Series 485

Sontag, S. 1966. *Against Interpretation: And Other Essays*. New York: Farrar, Strauss and Giroux

Stewart, S. 1993. *On Longing: Narratives of the Miniature, the Gigantic, the Souvenir, the Collection*. Durham, NC: Duke University Press

Thomas, J. 1993. The politics of vision and the archaeologies of landscape. In B. Bender (ed.), *Landscape: Politics and Perspectives*, 19–48. Oxford, UK: Berg

Webmoor, T. 2005. Mediational techniques and conceptual frameworks in archaeology: a model in "mapwork" at Teotihuacan, Mexico. *Journal of Social Archaeology* 5(1), 52–84

Wilkinson, K. & Stevens, C. 2003. *Environmental Archaeology: Approaches, Techniques and Applications*. Stroud, UK: Tempus

Witmore, C. 2004. On multiple fields. Between the material world and media: two cases from the Peloponnesus, Greece. *Archaeological Dialogues* 11(2), 133–64

Wolff, J. 1981. *The Social Production of Art*. London: Macmillan

Wolff, J. 2012. After cultural theory: the power of images, the lure of immediacy. *Journal of Visual Culture* 11(1), 3–19

Wylie, A. 2010. Archaeological facts in transit: the "Eminent Mounds" of Central North America. In P. Howlett & M.S. Morgan (eds.), *How Well Do Facts Travel? The Dissemination of Reliable Knowledge*, 301–22. Cambridge: Cambridge University Press

Zeuner, F.E. 1942–43. New reconstructions of the mammoth and the straight-tusked elephant. *Proceedings of the Linnean Society of London* 155(3), 245–51

Zeuner, F.E. 1943–44. New reconstructions of the woolly rhinoceros and Merck's rhinoceros. *Proceedings of the Linnean Society of London* 156(3), 183–95

Zeuner, F.E. 1944. Reconstruction-models of Pleistocene mammals. *Proceedings of the Geologists' Association* 55(2), 118–19

Zeuner, F.E. 1945. *The Pleistocene Period: Its Climate, Chronology and Faunal Successions*. London: Ray Society

Zeuner, F.E. 1946. *Dating the Past: An Introduction to Geochronology*. London: Methuen

CHAPTER FIFTEEN

Articulating Relations: A Non-Representational View of Scandinavian Rock Art

Fredrik Fahlander

A popular cliché when it comes to the interpretation of images is that meaning lies in the eye of the beholder, suggesting that meaning is, if not individual, at least culture specific. This echoes a traditional approach in the history of art according to which the meaning of an image is only understandable through context—that is, through its secondary or conventional meaning (e.g., Panofsky 1972, 4). Archaeological studies of imagery have generally addressed meaningful content and tried to understand what they depict, represent, illustrate, or symbolize (Aldhouse-Green 2004). There is little discussion of what images can do, or how they may affect future understandings of a place or artifact that has been "adorned" with them. Images of past worlds are, however, always tricky to handle because they seem to "talk back" to us in a fairly direct tone—sometimes even surpassing the rhetorical power of written text. They are not simply depicting something, but also communicating with the observer in elaborate and unconscious ways. This aesthetic property—or agency, if you like—is an underdeveloped field in studies of prehistoric imagery (Cochrane & Russell 2007). However, as Thomas Mitchell (1996) and Alfred Gell (1992) among others have argued, the study of the pictorial need not be primarily concerned with decoding the meaning of an image or exploring the intentions behind it. To bypass the problems of being led astray by aesthetics and apparently figurative aspects, we may approach imagery as "objects of encounter" rather than as "objects of recognition" (O'Sullivan 2005, 1). An object of recognition is merely a representation of something always already in place; but

Archaeology after Interpretation: Returning Materials to Archaeological Theory, edited by Benjamin Alberti, Andrew Meirion Jones, and Joshua Pollard, 305–24. ©2013 Left Coast Press, Inc. All rights reserved.

as an object of encounter it "produces a cut, a crack" that obliges us to think otherwise about what we see (ibid.).

Mats Rosengren's (2012) discussion of Paleolithic cave art is a good illustration of this distinction. As a professor of rhetoric, he found it curious that archaeologists have primarily been occupied with the origins and the background of the paintings—that is, what animals the paintings depict, how naturalistic and accurately they are portrayed, and how representative the paintings are of "their worlds." There has been much less discussion of what the practice of making images can tell us about the people crafting them. Why were they made, and what did it do to the people who saw them? How do they change the experience of the caves? To "encounter" past imagery, however, does not simply mean that we should approach them with "an open mind" or be more reflective about what we see. On the contrary, such a non-representational approach suggests that images can be perceived as integrated actants with a potential to affect the worlds that produced them. The images and shapes that surround us are not simply something that reflects past worlds; they are also to varying extents integrated in the course of events. Producing imagery affects things, whether in the form of paintings on a cave wall, pecked motifs on the bedrock, or punched elements on an artifact.

In this chapter I will attempt to discuss south Scandinavian petroglyphs as "material articulations." This means to emphasize the relationships that they help to integrate and to focus on their material conditions, their production process (in its technical and multi-sensuous aspects), and on how new and old motifs relate to each other, the rock face, and the local environment. In a similar way as Rosengren approaches Paleolithic cave art and Mitchell approaches modern day pictures, I will discuss the petroglyphs as objects of encounter and elaborate on the various ways they may be entangled in different social worlds.

MATERIAL IMAGES, MATERIAL RELATIONS

Petroglyphs have been carved and pecked on exposed rock faces in Scandinavia more or less continuously from c. 8000 BC to the present day (Vogt 2006). In Scandinavian rock art research, a distinction is generally made between a northern hunter-gatherer tradition and a southern tradition emerging at the beginning of the Bronze Age (c. 1700–500 BC). The south Scandinavian petroglyphs have traditionally been interpreted as a cultural expression of Bronze Age ideology, religion, or cosmology (e.g., Kristiansen 1990; Kaul 1998; Bradley 2009, 125). Besides general questions of chronology, the petroglyphs have thus been discussed primarily in terms of what they represent, mean, or symbolize

(Goldhahn 2008a). In recent research the focus has shifted somewhat from the petroglyph's pictorial content to also include the context in terms of regional niches, places, and the micro-topography of the rock (e.g., Tilley 2004; Ling 2008; Coles 2011). However, also in these studies the motifs are understood as images of real or ideal objects (boats, the sun, foot soles, etc.). In order to approach the petroglyphs as objects of encounter, an alternative approach is to downplay the figurative content and to focus more on how aspects of production and appropriation are related to place and materiality. From such a perspective, petroglyphs can be considered as material articulations that do not simply represent or reflect a social backdrop, but also play an active role in social formation and change.

In one sense it may seem strange to discuss petroglyphs as material articulations, since in a strict sense they constitute a void or inverted materiality. This property of being based on removal rather than com-position of matter is far from uninteresting. It is a point I will return to. It is quite evident that the "canvas," the rock face itself and its material properties, is important for understanding what petroglyphs "want." In Gibsonian terms the bedrock offers several properties that may or may not have been viewed as significant when making the images. Immov-ability is one obvious aspect of the rock, which ties the imagery to a certain place in space (and probably also to a certain landscape niche). The resilient aspect of the rock is another affordance of central impor-tance. It provides a long-lasting, perhaps even eternal, life to the images. There are examples of petroglyphs that seem to have been deliberately destroyed and others that have been covered up, intentionally or not, with rocks and soil (e.g., Goldhahn 2008b, 47; Nilsson 2012), but the fact that thousands of images pecked in rock survived into the present says a great deal. Another aspect of these resilient properties may be that it took time and effort to make petroglyphs. The typical smooth surfaces and formations created during the Ice Age are also important aspects of the rock surface, which may have been employed to relate the images and connect them to other places and locales. For example, in his analysis of the Simris petroglyphs in the southernmost of Sweden, Tilley (2004, 214) suggests that the ripples in the surface caused during the Ice Age may represent metaphorical waves of a "frozen sea." Others have discussed the audible properties of the rock as an important aspect in the process of making of the images (e.g., Nordström 1999; Whitley 2011, 156), as well as other aesthetic aspects like the feel or touch of the rock (Heyd & Clegg 2003; Tilley 2008, 201).

The material properties of the rock may play a different role in the renaissance of making petroglyphs during the Early Bronze Age in southern Scandinavia—perhaps even inviting and encouraging it due to the rock's special affordances. These material properties certainly also affect the way images were appropriated over time. It is of course difficult to wholly bypass issues of representation when discussing images like petroglyphs; the issue of representation is, however, far from unproblematic and can work in different ways. Mitchell (1994, 419–20) argues that the relation between original and representation may not be straightforward, but rather resemble an activity or process. Instead of viewing representation as a homogeneous field of relations governed by a single principle, representation may be viewed as "a heterogeneous terrain, a collage or patchwork quilt assembled over time out of fragments" (ibid.).

The idea that an image, thing, or practice can be entangled in a multitude of relationships is perhaps most frequently discussed within various strands of Actor-Network Theory (Law 1999, 3–5). Such relational and non-representational perspectives favor relational connections before categorical thinking. This view has also been explored in anthropology (Henare et al. 2007), geography (Anderson & Harrison 2010), and archaeology (e.g., Pollard 2005; Jones 2006; Ojala 2009). Being a relatively new approach, it offers by no means a coherent method or consistent theoretical framework. In a sense it can be characterized as a radicalization of social constructionism that attempts to view the social in terms of a "meshwork" of humans *and* things, real *or* ideal aspects (Ingold 2007, 80–84). Bruno Latour illustrates this point in his discussion of the hyphen between the terms "actor" and "network" in Actor-Network Theory. The main thing, he argues, is not really about actors, networks, or theory, but rather about what lies behind the hyphen between the terms (Latour 1999). The hyphen is a silent signifier of what lies between, the "dark matters" of fluid networks of relations. In a similar vein, this text will not focus on the "rock" or the "art," but on the "dark matter" between the material and the figurative (Latour 2005, 177). Although the medium, the rock, and the figurative content, the art, are certainly important, it is the space between the material and the imagery that really matters.

Having said this, it is important to point out that non-representational perspectives need not be anti-representational per se. Rather, as Anderson and Harrison (2010, 19) put it: "What pass for representations are apprehended as performative presentations, not reflections of some *a priori* order waiting to be unveiled, decoded, or revealed." Emphasizing the ways images are entangled in different sets of relations instead of defining meaning from context allow us to bypass much of the kind of binary thinking that has plagued rock-art research (e.g., real/imaginary, mobile/sedentary, Bronze Age/Neolithic, material/immaterial, general/particular, local/global, death/fertility, ritual/social, etc). A relational perspective allows for many simultaneous sets of relations, in which petroglyphs need not primarily represent something ideal or real but may in fact depend on varying circumstances (see Henare et al. 2007, 8).

BETWEEN THE REAL AND THE MAGICAL: ANIMATED IMAGERY

Throughout the history of research on them, south Scandinavian petroglyphs have been related to a varying extent to real and social circumstances. Mats Malmer suggested that they represent offerings to the gods and that petroglyphs were made as substitutes for real objects in metal (Malmer 1989, 27). Recently, Courtney Nimura (2012) has suggested that the southern tradition of mainly coast-bound petroglyphs coincides with the general land rise, and that the practice was evoked by the stress caused by the declining waters; the production of images was thus intensified during the Bronze Age, presumably in order to stop the water level from going down. Johan Ling (2008) connects the same production of images with the increasing importance of bronze, and suggests that especially the boat figure in particular is related to the import of metal to southern Scandinavia (see Ballard et al. 2003). Magical thinking may indeed be employed to evoke response from both man and nature. However, besides Malmer, very few actually argue why petroglyphs were used for such purposes instead of other means and practices. For instance, we could draw an analogy with the modern-day cargo cult of certain islands of the Pacific Ocean, whereby symbolic landing strips complete with airplanes and control towers were constructed to evoke the return of the flying colonialists (Lindstrom 1993). A landing strip, albeit fake, surely makes more sense in evoking a return than repeatedly hammering out petroglyphs on the bedrock.

A most important but often neglected aspect is that the practice of making petroglyphs has been used by the circumpolar hunter-gatherers for many millennia before it appeared in southern Scandinavia during the Early Bronze Age. At several localities, such as Alta, Kanozero, Nämforsen, and Vyg, the two traditions coincide and overlap (Gjerde 2010, 346, 381, 386; see Vogt 2006, 225), but few attempts have been made to relate them in ways other than stylistically and typologically (but see for example Sognnes 2001, 124). It would, however, seem logical that the "innovation" of a southern tradition would be related, at least in some ways, to the older (but contemporary) northern one. There are indeed a number of differences between the two, but they also have more in common than meets the eye (see Nordbladh 1980, 16; Vogt 2006, 226; Bradley 2009, 140–1; 2010, 197). The point here is that a sharp distinction between them is difficult to maintain, especially since the dating methods for petroglyphs are rather crude (e.g., Sognnes 2001, 36–38; Fahlander 2012a, 105). Instead of interpreting the petroglyphs as coming from either a Stone Age or a Bronze Age context, a non-representational approach may succeed in opening up a space in which the two traditions are allowed to intersect.

An alternative scenario could thus be that images were made in certain areas in order to relate to something or someone to whom they made sense. The Bronze Age petroglyphs have been traditionally associated with continental or even Mediterranean worlds (Kristiansen 1990; Malmer 1999; Kristiansen & Larsson 2005), but in this particular case it is perhaps more likely that they were directed to the northern hunters—after all it is "their" traditions of making petroglyphs that experience a renaissance in southern Scandinavia during this period. The newfound interest in making petroglyphs may thus have originally been a case of archaization—a way to establish connections to a semimythical past or to create a relation with others by appropriating "their" modes of articulation.

Certainly petroglyphs change according to the changing relationships of the worlds they are a part of. It is, however, important to recognize that the petroglyphs can be something more than silent representations reflecting social and natural events. It may be more useful to employ perspectivist thinking, exploring ontologically different ways of perceiving the material world (Alberti & Bray 2009). For instance, if we leave aside the asymmetrical ontology in which the human and material are separated, we may consider the prospect by which certain materialities (objects, animals, images, etc.) may be "animated" and charged with certain powers (Viveiros de Castro 2004; Ingold 2006; Hill 2011). Instead of only representing such entities, the petroglyphs may be considered ontologically "real" in a similar sense as any living entity. For example, the difference between painting or engraving an image in stone and the tedious process of pecking a petroglyph have different properties that may or may not be intentional. Whereas a rock painting may be done with a mixture of animal or human substances, the grooves of the petroglyph offer a void to be filled. It is known, for example, that in the past cup marks were greased or provided space for coins and other valuables (Goldhahn 2008b, 129). Following a similar logic, an anthropomorph or a zoomorph may be fed (or inseminated), and a boat image anointed, by filling the grooves with appropriate substances. The carefully sculptured figures, often with great emphasis on detail, make evident that the image is a critical component of the practice. However, as previously argued, petroglyphs are by definition constituted by a void, being hammered out of the rock. We may thus consider that the practice takes something away from the rock as much as it carves something on it. We have no proper means to investigate what actually happened with the dust and sand pecked from the rock, but this might have been important material, charged with powers used to create relations between different places and individuals or with the supernatural.

It is generally recognized that the practice of making petroglyphs has probably many reasons and encompasses many meanings (e.g., Goldhahn 2008b, 71). It would thus be pointless to emphasize one aspect of the practice as valid across an entire region or throughout the Bronze Age. In order to continue to discuss the tacit aspects of the petroglyphs, it is necessary to move away from generalizations and relate to a specific body of material. In particular, I wish to discuss a cluster of petroglyphs outside the modern city of Enköping, about 100 kilometers northwest of the Swedish capital Stockholm (see Figure 15.1). At the parish of Boglösa there is an interesting cluster of petroglyphs, mainly from the

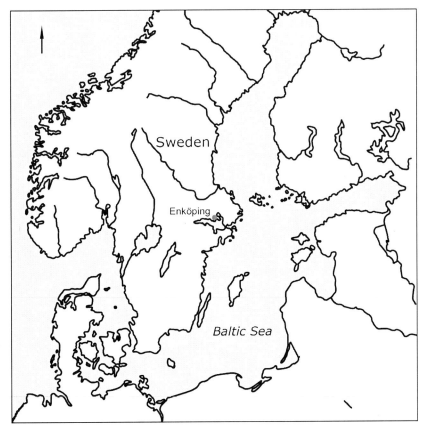

Figure 15.1 Map of southern Scandinavia with the location of the Enköping area

Late Neolithic and Early Bronze Age (Kjellén & Hyenstrand 1977; Coles 2000; Ling 2012).

A BAY OF IMAGES: THE PETROGLYPHS AT BOGLÖSA, UPPLAND

The county of Uppland comprises one of the densest concentrations of petroglyphs in southern Sweden. Hitherto 7721 boats, 309 "foot soles," 190 anthropomorphs, 185 zoomorphs, 128 circle features, and 612 other/undeterminable motifs, along with over 19000 cup marks, have been registered in this area alone (Goldhahn et al. 2010, 7). The area around Enköping encompasses a majority of the figurative petroglyphs, which cluster on the eastern mainland side of what during the Early Bronze Age (c. 1700–1100 BC) was a shallow cove. Why this particular place became filled with images in stone is by no means apparent. There are no particular settlement structures, burials, or other cultural remains that suggest that this place was much different from any other along the east coast. Some have suggested that it may have been an aggregation site where different maritime groups met and interacted and manifested their relations by making images in the bedrock (Wessman 2010; Ling 2012; see also Fahlander 2012a).

However, instead of viewing the appearance of petroglyphs as merely a result of social circumstances, it is also important to emphasize the different ways in which these images may have been integral parts of such a social process. For instance, what happened in this particular corner of the world when the rocks at the water's edge began to be filled with images? How did it begin, and what were the consequences of such a development? Is it meaningful to equate the sheer number of images with a similar number of people? Can we even suggest that the abundance of petroglyphs is relative to the importance of the site? Or is it perhaps something analogous to modern day graffiti, something forbidden that is performed secretly at non-places and hidden areas?

For the Kilmartin region of Scotland, Andrew Jones has suggested that the making of petroglyphs draws attention to places and also relates different places to each other, creating relational links by means of imagery: "The production of images is a form of poeisis, a way of weaving a sense of belonging and place, just as images are visually woven into the rock surface. More than this, it is a way of objectifying or visualizing the relationship between people and place" (Jones 2006, 222). In order to pursue such facets of the practice we need to consider in greater detail the particular circumstances in which the images were made.

Unfortunately, the shore displacement calculations in the area are not very precise because they are either not local or not detailed enough. The most recent one for southwest Uppland by Plikk (2010) ends at 1400 BC, and we can only roughly estimate the water level for the Late Neolithic and Early Bronze Age to c. 20–25 meters above the current sea level. The shore displacement rate is important because it suggests that the first petroglyphs were likely to be pecked very close to the water's edge. This is imperative for our understanding of the practice and of the role the images may have played. The green dots on Figure 15.2 mark sites with figurative petroglyphs along a shoreline c. 20 meters above the present-day level. The actual water level during the Early Bronze Age may have been a few meters higher. It is clearly evident that the petroglyphs tend to cluster at the water's edge at small creeks and coves and within the shallow bay. When studying the micro-topography of the sites it is also obvious that the majority of images face the water world, and when placed on islets they only rarely face the mainland. These circumstances imply that they were either made to be seen while approaching by boat or that they were directed to the seascape itself.

The audible aspects may have been of importance here. From ethnographic accounts we know that the sound of making images normally does not go unnoticed by people in the vicinity (Whitley 2011, 156–57).

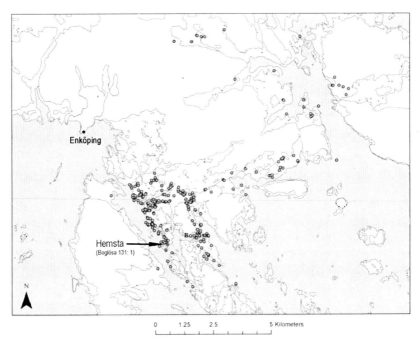

Figure 15.2   Boglösa Bay of Images (modified after Wessman 2011)

Pecking can often be heard from far away, which makes the practice noticeable. Patrik Nordström suggests that the sound of pecking petroglyphs was an important aspect that connected the imagery to the place and echoed relations to previous generations. The association with sound, he continues, implies that the sight of the images could have evoked audible memories, making the images more alive than simple silent representations (Nordström 1999, 134). Since the petroglyphs were made at the water's edge, the sound was likely to be heard over greater distances over the water than over the land. This may be an important hint of the image-making process and support the idea that the images were directed toward the seascape. However, in this particular case the bay may actually have been chosen to avoid the sound from being heard, since the large island to the west must have dampened the noise. These circumstances hint that the bay may have been chosen because of its secluded properties, suggesting that the images should not be heard nor seen.

Following the logic of these considerations, the production of petroglyphs by the water's edge can thus be seen either as a way of relating the local inhabitants with the wider world (real and/or imagined) or as a way for maritime groups to relate to the unknown worlds on the mainland (real and/or imagined). To complicate issues further, the petroglyphs might have been produced by both "locals" and "visitors." The manner in which certain motifs of different style and date relate to each other indicates that they can be interpreted as a case of an iconoclastic clash (an iconoclash) between different groups. Elsewhere I have suggested that the typical southern tradition of petroglyphing emerged in a hybrid flux between different ways of life during the Late Neolithic and Early Bronze Age (Fahlander 2012a; see Sognnes 2001, 131). From such a perspective it is easy to picture different groups, with both maritime and terrestrial lifestyles, moving about in the area and making images in stone to create and negotiate their relations with the different niches of the region. Some of the images may thus articulate a relation to the land world and others relate to the water world. The Boglösa "bay of images" becomes a material articulation of hybridity (Fahlander 2007, 2012b).

The idea that the Boglösa area may have been a kind of middle ground of hybrid relations may be substantiated by focusing in greater detail on how subsequent images relate to each other and to the properties of the bedrock. At the beginning of the Early Bronze Age, the Hemsta outcrop was a small islet at the southern entrance to the Boglösa bay. The altitude above sea level suggests that this outcrop was submerged until about 2500 BC, when it gradually became visible above the surface (see Figure 15.3).

Figure 15.3 A tentative illustration of how the Hemsta outcrop may have looked at the beginning of the second millennium BC. View from the mainland toward the island in the west.

A broad range of different motifs are present at the site, including anthropomorphs, zoomorphs, and geometric figures, but the vast majority of the images consist of various boat-like figures. What makes this small outcrop particularly interesting is that it has recently been subject to detailed documentation that not only recorded the varying depth of the images but also the natural cracks, fissures, and ores in the bedrock. This has made it feasible to establish a horizontal stratigraphy of a sequence of phases (Fahlander 2012a). Figure 15.4 illustrates the main phases. The earliest motifs are two shallowly pecked boats with hatched hulls and a group of animals, one of which is merged with one of the boats (light gray). The second phase consists of two columns of distinctly cut stacked boats (black); these superimpose the hatched boats. The third phase (gray) consists of a number of smaller boat images that also superimpose the earliest motifs but are adjusted to fit the gaps between the stacked boats.

In more detail, the first phase (light gray) consists of two boat figures and a number of zoomorphs and is distinguished by the following aspects: the cut is thin and shallow, the type and design of the boats are rare (only found at a few other sites), the two boats and the animals vary in alignment, and one boat extends over a natural crack in the bedrock. An interesting aspect of this is that one of the animals is incorporated

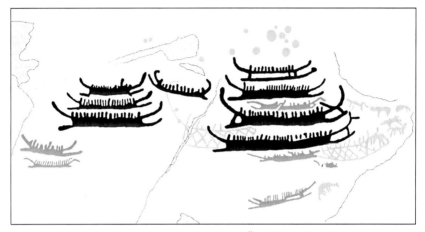

Figure 15.4 Part of the Hemsta outcrop (RAÄ Boglösa 131) and the sequence of phases illustrated in shades of gray. Image retouched based on a documentation made by Broström (2011).

into one of the boats, a phenomenon commonly found in the northern Neolithic tradition (e.g., Sjöstrand 2011, 123). The motifs of the second phase (black), by contrast, are distinctly and deeply cut, they have a similar design with hammered-out hulls, they share an alignment, and are stacked on top of each other. They do not avoid interfering with the previously cut boats but do not extend over the natural cracks of the bedrock. It is interesting how they relate in size to each other. Although they differ slightly in length, their size is maximized in relation to the available space between the cracks in the bedrock. The third phase is characterized by a number of boats of smaller size and slightly different style. These figures too are adjusted to the natural cracks in the bedrock, and they superimpose the images of the first phase. They do, however, avoid the previously carved images of the second phase.

The rather abrupt change from the first two delicate pecked boats found on a recently submerged rocky island in the Enköping archipelago to the columns of distinctly cut boat motifs filling the available surface may constitute a classic example of an iconoclash (Latour 2002). The two columns of large boats dominate the space, not only by size and depth, but also by their consistent alignment: in a sense they "kill" the previous images. The subsequent third phase of smaller boats seemingly adjusted to the large ones may represent a case of relating to something of the past, perhaps in a similar way that secondary burials sometimes relate to a previous burial mound. This superimposition also indicates the importance of a particular space, in this case the uppermost area of the impediment, since there were a lot of suitable areas to make new petroglyphs just meters away.

The displacements in size, depth, alignment, and superimposition suggest that the panel is not likely to be a planned composition. The sequence rather shows a cumulative development between phases, again not too different from the development of burial grounds in which new burials need to relate to previous ones (see Moberg 1965). Two of the boat figures illustrate the careful adjustment of subsequent images. One is a boat of the third phase that has been crammed to fit in between two larger boat images of the previous phase. The prows of the boat have been bent to fit the available space. It is interesting that the extended size of the prow and keel lines were regarded as so important that they were not simply reduced in size but were rather bent in an unusual manner. The other example is the topmost boat on the left column of boat images (light blue). Here the diagonal crack in the bedrock has prevented it from being placed on top of the other three boats, as in the right column. Instead, the boat has been placed at an angle at the side of the left column. These priorities have resulted in a figure that has a more curved shape and thus an apparently different style. It may be noted that this phenomenon is not unique to this particular rock. Another example of this type of adjustments to the column format is also found on another panel (RAÄ Boglösa 73:1)[1] a few kilometers north of Hemsta. Again this panel consists of two columns of boat images fitted between natural cracks of the rock, and the stacking of images is disrupted. In this case an anthropomorph figure is placed above the two lowermost boats and thus forces the third to be placed at an angle at the side of the left column.

The apparent importance of the natural cracks in the bedrock is interesting in several ways. The relations between different images and the rock seem to be randomly dispersed. They obviously relate to each other as well as to the cracks and fissures of the bedrock. The apparent importance of the Hemsta panel discussed here may thus not be necessarily due to its location at the entrance of the bay, nor to its being the highest space on the outcrop, but to the way the bedrock offers a suitable space between the cracks. This is informative, since it reveals aspects of the boat motif that were important to those who made the images.

MATERIAL RELATION-SHIPS (OR, WHAT THIS "BOAT" MEANS)

It is interesting to note the small but significant displacements in the way in which new motifs have been added to the Hemsta outcrop. Seen from an iconological perspective, most images on this particular panel are of roughly the same style and are dated to the first period of the Bronze Age—except the images of the first phase, which show some differences in style and are of Neolithic date (Ling 2012, 52). Of all the figurative petroglyphs in Uppland, the boat motif is by far the most common. Of 472 figurative panels, 408 contain one or more boats (ibid., 4). I have used the descriptive term "boat" in this text for convenience, but without subscribing to any *a priori* ideas of what they may or may not represent. Indeed, what these iconic figures really represent, symbolize, or mean is far from evident. The close spatial relation to the water's edge is one indication of a maritime interpretation, and there are also a few petroglyphs that portray in greater detail a crew of paddlers (e.g., Coles 1995, 27). One obvious examples of this, the huge Brandskog boat, is also found in the Boglösa area (see Figure 15.5). However, images always carry a potential to be something other than what they seem to depict (Ginzburg 2002, 63ff; Wittgenstein 2009). There are few means for us to understand if the petroglyphs are pictures, pictograms, or ideograms (e.g., Mitchell 1987, 27).

Since we do not know the ontological status of the petroglyphs, it is problematic to assume that a boat image made in stone is a boat (whether it is supposed to represent a real vessel of a mythological one).

Figure 15.5 The big Brandskog boat (RAÄ Boglösa 109), c. 4.2 meters long. The date is uncertain but is stylistically attributed to the Late Bronze Age. Photo by Einar Kjellén (Enköpings Museum, ID:109M CBekBoglosaby).

The boat figure is interesting for other reasons than its representational features of image content. An important aspect of the boat motif lies in its overall consistency. It is striking how uniform the basic boat motif is over great distances and over long periods of time (see Ljunge, in press). Although they come in many different shapes and forms, these boats are generally recognizable to us as similar. But was it evident to the circumpolar hunter-gatherers that their boats were the same as those of the Bronze Age communities? If these images represent actual sea vessels, their importance must have been quite diverse according to different ways of life.

I do not question the boat interpretation nor that these figures mean something, or perhaps even illustrate and represent something. However, to treat the petroglyphs from a representational perspective as "objects of recognition" masks and renders invisible other aspects of the motif. Whether one wishes to understand these images as depictions of real vehicles indicating primarily maritime activity (Ling 2008), as ideal vessels transporting the dead to the other side (Ekholm 1916), as vessels transporting the sun (Kaul 1998), or as representing "boat-loads of people" (Tilley 2004, 195), such categorical way of thinking is problematic.

An alternative way of looking at this motif is as something similar to an iconic key symbol (Ortner 1973). As such it need not have a particular essence but can be employed as a vehicle for the mind for a variety of purposes (see Sjöstrand 2011, 160). From such a perspective, the apparent importance of certain details (e.g., the bent prows) and the overall great variability of the boat motif make better sense (e.g., figures mixed with both contour and hammered-out hulls, boats with or without "crew strokes," etc.). The boat figure may thus have been a way of articulating a great numbers of things. This allows for quite a lot of creativity in varying and combining different elements and figures with each other and the rock. The variability is thus also part of "the message."

The category of "boats" and the conclusions drawn from such an interpretation not only illustrate the difficulties with viewing the imagery as objects of recognition; it also underlines the perils of being trapped by the aesthetic appearance of the imagery and its presumed social context. For example, it is indicative how the visual worlds of the Bronze Age differ between the Irish/British contexts and those of southern Scandinavia. In studies of the former, the period is discussed in almost mundane terms, whereas research on the south Scandinavian petroglyphs focuses much more on grand narratives of cosmology or ideology. As Jones (2006, 214) has indicated, this might partly be due to the fact that Irish/British rock art consists of abstract motifs, whereas the southern Scandinavian art is figurative and "recognizable." The binary division of Scandinavian rock art in a northern and a southern tradition comprises an analogous case. It is not surprising that the northern tradition is largely argued to be a shamanic articulation, whereas the southern tradition is charged with a much more complex cosmology with ideological underpinnings (e.g., Malmer 1981; Kaul 1998). For instance, when Tilley writes about making petroglyphs of swords, lures, and other metal objects as "bronzing the rock" (2008, 253), a parallel way or reasoning would be to see petroglyphs in the northern tradition as "elking the rock." Clearly our preconceived understandings of the society in question direct our interpretations of the practice and the meaning of rock art.

However, contrasting interpretations across contexts can also be illustrative when it comes to different uses of similar motifs or techniques, relations, and combinations—for instance, the way boat motifs are made and arranged in the northern and southern tradition, respectively. What does it mean that the northern tradition is dominated by elk figures and the southern tradition by boat figures? Indeed, there seems to be a much more integrated relation between those two types of figures. In the northern tradition of circumpolar hunters, petroglyphs of four-legged zoomorphs ("elks") and boats are frequently mixed and combined in various ways. Some boat images have what looks like animal heads on the prow. A number of figures have also been transformed from boats to elks and vice versa by later manipulations and additions (e.g., Bolin 2000, 167–69; Sjöstrand 2011, 123). Examples of similar hybrids are, as mentioned, found at the Hemsta outcrop (Boglösa 131). The large Brandskog boat has unmistakable animal heads on its prows, and there are other examples of more stylized "elk-boats" in the area as well (e.g., Boglösa 73 and 123).

It is also intriguing that a relation (elk-boat) that apparently emerged within a mobile hunting and gathering life style has survived in the more sedentary, farming lifestyle of the Bronze Age. It is difficult to understand which unknown "dark matters" lie in this particular hyphen, but the elk-boat motif illustrates the problems with categorical thinking and typological approaches to imagery. Another transformation common to the two seemingly different traditions of making petroglyphs is the practice of exaggerating and prolonging certain elements of the figure. In the northern tradition it can be the necks of bird figures, whereas in the southern tradition it is human extremities and artifact depictions that are exaggerated (Fahlander 2012b, 2013).

The use of similar, though not identical, motifs in both traditions is interesting since it may provide a link between different ways of life as well as between the past and the present. It is probably no coincidence that the southern tradition emerged during the Early Bronze Age. It is an old tradition that was probably made deliberately in a different style to mark a break, a distinction. This is illustrated by the "killing" of the first pair of boats at Hemsta by the new boat figures, distinctly cut in a new style. Thus, the use of an archaic tradition signals a relation to the old ways at the same time as it emphasizes a break with them.

CONCLUSIONS

In this chapter, I have discussed the prospects of a relational and non-representative analysis of south Scandinavian petroglyphs as an alternative to traditional contextual and stylistic approaches to image analysis. This perspective is not necessarily better and does not entirely replaces contextual and interpretive approaches, but it has the potential to emphasize the relational aspects of images, practices, and materialities that tend to be made invisible in categorical and contextual approaches. By analyzing petroglyphs as material articulations rather than representations, it is possible to see them as part of social structuration rather than a simple reflection of it. The focus is placed here on the possible magical aspects of the practice of making images in stone and of their unintended and unforeseen effects.

My analysis of the Hemsta outcrop emphasized the materiality of the medium, the rock. The resilient nature of the bedrock offers the images almost eternal life and binds them to a certain place. Such an impression is also supported by the Hemsta panel, which shows how boat images are adjusted to the natural cracks and fissures in the rock in order to be intact. The rock also provides a resistance and demands an effort to make images, which also places emphasis on aspects such as size and depth, level of detail, and aesthetic appearance. In particular the common boat figure, as an iconic key symbol, is nested in various sets of relationships. The making of petroglyphs in south Scandinavia during the Early Bronze Age was an active component in a series of material "meshworks" connecting sea and land, human and material, farming and hunting, past and present, as well as different places.

NOTE

1. RAÄ number according to the ancient monuments registry (Fornminnesregistret), based on parishes and current number within the parish.

REFERENCES

Alberti, B. & Bray, T. 2009. Introduction. Animating archaeology: of subjects, objects and alternative ontologies. *Cambridge Archaeological Journal* 19(3), 337–43

Aldhouse-Green, M.J. 2004. *An Archaeology of Images: Iconology and Cosmology in Iron Age and Roman Europe*. London: Routledge

Anderson, B. & Harrison, P. 2010. *Taking Place: Non-Representational Theories and Geography*. Farnham, UK: Ashgate

Ballard, C., Bradley, R., Nordenborg Myhre, L. & Wilson, M. 2003. The ship as symbol in the prehistory of Scandinavia and South-east Asia. *World Archaeology* 35(3), 385–403

Bolin, H. 2000. Animal magic: the mythological significance of elks, boats and humans in North Swedish rock art. *Journal of Material Culture* 5(2), 153–76

Bradley, R. 2009. *Image and Audience: Rethinking Prehistoric Art*. Oxford: Oxford University Press

Bradley, R. 2010. Epilogue: drawing on stone. In J. Goldhahn, I. Fuglestvedt & A. Jones (eds.), *Changing Pictures: Rock Art Traditions and Visions in Northern Europe*, 197–205. Oxford, UK: Oxbow Books

Broström, S-G. 2011. *Hällristningarna Raa 130 och 392 samt två nyfynd i Hemsta hage, Boglösa socken Uppland: redogörelse över ny dokumentation 2009*. Tumba, Swed.: Botark AB

Cochrane, A. & Russell, I. 2007. Visualizing archaeologies: a manifesto. *Cambridge Archaeological Journal* 17(1), 3–19

Coles, J. 1995. *Hällristningar i Uppland. En vägledning*. Uppsala, Swed.: University of Uppsala

Coles, J. 2000. *Patterns in a Rocky Land: Rock Carvings in South-West Uppland*. Uppsala, Swed.: Department of Archaeology and Ancient History, University of Uppsala

Coles, J. 2011. A theatre of imagery: the rock carving of Döltorp, Skee Parish, Bohuslän, Sweden. *Antiquaries Journal* 91, 1–25

Ekholm, G. 1916. De skandinaviska hällristningarna och deras betydelse. *Ymer* 1916, 275–308

Fahlander, F. 2007. Third space encounters: hybridity, mimicry and interstitial practice. In P. Cornell & F. Fahlander (eds.), *Encounters-Materialities-Confrontations: Archaeologies of Social Space and Interaction*, 15–43. Newcastle, UK: Cambridge Scholars Publishing

Fahlander, F. 2012a. Articulating stone: the material practice of petroglyphing. In I.-M. Back Danielsson, F. Fahlander & Y. Sjöstrand (eds.), *Encountering Imagery: Materialities, Perceptions, Relations*, 97–116. Stockholm: University of Stockholm

Fahlander, F. 2012b. Articulating hybridity: structurating situations and indexical events in north-European rock art. In N.M. Burström & F. Fahlander (eds.), *Matters of Scale: Processes and Courses of Events in Archaeology and Cultural History*, 53–74. Stockholm, Swed.: University of Stockholm

Fahlander, F. 2013. Skillnadens dimensioner: storlek och materialitet i hällbildspraktik. *Primitive Tider* 16, 7–20

Gell, A. 1992. The technology of enchantment and the enchantment of technology. In J. Coote & A. Shelton (eds.), *Anthropology, Art and Aesthetics*, 40–63. Oxford, UK: Clarendon Press

Ginzburg, C. 2002. *Wooden Eyes: Nine Reflections on Distance*. Translated by M. Ryle & K. Soper. London: Verso

Gjerde, J.M. 2010. *Rock Art and Landscapes: Studies of Stone Age Rock Art from Northern Fennoscandia*. Tromsø, Nor.: University of Tromsø

Goldhahn, J. 2008a. Rock art research in northernmost Europe, 2000–2004. In P. Bahn, N. Franklin & M. Strecklin (eds.), *Rock Art Studies: News of the World III*, 16–36. Oxford, UK: Oxbow Books

Goldhahn, J. 2008b. *Hällbildsstudier i norra Europa*. 2nd edition. Gothenburg, Swed.: University of Gothenburg

Goldhahn, J., Fuglestvedt, I. & Jones, A. 2010. Changing pictures: an introduction. In J. Goldhahn, I. Fuglestvedt & A. Jones (eds.), *Changing Pictures: Rock Art Traditions and Visions in Northern Europe*, 1–22. Oxford, UK: Oxbow Books

Henare, A., Holbraad, M. & Wastell, S. 2007. Introduction: thinking through things. In A. Henare, M. Holbraad & S. Wastell. (eds.), *Thinking Through Things: Theorising Artefacts Ethnographically*, 1–31. London: Routledge

Heyd, T. & Clegg, J. (eds.) 2003. *Aesthetics and Rock Art*. Burlington, VT: Ashgate

Hill, E. 2011. Animals as agents: hunting ritual and relational ontologies in prehistoric Alaska and Chukotka. *Cambridge Archaeological Journal* 21, 407–26

Ingold, T. 2006. Rethinking the animate, re-animating thought. *Ethnos* 71(1), 9–20

Ingold, T. 2007. *Lines: A Brief History*. London: Routledge

Jones, A. 2006. Animated images: images, agency and landscape in Kilmartin, Argyll. *Journal of Material Culture* 11(1–2), 211–26

Kaul, F. 1998. *Ships on Bronzes: A Study in Bronze Age Religion and Iconography*. Copenhagen, Den.: National Museum

Kristiansen, K. 1990. *Europe before History*. Cambridge: Cambridge University Press

Kristiansen, K. & Larsson, T.B. 2005. *The Rise of Bronze Age Society: Travels, Transmissions and Transformations*. Cambridge: Cambridge University Press

Kjellén, E. & Hyenstrand, Å. 1977. *Hällristningar och bronsålderssamhälle i sydvästra Uppland*. Uppsala, Swed.: Upplands fornminnesfören

Latour, B. 1999. On recalling ANT. In J. Law & J. Hassard (eds.), *Actor-Network Theory and After*, 15–25. Oxford, UK: Blackwell

Latour, B. 2002. What is iconoclash? Or is there a world beyond the image wars? In B. Latour & P. Weibel (eds.), *Iconoclash*, 16–38. Karlsruhe, Germ.: ZKM Centre for Art and Media

Latour, B. 2005. *Reassembling the Social: An Introduction to Actor-Network Theory*. Oxford: Oxford University Press

Law, J. 1999. After ANT: complexity, naming and topology. In J. Law & J. Hassard (eds.), *Actor-Network Theory and After*, 1–14. Oxford, UK: Blackwell

Lindstrom, L. 1993. *Cargo Cult: Strange Stories of Desire from Melanesia and Beyond*. Honolulu: University of Hawaii Press

Ling, J. 2008. *Elevated Rock Art: Towards a Maritime Understanding of Bronze Age Rock Art in Northern Bohuslän, Sweden*. Gothenburg, Swed.: University of Gothenburg

Ling, J. 2012. *Rock Art and Seascapes in Uppland*. Oxford, UK: Oxbow Books

Ljunge, M. In press. Mellan stil och symbolik: om estetiska och konsthistoriska perspektiv på hällbilder. In M. Ljunge & A. Röst (eds.), *Aktuell Bronsålder*. Stockholm, Swed.: University of Stockholm

Malmer, M.P. 1981. *A Chorological Study of North European Rock Art*. Stockholm, Swed.: University of Stockholm

Malmer, M.P. 1989. Bergkonstens mening och innehåll. In S. Janson, E.B. Lundberg & U. Bertilsson (eds.), *Hällristningar och hällmålningar i Sverige*, 9–28. Stockholm, Swed.: Forum

Malmer, M.P. 1999. How and why did Greece communicate with Scandinavia in the Bronze Age? In C. Orrling (ed.), *Communication in Bronze Age Europe: Transactions of the Bronze Age*, 33–42. Stockholm, Swed.: Statens Historiska Museum

Mitchell, W.J.T. 1987. *Iconology: Image, Text, Ideology*. Chicago, IL: University of Chicago Press

Mitchell, W.J.T. 1994. *Picture Theory: Essays on Verbal and Visual Representation*. Chicago, IL: University of Chicago Press

Mitchell, W.J.T. 1996. What Do Pictures Really Want? *October* 77, 71–82

Moberg, C-A. 1965. Historia ur fornlämningar. In S. Janson & C-A. Moberg (eds.), *Med Arkeologen Sverige Runt*, 7–44. Stockholm, Swed.: Forum

Nilsson, P. 2012. The beauty is in the *act* of the beholder: South Scandinavian rock art sites from a uses of the past–perspective. In F. Fahlander, I-M. Back Danielsson & Y. Sjöstrand (eds.), *The Materiality of the Perceptible*, 77–96. Stockholm, Swed.: University of Stockholm

Nimura, C. 2012. Rock art and coastal change in Bronze Age Scandinavia. In F. Fahlander, I-M. Back Danielsson & Y. Sjöstrand (eds.), *The Materiality of the Perceptible*, 117–32. Stockholm, Swed.: University of Stockholm

Nordbladh, J. 1980. *Glyfer och rum kring hällristningar i Kville*. Gothenburg, Swed.: University of Gothenburg

Nordström, P. 1999. Ristningarnas rytm. Om hällristningar och landskap: exemplet Boglo¨sa i Uppland. In P. Nordström & M. Svedin (eds.), *Aktuell Arkeologi VII*, 127–36. Stockholm, Swed.: Stockholm Archaeological Report 36

O'Sullivan, S. 2005. *Art Encounters Deleuze and Guattari: Thought beyond Representation*. Basingstoke, UK: Palgrave Macmillan

Ojala, C-G. 2009. *Sàmi Prehistories: The Politics of Archaeology and Identity in Northernmost Europe*. Uppsala, Swed.: University of Uppsala

Ortner, S.B. 1973. On key symbols. *American Anthropologist* 75(5), 1338–46

Panofsky, E. 1972. *Studies in Iconology: Humanistic Themes in the Art of the Renaissance*. New York: Oxford University Press

Plikk, A. 2010. *Shore Displacement in Fjärdhundraland, SW Uppland, and the Northern Coastal Areas of Lake Mälaren since c. 1000 BC*. Unpublished master's thesis, Department of Physical Geography and Quaternary Geology, Stockholm University

Pollard, J. 2005. The art of decay and the transformation of substance. In C. Renfrew, C. Gosden & E. DeMarrais (eds.), *Substance, Memory and Display: Archaeology and Art*, 47–62. Cambridge, UK: McDonald Institute Monographs

Rosengren, M. 2012. *Cave Art, Perception and Knowledge*. London: Palgrave Macmillan

Sjöstrand, Y. 2011. *Med älgen i huvudrollen: om fångstgropar, hällbilder och skärvstensvallar i mellersta Norrland*. Stockholm, Swed.: University of Stockholm

Sognnes, K. 2001. *Prehistoric Imagery and Landscapes: Rock Art in Stjørdal, Trøndelag, Norway*. Oxford: British Archaeological Reports, International Series 998

Tilley, C. 2004. *The Materiality of Stone*. Oxford, UK: Berg

Tilley, C. 2008. *Body and Image: Explorations in Landscape Phenomenology II*. Oxford, UK: Berg

Viveiros de Castro, E. 2004. Exchanging perspectives: the transformation of objects into subjects in Amerindian ontologies. *Common Knowledge* 10(3), 463–84

Vogt, D. 2006. *Helleristninger i Østfold og Bohuslän: en analyse av det økonomiske og politiske landskap*. Oslo, Nor.: Oslo University

Wessman, A. 2010. *Hällbilder, landskap och sociala logiker*. Unpublished master's thesis, Department of Historical Studies, University of Gothenburg

Whitley, D. 2011. *Introduction to Rock Art Research*. 2nd edition. Walnut Creek, CA: Left Coast Press

Wittgenstein, L. 2009. *Philosophical Investigations*. New York: Wiley

CHAPTER SIXTEEN

Materials of Affect: Miniatures in the Scandinavian Late Iron Age (AD 550–1050)

Ing-Marie Back Danielsson

This paper discusses Scandinavian gold-foil figures—small human-like figures hammered or cut out of thin foil—from the early part of the Scandinavian Late Iron Age (AD 550–1050) from a relational perspective. Earlier interpretations largely approach them as symbols and representations, which downplays their practical or performative role and results in static or embalmed objects. In this paper I discuss the affective dimensions of the figures, as well as some of the myriad rhizomatic relations that were generated through the processes of manufacture, manipulation, and visual encounter. I will argue that during the Late Iron Age in Scandinavia certain human beings and gold-foil figures were ontological equivalents, and that gold-foil figures go far beyond our contemporary understanding of representations.

THEORETICAL CONSIDERATIONS: FROM REPRESENTATION TO PRACTICE

Like other archaeological materials that come in miniature form, gold-foil figures are commonly interpreted as symbols and representations of different sorts. Since they also come in human/oid form, they are interpreted as representations of specific gods, known through later, medieval written sources. However, such interpretations are problematic. One of their most problematic aspects is the disregard of the variety of bodily manipulations the figures have undergone. In other words, the practices and the events in which the figures partook are neglected, and

Archaeology after Interpretation: Returning Materials to Archaeological Theory, edited by Benjamin Alberti, Andrew Meirion Jones, and Joshua Pollard, 325–43.

as a result the possibility to understand the figures in terms of affect is precluded. I argue, following Harrison (2000), Thrift (2000), and Whatmore (2002), that interpretations that focus on representation and meaning tend to downplay practice to the extent that the objects, or events, of study become "drained for the sake of orders, mechanisms, structures and processes" (Dewsbury et al. 2002, 438).

When we consider an object as a representation, the lived present is ignored and, more importantly, is not considered as "an open-ended and generative process" (Harrison 2000, 499). Instead we need to understand what Anderson & Harrison (2010, 10) describe as things taking place; we need to recognize the movement and change of things and how an increased focus on practices and events results in discovering "new potentialities for being, doing and thinking." From a feminist point of view, the focus on the lived present as an open-ended and generative process is attractive (see, for instance, Harding 1987, 1993; Longino 1994, 483). Feminists in archaeology have long since pointed to the delimiting ontological and epistemic norms that underlie and prefigure archaeological practice in all forms. These norms include the impulse to seek closure and to reduce ambiguity and complexity (Wylie 2007, 212–13, with references), which I consider to be characteristic traits of theories that are exclusively devoted to representation and meaning. Thus the criticism against representational theories, which is nascent in some disciplines, such as archaeology, and more or less established in others, such as geography, is not revolutionary or new to feminists. These critical approaches are often labeled as non-representational theories; some of them, especially in response to feminist concerns, prefer the somewhat more nuanced notion of "more-than-representational" (Cadman 2009, 7; see also Dewsbury et al. 2002, 438; Lorimer 2005).

This shift in focus has also resulted in the elaboration of different methodologies, striving to "coproduce" the world (Thrift 2000; see Latour 1991; Dewsbury et al. 2002; Keane 2003; Meskell 2006). Dewsbury (2003) describes one such method as witnessing, with the purpose of presenting descriptions "that are infused with a certain fidelity to what they describe" (Latham 2003, 1903). This means that the leap towards an overarching meaning, interpretation, and/or representation is avoided. In what follows, Scandinavian Late Iron Age gold-foil figures will be discussed through the lenses of witnessing, in an effort to unfold the different practices these figures were involved in and, perhaps, instigators of. Necessarily, I will also discuss the ontological status of these crafted things and of the different sets of relationships that produced their being and becoming. Whereas witnessing may be perceived as a passive, unreflexive, and irresponsible practice, the witnessing conducted in this chapter does not strive to be modest, unaccountable, or unreflexive. My hope is that this will allow me to deal with the concern that non-representational theories would neglect, and perhaps deny, power relations as well as bodily differences (Colls 2011, with references).

My approach to materials is influenced by the recent work of Conneller (2011), who has advocated a processual understanding of materials. "Raw" materials need not necessarily be understood using contemporary physical or chemical descriptions (e.g., on the basis of the periodic table of elements). Conneller argues that materials are best understood through what they do, rather than what they are. This approach to materials can be followed by tracing "the processes by which the properties of past materials emerge reveals configurations of past worlds; particular articulations of the cultural, the natural and the supernatural" (ibid., 125). The figures are examined, or witnessed, here from two different but interrelated perspectives: *materials* and *relations*. First, I pay attention to the material aspect of the figures, highlighting also how they worked as materials of affect. Second, by examining the different relationships prompted and produced by the figures, I discuss them in terms of the different scales and power dimensions they affect. It is worth pointing out that these two witnessing perspectives at times naturally intersect.

MATERIALS

THE FIGURES

Gold-foil figures are very small figures stamped on or cut out of thin foil, known only from Scandinavia (see Figure 16.1). They are mainly attributed to the Vendel Period (AD 550–800), although their chronological span might begin in the Migration Period (AD 400–550) and end in the Viking Age (AD 800–1050) (Lamm 2004, 130). The figures have a length of c. 1–2.5 centimeters and weigh less than one gram, commonly c. 0.1–0.15 grams (Gullman 2004). Despite their small size, the figures are usually very detailed in their execution. The thin gold foils may show human-like single figures, pairs, and at times also animals (see Figures 16.2–16.5). A few may be highly stylized (see Figure 16.6).

The majority of the figures are stamped with the use of patrices of bronze, whereas others may be cut out of a very thin gold foil (Lamm 2004, 109). Whereas a matrix has a depression into which the material is pressed, a patrix has a raised motif over which thin material, in this case thin gold foil, is pressed or molded. A solid bronze patrix produced the gold foil figure with a positive image in relief. Occasionally, patrices

Figure 16.1 Map of Scandinavia with the geographical locations of patrices and gold-foil figures

equipped with a helping handle have been found (Lamm 2004, 105). The most frequent places of recovery of the figures are in connection to special buildings or workshops (e.g., Helgö, Slöinge, Borg, Uppåkra, Svintuna, Vä, Husby), some of which are considered to be aristocratic halls. The

Figure 16.2   Gold-foil figures from Bornholm, Denmark

Figure 16.3   Gold-foil figure from Bornholm, Denmark

figures have also been recovered in a bog (Tørring), in secondary burials (Bolmsö, Visingsö, Ulltuna), and in or as components of hoards (Hög Edsten, Nørre Hvam) (Andréasson 1995; Lamm 2004).

Efforts are commonly made by archaeologists to sex the figures and to attribute them to divine identities found in later medieval written

Figure 16.4   Gold-foil couple from Östergötland, Sweden

Figure 16.5   Figure from Uppåkra, Sweden, "dressed" with golden necklace

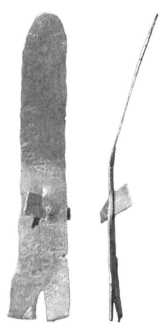

Figure 16.6 Figure from Uppåkra, seemingly stabbed by a golden item in its abdomen

sources (e.g., Hauck 1992, 1993a, 1993b; Watt 2001). Almost every archaeological publication presenting and discussing gold-foil figures, or any figure for that matter, seems to concentrate on the figures per se and their possible identities, almost as if they were contemporary photographs (e.g., Hauck 1992, 1993a; Watt 2001; see also criticism of this in, for instance, Bailey 2005, 12–13; Back Danielsson 2012). Further, a prevailing interpretation of the gold-foil figures is that they represent gods and heroes and that they worked as temple coins, a way of paying for ritual services (e.g., Hauck 1994, 302; Watt 1992; 2004, 216).

GOLD

When we turn our attention to the material itself, and adopt a witnessing stance, the following traceable events are unfolded. The analysis of the gold in the foil figures has shown that the precious material was smelted many times and came from different origins (Gullman 2004, 113). We can already notice here the motility of gold as a material; the gold has been transformed in a variety of circumstances to become a variety of objects, which in turn were used for a number of transformational purposes in both human and supernatural worlds. As we shall see below, the processes by which the gold was transformed is interrelated to other technical processes that emphasized properties of wealth and regeneration.

The smith or artisan would make the figures by first melting small quantities of gold (alloy) with a flame and a blowpipe (Gullman 2004). Although gold is ductile, its casting required the use of bellows or another air source for the furnace; pure gold melts at 1064 degrees Celsius (Jørgensen & Vang Petersen 1998, 29). In order to work a drop of gold into thin foil, repeated heating and steeping was demanded; if this was not done, the metal would easily fracture (Gullman 2004, 113). Since the copper content of the foil might oxidize, the artisan must put the foil into some kind of a cleansing bath, perhaps fruit juice (ibid.). When this was accomplished, patrices were employed to give birth to the figures. Bodily senses participated in these processes through seeing, hearing, sensuous touch, and perhaps even through smelling and tasting. Touch and taste are known to have been used in order to distinguish different qualities of ore used for iron production (Lindeberg 2009, 59).

The gold content of gold-foil figures has been scientifically measured, and it has been conclusively shown that the people who manufactured and used the foils showed very little, if any, concern with the gold content (Gullman 2004, 112–13). Gold foils within one and the same context demonstrate a great variety as regards the purity of the gold. Even die-identical figural foils from the same place may differ in gold content, such as gold foil numbers 737 and 1860 from Helgö, Sweden, containing 63 percent and 88.6 percent gold, respectively (ibid., 113). From this it can be concluded that other features of the foils, and not their purity, were deemed significant and important—such as the detailed production and formation of the figures themselves, the metal's shiny quality, and the overall visual impression. This argument for the aesthetic significance of gold is further supported by the fact that figures were also occasionally made of other shining metals, such as silver and bronze (see Conneller on skeumorphs, in this volume).

When gold-foil figures were produced, gold was perceived to be the metal of gods, to the extent that the words "golden" and "godly" or "divine" were used interchangeably (Jørgensen & Vang Petersen 1998, 82). The ancient Swedish/Scandinavian word for gold was *gul* or *gull*. The word gold (*guld*, in contemporary Swedish) is thus etymologically related to the color yellow (*gul* in Swedish). Gold consequently translates as "the yellow metal" (Hellquist 1980). Conclusively, gold expressed a coemergence of color-and-thing/metal and divinity (see Casson 1997).

THE GOLD FOIL FIGURES: MATERIALS OF AFFECT

In previous analyses (Back Danielsson 2012) I have described the manipulations that gold-foil figures have undergone as *incorporated* and *added* manipulations. Incorporated manipulations are made when the figure itself is produced. These include the exaggerations or abbreviations (manipulations) of bodily attributes on the patrix used to make the foil figure. The most common exaggerations concern the eyes, the nose, and jewelry. Since it is known that jewelry carried significant details in pivotal stories or ceremonies (e.g., Magnus 2001), it is not surprising to find these elements in larger sizes. It is only the artisan/smith that can make these incorporated manipulations, since this person is likely to be the one making the patrix.

By contrast, added manipulations are made after the birth or manufacture of the figure, and they may consist of adding details to it. The same artisan who created the figure could add a great variety of manipulations, but, importantly, added manipulations could also be made by other people during a single or multiple performances over the life of the figures.

The incorporated manipulations may be summarized as follows (Back Danielsson 2007, with references):

- Protuberant eyes: suggesting far sightedness?
- Exaggerated nose: focus on smelling/breathing?
- Drinking from horns: suggestive of transcending experiences?
- Pointed chin: It does not have to be a beard (see also Watt 2004, 201), but rather could imply a leaning-back position, as in trance, where the chin is lifted up.
- Lips: visible when couple is eating (gold foil from Helgö, Sweden).
- Vocal production (Eketorp, Sweden).
- Kissing (Helgö, Sweden).
- Moving legs and feet (e.g. Ravlunda, Sweden).
- Seated postures: They may additionally be linked to sitting in the high seat, that is, having political, religious, and legal significance (e.g., Bolmsö, Sweden).
- Touching by arms and hands (e.g., Slöinge, Sweden).
- Wearing an assortment of garments: Some are in the form of bird's wings or animal furs (e.g., Tørring, Denmark, and Eketorp, Sweden).

The added manipulations, realized by one person or several people in one or multiple performances, may be summarized as (Back Danielsson 2007, with references):

- Piercing the vital organs (e.g., Uppåkra).
- Cutting the figures (e.g., Uppåkra).

- Equipping the figures with props, such as necklaces (e.g., Bornholm and Uppåkra), belts (Bornholm and Uppåkra), and maneuverable phalluses (Uppåkra).
- Crumpling up the figures (several locations).
- Turning the foil into a cylinder, then treading it among beads on a necklace (Tørring).
- Folding the figure (e.g., Bornholm, Denmark, and Lillehammer, Norway).
- Ripping the figure apart (e.g., Bornholm).
- Folding the figures together with other golden items/strips into small packages (Bornholm).
- Adding loops enabling the figures to be hung (several locations).

Overall, pricks, scratches, and punctures can be observed on specific body parts, such as head, heart, and genitalia on both gold foil figures and some gold bracteates (Back Danielsson 2007, 124–27; see also Williams & Nugent 2012). It must further be noted that eyes and eyesight are prominent, multifaceted narrative features expressed through material culture in the Scandinavian Late Iron Age (Nordbladh 2012). In fact, it has been suggested that reduced (but in other respects enhanced) visual capacity was desirable, illustrating a body normativity that differs from the one prevailing today.

The multiple actions and events described above speak against a description of the figures as simple representations. The miniscule bodies need to be taken seriously, and their visual potency introduces phenomenological registers that exceed the simple notion of representation (see Cochrane 2005, 2008, 2009; Jones 2006). Mitchell (1996, 2005) recognizes that images make demands, awake desires, repulsions, etc., and as such they may be apprehended as living entities; however, it is important to understand that images, in this case figures, are only living because of our apprehensions of them. Indeed the living image is a metaphor, a meta-picture, "a secondary, reflexive image of images" (Mitchell 2005, 10), highlighting the relationality of image and beholder.

In the case of the gold-foil figures, the manufactured figure, its wearer or handler, and the person who gazed at the figures all seemingly had to do things. It is as if the figures/images (or rather the meta-things or meta-pictures) evoked certain actions that were dictated by the images themselves. A human-like figure engaged in different activities, perhaps experienced as divine, godly, uncanny, and human as well as animal-like or even vegetal-like—perhaps all these aspects at the same time—resulted in the person's doing things to the artifact. In the following, I will delve deeper into the relations between different bodies, makers, and manipulators and will further consider how the ontological status of the figures in their animated states had an equivalence among certain human beings.

RELATIONS

SIZE AND AFFECT

Gold-foil figures are small. However, this does not mean that they are miniatures (i.e., they are not representations in a smaller scale of something larger). Using the word miniature is delimiting: it implies a certain distance, or rather a specific relation, between beholder and figure. For one thing, it automatically implies that something is *represented*. Second, what is represented can be found materially or immaterially, for real, elsewhere. Such reasoning does indeed downplay practice and it silences, or embalms, the object of study (see also Alberti, in this volume).

The size choice brings with it certain desirable and perhaps also unintended effects. Small figures or bodies may evoke emotions in the handler or viewer, such as wonder, awe, and/or empowerment (see Bailey 2005, 29, 33). But at the same time, encountering something small, a reminder of human-like, or god-like, bodies may engender feelings of humbleness, because the tiny entity/living being needs you to take care of it. Thus these figures may not only protect a person (if they do) but may also require protection.

Making things/entities in smaller sizes requires expertise, and very often certain characteristics of the body are abbreviated. Abbreviation commonly holds that only certain marks or elements are considered necessary (Proschan 1983, 14). This abbreviation invites disparate *significata*, which opens the images to interpretational plurality (Tonkin 1979, 245). With such techniques, paradox and power are manifested and exerted, inviting and generating a possible array of mixed and (importantly) enhanced feelings, such as fear, relief, anxiety, and joy. To be able to relate to such *significata* is to be powerful (ibid.). This, I would argue, is especially pertinent in the case of stylized gold-foil figures. These luminous, crude, and abbreviated figures would be hard to relate to for an uninitiated person.

ONTOLOGICAL EQUIVALENTS

Gold had a mythological origin during the Iron Age in Scandinavia and thereby also magical powers (Holtsmark 1960). It is thus possible to describe the gold-foil figures as divine miniature beings with luminous properties that also attracted a numinous presence (Back Danielsson

2010). The divine miniature beings were probably dressed up by the artisan, either through incorporation of the jewelry already in the patrix, or at a later stage by the smith or other person/people through the addition of, for instance, golden necklaces. The artisan making gold-foil figures was also responsible for giving divine powers to certain human beings by equipping them with arm rings, disc-on-bow brooches, and necklaces—all with luminous properties.

Consequently, the artisan furnished both humans and divine beings with paraphernalia necessary for performing certain ceremonies, such as weddings, prophesy making, or initiations rituals. What is more, the artisan was also so powerful and in possession of such specific knowledge as to produce and deliver the miniature gods. This is indeed in agreement with the Norse anthropogenic myth *Voluspà*, which recounts that the gods created smiths or artisans that in turn made *manlikon*, human or human-like beings in the shape of statues or something similar (Steinsland 1983, 85). This highlights the special position and role the artisan held during this period. Only through the expertise of the smith/artisan could certain human and divine bodies receive the correct treatment/paraphernalia that were required for them to perform in intended, and, perhaps, unintended ways. Through the artisan's acts, both figures and humans could create, explain, and protect the world and the cosmos. For instance, specific gold-foil figures deposited in certain postholes in connection with the inauguration of special buildings could work as protective forces (Back Danielsson 2010); and certain human beings would require certain paraphernalia and bodily treatments to be able to perform prophesy making (*sejdr*) (e.g., Price 2002). This suggests that the gold-foil figures and (certain) human bodies were ontological equivalents. Such equivalency is known from other prehistoric societies, such as the Early Formative Candelaria in Northwest Argentina, where bodies and ceramic pots were considered ontological equivalents (Alberti 2012; see also Alberti & Bray 2009; Alberti et al. 2011).

ONTOLOGICAL RELATIONS

The artisan making the gold-foil figures (and other objects) had extraordinary skills in transforming metals into objects. However, this knowledge also entailed the possession, or rather the control, of magical powers (e.g., Haaland et al. 2002; Hedeager 2002, 7; Herbert 1984, 1993). As reiterated above, the luminous gold metal was considered endowed with numinous and divine qualities, so the person who was able to transform this heavenly metal would be special, perhaps even imbued with supernatural powers (Helms 1993, 19; Källén 2004, 192; Lindeberg 2009, 59–60). Indeed, in Late Iron Age Scandinavia gods were considered artisans or craftsmen, a trait Scandinavia shares with many other cultures (Hed Jakobsson 2003, 144; see also Eliade 1971; Helms 1993).

The fact that the garments and jewelry of the figures had their counterparts among human beings (Mannering 2004, 212) underscores the specialized knowledge of the artisan, who would have close encounters with these clothes and the ceremonies in which they participated. The gold-foil figures point to the Late Iron Age materialization of something immaterial, a divine being. The figures worked as performing objects that were manipulated in different ways during performances or storytelling. The smith/artisan was the creator of these being with agency. Without the artisan's abilities, expertise, and intimate knowledge of human and divine ceremonies, performances, and bodily practices, there would be no gold-foil figures.

Researchers have suggested that the contexts where the figures have been recovered, and specifically the workshop locations, were associated with particular aristocratic networks (Söderberg 2005, 181). These places show extensive evidence of workshop activities, often highly advanced. This means that the smiths/artisans and their products were prominent features in these places, because of their role in manufacturing not only gold-foil figures but also a variety of precious metal goods. Importantly, these same contexts are also associated with other transformational changes or processes—those connected to crops, harvesting, and grinding. Very different activities such as smithing and the preparation of food were considered analogues during the Scandinavian Iron Age (Hed Jakobsson 2003, 173). The same was true for finished products and prepared food: they were kennings for one another. A kenning is a particular kind of common imagery in language, which defines in particular Norse poetry (Marold 1983); it indicates a descriptive term that embodies a kind of affect. For instance, blood could be named "the river of the sword" or "wound-sea," and a shield could be named "headland of swords" (Faulkes 1997, 24).

Food, jewelry, and presumably gold-foil figures circulated in the relationships among human beings and other beings/entities (see Hed Jakobsson 2003, 116). To be able to assist in such transformations, becomings, and expanding relationships was to be powerful, and it also indicated the possession of certain abilities and consequently the capacity to produce wealth and in return offer regeneration and reproduction. Leading families and rulers were connected to such processes and as a result were considered producers of wealth (ibid.).

The foregoing discussion of gold-foil figures in the Scandinavian Late Iron Age suggests that it is the processes of formation that are primary, not the states of matter. The focus here is not on the substances involved, but rather on the relations they produce. In Ingold's terms (2010, 92), we are looking at an ontology of relations, not of substances (on alternatives to an ontology of substances, see Latour 1999, 2005; Barad 2003, 2007; Alberti & Bray 2009).

CONCLUSIONS: GOLD-FOIL FIGURES BEYOND REPRESENTATION

In this paper I have adopted a witnessing stance to describe the lives of Scandinavian Late Iron Age gold-foil figures, in order to question the prevailing approach to archaeological interpretations. The archaeological study of material culture tends to be primarily concerned with representational meanings. Such approaches to the study of archaeological materials tend to downplay practice, to the extent that the lives and loves of the figures (paraphrasing Mitchell's [2005] work on images) are not considered—and are in fact obliterated. This is evident in earlier interpretation of the gold-foil figures as representations of gods known from later, written medieval sources, or as a sort of temple coins. Equally, their small sizes frequently lure the interpretive archaeologist into thinking in terms of representation—into seeing the figures as miniatures, that is, as representations of something else that is materially or immaterially greater/other. Here I contend that rather than be thought of as miniatures, their bodies need to be taken seriously, in their own rights.

A focus on practice also highlights the importance of recognizing the human body, and the manipulations it has made and experienced, as a central device for relating to the ongoing nature of the world. The processes of becoming of which the figures are part do not involve transformations into easily identifiable Western categories such as, for instance, male and female. For example, Denmark has produced thousands of gold-foil figures (mainly from the island of Bornholm); of these less than 10 percent could be categorized as being of either of the sexes and having corresponding clothes (Mannering 2006, 42–43). In Sweden's circa 40 percent of the gold-foil figures could be categorized by sex. The material begs for other understandings. Garments, bodily characteristics, and other paraphernalia invite other realms, such as those connected to the animal and vegetal worlds but also to constant movement and transformation. This resonates well with the ways of living in the Late Iron Age in Scandinavia as described by the history of religion. For instance, all human beings had a *hugr*, a dimension of their soul, which under certain conditions could act on its own (Steinsland 1990, 62). Frequently, it would materialize itself in the form of an animal. Gifted humans could practice this form of shape shifting.

Another dimension of the soul was the *fylgja*, which could be observed either in a female or in an animal shape (Price 2002, 59). The *fylgja* as an animal gestalt was born with the human and functioned like his/her alter ego, and it has been interpreted as reflecting a genuinely Nordic perception of the soul (Steinsland 1990, 62–63).

Another way to approach what I would describe as a discrepancy between material and interpretation is to think through practices and bodies by following Viveiros de Castro's perspectivism (e.g., Viveiros de Castro 1998, 2004). Described by Bruno Latour (2009) as a bomb designed to shatter Western philosophy and specifically Kantian ideals, perspectivism was developed by Viveiros de Castro in his studies of Amerindians in Amazonia. Here human culture is something that binds together all beings, including animals, plants, and other things/ phenomena. What separates them from one another are their bodies, resulting in different perspectives. Such an approach makes a nonsense of traditional divisions such as nature versus culture. Returning to the gold-foil figures, it is the transformation per se that is important, and the transformation (or rather the change of ongoing relations) is enabled only through different bodily practices/processes. Gold-foil figures are figures in action—they are not static and do not stand still; they are meant to be in constant movement. They are not about fixity, durability, and universality, but are instead figures in flux, fickle and distinctive (Back Danielsson 2012). As such, they share central characteristics with other beings in constant motion: humans. The activities the figures partook in, and perhaps instigated, were also experienced by certain upper-class humans—presumably those that visited the transit halls and workshops where the foils were deposited. They ate, met, feasted, drunk, ruled, participated in weddings, initiation rituals, etc. An upper-class person in Late Iron Age Scandinavia was far different from our modern sense of an individual, since he/she had different relations and engagements with material and immaterial worlds. Gold-foil figures and humans also shared the same characteristics and paraphernalia, which were provided to them by artisans/smiths.

Finally, in this chapter I have argued that the figures and certain humans were ontologically equivalent. An example of this ontological equivalence is that Iron Age ritual specialists in Norway played the role of transformers and were involved in both the cremation of people and the melting of iron (Goldhahn & Oestigaard 2007). However, the equivalence does not stop there. It also encompasses, for instance, the preparation of products and food. The creation of crops and the manufacture of things were seen as ontologically equivalent. Both processes resulted in finished products and edible food, and both revealed desirable and attractive properties of the materials: wealth and regeneration.

A change in perspective from a representational mode of thinking to a more-than-representational mode of thinking—from understanding materials as substances to a processual understanding of their affects— inevitably results in the conclusion that gold-foil figures are much more than simple representations.

ACKNOWLEDGMENTS

I would like to thank the editors for inviting me to participate in this inspirational volume. In particular, I would like to thank Andy Jones for making most valuable comments on an earlier version of this chapter. This work was written while I was suffering from an atypical infection that took months to heal, and I am very grateful for the understanding and sympathy I received from the editors, and especially Andy Jones, during this time. I am also grateful to Finn Ole Nielsen and René Laursen, of the Bornholm Museum, for generously sharing photos of gold-foil figures. As always, Milton and Per, you are the best there is. I would also like to express my deepest gratitude to the Torsten Söderberg Foundation for generously supporting my research on miniatures.

REFERENCES

Alberti, B. 2012. Cut, pinch and pierce: image as practice among the Early Formative La Candelaria, first millennium AD, Northwest Argentina. In I.-M. Back Danielsson, F. Fahlander & Y. Sjöstrand (eds.), *Picture This! The Materiality of the Perceptible*, 13–28. Stockholm, Swed.: Stockholm University

Alberti, B. & Bray, T.L. 2009. Animating archaeology: of subjects, objects and alternative ontologies. *Cambridge Archaeological Journal* 19(3), 337–43

Alberti, B., Fowles, S., Holbraad, M., Marshall, Y. & Witmore, C. 2011. "Worlds otherwise": archaeology, anthropology and ontological difference. *Current Anthropology* 52(6), 896–912

Anderson, B. & Harrison, P. (eds.) 2010. *Taking-Place: Non-Representational Theories and Geography*. Farnham, UK: Ashgate

Andréasson, A. 1995. *Skandinaviens guldgubbar—med kända fynd och fyndplatser från 1740 till 1994*. Unpublished BA thesis, Department of Archeology, Göteborg University

Back Danielsson, I.-M. 2007. *Masking Moments: The Transitions of Bodies and Beings in Late Iron Age Scandinavia*. Stockholm, Swed.: Stockholm University

Back Danielsson, I.-M. 2010. Go figure! Creating intertwined worlds in Late Iron Age Scandinavia. In D. Gheorgiou & A. Cyphers (eds.), *Anthropomorphic and Zoomorphic Miniature Figures in Eurasia, Africa and Meso-America: Morphology, Materiality, Technology, Function and Context*, 79–90. Oxford: British Archaeological Reports, International Series

Back Danielsson, I.-M. 2012. The rape of the lock: or a comparison between miniature images of the eighth and eighteenth centuries. In I.-M. Back Danielsson, F. Fahlander & Y. Sjöstrand (eds.), *Picture This! The Materiality of the Perceptible*, 29–50. Stockholm, Swed.: Stockholm University

Bailey, D. 2005. *Prehistoric Figurines: Representation and Corporeality in the Neolithic.* London: Routledge

Barad, K. 2003. Posthumanist performativity: towards an understanding of how matter comes to matter. *Signs: Journal of Women in Culture and Society* 28(3), 801–31

Barad, K. 2007. *Meeting the Universe Halfway: Quantum Physics and the Entanglement of Matter and Meaning.* Durham, NC: Duke University Press

Cadman, L. 2009. Nonrepresentational theory/nonrepresentational geographies. In R. Kitchin & N. Thrift (eds.), *International Encyclopaedia of Human Geography*, 456–63. Amsterdam, Neth.: Elsevier

Casson, R.W. 1997. Color shift: evolution of English color terms from brightness to hue. In C.L. Hardin & L. Maffi (eds.), *Color Categories in Thought and Language*, 224–39. Cambridge: Cambridge University Press

Cochrane, A. 2005. A taste of the unexpected: subverting mentalities through the motifs and settings of Irish passage tombs. In D. Hofmann, J. Mills & A. Cochrane (eds.), *Elements of Being: Mentalities, Identities and Movements*, 5–19. Oxford: British Archaeological Reports, International Series 1437

Cochrane, A. 2008. We have never been material. *Journal of Iberian Archaeology* 9, 137–57

Cochrane, A. 2009. Additive subtraction: addressing pick-dressing in Irish passage tombs. In J. Thomas & V. Oliveira Jorge (eds.), *Archaeology and the Politics of Vision in a Post-Modern Context*, 163–85. Newcastle, UK: Cambridge Scholars Publishing

Colls, R. 2011. Feminism, bodily difference and non-representational geographies. *Transactions of the Institute of British Geographers* 37, 430–45

Conneller, C. 2011. *An Archaeology of Materials: Substantial Transformations in Early Prehistoric Europe.* London: Routledge

Dewsbury, J.-D. 2003. Witnessing space: knowledge without contemplation. *Environment and Planning A* 35, 1907–32

Dewsbury, J.-D., Harrison, P., Rose, M. & Wylie, J. 2002. Enacting geographies. *Geoforum* 33, 437–40

Eliade, M. 1971. *Patterns in Comparative Religion.* London: Sheed and Ward

Faulkes, A. 1997. *Poetical Inspiration in Old Norse and Old English Poetry.* London: Viking Society for Northern Research

Goldhahn, J. & Oestigaard, T. 2007. *Rituelle spesialister i bronse- og jernalderen.* Göteborg, Swed.: Department of Archaeology & Classical Studies, Göteborg University

Gullman, J. 2004. The gold of the figural gold foils. In H. Clarke & K. Lamm (eds.), *Excavations at Helgö XVI: Exotic and Sacral Finds from Helgö*, 112–13. Stockholm, Swed.: Almqvist and Wiksell International

Haaland, G., Haaland, R. & Rijal, S. 2002. The social life of iron. *Anthropos* 97, 35–54

Harding, S. 1987. *Feminism and Methodology.* Bloomington, IN: Indiana University

Harding, S. 1993. Rethinking standpoint epistemology: what is "strong objectivity"? In L. Alcoff & E. Potter (eds.), *Feminist Epistemologies*, 49–82. New York: Routledge

Harrison, P. 2000. Making sense: embodiment and the sensibilities of the everyday. *Environment and Planning D* 18, 497–518

Hauck, K. 1992. *Der historische Horizont der Götterbild-Amulette aus der Übergangsepoche von der Spätantike zum Fühmittelalter: Bericht über das Colloquium vom 28.11–1.12 1988 in der Werner-Reimers Stiftung, Bad Homburg.* Abhandlungen der Akademie der Wissenschaften in Göttingen/Phi-lologisch-historische Klasse F. 3, 200. Göttingen, Germ.: Vandenhoeck und Ruprecht

Hauck, K. 1993a. Die bremische Überlieferung zur Götter-Dreiheit Altuppsalas und die bornholmischen Goldfolien aus Sorte Muld. *Frühmittelalterliche Studien* 27, 409–79

Hauck, K. 1993b. Das Aufkommen des erfolgreichsten Motivs der völkerwanderungszeit-lichen Brakteaten. In G. Arwidsson et al. (eds.), *Sources and Resources: Studies in Honour of Birgit Arrhenius*, 403–34. Rixensart: Pact Belgium

Hauck, K. 1994. Götterbilder des spätantiken Polytheismus im Norden auf Votivgoldminia-turen. *Zeitschrift für Kunstgeschichte* 57, 301–5

Hed Jakobsson, A. 2003. *Smältdeglars härskare och Jerusalems tillskyndare. Berättelser om vikingatid och tidig medeltid.* Stockholm, Swed.: Stockholm University

Hedeager, L. 2002. Scandinavian "central places" in a cosmological setting. In B. Hårdh & L. Larsson (eds.), *Central Places in the Migration and Merovingian Periods*, 3–18. Stockholm, Swed.: Almqvist and Wiksell International

Hellquist, E. 1980. *Svensk Etymologisk Ordbok.* Malmö, Swed.: Gleerups Förlag

Helms, M. 1993. *Craft and the Kingly Ideal: Art, Trade, and Power.* Austin: University of Texas Press

Herbert, E.W. 1984. *Red Gold of Africa: Copper in Precolonial History and Culture.* Madison: University of Wisconsin Press

Herbert, E.W. 1993. *Iron, Gender and Power: Rituals of Transformations in African Societies.* Indianapolis: Indiana University Press

Holtsmark, A. 1960. Gull i västnordisk litteratur. *Kulturhistoriskt Lexikon över Nordisk Medeltid* 5, 573–5

Ingold, T. 2010. The textility of making. *Cambridge Journal of Economics* 34(1), 91–102

Jones, A.M. 2006. Animated images: images, agency and landscape in Kilmartin, Argyll. *Journal of Material Culture* 11(1–2), 211–26

Jørgensen, L. & Petersen, P.V. 1998. *Guld, Magt og Tro. Danske skattefund fra oldtid og middelalder.* Copenhagen, Den.: Nationalmuseet

Källén, A. 2004. "And Through Flows the River: Archaeology and the Pasts of Lao Pako." *Studies in Global Archaeology* 6, monographic issue. Uppsala, Swed.: Uppsala University

Keane, W. 2003. Semiotics and the social analysis of material things. *Language and Communication* 23(2–3), 409–25

Lamm, J.P. 2004. Helgös guldgubbar. In H. Clarke & K. Lamm (eds.), *Excavations at Helgö XVI. Exotic and Sacral Finds from Helgö*, 41–142. Stockholm, Swed.: Almqvist and Wiksell International

Latham, A. 2003. Research, performance, and doing human geography: some reflections on the diary-photograph, diary-interview method. *Environment and Planning A* 35, 1993–2017

Latour, B. 1991. *We Have Never Been Modern.* Cambridge, MA: Harvard University Press

Latour, B. 1999. *Pandora's Hope: Essays on the Reality of Science Studies.* Cambridge, MA: Harvard University Press

Latour, B. 2005. *Reassembling the Social: An Introduction to Actor-Network Theory.* Oxford, UK: Clarendon Press

Latour, B. 2009. Perspectivism: "type" or "bomb"? *Anthropology Today* 25(2), 1–2

Lindeberg, M. 2009. *Järn i jorden. Spadformiga ämnesjärn i Mellannorrland.* Stockholm, Swed: Stockholm University

Longino, H.E. 1994. In search of feminist epistemology. *The Monist* 77(4), 472–85

Lorimer, H. 2005. Cultural geography: the busyness of being "more-than-representational." *Progress in Human Geography* 29(1), 83–94

Magnus, B. 2001. The enigmatic brooches. In B. Magnus (ed.), *Roman Gold and the Development of Early Germanic Kingdoms*, 279–96. Stockholm, Swed.: Kungliga Vitterhets—Historie och Antikvitetsakademien

Mannering, U. 2004. Dress in Scandinavian iconography of the 5–10th centuries AD. In M. Jerzy (ed.), *Priceless Invention of Humanity—Textiles*, 67–74. Acta Archaeologica Lodziensia, No. 50. Lódz, Pol.: Łódzkie Towarzystwo Naukowe

Mannering, U. 2006. *Billeder af dragt. En analyse af påklaedte figurer fra yngre jernalder i Skandinavien*. Copenhagen, Den.: Københavns Universitet

Marold, E. 1983. *Kenningkunst. Ein Beitrag zu einer Poetik der Skaldendichtung*. Berlin & New York: Walter de Gruyter

Meskell, L.M. (ed.) 2006. *Archaeologies of Materiality*. Malden, MA: Blackwell

Mitchell, T. 1996. What do pictures really want? *October* 77, 71–82

Mitchell, T. 2005. *What Do Pictures Want? The Lives and Loves of Images*. Chicago, IL: University of Chicago Press

Nordbladh, E. 2012. Ability and disability: on bodily variations and bodily possibilities in Viking Age myth and image. In I.-M. Back Danielsson & S. Thedéen (eds.), *To Tender Gender: The Pasts and Futures of Gender Research*, 33–60. Stockholm, Swed.: Stockholm University

Price, N. 2002. *The Viking Way: Religion and War in Late Iron Age Scandinavia*. Uppsala, Swed.: Uppsala University

Proschan, F. 1983. The semiotic study of puppets, masks, and performing objects. *Semiotica* 47(1–4), 3–44

Söderberg, B. 2005. Aristokratiskt rum och gränsöverskridande: Järrestad och sydöstra Skåne mellan region och rike 600–1100. *Arkeologiska undersökninger skrifter* 62. Stockholm, Swed.: Riksantikvarieämbetet

Steinsland, G. 1983. Antropogonimyten i Voluspá. En tekst- og tradisjonskritisk analyse. *Arkiv för nordisk filologi*, 80–107

Steinsland, G. 1990. De nordiske gullblekk med parmotiv og norrøn fyrsteideologi. *Collegium Medievale* 1990–91, 73–94

Thrift, N. 2000. Dead or alive? In I. Cook, D. Crouch, S. Naylor & J. Ryan (eds.), *Cultural Turns/Geographical Turns: Perspectives on Cultural Geography*, 1–6. Harlow, UK: Prentice Hall

Tonkin, E. 1979. Masks and powers. *Man* (N.S.) 14, 237–48

Viveiros de Castro, E. 1998. Cosmological deixis and Amerindian perspectivism. *Journal of the Royal Anthropological Institute* 4(3), 469–88

Viveiros de Castro, E. 2004. Exchanging perspectives: the transformation of objects into subjects in Amerindian ontologies. *Common Knowledge* 10(3), 463–84

Watt, M. 1992. Die Goldblechfiguren ("guldgubber") aus Sorte Muld, Bornholm. *Der historische Horizont der Götterbild-Amulette aus der Übergangsepoche von der Spätantike zum Fühmittelalter: Bericht über das Colloquium vom 28.11–1.12 1988 in der Werner-Reimers Stiftung, Bad Homburg*, 195–227. Göttingen, Germ.: Vandenhoeck und Ruprecht

Watt, M. 2001. "Gummor" og "grodor." Om könsbestemmelse af guldgubber. In J.P. Lamm & B. Magnus (eds.), *Vi får tacka Lamm*, 219–28. Stockholm, Swed.: Statens Historiska Museum

Watt, M. 2004. The gold-figure foils ("Guldgubbar") from Uppåkra. In L. Larsson (ed.), *Continuity for Centuries: A Ceremonial Building and Its Context at Uppåkra, Southern Sweden*, 167–222. Stockholm, Swed.: Almqvist and Wiksell International

Whatmore, S. 2002. *Hybrid Geographies*. London: Sage

Williams, H. & Nugent, R. 2012. Sighted surfaces: ocular agency in Early Anglo-Saxon cremation burials. In I.-M.Back Danielsson, F. Fahlander & Y. Sjöstrand (eds.), *Picture This! The Materiality of the Perceptible*, 187–208. Stockholm, Swed.: Stockholm University

Wylie, A. 2007. Doing archaeology as a feminist: introduction. *Journal of Archaeological Method and Theory* 14, 209–16

CHAPTER SEVENTEEN

Representational Approaches to Irish Passage Tombs: Legacies, Burdens, Opportunities

Andrew Cochrane

> Leonard Bilsiter was one of those people who have failed to find this world attractive or interesting and have sought compensation in an "unseen world" of their own experience or imagination—or invention.
>
> —Saki

After spending time in his tool shed, C.S. Lewis (1971) stated that there was a profound difference between looking *at* and looking *along* a particular idea. By looking along, one could bypass scientific realism and appreciate more experiential modes of being. In a similar vein, and with some Neolithic passage tombs from Ireland, here we will move along and through some things in the world. Such an approach is stimulated by reactions to the dominance of representational narratives within archaeology.[1] This chapter moves beyond mere representation and the idea that things are passive, and instead offers a narrative of the Fourknocks complex that is more compositional and collaborative. Fourknocks is superb in that it presents opportunities to discuss images with archaeologically contextualized materials.

IMPROPER STORIES

Since the seventeenth century, the past has been understood in terms of a politics of display and visual documentation—for example, cabinets of curiosities, woodcut iconographies, paintings, archives, publications, private collections, and museum exhibits (see Perry, in this volume). Indeed, many of the origins of archaeology lie in art historical traditions,

Archaeology after Interpretation: Returning Materials to Archaeological Theory, edited by Benjamin Alberti, Andrew Meirion Jones, and Joshua Pollard, 345–68.

sharing commonalities for visualizing the world. Archaeological practice has progressed through modern visual technologies and scientific revolutions, such as section drawings and single-context plans, that have created standardized media. Such developments, however, have often generated a perceived gap between the "objectivity" and "subjectivity" of images (Thomas 2009). Since the nineteenth century, many practitioners have sought to observe and objectively document the world, be it the changing colors of soils or similarities of form. Archaeologists are trained in technical practices as a means of rendering things objective and allowing comparative analyses (e.g., Westman 1994). After the acceptance of positivism in archaeology during the mid-twentieth century, image-making tools (e.g., photography, LiDAR, laser scanning) have increasingly been used to truthfully represent and document elements of the past (see Cochrane & Russell 2007; Bradley 2009; Jones 2012a; Russell 2013; Perry, in this volume). Such visual movements are not only persuasive but also essential to contemporary archaeology. They have, however, helped create a situation whereby representational interpretations of *all* things in the past dominate; to end with a representational interpretation is understandable, to begin with one is problematic.

That representational approaches are used in archaeology is not a bad thing; for instance, they are integral to fieldwork. I am, however, concerned that some researchers approach data with the expectation that all things represent things not present—invisible and intangible conceits.[2] In such models, materials are passive and inert, patiently waiting for meanings to be overlaid onto them by thoughtful people (see Cochrane & Jones 2012; Jones 2012b; Fahlander, in this volume). The encoding and then decoding of things is deemed a universal human activity, being as popular in the past as it is in archaeology today. That things do represent is a *fait accompli*. In many accounts, people seem to step from intangible worlds in order to represent their experiences as visual symbols. In such proposals the material world—separate from humans— influences little in the process of representation. What would archaeology look like if we did not *start* with such conceptions of imagery? What happens when we consider different elements in the world as influential partners in the process of expression? Would we still draw the same conclusions, or would other narratives be possible? In attempting to answer such questions, instead of promoting a "non-representational" approach to archaeology (which is tempting), I collaborate with the dominant positions to help compose new narratives that are "more than representational."[3] Such movement draws attention away from the differences between what things or images symbolize or do not symbolize. It also means that I am not a representational iconoclast.

FOURKNOCKS

Named from the Irish words *fornocht* or *fuar cnuic*, meaning "exposed place" or "cold hills," the Fourknocks I passage tomb, Fourknocks II tomb, and Fourknocks III mound/barrow are located near the modern village of Naul, County Meath (Hartnett 1957, 197, 272; see Figure 17.1). These sites form a complex and are located on the summit of a broad-backed ridge orientated northeast to southwest and situated at 152 meters above sea level.

The views from the summit are spectacular; on a clear day one can see the Dublin/Wicklow Mountains to the south, the Cooley and Mourne Mountains to the north, and the distant Loughcrew passage tomb complex to the northwest (Hartnett 1957, 198; Herity 1974, 39). Although closer in distance, the Hill of Tara with the Mound of the Hostages passage tomb in County Meath is harder to see, and the Bellewstown Ridge conceals the more immediate Boyne Valley complex (e.g., Newgrange, Knowth, and Dowth), which is c. 15 kilometers away. The hills also overlook the Delvin River to the south (Shee Twohig 1981, 220); such proximity to water is reminiscent of the Boyne Valley complex. The siting of the passage tombs suggests a desire for visual dominance, and this effect is particularly enhanced if one approaches the summit from the lower grounds to the north, and to a slightly lesser extent if one comes from the south (Cooney 1997, 17, 19).

I will explore the personality of the Fourknocks complex (see also Robinson 2012); this is something that I have investigated elsewhere, in Loughcrew, County Meath (Cochrane 2012a). Such an approach is equally viable at Fourknocks, because here too we can witness relationships among the varied elements present (e.g., the architecture,

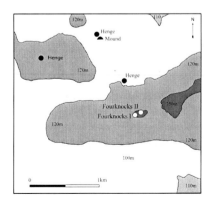

Figure 17.1 Schematic map of the mounds Fourknocks I and II (adapted from Cooney 1997, 19)

the mound, the imagery, the cremations). The emergence of the complex was an ongoing process and it involved things that needed to be worked with. My primary focus will be on Fourknocks I, as it is the only feature on the hill that is currently known to contain motifs. I will, however, also briefly consider the nearby Fourknocks II, to enhance some of the complex histories that these mounds may have experienced (see also discussions in Cooney 1997, 19; 2000, 106). In doing so, I introduce some of the impacts that the imagery produces and stimulates, and consider the differences that it makes.

Fourknocks I is dated to c. 3000 BC. The passage tomb itself was re-brought to the public attention by Mrs. Liam O'Sullivan in the mid-twentieth century and was excavated by Hartnett (1957). It was later (re)constructed by the Office of Public Works, with a concrete covering dome topped with turf, designed to protect the interior and simulate an earthen mound. Upon entering the passage tomb from the northeast, one soon traverses the passage and is led into a central pear-shaped, beehive-fashioned roofed chamber (c. 5.5 to 6.4 meters in diameter), which has three smaller chambers in a cruciform plan with linteled roofs (Hartnett 1957, 201; Herity 1974, 39; Shee Twohig 1981, 221; see Figure 17.2).

There are corbel stones above the orthostats of the central area that were originally kept in place by retentive clay, reaching a height of 2.75

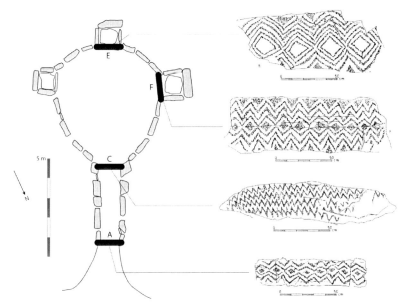

Figure 17.2 Plan of Fourknocks I highlighting the decorated lintels (with kind permission of Guillaume Robin)

meters; it has been proposed that the main roof space was not completely corbeled, and that instead the structure contained a framework of radial wooden rafters forming a roof, supported by a timber post (Hartnett 1957, 201; Herity 1974, 39). Evidence for this rests with the discovery during excavation of a posthole 0.65 meters wide and 0.40 meters deep, located in the center of the main chamber, to the east of the passage and near the inner side of the stone that forms the east wall of the southern chamber. Impressions on the floor were also interpreted as marks left by fallen timbers that decayed in situ (Hartnett 1957, 212; Herity 1974, 40). Hartnett (1957, 212) argued that if there was indeed a wooden structure, it was likely conceived to be temporary and impermanent. It has also been suggested that the post pre-dates the passage tomb, providing a focus within the environment (Cooney 2000, 104). Either way, its spatial relationship to the structure of the passage and the southern chamber suggests a degree of importance (Cooney 2000).

The hill itself incorporates outcrops of blue carboniferous limestone containing nodular concretions of chert, from which the structure of this passage tomb (i.e., uprights and roof corbels) was built, with grey/green gritty shale being used for the decorated stones[4] and thus creating distinctive color differences (Hartnett 1957, 198, 228; Shee Twohig 1973, 164; 1981, 222; Herity 1974, 41; Cooney 2000, 109). The mound (20 meters in diameter and c. 4 meters high) was composed of earth and grass turfs and was demarcated by a low dry-built sandstone kerb (Hartnett 1957, 200, 203; Herity 1974, 39; Shee Twohig 1981, 221).

SO HOW ARE THINGS?

The closure of Fourknocks I passage tomb was marked by the deposition of materials in the passage way, including inhumed bones of children and cremated bones, held in situ by covering stones. The human remains can broadly be split into two groups, with children occurring as inhumations (only three children were cremated in Fourknocks I) and adults as cremations (Hartnett 1957; Cooney 1992; Finlay 2000). There are deposits of human bone in all three chambers and the entrance passage, with evidence of human bone placed above the pre-excavated and restored roof over the central area of the mound. Inside the chambers there were cremation layers, c. 10–25 centimeters deep, covering the flagstone floors and sealed by thin stone slabs. The cremations were possibly washed or cleaned, and therefore the pyre debris is mostly absent. The deposits did, however, contain stone and bone artifacts, including miniature hammer-pendants, chalk balls, and bone pins that were heat damaged. This may suggest that they were burnt with the bodies (Herity 1974, 124). These smaller assemblages have previously been interpreted as personal objects that were worn by the dead, dressed as in life (ibid., 126). Yet, instead of being just personal goods for a particular person, or functional fasteners for hair buns on the back of the head or "ceremonial cloaks" (Herity 1974, 134; Eogan 1986, 181), they may have performed in alternative fashions. This is not to suggest that some people did not adorn themselves in life, but rather that in the context of Fourknocks, in association with human remains and decorated stones, these things may have operated in more complex ways (Cochrane 2008, 139). Very few things occur in the tombs by chance, coming together instead through deliberate acts. What we might be witnessing therefore are episodes of deposition that may have been related to the construction/disruption of identities and the personalities of place (Pollard 2001, 316).

Cremation dominates as a way of depositing human remains within passage tombs in Ireland (Eogan et al. 2012, 40). That non-burnt human bones were incorporated not only highlights the particular personality of Fourknocks, but also suggests alternating modes of illumination. The cremation of human bodies may not have been accomplished merely for functional perseveration and ease of transportation (e.g., Herity 1974, 122). At some level, the mixing of substances in differing states may reflect the beliefs that human bodies are porous, with elements, sensations, and emotions continually flowing (Grosz 1994, 165; Fowler 2004). We may at some level be witnessing the residue of performances that sought to express how some things were enmeshed within relationships. By blending, circulating, and depositing fragmented human remains, such connections may have been magnified. The act of de-totalizing the body into fragments via cremation may have brought a new integrity to the dead as a whole, with the placement in the tomb completing/ commencing transitions. In such scenarios, cremation is cosmogony, with death being assimilated in the processes of transformation (Parry 1982, 76). Such fluid practices would have been intimately linked with sensations, emotions, and being with Fourknocks in general.

Cremations can create numerous performances. At Fourknocks, these may have included: preparing and purifying the body via hair removal, excoriation, and washing; collecting the correct fuels to burn; constructing a trench (e.g., Fourknocks II); collaborating with things (e.g., bone pins and pendants); burning and breaking up the parts; washing the cremations; and transportation with eventual deposition (Bloch 1982; Parry 1982; Gell 1995; Parker Pearson 1999; Fowler 2004). Ultimately, the reshaping of the deceased via the cremation and depositional processes may have created interconnected relationships that punctuated how some saw and expressed themselves. If the human remains were thought of as powerful, then their inclusion within enclosed spaces that inhibit movements (especially the recesses and passage) may highlight attempts to make them less disturbing. Scale and architecture can often reassure (Doss 1977).

The minimum number of persons found inside is 65, with 31 of these being cremated and 34 unburned (Hartnett 1957, 269–70; Eogan 1986, 138; Cooney & Grogan 1994, 68; Cooney 2000, 108–9). The cremated bones occurred mostly on the lower layers, whereas the unburnt child bones appeared mostly on the top deposits. These upper child/infant deposits included seven neonates, six infants in their first year, three in their second, a child of approximately five years, and one of indeterminate age (Hartnett 1957, 270; Finlay 2000, 414). That the passages were deliberately blocked with human remains, a high proportion of these being children, may mark a change in the ways in which some people may have thought about the site in its later stages of use, and may have created new narratives and conversations about the place (Cooney 1997, 19; Finlay 2000, 416, 419; Davidsson 2003, 240). In considering these possible situations one should not, however, automatically assume that they incorporated the perpetuation and presentation of "individual" persons within particular burial activities (see Gell 1999; Whittle 2003; Fowler 2004; Hofmann 2005; Jones 2005). Nor should we regard the cremated remains as passive objects merely operating within representational systems of citation and memory (be it the remembrance or forgetting of past people or "ancestors"). Instead, it may be more profitable to consider the cremated elements as affecting, even after fragmentation and dispersion. These (re)active acts could possibly stimulate new tensions that dislocated and supported various frames of reference (Bailey 2005, 33). Articulation and disarticulation, composition and decomposition: here we have the montage.

Some of the pendants have been interpreted as miniature facsimiles of larger stone technologies, such as pestle hammers or axe heads (Herity 1974, 126–29; Eogan 1986, 142–44). If, indeed, they are small-scale versions of something else, many interesting proposals can be explored. For instance, they may have actively influenced particular people in novel ways, rather than being merely passive ornaments of the deceased. As such, the miniaturization of things might be less about accuracy through representation and more about experimentation (Bailey 2005, 29; see also Bailey et al. 2010). Scale often works as a series of impressive strategies that charge things with psychological tensions, generating intense sensory and emotional experiences. It can also influence understandings of time and enhance cognitive speeds (Delong 1981, 1983). This can result in feelings that are empowered and engaged, but also unsettled or alienated (Nakamura 2005, 32). With the smaller scale, only certain traits of the full size are ever present, rendering the diminutive a compressed and powerful version of the larger one. These interactions operate within an intimate sphere and offer different ways of experiencing (Bailey 2005, 32; Cochrane 2007, 143; Jones 2012a, especially chapter 3). The pendants invite being picked up, held in the hand, turned around, and felt (smelt and tasted?), allowing many of their textures and details to be absorbed. Such an encounter immediately distinguishes itself from performances with the larger passage tombstones, since once the latter were set within the structure it is unlikely that they were moved again (although see discussions of Stone A below).

According to such a perspective, the chalk balls that have been discovered may have been more than "marbles," or specifically "children's marbles" (Hartnett 1957, 235–37; Herity 1974, 136), and may be better understood instead through tactile habits. For example, it has been suggested that the ball shapes found at the relatively close Loughcrew complex were involved in performances with the motifs on the orthostats, being often inserted into cup marks (McMann 1993, 28; 1994, 541). The lack of cup mark motifs in the passage tomb suggests that such acts were not a character trait of Fourknocks. Their form as durable, portable, possibly miniature, three-dimensional things does, however, create corporeal choreographies. These engagements can result in the handlers feeling empowered as they easily manipulate a pendant or chalk ball, but at the same time being uneasy, as they may feel gigantic in relation to it (Tilley 2004, 137; Bailey 2005, 33; Nakamura 2005, 33).

Animal remains were also present, and included cattle, sheep, pig, bat, and dog (Hartnett 1957, 271). The presence of bat is most likely the result of roosting inside the tomb, rather than being a deliberate anthropogenic deposit. If indeed this is the case, it suggests that the tomb was accessible and roofed for a season, at the very least. Pottery is almost absent, with only two sherds being found in the body of the mound (ibid., 270). Interestingly, and uncommon for passage tombs in Ireland, unburned or inhumed human bones are also present in the form of skulls and long-bone fragments. The lack of pottery and the inclusion of inhumed human bones highlight that although specific amalgamations of materials regularly occurred within passage tombs, apparently there were no universal imperatives governing precise combinations. This suggests that although general principles were at play, particular assemblages were mostly interacted with and juxtaposed in improvised ways.

VOYAGES EN ZIGZAG

> I curse and bless Engraving alternatively, because it takes so much time and is so intractable, tho' capable of such beauty and perfection.
>
> —William Blake

The flat-surfaced stones within this passage tomb are mostly decorated with distinctive angular motifs, which are often referred to as the "Fourknocks style" (Hartnett 1957, 227), whereas curvilinear motifs are found when the surface is convex (O'Sullivan 1993, 27). The imagery was created with flint engravers and quartz pebbles (Hartnett 1957, 221). The process of production was probably a sensual engagement involving vision, hearing, touch, and maybe smell (Cochrane 2008, 2009; Lamdin-Whymark 2011a, 2011b). The finest examples of imagery are arguably found on the lintel stones (O'Sullivan 1993, 27). With the exception of Stone G, all the decorated stones are sandstone. There are only five orthostat stones decorated with motifs in Fourknocks I (L4, R2, R5, C1, and C5). Other decorated stones in the passage tomb include stones A, B, C, D, E, F, and G (Hartnett 1957, 224–28; Shee Twohig 1981, 221). Rather than detailing the motifs on each particular stone, I will briefly illustrate specific images and their location in the passage tomb.

Orthostat C1 is one of the most famous stones in Fourknocks I, and possibly Ireland in general. The front face of the stone is crossed near the top by two long lines. The top of one line turns downward at its terminal and connects with the top of a double lozenge shape. Below the apex where the two main lines cross is positioned a wide V incision, forming another loose lozenge. Directly beneath this is a wide crescent that turns upward at the ends. Under this are positioned several short lines and curve shapes (Shee Twohig 1981, 221). Some have suggested that this imagery may demonstrate anthropomorphic qualities, representing a face with eyebrows, hair, mouth, torso, possibly limbs, and a belt (Hartnett 1957, 222; Herity 1974, 94; O'Sullivan 1993, 28; see Figure 17.3). This resemblance might or might not have been intentional (Shee Twohig 1981, 221). Interestingly, the excavators of Fourknocks I often referred to this stone as "The Clown" (Hartnett 1957, 222), possibly evoking subversive notions, albeit modern, within the passage tomb.

Stone A was rediscovered by Hartnett (ibid., 224) lying decorated face-down, situated northwest on the outside of the mound; apparently, twenty years before Hartnett's excavations it was located further north of the mound. The stone is roughly rhomboidal shaped, with parallel flat smooth sides, both of which are decorated. On the side, which is sometimes considered as the main surface, there are three joining motifs, comprising circles, spirals, cup marks, bent zigzags, short lines, and angular lines; all the composite designs are poorly executed, with no effort made to smooth the edges of the lines (Hartnett 1957, 224; Shee Twohig 1981, 221). Interestingly, Hartnett described this ambiguous image as "an 'impressionist' representation of a . . . rather animated female figure" (1957, 224). Although I agree that the image suggests

Figure 17.3 Architecture as process. Looking out along the passageway, Orthostat C1 is to the right, with Stone A and Stone C in their current locations (digital photograph by Ken Williams)

fluid movements and actions, I fail to see this as representing a female form (and I have really tried). The long-axis edge of this stone is covered in imagery, comprising eight heavily picked lozenge designs that are flanked by double lines of zigzags. Based on the assumed importance of the "female image," Hartnett (ibid., 225) suggested that both sides of this stone were intended to be seen, with Stone A being originally set vertically as an orthostat near the entrance. Similar to the roof-box lintel at Newgrange Site 1, it is more likely that this stone was part of the missing passage lintels, with the more ornate edge being designed to be seen and the other images remaining hidden in the architecture of the passage tomb (see discussions in Shee Twohig 1981, 221–22). Hartnett (1957, 225) was unsure of its original position; it is now firmly located within the passage tomb. It would appear that some decorated stones were apt to move around, thus defying static and concrete interpretation.

Stone B rests upon the dry-stone corbelling above Orthostat L6. The exposed overhanging part of this stone is decorated. The imagery consists of four groupings of concentric circles sequentially positioned across the stone, with smaller circles embedded in the angles of the connecting points. Located on the left portion of the stone are three parallel lines. All the main circles are linked via a continuous line that doubles itself at the left terminal. The overall design is very precise, and its definition is enhanced by raised bands between the picked areas (Shee Twohig 1981, 222), resulting in a kind of bas-relief. Due to the effects achieved by the meticulous execution of this piece, Hartnett (1957, 226) suspected that a metal punching tool was used to produce the design. Recent experiments, however, have demonstrated that similar results can be achieved with sharp pointed flints or quartzite implements struck with a stone, wooden mallet, or hammer (Shee Twohig 2004, 45).

Stone C is another stone that has moved around; it is thought that is was positioned as a lintel that rests on R5 and L6, spanning the passage (see Figures 17.4 and 17.5). It currently resides off to the right-hand side of the chamber as you enter (see Figure 17.3 above). It was discovered at the inner mouth of the entrance passage, with one edge dipped downwards into the materials that filled the passage (Hartnett 1957, 226, Plate LXVII).

Architecture is a fluid and ongoing process. A medium point was possibly used to execute the majority of motifs on this stone. The imagery comprises four tightly nested horizontal bands of fairly parallel angular zigzags. Their combination can create an experience that is unsettling—I think this is because they project confidence, agitation, and frenzy. For a less subjective interpretation, it may be because they form dense optical patterns, which can cause the neuro-visual system to malfunction. The extreme intensity of the pattern of

Figure 17.4 Fourknocks I with its recessed chambers (digital photograph by Ken Williams)

Figure 17.5 Stone C (digital photograph by Ken Williams)

zigzag lines overloads the contrast/orientation neurons of the primary visual cortex (area V1), causing them to "leak" and cross-stimulate neighboring neurons; this is termed the "contextual effect" (Wilkins et al. 1984; Zeki 1999; Hoffman 2000). If viewed for sufficiently long periods, this effect can cause optical illusions, headache, and dizziness. Furthermore, it can result in migraine and epileptic seizures in photosensitive sufferers (Wilkins et al. 1984). When the motifs were fresher, there may have been greater contrasts between line and space, heightening such effects (Cochrane 2008).[5] These might have been further magnified if the engraving interacted with flickering lights. Such illumination may have come from the fires lit on the extensive spreads of charcoal around the center of the chamber and in front of western recess (Cell 3) (Hartnett 1957, 210, Plate LXV).

That all these angles meet at their apexes suggests that they are not entoptic motifs (subjective visual phenomena) as defined by Dronfield (1994, 1995, 1996). Regarding other passage tomb images in Ireland as possibly representing entoptic motifs, I no longer believe this is the case (contra Cochrane 2001). I still think that it is possible that some people engaged in altered states of consciousness and that particular images collaborated in these experiences. I do not, however, think that the images represent entoptics *per se*. Some may have the active ability to remind us of entoptic motifs (especially the earliest ones), but they do not passively represent such motifs (Cochrane 2006a, 83; see also

Jones 2004, 202; Hensey 2012, 168; Robin 2012, 166). The images are things in their own right, rather than mere facsimiles or auras of other things that humans have experienced elsewhere. What we do have here are episodes of application over time. The motifs are incomplete near the right-hand edge due to the possible flaking of the surface; these were poorly restored with images applied at a later date (Hartnett 1957, 226; Shee Twohig 1981, 222; see Figure 17.3). We can also witness re-pecking overlaying the second line of zigzags—an example of the removal of surface to create surface, or additive subtraction (Cochrane 2009). That reimaging occurred may suggest that existence precedes essence (Latour & Lowe 2010), meaning that for images to have ongoing substance they need to be able to subsist (as with many things in the world). Such a proposition regarding passage tomb motifs is not as esoteric as it might appear at first. The fact the motifs are still present today is contingent upon many complex engagements over time. These include the flaking of the surface, the overlaid pecking, the sealing of the tomb, the collapse of the roof, the late twentieth-century restorations, and the current management plans. Such collaborative ecologies are part of Fourknocks' personality.

Stone E (Figure 17.6) is the lintel over the southern recess (Cell 2), the innermost chamber that faces the passage. The largest amounts of material were found here, including burnt fragments of an ornate antler pin, made from the shed tine of a young red deer (Hartnett 1957,

Figure 17.6 Stone E (digital photograph by Ken Williams)

214–15). Although damaged on one end, the stone is still impressively decorated in the angular "Fourknocks style" (ibid., 227).

The imagery is formed by four large picked double lozenges, which are flanked by five rows of parallel zigzags above and two below. Inserted into these zigzags are picked triangular shapes; the central lozenge designs are solid, and the surrounding ones are formed by false relief bands (Hartnett 1957, 227; Shee Twohig 1981, 222). Here, the lines are harmonious with each other and the surface of the stone (Hartnett 1957, 227), delivering a sense of surety and confidence. The zigzags are sublime—their elegance is matched only by their violence. Interestingly, the motifs on the antler pin are reminiscent of the angular zigzags. That the pin was broken before being burnt and deposited (ibid., 242) may attest to its potency. Certainly, emotional commitments are often involved in deliberately fragmenting things, together with the sounds, sensations, and affects of the breakage. After fragmentation, and especially after burning, these disjointed elements may have provided cognitive indecipherability, helping to confuse the spectator (and excavator), who is unable to distinguish at once parts and wholes.

Similar in detail is Stone F, the lintel capstone of the western recess (Cell 3) that is visible on the right-hand side upon entering the chamber; it is the largest of the three cells. The imagery comprises ten independent solidly picked lozenges that form a central band. Above and below the lozenges are positioned three parallel rows of angular zigzags, which have solid triangular shapes inserted into the external edges of the composition (Hartnett 1957, 227; Shee Twohig 1981, 222; see Figure 17.3). The images here appear rapid—they suggest adaptation. Although worn from exposure to weathering (Hartnett 1957, 197–98, 227), the lines themselves have depth, and this allows them to act as a sculpture. They create a feeling of texture, suggesting rather than rendering. Here, we have flexibility with resilience, possessing a character of life; there is not a limp or dead line in sight.

If we accept that the current locations of the lintel stones reflects their positions during the later stages of the life of Fourknocks I in the Neolithic—which I do, with the possible exception of Stone A—then the motifs within the architecture of the tomb are collaborating. Robin (2010, 389) terms such images threshold motifs, occurring at significant junctions or liminal crossings (see also Sharples 1984, 116–17; Cochrane 2006a, 169). Such relationships are powerful and enhance a feeling of movement within the tomb (Thomas 1990, 1992; Lewis-Williams & Dowson 1993; Cochrane 2006b, 2012b). It can also be humbling and overwhelming—visual saturation. Decorated lintels can stimulate senses of isolation (Lewis-Williams & Dowson 1993, 60; Robin 2012, 390). Interestingly, the easternmost chamber (Cell 1) to the left as one enters, has no decorated lintel and contains the lowest comparable quantities of cremated bone and artifacts (Cooney 2000). This may be part of the preference for *dexter* over *sinister* in the passage tombs of Ireland (Herity 1974, 123; see also Eogan et al. 2012, 36). With Fourknocks I, things are involved in processes of adaption and change. The diversity of archaeological narratives surrounding the place attests to this aspect of its character. Such fluidity means that static interpretations of what the site might represent become inappropriate. Instead, creative acts with placements and displacements take center stage.

FOURKNOCKS II

The excavator Hartnett (1971, 38) described the site as a "composite monument." The ruinous and un-restored mound of Fourknocks II is located c. 100 meters to the east of Fourknocks I, and it is built on slightly higher ground; it is ovoid shaped and measures 28 by 24 meters (ibid., 35–36). The mound, which was surrounded by a ditch, covers several features: a bell-shaped cairn, a cairn ditch, a megalithic passage, and a trench (ibid., 35–42). The elongated trench (10.6 by 1.6 meters) was constructed before the mound and is possibly contemporary with the cairn. This was an open-air location where bodies were cremated (ibid., 44, 63); the fill also included worked antler, burnt clay, and charcoal produced from ash (*Fraxinus*), hazel (*Corylus*), oak (*Quercus*), and willow/poplar (*Salix/Populus*) (ibid., 42).[6] The trench may have been developed to aid protection from the elements during the performance of cremation. Fourknocks is after all an exposed place, and cremations are generally acts that can be only partly controlled, with weather, wind, and the body's reaction to heat all interacting in unpredictable ways (Hofmann 2012, 232). The minimum number of people identifiable in the human remains is circa 21, with about 11 children and 10 adults (Cooney 2000, 106–8). Sometime after the last cremation was deposited, a megalithic passage roofed with limestone and blue flag (4.3 meters long and c. 1 meter wide) was erected; this was orientated to face northeast, dipping down to terminate at the cremation trench and creating a T-shaped plan. The passage was constructed from seven undecorated orthostats on the southeastern side and six undecorated ones on the northwestern side, and it was filled with stone, shingle, and earth with deposits of fragmented and cremated human bone; the fill included adult and large amounts of children deposits (Hartnett 1971, 40–41). Inhumation and children seem to dominate this passage area (ibid., 63). Burnt antler and bone pins were also discovered that may have been associated with a sheep's metacarpal. The final addition was an earthen mound placed to cover the entire feature (ibid., 44). The mound consisted of: boulder clay, rock chippings, redeposited sods with associated vegetation, blue-colored soil, cairn material, occasional pieces of quartz, fragmented pottery, and some stone tools (ibid., 47–62).

INTERNAL RUMORS

> Always there was this feeling . . . a fine net drawn round us with infinite skill and delicacy, holding us so lightly that is was only at some supreme moment that one realized that one was indeed entangled in its meshes.

—Dr. Watson

Fourknocks I and II face northwards, and both are located on the northern extreme of the hill's ridge; this renders them more visible when approached from the north (Cooney 1997, 17; 2000, 111). The original earthen covers over the mounds would have made them appear similar in stature and size; for instance, Fourknocks I was c. 20 meters and Fourknocks II was c. 28 meters in circumference (Hartnett 1971, 35; Cooney 2000, 111). The reconstructed Fourknocks I is still noted for being striking (Kador & Ruffino 2010). In both mounds access through the passages was eventually impeded by the packing of human bone. Collaborations between the mounds are also threaded through the proposition that the sites were contemporaneous. It has been suggested that during the earlier phases, the deposits of human bone discovered in Fourknocks I had been originally burnt within the open-air cremation trench (Hartnett 1957, 250; 1971, 63; Herity 1974, 163; Cooney 2000, 111). At some point it would appear that Fourknocks II was transformed into a structure that resembles a passage tomb in order not to remain exposed to the elements. Both sites were demarcated by specific yet different features: Fourknocks I by a low kerb and Fourknocks II by a ditch. The ditches may at some level play a delineating role similar to megalithic kerbs (O'Sullivan 2005, 236). Interestingly, in both these sites closure was accompanied by the placement of human remains. The usage of the passage at Fourknocks II parallels that at Fourknocks I; for instance, both contained child remains (Hartnett 1971, 63). At both sites children under five years old were mostly inhumed. One of the most striking differences between the mounds is the presence or absence of imagery on the passage orthostats. Fourknocks II is undecorated, and this may be a result of the placement of the orthostats to indicate the closure of the feature rather than its perpetuation. By contrast, it would appear that repeated engagements occurred within Fourknocks I, which necessitated visual stimulation and regeneration.

Such performances involving mixtures of mixtures (e.g., motifs, cremated bones, animal bones, burnt things; see Cochrane 2007) and the closing of the mounds at Fourknocks might be about more than forgetting pollutants or commemorating the dead and the "ancestors" (see further discussions in Mullin 2001; Fowler 2010; Harris 2010). We should not reduce these actions to mere acts of remembrance or forgetting. The two processes are not necessarily oppositions; repeated performances can sometimes assist in actively remembering to forget. Within such actions, remembering and forgetting are not clashing imperatives; rather, they are differing perspectives collaborating simultaneously (Russell 2012, 252).[7] Such movements may account for repeated and similar activities over time. Although not contemporary with Fourknocks I and II, it is interesting to note that the later Bronze Age monument at Fourknocks III (Hartnett 1971, 81) mimicked the mound shape of its predecessors. It may have been attempting to imitate them at some level, thereby enhancing the significance of the ridgeway. Such emulation in itself might have been part of ongoing and staged performances (ibid.), and might also account for the series of late Neolithic pits containing grooved ware pottery and burnt matrices located c. 550 meters east of the complex (King 1999, 176–77). Such motivations may explain why Fourknocks I and II also acted as cemeteries during the Bronze Age (Hartnett 1957, 1971; Cooney 2000).

The mounds were not merely protective covers for the tombs (Robin 2010, 373–74); the tomb architecture, the kerb, the ditch, the images, the things within, and varied layers of mound material were part of working nets of performances. Hartnett (1957, 203) commented on the symmetrical relations of tomb and kerb at Fourknocks I, and of cairn and trench at Fourknocks II (Hartnett 1971, 64). Although the mounds appear less symmetrical, they are not asymmetrical, since there are no overarching divisions suggesting a predominance of right over left, as seen in the passage tombs (Robin 2010, 400). The mounds were composed of deposits including: yellow clay, brown, red, shingle and sandy soils, cairn material, and turf layers (Hartnett 1957, 209; 1971, 44). It appears that the construction of the mounds was not random; some elements may have been incorporated for their abilities to stem water percolation (O'Kelly 1982, 22; Robin 2010, 383), and others for their smell, texture, and visual impact (e.g., the yellow clay). Why would people invest so much time and effort into developing a sequence within a mound that could not be seen? One answer might be that it was the performance of creating the mound that was important. It was the interaction with different things that brought forth particular significances, beyond what could or could not be seen when it was "finished." These engagements may include: stiffness from exertion, hot sweat on a cold morning, the stone that cuts the finger, and emotional satisfaction. Such events move beyond representation and involved things coming together, collaborating, and building a common world.

COMPOSING FOURKNOCKS

What's interesting about you is you.

—Alonzo King

By looking in detail at the assemblages and blending of essences in Fourknocks, we have "looked along" some of the threads that permeate these amalgamations. My aim in this chapter was not to present a critique of representational approaches—to deconstruct, break, or wipe the slate clean. Instead, I wanted to create and compose, to work with and collaborate; in essence, to feel that there are other ways to talk with Fourknocks. Sometimes this is best achieved by acknowledging that things are what they are, that images are what they are, and that life is often messy. The compositions at Fourknocks are not merely matters *of* symbolic meaning that humans determine; rather, they live *within* matters of ongoing concern.

ACKNOWLEDGMENTS

Some of the ideas in this chapter were developed during a research trip in Sofia, Bulgaria, kindly funded by the Sainsbury Institute. Back in Ireland, discussions with Fumihito Nagase and Professors Tetsuo Kobayashi and George Eogan helped my thinking. Special thanks go to the Museum of London Archaeology, which funded me to attend the workshop. Guillaume Robin was very kind in helping me with Figure 2—Ken Williams is as ever amazing! A big thank you to Elizabeth Shee Twohig, Muiris O'Sullivan, Douglass Bailey, and Alasdair Whittle, for commenting on early versions. Andy Jones and Lesley McFayden guided me to think in new ways. Thank you to Tony Todd for introducing me to "Onkalo," and to Ian Russell for stimulating insights. Ben Alberti, Andy Jones and Josh Pollard are all legends, as are all the participants of the workshop. It was a wonderful weekend and a wonderful way to do archaeology!

NOTES

1. It is also stimulated by Cooney (2000), Ingold (2007), Jones et al. (2012).
2. Such approaches to passage tombs have been dominant for over 150 years. They are representational and stipulate that things and meanings lie behind or just beyond the image—through the cracks, if you like. They mostly subscribe to textual understandings, and can often be very expressionistic and poetic. Ultimately they are based on the idea that an image can represent something else—be it an ancestor, text, creature, hybrid, language, face, god, swastika, plant, celestial phenomenon, worldview, or another image,

like a hallucination. The following list of proponents of these approaches is by no means exhaustive: Wilde (1849), Deane (1889–91), Coffey (1912), Breuil (1921), Macalister (1921), Mahr (1937), Crawford (1957), Herity (1974), Brennan (1983), Thomas (1992), Lewis-Williams & Dowson (1993), Dronfield (1995), Tilley (1999), Nash (2002), McCormack (2012). For a comprehensive review see Hensey (2012, 161–68).

3. For further reading see Baudrillard (1994), Lorimer (2005), Thrift (2008), Anderson & Harrison (2010).

4. Stone G, the non-orthostatic limestone found outside the passage on the eastern edge of the mound, is the possible exception. Although Hartnett (1957, 228) once saw faint incised lines, few have been able to see them since (e.g., Shee Twohig 1981, 222).

5. Such affects would be further enhanced by the application of color. For discussions of the possible occurrence of pigment on stone see Breuil & Macalister (1921, 4), Shee Twohig (1981, 32–35), Bradley et al. (2000), Card & Thomas (2012).

6. Such floral remains indicate that there was considerable scrub in the area at the time of construction. Hazel was also the predominant wood found at Fourknocks I (Hartnett 1957, 271–72; 1971, 64).

7. For instance, in Michael Madsen's documentary *Into Eternity: A Film for the Future* (2010), we are introduced to "Onkalo," a depositional project in Finland. Onkalo is a deep mine created to store nuclear waste. The intention is that the placed material will remain undisturbed for 100,000 years, after which time it will no longer be harmful. The greatest threat to the success of the material being left alone is human curiosity. Since contemporary representational signs and markers are unlikely to be decipherable over such time spans, other methods are being sought. These include repeated performances of actively remembering to forget about the place (see detailed discussions in Russell [2012]). Dead children may have been considered dangerous for some during the Neolithic (Finlay 2000). The infant remains placed into Fourknocks I/II, and the later creation of Fourknocks III (which also had a child burial) might respond to perspectives similar to those highlighted by the Onkalo project.

REFERENCES

Anderson, B. & Harrison, P. 2010. The promise of non-representational theories. In B. Anderson & P. Harrison (eds.), *Taking-Place: Non-Representational Theories and Geography*, 1–34. Farnham, UK: Ashgate Publishing

Bailey, D. 2005. *Prehistoric Figurines: Representation and Corporeality in the Neolithic*. Oxford, UK: Routledge

Bailey, D., Cochrane, A. & Zambelli, J. 2010. *Unearthed: A Comparative Study of Jōmon Dogū and Neolithic Figurines*. Norwich, UK: SCVA

Baudrillard, J. 1994. *Simulacra and Simulation*. Translated by S.F. Glaser. Ann Arbor: University of Michigan Press

Bloch, M.E.F. 1982. Death, women and power. In M.E.F. Bloch & J. Parry (eds.), *Death and the Regeneration of Life*, 211–30. Cambridge: Cambridge University Press

Bradley, R. 2009. *Image and Audience: Rethinking Prehistoric Art*. Oxford: Oxford University Press

Bradley, R., Phillips, T., Richards, C. & Webb, M. 2000. Decorating the houses of the dead: incised and pecked motifs in Orkney chambered tombs. *Cambridge Archaeological Journal* 11(1), 45–67

Brennan, M. 1983. *The Stars and the Stones: Ancient Art and Astronomy in Ireland*. London: Thames and Hudson

Breuil, H. 1921. Les pétroglyphes d'Irlande. *Revue Archéologique* 13, 75–78

Breuil, H. & Macalister, R.A.S. 1921. A study of the chronology of Bronze Age sculpture in Ireland. *Proceedings of the Royal Irish Academy* 36C, 1–9

Card, N. & Thomas, A. 2012. Painting a picture of Neolithic Orkney: decorated stonework from the Ness of Brodgar. In A. Cochrane & A.M. Jones (eds.), *Visualising the Neolithic: Abstraction, Figuration, Performance, Representation*, 111–24. Oxford, UK: Oxbow Books

Cochrane, A. 2001. *Between Heaven and Earth: Contextualising the Alien Art of Irish Passage Tombs.* Unpublished MA dissertation, School of History and Archaeology, Cardiff University

Cochrane, A. 2006a. *Irish Passage Tombs: Neolithic Images, Contexts and Beliefs.* Unpublished PhD thesis, School of History and Archaeology, Cardiff University

Cochrane, A. 2006b. The simulacra and simulations of Irish Neolithic passage tombs. In I. Russell (ed.), *Images, Representations and Heritage: Moving beyond a Modern Approach to Archaeology*, 251–82. New York: Springer-Kluwer

Cochrane, A. 2007. We have never been material. *Journal of Iberian Archaeology* 9–10, 138–57

Cochrane, A. 2008. Some stimulating solutions. In C. Knappett & L. Malafouris (eds.), *Material Agency: Towards a Non-Anthropocentric Approach*, 157–86. New York: Springer-Kluwer

Cochrane, A. 2009. Additive subtraction: addressing pick-dressing in Irish passage tombs. In J. Thomas & V. Oliveira Jorge (eds.), *Archaeology and the Politics of Vision in a Post-Modern Context*, 163–85. Newcastle, UK: Cambridge Scholars Publishing

Cochrane, A. 2012a. The immanency of the intangible image: thoughts with Neolithic expression. In I.-M. Back Danielsson, F. Fahlander, & Y. Sjöstrand (eds.), *Encountering Imagery: Materialities, Perceptions, Relations*, 133–60. Stockholm, Swed.: Stockholm University

Cochrane, A. 2012b. Composing the Neolithic at Knockroe. In A. Cochrane & A. Jones (eds.), *Visualising the Neolithic: Abstraction, Figuration, Performance, Representation*, 179–97. Oxford, UK: Oxbow Books

Cochrane, A. & Jones, A.M. 2012. Visualising the Neolithic: an introduction. In A. Cochrane & A.M. Jones (eds.), *Visualising the Neolithic: Abstraction, Figuration, Performance, Representation*, 1–14. Oxford, UK: Oxbow Books

Cochrane, A. & Russell, I. 2007. Visualizing archaeologies: a manifesto. *Cambridge Archaeological Journal* 17(1), 3–19

Coffey, G. 1912. *Newgrange and Other Incised Tumuli in Ireland: The Influence of Crete and the Aegean in the Extreme West of Europe in Early Times.* Dublin, Ire.: Hodges, Figgis & County Ltd

Cooney, G. 1992. Body politics and grave messages: Irish Neolithic mortuary practices. In N. Sharples & A. Sheridan (eds.), *Vessels for the Ancestors: Essays on the Neolithic of Britain and Irelands in Honour of Audrey Henshall*, 128–42. Edinburgh, UK: Edinburgh University Press

Cooney, G. 1997. A tale of two mounds: monumental landscape design at Fourknocks, Co. Meath. *Archaeology Ireland* 11(2), 17–19

Cooney, G. 2000. *Landscapes of Neolithic Ireland.* New York: Routledge

Cooney, G. & Grogan, E. 1994. *Irish Prehistory: A Social Perspective.* Bray, Ire.: Wordwell

Crawford, O.G.S. 1957. *The Eye Goddess.* London: Phoenix House

Davidsson, M. 2003. On the anatomy of megaliths—the interrelation between physical interment and morphology in Irish megalithic tombs. In G. Burenhult (ed.), *Stones and Bones: Formal Disposal of the Dead in Atlantic Europe during the Mesolithic-Neolithic Interface 6000–3000 BC. Archaeological Conference in Honour of the Late Professor Michael J. O'Kelly*, 235–41. Oxford, UK: British Archaeological Reports, International Series 1201

Deane, T.N. 1889–91. On some ancient monuments scheduled under Sir John Lubbock's Act, 1882. *Proceedings of the Royal Irish Academy* 1 (Third Series), 161–65

Delong, A.J. 1981. Phenomenological space-time: towards an experiential relativity. *Science* 213, 681–82

Delong, A.J. 1983. Spatial scale, temporal experience and information processing: an empirical examination of experiential reality. *Man-Environment Systems* 13, 77–86

Doss, E. 1977. Making imaginations age in the 1950s: Disneyland's fantasy art and architecture. In K.A. Marling (ed.), *Designing Disney's Theme Parks: The Architecture of Reassurance*, 179–89. New York: Flammarion

Dronfield, J. 1994. *Subjective Visual Phenomena in Irish Passage Tomb Art: Vision, Cosmology and Shamanism.* Unpublished PhD thesis, Department of Archaeology, Cambridge University

Dronfield, J. 1995. Subjective vision and the source of megalithic art. *Antiquity* 69, 539–49

Dronfield, J. 1996. Entering alternative realities: cognition, art and architecture in Irish passage tombs. *Cambridge Archaeological Journal* 6(1), 37–72

Eogan, G. 1986. *Knowth and the Passage-Tombs of Ireland.* London: Thames and Hudson

Eogan, G., Shee Twohig, E. & Williams, K. 2012. Containing the dead in Irish passage tombs. In B. Britnell & B. Silvester (eds.), *Reflections on the Past: Essays in Honour of Frances Lynch*, 33–47. Welshpool, UK: Cambrian Archaeological Association

Finlay, N. 2000. Outside of life: traditions of infant burial in Ireland from *cillín* to cist. *World Archaeology* 31(3), 407–22

Fowler, C. 2004. *The Archaeology of Personhood: An Anthropological Approach.* London: Routledge

Fowler, C. 2010. Pattern and diversity in the Early Neolithic mortuary practices of Britain and Ireland contextualising the treatment of the dead. *Documenta Praehistorica* 37, 1–22

Gell, A. 1995. Closure and multiplication: an essay on Polynesian cosmology and ritual. In D. de Coppet & A. Iteanu (eds.), *Cosmos and Society in Oceania*, 21–56. Oxford, UK: Berg

Gell, A. 1999. Strathernograms, or, the semiotics of mixed metaphors. In A. Gell, *The Art of Anthropology: Essays and Diagrams*, 29–75. London: Routledge

Grosz, E. 1994. *Volatile Bodies: Towards a Corporeal Feminism.* Bloomington: Indiana University Press

Harris, O.J.T. 2010. Emotional and mnemonic geographies at Hambledon Hill: texturing Neolithic places with bodies and bones. *Cambridge Archaeological Journal* 20(3), 357–71

Hartnett, P.J. 1957. Excavation of a passage grave at Fourknocks, Co. Meath. *Proceedings of the Royal Irish Academy* 58C, 197–277

Hartnett, P.J. 1971. The excavation of two tumuli at Fourknocks (Sites II and III), Co. Meath. *Proceedings of the Royal Irish Academy* 71C, 35–89

Hensey, R. 2012. Assuming the jigsaw had only one piece: abstraction, figuration and the interpretation of Irish passage tomb art. In A. Cochrane & A.M. Jones (eds.), *Visualising the Neolithic: Abstraction, Figuration, Performance, Representation*, 161–78. Oxford, UK: Oxbow Books

Herity, M. 1974. *Irish Passage Graves: Neolithic Tomb-Builders in Ireland and Britain, 2500 BC.* Dublin, Ire.: Irish University Press

Hoffman, D. 2000. *Visual Intelligence: How We Create What We See.* New York: W.W. Norton

Hofmann, D. 2005. Fragments of power: LBK figurines and the mortuary record. In D. Hofmann, J. Mills & A. Cochrane (eds.), *Elements of Being: Mentalities, Identities and Movements*, 58–70. Oxford, UK: British Archaeological Reports, International Series 1437

Hofmann, D. 2012. The life and death of Linearbandkeramik figurines. In A. Cochrane & A.M. Jones (eds.), *Visualising the Neolithic: Abstraction, Figuration, Performance, Representation*, 226–42. Oxford, UK: Oxbow Books

Ingold, T. 2007. *Lines: A Brief History*. London: Routledge

Jones, A.M. 2004. By way of illustration: art, memory and materiality in the Irish Sea and beyond. In V. Cummings & C. Fowler (eds.), *The Neolithic of the Irish Sea: Materiality and Traditions of Practice*, 202–13. Oxford, UK: Oxbow Books

Jones, A.M. 2005. Lives in fragments? Personhood and the European Neolithic. *Journal of Social Archaeology* 5(2), 193–224

Jones, A.M. 2012a. *Prehistoric Materialities: Becoming Material in Prehistoric Britain and Ireland*. Oxford: Oxford University Press

Jones, A.M. 2012b. Living rocks: animacy, performance and the rock art of the Kilmartin region, Argyll, Scotland. In A. Cochrane & A.M. Jones (eds.), *Visualising the Neolithic: Abstraction, Figuration, Performance, Representation*, 79–88. Oxford, UK: Oxbow Books

Jones, A.M., Freedman, D., O'Connor, B., Lamdin-Whymark, H., Tipping, R. & Watson, A. 2011. *An Animate Landscape: Rock Art and the Prehistory of Kilmartin, Argyll, Scotland*. Oxford, UK: Windgather Press

Kador, T. & Ruffino, J. 2010. Teletubbylandscapes: children, archaeology and the future of the past. In S. Koerner & I. Russell (eds.), *Unquiet Pasts: Risk Society, Lived Cultural Heritage, Re-Designing Reflexivity*, 327–42. London: Ashgate

King, H.A. 1999. Excavation on the Fourknocks Ridge, Co. Meath. *Proceedings of the Royal Irish Academy* 99C, 157–98

Lamdin-Whymark, H. 2011a. Lithics, landscape and performance. In A.M. Jones, D. Freedman, B. O'Connor, H. Lamdin-Whymark, R. Tipping & A. Watson (eds.), *An Animate Landscape: Rock Art and the Prehistory of Kilmartin, Argyll, Scotland*, 178–201. Oxford, UK: Windgather Press

Lamdin-Whymark, H. 2011b. The experience of manufacturing rock art. In A.M. Jones, D. Freedman, B. O'Connor, H. Lamdin-Whymark, R. Tipping & A. Watson (eds.), *An Animate Landscape: Rock Art and the Prehistory of Kilmartin, Argyll, Scotland*, 334–35. Oxford, UK: Windgather Press

Latour, B. & Lowe, A. 2010. The migration of the aura or how the original through its facsimiles. In T. Bartscherer (ed.), *Switching Codes*, 275–98. Chicago, IL: University of Chicago Press

Lewis, C.S. 1971. Meditation in a toolshed. In W. Hooper (ed.), *Undeceptions: Essays on Theology and Ethics*, 171–74. London: Geoffrey Bles

Lewis-Williams, J.D. & Dowson, T.A. 1993. On vision and power in the Neolithic: evidence from the decorated monuments. *Current Anthropology* 34(1), 55–65

Lorimer, H. 2005. Cultural geography: the busyness of being "more-than-representational." *Progress in Human Geography* 29(1), 83–94

Macalister, R.A.S. 1921. *Ireland in Pre-Celtic Times*. Dublin, Ire.: Maunsel and Roberts

Mahr, A. 1937. New prospects and problems in Irish prehistory: presidential address for 1937. *Proceedings of the Prehistoric Society* 3, 201–436

McCormack, L. 2012. Thoughts on the Loughcrew autumn equinox. *Archaeology Ireland* 26(1), 9–11

McMann, J. 1993. *Loughcrew the Cairns: A Guide to an Ancient Irish Landscape*. Oldcastle, Ire.: After Hours Books

McMann, J. 1994. Forms of power: dimensions of an Irish megalithic landscape. *Antiquity* 68, 525–44

Mullin, D. 2001. Remembering, forgetting and the invention of tradition: burial and natural places in the English Early Bronze Age. *Antiquity* 75, 533–37

Nakamura, C. 2005. Mastering matters: magical sense and apotropaic figurine worlds of Neo-Assyria. In L. Meskell (ed.), *Archaeologies of Materiality*, 18–45. Oxford, UK: Blackwell

Nash, G. 2002. The landscape brought within: a re-evaluation of the rock-painting site at Tumlehed, Torslanda, Göteborg, west Sweden. In G. Nash & C. Chippindale (eds.), *European Landscapes of Rock-Art*, 176–94. London: Routledge

O'Kelly, M.J. 1982. *Newgrange: Archaeology, Art and Legend*. London: Thames and Hudson

O'Sullivan, M. 1993. *Megalithic Art in Ireland*. Dublin, Ire.: Country House

O'Sullivan, M. 2005. *Duma na nGiall: The Mound of the Hostages, Tara*. Bray, Ire.: Wordwell

Parker Pearson, M. 1999. *Archaeology of Death and Burial*. Stroud, UK: Sutton

Parry, J. 1982. Sacrificial death and the necrophagous ascetic. In M.E.F. Bloch & J. Parry (eds.), *Death and the Regeneration of Life*, 74–110. Cambridge: Cambridge University Press

Pollard, J. 2001. The aesthetics of depositional practice. *World Archaeology* 33(2), 315–33

Robin, G. 2010. Spatial structures and symbolic systems in Irish and British passage tombs: the organization of architectural elements, parietal carved signs and funerary deposits. *Cambridge Archaeological Journal* 20(3), 373–418

Robin, G. 2012. The figurative part of an abstract Neolithic iconography: hypotheses and directions of research in Irish and British Passage tomb art. In A. Cochrane & A.M. Jones (eds.), *Visualising the Neolithic: Abstraction, Figuration, Performance, Representation*, 140–60. Oxford, UK: Oxbow Books

Robinson, D.W. 2012. Discussion: personality and Neolithic visual media. In A. Cochrane & A.M. Jones (eds.), *Visualising the Neolithic: Abstraction, Figuration, Performance, Representation*, 291–300. Oxford, UK: Oxbow Books

Russell, I.A. 2012. Towards an ethics of oblivion and forgetting: a parallax view. *Heritage & Society* 5(2), 249–72

Russell, I.A. 2013. Cultural heritage management and images of the past. In C. Smith (ed.), *Encyclopedia of Global Archaeology*, 323–24. New York: Springer

Sharples, N. 1984. Excavations at Pierowall Quarry, Westray, Orkney. *Proceedings of the Society of Antiquaries of Scotland* 114, 75–125

Shee Twohig, E. 1973. Techniques of Irish passage grave art. In G. Daniel & P. Kjærum (eds.), *Megalithic Graves and Ritual: Papers Presented at the III Atlantic Colloquium, Moesgård 1969*, 163–72. Copenhagen, Den.: Jutland Archaeological Society

Shee Twohig, E. 1981. *The Megalithic Art of Western Europe*. Oxford, UK: Clarendon Press

Shee Twohig, E. 2004. *Irish Megalithic Tombs*. 2nd edition. Princes Risborough, UK: Shire Books

Thomas, J. 1990. Monuments from the inside: the case of the Irish megalithic tombs. *World Archaeology* 22(2), 168–78

Thomas, J. 1992. Monuments, movement and the context of megalithic art. In N. Sharples & A. Sheridan (eds.), *Vessels for the Ancestors: Essays on the Neolithic of Britain and Irelands in Honour of Audrey Henshall*, 143–55. Edinburgh, UK: Edinburgh University

Thomas, J. 2009. On the ocularcentrism of archaeology. In J. Thomas & V. Oliveira Jorge (eds.), *Archaeology and the Politics of Vision in a Post-Modern Context*, 1–12. Newcastle, UK: Cambridge Scholars Publishing

Thrift, N. 2008. *Non-Representational Theory: Space, Politics, Affect*. New York: Routledge

Tilley, C. 1999. *Metaphor and Material Culture*. Oxford, UK: Blackwell

Tilley, C. 2004. *The Materiality of Stone: Explorations in Landscape Phenomenology 1*. Oxford, UK: Berg

Westman, A. (ed.) 1994. *MOLAS Archaeological Site Manual.* 3rd edition. London: Museum of London

Whittle, A. 2003. *The Archaeology of People: Dimensions of Neolithic Life.* London: Routledge

Wilde, W. 1849. *The Beauties of the Boyne and the Blackwater.* Reprinted 2003. County Galway, Ire.: Kevin Duffey

Wilkins, A., Nimmo-Smith, I., Tait, A., McManus, C., Della Sala, S., Tilley, A., Arnold, K., Barrie, M. & Scott, S. 1984. A neurological basis for visual discomfort. *Brain* 107, 989–1017

Zeki, S. 1999. *Inner Vision: An Exploration of Art and the Brain.* Oxford: Oxford University Press

CHAPTER EIGHTEEN

Afterword: Archaeology and the Science of New Objects

Gavin Lucas

ON ARCHAEOLOGICAL ASEPSIS

Since the middle of the eighteenth century, it has been estimated that about 2 million species have been recorded on our planet. According to the International Institute for Species Exploration based at Arizona State University, about 18,000 new species are catalogued every year, including fossil species (www.species.asu.edu). Beyond the earth, new planets and stars are being discovered rapidly through new space telescopes, like the Kepler observatory. Meanwhile, each year archaeologists unearth hundreds of thousands of objects from the ground all over the world. It is odd that when we think about what science does, as scientists we tend to focus on new interpretations, new theories, new knowledge. Yet what the public sees—and what we too easily forget—is that more than anything, we find new objects. Perhaps it is so obvious we simply don't see it. Or we refuse to acknowledge it because it would seem to smack of a naïve empiricism or inductivism that equates new knowledge with the accumulation of new facts. The only time such an acknowledgment is made is when the very existence of such new objects is controversial, whether it is a new species, planet, or subatomic particle. Indeed, the heated discussions around scientific realism that were very popular between the 1960s and 1980s revolved precisely around invisible or theoretical objects like electrons (e.g., see Wylie 1986). Yet, as one of the earliest and still most lucid discussions put it: "One of the exciting aspects of the development of science has been the emergence of reference to strikingly new kinds of entities. . . . The compulsion toward

Archaeology after Interpretation: Returning Materials to Archaeological Theory, edited by Benjamin Alberti, Andrew Meirion Jones, and Joshua Pollard, 369–80.

metaphysical asepsis . . . seems to have arisen from a pre-occupation with metaphysical pseudo-problems, e.g. the conviction that there are very few ontologically legitimate kinds of entities, perhaps only one" (Maxwell 1962, 27).

Such discussions of scientific realism should perhaps make us sit up and reflect on what we do in archaeology. It is one thing to point out that archaeologists might discover new types of pottery, a previously unknown form of burial—or, if you are really lucky, a new civilization. But what the debates over scientific realism involve is not simply new types or new species, but new kinds of objects altogether. Is this possible in archaeology? Is there an archaeological equivalent of the electron? This is the question I want to engage with in this chapter. But to start, we might be wise to heed Maxwell's point in the quotation given above, specifically: What kind of metaphysical asepsis is involved in archaeology? That is, what *implicit* acts of ontological purification are routinely made in archaeology so that we always end up reducing reality to just two kinds of entities—humans and things? What possibilities are we not realizing because of such asepsis?

These questions relate very closely to the ones that are being increasingly raised by a number of archaeologists embracing what might be called the ontological turn (e.g., Olsen 2010; Alberti et al. 2011; Olsen et al. 2012). This is one specific manifestation of the reaction against two decades of semiotic and hermeneutic interpretation in archaeology, but it is enjoined by other scholars who for example focus on the performative or agential aspects of things (e.g., Knappett & Malafouris 2008; Conneller 2011; Jones 2012) or simply engage in a general rethinking of the relations between people and things (Knappett 2005; Boivin 2008; Hodder 2012). The contributions in this volume testify to the variety of research in this broad domain. My particular focus, though, is with ontology, and as Alberti has pointed out, it is not enough to simply redescribe all our familiar objects in a new theoretical language. We need to rethink our objects as part of "worlds otherwise"; we need to think about ontology in relation to alterity (see Alberti et al. 2011). However, the alterity I am thinking of is not related to "other" ontologies; my position is more about an *open* ontology than a multiple one. Thus I am not going to approach this argument in terms of a kind of paleo-ethnography, which is the inspiration for much of this work in archaeology (e.g., Viveiros de Castro 2004; Henare et al. 2007). Rather, I will follow Maxwell's position in relation to scientific realism. Furthermore, unlike many of the contributions in this book, I will not choose examples from prehistory, but rather studies much closer in time. My examples come from my research in Iceland in the modern period. So let me begin with an archaeological fable.

EXTRACTS FROM AN AUTOPSY

In May 2002, archaeologists discovered the buried remains of an extinct organism in the southwest of Iceland, an island just south of the Arctic Circle. When I say discovered, I am being somewhat liberal with the term: documented accounts and even visual depictions of the being were recorded while this organism was still alive, so we already knew of its prior existence. Moreover, several prior archaeological investigations during the twentieth century had confirmed its presence. But it was only in 2002 that a more extensive project was initiated to recover its remains, and only in the last year has its unique nature been fully appreciated. The exhumation and autopsy of the organism's body was performed each time by a team of around ten people, most of whom remained present throughout the six years; the team was led by Dr. Gavin Lucas, with the assistance of Mjöll Snæsdóttir.

Circumstances

The site where the remains were found lies in the southwest of Iceland, about an hour and a half's drive from the capital city, Reykjavík. The area is rural farmland (pasture) and presently there are a church, a cultural center, a hotel, and associated dwellings near the site. The present community was aware of the remains and was very supportive of the exhumation; it also helped raise funds for its preservation and presentation to the public. The area sees lots of tourists, especially in the summer months, and is on a fixed route of attractions in the area called the Golden Circle. During the two months of fieldwork every summer, the team working on the exhumation lived on location. All samples and removable parts were taken back to Reykjavík for further analysis.

Protocols

A formal system of conducting the exhumation and autopsy was followed, producing a number of standardized records . . . following accepted protocols. . . .

External Examination

Prior to exhumation, an external examination of the area was undertaken: the surface ground was surveyed using a differential GPS, and prior documented records from previous centuries were located and collated. This gave valuable background information prior to exhumation.

(Contd.)

(Contd.)

Internal Examination

The first incision removed the surface turf with a mechanical excavator. Thereafter, investigation proceeded with hand tools . . . removing elements of the organism in correct anatomical sequence, as far as possible. What follows is a summary of the key systems/organs that comprise the creature.

Systemic and Organ Review

There were a number of recognizable systems for the circulation of various micro-organisms and other substances within the body remains, chiefly those involving people, water, air, light, and heat. Beyond that, however, identifying the function of specific organs was problematic; there was certainly a clear division between components, but how these functioned is not entirely clear as yet. However, reports contemporary with the last years of the life of the organism are of some assistance. . . . Although much of the internal anatomy of the organism can be related to such systems, there is clearly more going on. At a very coarse level, one might identify other systems that were more localized in their operation. . . . Each of these systems was dependent on a controlled exchange of substances and micro-organisms with the external environment, in particular humans, wood, ceramic and glass vessels, tobacco pipes, clothing, writing implements, meat, beans, grain, fish, milk products, and so on. . . . Remains of all these objects and more have been found within different parts of the organism's body, although a lot more work is still to be done on their distribution and precise function within the organism.

It is quite clear from this summary that the organism can be seen in many ways as a host for the human micro-organism or parasite. Based on documented accounts and visible organ differentiation, these micro-organisms clearly vary in their status. Some were there for behavioral modification (short-term treatment) and were temporary inhabitants; others may have been more permanent (long-term committed) . . . while a smaller number may have been fairly long-term occupants, though their role remains obscure. . . . Yet still, the organism was an independent being, its functioning and existence greater than its parts, most of which had much shorter life spans and/or presence.

Cause of Death (CoD)

It was quite clear that we were dealing with a very long-lived organism before its death; our investigation only dealt with the last three hundred years of its life, but it is likely that it was nearly a thousand years old when it died. Age estimations

(Contd.)

(Contd.)

> are fortunately quite easy, since such beings have a tendency to
> preserve signs of their earlier life in the form of defunct or
> vestigial organs, some of which undergo clear signs of repair
> and are incorporated into later organs, whereas others lie inert
> and inactive and are completely shed off. The question remains
> concerning the CoD. This is not always apparent; certainly it
> is very difficult, if not impossible, to ever ascribe a natural
> term of life to such beings, since they have the potential to
> live for an unlimited duration. We are still working on this
> question, but issues of internal organ/system failure cannot be
> ruled out and also need to be related to environmental changes.
> This was a being that regularly and promiscuously exchanged
> substances with other beings in its environment, and therefore
> its fate must have been closely entangled with them. What we
> do know is that the time of its demise roughly coincides with
> the emergence of a completely new type of entity seen in these
> regions, a super-entity which evolved . . . to the east in an
> area now known as Reykjavík. This new organism (or colony,
> the attribution is uncertain) may have acted as an attractor
> for the human micro-organisms that would be essential to the
> maintenance of our entity—their departure ultimately causing
> its death.

TOWARDS AN OPEN ONTOLOGY

The extract you have just read is no fable but a factual description. It is meant as a serious reflection on what we think the object—or subject—of archaeological interpretation is meant to be. There is a lot at stake here. For many archaeologists, the goal of archaeology is to get at "the Indian behind the artefact," a phrase coined by Braidwood in his obituary of Gordon Childe (Braidwood 1958). This focus on people was an obvious corrective to the endless, dry texts on typologies produced by orthodox cultural history accounts, which seemed to forget who their proper subject was. The concern was also repeated against the wave of statistics and system-thinking ushered in by the New Archaeology and prompted Jacquetta Hawke's famous essay in which she underlined that the proper study of mankind is man (Hawkes 1968). As if to counterattack, Kent Flannery then rephrased Braidwood to argue that the goal of archaeology was to get at the system behind both the Indian and the artifact (Flannery 1967). Today's theoretical orthodoxy is a blend of both Indian and system as structure and agency generally define the ontological parameters of the social; both are still articulated with the artifact, but the latter is now given a more active role.

For some archaeologists, this triangulation of people, social structure, and objects still denies objects an equal treatment within archaeology, their existence and meanings ultimately depending on and deriving from the other two terms (Olsen 2010; Olsen et al. 2012). There is a great deal of important insight that has emerged from this critique, but what tends to get reinforced is an oppositional stance of humans and things, with some scholars arguing for an archaeology that focuses on things (Oslen 2010), and others arguing for their mutual entanglement (Hodder 2012). I feel neither approach goes far enough insofar as both preserve what Maxwell (in the quotation at the start of this chapter) called a metaphysical asepsis: the idea that there are only two kinds of entities, i.e., humans and things. Though I appreciate that this dichotomy has been critiqued by these same archaeologists, their arguments—to me at least—appear to actually perpetuate it. The only way to move on is to take Maxwell's point seriously and ask: What *new* entities can archaeology propose? We *already* know humans exist; we *already* know pots and arrowheads exist. What does archaeology show us that we did *not* know already? This is what my fable is intended to sketch out: a view of the archaeological record as something that gives us access to unfamiliar, new types of entities. And this is not simply about proposing new objects, but about seeing familiar things in unfamiliar ways; a building is not quite what we thought it was.

There exists an organism which is able to change its appearance almost at will, to modify the functionality of its organs, to add and subtract from its body, and to transform its powers to act. I am talking about humans, of course. Clothing, tools, and machines can be attached and detached to the human body like prosthetics. Humans as cyborgs: this is a familiar idea (e.g., Haraway 1991; Pearson & Shanks 2001; Clark 2003), but I have always been especially drawn to Crawford's idea of archaeological remains as *disjecta membra* (cast-off limbs), which he proposed back in the 1920s (Crawford 1921). If we take this idea quite literally, it means that humans are entities that can reassemble themselves into different kinds of beings according to their prosthetics. But the idea of prosthetics and cyborgs does not quite go far enough; it might apply to a warrior equipped with shield, sword, and helmet going into combat, but it applies less adequately to an activity like making pottery. Where do the potter end and the clay pot begin? In this case or indeed the previous one, is it not fairer to say that a more complex, composite entity emerges consisting of the potter-wheel-clay (etc.)? We could conceptualize it as a machine in the sense discussed by Canguilhem—as an extended organism (Canguilhem 1992; Hacking 1998). A much better way to articulate what is happening in both these cases is to think of this as a process of assemblage (see also Fowler, in this volume).

I would suggest that assemblages are collectives or systems of usually familiar entities (which include humans, pots, arrowheads etc.) that cohere in stronger or weaker ways and for longer or shorter durations. I have discussed this concept in greater detail elsewhere, especially how it relates to our conventional understanding of archaeological assemblages (see Lucas 2012, in particular chapter 5). In the context of this chapter, however, I want to focus more on the issue of when such assemblages start to act like independent entities themselves—when their connections stabilize or ossify so that there is a sense of interior and exterior. It is at this point that we can cease talking in terms of networks or connections and must start talking of a new and emergent entity (see DeLanda 2006). This is not to suggest that such entities are not still composed of parts with relations, but simply that such relations now become defined in terms of exteriority and interiority. These phenomena of assemblage and emergence, I suggest, are what we can explore archaeologically; and indeed, they are arguably what archaeology is best suited to explore. By way of an example, I want now to introduce a different archaeological site I have been working on in Iceland and explore the processes of assembly (and disassembly) through the ideas of containment and enchainment (see Lucas 2012 for a detailed discussion of these terms).

Björnshús ("the house of Björn") was a stone-and-timber house built on the island of Viðey in the bay of Reykjavík in 1907, which was pulled down in 1943. It was one of several worker houses constructed at a new harbor and fish factory in connection to the industrialization of fishing in Iceland at the beginning of the twentieth century (see Lucas & Hreiðarsdóttir 2012). The building is an assemblage, a conjunction of parts. Many of these parts came from other assemblages elsewhere; for example, the timber came from warehouses in Norway and buildings at another fishing village in the northwest of Iceland. But many parts were themselves autonomous assemblages, such as the people who moved from different parts of the country or the objects such as plates, stoves, and toys. As an assemblage, this building both *contained* its parts and was *enchained* by them. Through containment, it created a boundary between inside and outside, and in effect it became an autonomous entity that lived for thirty-six years. Its walls, roof, and foundations acted as physical barriers to some entities (wind, rain, wildlife), whereas its doors and windows acted as conduits for others to come in and out (people, food, goods). Containment is never total; no object is impervious to others, which is why relations between objects are possible. And such relationality is not exclusively defined by the demarcation of barriers and conduits; a gust of wind may blow past the walls without effect, but the rain steadily and surely wears down its surface, as may particles of sand or sea salt in the wind. The door may permit access to people, but not all people may want or feel the right to enter. An object establishes its relation to the world, but the world is after all composed of other objects with their own properties that may breach firewalls or ignore open windows.

But this house is not just a container for its parts—it *is* its parts. The house as an assemblage or entity *is* the stone foundations, the iron stove, the timber door, the cups and plates, the people, the window glass. It is not just the immobile parts, but also all the mobile ones that come and go or move around inside. Indeed mobility, like containment, is not absolute but relative. Some parts stay put for long periods, some for shorter. The iron stove may not move for decades, the plate may move around daily. But nothing remains fixed forever, not even the walls and roof. The timber part of the house was assembled from parts of other houses; in 1943 the building was dismantled and reassembled on a lot in Rekjavík, and then moved again decades later, this time to a village miles away, where it still stands today. I have explored some of these mobilities through specific examples elsewhere (Lucas, forthcoming) so I will not dwell on them here. Suffice to say that the house is an enchainment of its parts, by which I mean the iterative process of parts linked together toward a common performance or practice. These processes are multiple (like the multiple processes occurring in your body now—digestion, respiration, etc.) and include routinized practices such as cooking, eating, or cleaning. Insofar as these iterative processes take place within and by parts of the house, they help to stabilize it and to maintain its integrity and autonomy. Without them, the house dies, even if its walls and roof remain intact. And slowly, even these soon crumble without maintenance routines.

Through the processes of containment and enchainment, and their respective properties of impermeability and durability, we can begin to see the archaeological record in terms of new kinds of entities. This does not mean that the old, familiar objects disappear; we still have humans, pots, and arrowheads, but we also have the emergence of new objects that incorporate these older ones and generally exist at a scale *above* the human organism. What makes my account of entities in the last two examples not simply about buildings, though, is that these entities are more than the walls, fixtures, and fittings; they are a functioning whole that like an organism exchanges substances with its environment and has an internal system of organs (for a comparable approach on buildings as assemblages, which also draws on the work of DeLanda, see Normark 2009). The organic metaphor has been used most recently in the context of nanoarchitecture, a field that develops close links between buildings and materials technology, and also following the development of "smart" rooms or "smart" spaces (e.g., Johansen 2002; Eng et al. 2003). However, I am using it in a much broader sense to incorporate any building that is partially self-sustaining or autonomous. This approach serves as a complement to those studies that look at buildings in terms of design and construction, in relation to performance and practice (e.g., Yaneva 2009, forthcoming; Jacobs & Merriman 2011; McFadyen, in this volume).

The focus on buildings as organisms or entities in this chapter should not be read as an indication that I consider these as the only form of new entities. However, they are a very dominant one, alongside even larger amalgamations like villages or cities. I should also repeat that they are not equivalent to what I mean by assemblage. Assemblages are far more numerous and diverse in their constitution, but they are also far more ephemeral. The issue here is when assemblages stabilize to an extent that they can be called autonomous entities—new kinds of things. It is the question of emergence. Arguably this focus on entities at a scale above the human displaces humans from any central role in archaeological narrative. But more important than de-centralizing humans is breaking down the dichotomy of humans and things, which the focus on emergence entails.

This is by no means a novel suggestion: the systems theory of the 1970s came close to suggesting this, especially in the work of David Clarke (1968), and whereas almost all archaeological perspectives adopt the idea of structures or processes operating above the level of human individuals, few make any ontological claims about these phenomena. Clarke was a rare exception. On the other hand, some archaeologists are suggesting that in studying the past, we need to focus more on the subhuman level. Just as the unit of biological evolution is the gene rather than the organism, so in human cultural evolution, according to contemporary Darwinian archaeologies (especially of the selectionist and dual inheritance kinds), the unit is the meme, conceived as cultural traits or traditions, rather than people *per se* (e.g., Cullen 2000; Shennan 2003; O'Brien et al. 2010). Whatever one thinks about the validity of applying Darwinian theory to human history, the idea that entities other than humans are the focus of analysis in a discipline like archaeology is a provocative move.

It does come at a cost, though: it raises questions over the status of archaeology as a humanist discipline. It is, if you like, quite explicitly post-humanist. Humans remain part of the story, but they are not *the* story. This may be too bitter a pill for some to swallow, but this is not to argue that there can be *no* science with humans at its center. It is only to suggest that *archaeology* may not be best suited to fulfill that role—largely because of the nature of its evidence, a point I develop in *Understanding the Archaeological Record* (Lucas 2012). However, paradoxically perhaps, I also suggest we can still preserve the idea of a social archaeology. But the societies we study are not those of Durkheim or Weber, Giddens or Bourdieu. They are closer to the societies of Latour and Callon: collectives, assemblages of agents of all stripes. Whereas Actor-Network Theory tends to retain the concept of assemblage as a loose, relational connection, for me the question is to explore when and how such networks become ossified, when connections become bound so tightly and iteratively that one can start to talk of a new, emergent entity that differentiates between an inside and outside. Under Actor-Network Theory, the flows seem endless. And sometimes surely they are. But sometimes they are not. We have to cut these networks (Strathern 1996). And where we do so is an empirical question, which brings me back to the central point of this chapter: archaeology as the science of new things.

What ontological status do these new things have? I have been pushing the organic metaphor quite far in this chapter because it is a useful middle ground between inert matter (brute things) and conscious subjects (humans). My intention is not to develop a kind of animist ontology (e.g., Alberti & Bray 2009), but rather to avoid conventional dichotomies. However, of course this perspective runs the risk of drawing on a different dichotomy between the organic and inorganic. But the distinction between the organic and inorganic is, like that between nature and culture or mind and matter, one we need to shed. As Jane Bennett argues, matter is vibrant, and although attempts in the early twentieth century to emphasize the life force in reality, such as Bergson's *élan vital* or Driesch's entelechy, are often dismissed as vitalism, they still challenge the separation of organic and inorganic (Bennett 2010; also see Canguilhem 1992). Bennett highlights in particular Driesch's connection to experimental science, and it is interesting to see how modern scientists have started to extend the notion of animacy to animal-built structures like termites nests (e.g., see Turner 2000, 2004). Such work on extended organisms resonates with others on the extended mind (e.g., Clark 2011) or with Leroi-Gourhan's extended organ (Leroi-Gourhan 1993). All of these perspectives challenge subject/object and mental/material dichotomies and are part of a much larger shift that cuts across these and other deep-seated divisions and help to bridge and bring closer the human and natural sciences. If archaeology can be part of this shift—and this seems to be a problem of increasing concern, not least in connection to archaeometry (e.g., Jones 2004; Pollard & Bray 2007)—this is surely a positive thing.

REFERENCES

Alberti, B. & Bray, T. 2009. Animating archaeology: of subjects, objects and alternative ontologies. *Cambridge Archaeological Journal* 19(3), 337–43

Alberti, B., Fowles, S., Holbraad, M., Marshall, Y. & Witmore, C. 2011. "Worlds otherwise": archaeology, anthropology and ontological difference. *Current Anthropology* 52(6), 896–912

Bennett, J. 2010. *Vibrant Matter: A Political Ecology of Things*. Durham, NC: Duke University Press

Boivin, N. 2008. *Material Cultures, Material Minds*. Cambridge: Cambridge University Press

Braidwood, R. 1958. J. Vere Gordon Childe 1892–1957. *American Anthropologist* 60, 733–36

Canguilhem, G. 1992. Machine and organism. In J. Crary & S. Kwinter (eds.), *Incorporations*, 44–69. New York: Zone Books

Clark, A. 2003. *Natural-Born Cyborgs: Minds, Technologies and the Future of Human Intelligence*. Oxford: Oxford University Press

Clark, A. 2011. *Supersizing the Mind*. Oxford: Oxford University Press

Clarke, D.L. 1968. *Analytical Archaeology*. London: Methuen & Co.

Conneller, C. 2011. *An Archaeology of Materials: Substantial Transformations in Prehistoric Europe*. London: Routledge

Crawford, O.G.S. 1921. *Man and His Past*. Oxford: Oxford University Press

Cullen, B. 2000. *Contagious Ideas: On Evolution, Culture, Archaeology, and Cultural Virus Theory*. Oxford, UK: Oxbow Books

DeLanda, M. 2006. *A New Philosophy of Society: Assemblage Theory and Social Complexity*. London: Continuum

Eng, K., Baebler, A., Bernardet, U., Blanchard, M., Briska, A., Costa, M., et al. 2003. Ada: buildings as organisms. Paper presented at "Game, Set and Match," Faculty of Architecture, TU Delft, Holland. At http://ada.ini.uzh.ch/presskit/papers/ada-gamesetandmatch.pdf

Flannery, K. 1967. Culture history v. culture process: a debate in American archaeology. *Scientific American* 217, 119–22

Hacking, I. 1998. Canguilhem amid the cyborgs. *Economy and Society* 27(2–3), 202–16

Haraway, D. 1991. *Simians, Cyborgs and Women: The Reinvention of Nature*. London: Free Association Press

Hawkes, J. 1968. The proper study of mankind. *Antiquity* 42, 255–62

Henare, A., Holbraad, M. & Wastell, S. (eds.) 2007. *Thinking Through Things: Theorising Artefacts Ethnographically*. London: Routledge

Hodder, I. 2012. *Entangled: An Archaeology of the Relationships between Humans and Things*. Oxford, UK: Wiley-Blackwell

Jacobs, J. & Merriman, P. 2011. Practising architectures. *Social and Cultural Geography* 12(3), 211–22

Johansen, J.M. 2002. *Nanoarchitecture: A New Species of Architecture*. New York: Princeton Architectural Press

Jones, A.M. 2004. Archaeometry and materiality: materials-based analysis in theory and practice. *Archaeometry* 46(3), 327–38

Jones, A.M. 2012. *Prehistoric Materialities: Becoming Material in Prehistoric Britain and Ireland*. Oxford: Oxford University Press

Knappett, C. 2005. *Thinking Through Material Culture*. Philadelphia: University of Pennsylvania Press

Knappett, C. & Malafouris, L. (eds.) 2008. *Material Agency: Towards a Non-Anthropocentric Approach*. New York: Springer

Leroi-Gourhan, A. 1993. *Gesture and Speech*. Cambridge, MA: MIT Press

Lucas, G. 2012. *Understanding the Archaeological Record*. Cambridge: Cambridge University Press

Lucas, G. Forthcoming. Conduits of Dispersal: dematerializing an early twentieth century village in Iceland. In B. Olsen & Þ. Pétursdóttir (eds.), *Ruin Memories*. London: Routledge

Lucas, G. & Hreiðarsdóttir, E. 2012. The archaeology of capitalism in Iceland: the view from Viðey. *International Journal of Historical Archaeology* 16(3), 604–21

Maxwell, G. 1962. The ontological status of theoretical entities. In H. Feigl & G. Maxwell (eds.), *Minnesota Studies in the Philosophy of Science*, 3–27. Minneapolis: University of Minnesota Press

Normark, J. 2009. The making of a home: assembling houses at Nocacab, Mexico. *World Archaeology* 41(3), 430–44

O'Brien, M.J., Lyman, R.L., Mesoudi, A. & VanPool, T.L. 2010. Cultural traits as units of analysis. *Philosophical Transactions of the Royal Society B* 365, 3797–806

Olsen, B. 2010. *In Defense of Things: Archaeology and the Ontology of Objects*. Walnut Creek, CA: AltaMira Press

Olsen, B., Shanks, M., Webmoor, T. & Witmore, C. 2012. *Archaeology: The Discipline of Things*. Berkeley: University of California Press

Pearson, M. & Shanks, M. 2001. *Theatre/Archaeology*. London: Routledge

Pollard, A. & Bray, P. 2007. A bicycle made for two? The integration of scientific techniques into archaeological interpretation. *Annual Review of Anthropology* 36, 245–59

Shennan, S. 2003. *Genes, Memes and Human History*. London: Thames & Hudson

Strathern, M. 1996. Cutting the network. *Journal of the Royal Anthropological Institute* 2(3), 517–35

Turner, J. 2000. *The Extended Organism: The Physiology of Animal-Built Structures*. Cambridge, MA: Harvard University Press

Turner, J. 2004. Extended phenotypes and extended organisms. *Biology and Philosophy* 19, 327–52

Viveiros de Castro, E. 2004. Exchanging perspectives: the transformation of objects into subjects in Amerindian ontologies. *Common Knowledge* 10(3), 463–84

Wylie, A. 1986. Arguments for scientific realism: the ascending spiral. *American Philosophical Quarterly* 23, 287–97

Yaneva, A. 2009. Making the social hold: towards an Actor-Network Theory of design. *Design and Culture* 1(3), 273–88

Yaneva, A. Forthcoming. Actor-Network Theory approach to the archaeology of contemporary architecture. In P. Graves-Brown, R. Harrison & A. Piccini (eds.), *The Oxford Handbook of the Archaeology of the Contemporary World*. Oxford: Oxford University Press

Index

and transmorphic affect in
Chumash rock art, 63–67, 71–72
correspondence theory of truth, 235
cosmic power
Avebury monument complex, 190
marae of Polynesia, 185–87
credibility, of IoA models, 293
cremations, Fourknocks complex,
349–51
Crick barrow, 260–61, 261*f*
cultural capital wielded by IoA
models, 295–96
culture, material. *See* material culture
Cummings, Vicki, 177

D

Danielsson, Ing-Marie Back, 279
datura, and Chumash rock art, 71
deceptive nature of skeuomorphs
in Early Upper Paleolithic Europe,
125–27, 126*f*, 126*t*
essentialist view of materials, 121
general discussion, 131–32
materials and technology, 127–29,
128*f*
overview, 116, 119–21
perspectivism, 129–31
privileging of form over material,
121–22
thinking productively about,
122–24
Deleuze, Gilles, 20–21, 28–29, 213
Deloria, V., Jr., 199, 200
dependent architecture, 145–46,
147–48
dependent material, in architecture,
139
deposition
in Irish passage tombs, 349–52
of pottery in Saxo-Norman
Southampton, 225–26, 229–30
of sherds in Castelo Velho site,
142–44, 143*f*, 145*t*
Derrida, Jacques, 28–29
design, in prehistoric architecture,
138–39

dietary habits, Mesolithic–Neolithic
transition in Britain, 160–62, 165
differences, use of term, 28–29
dioramas. *See* models, Institute of
Archaeology
Dirikoro area, Ethiopia, 268–69,
269*f*
Discours Admirables (Palissy), 123
divine miniature beings, Scandinavian
gold-foil figures as, 335–36
domestic settings, relational
ontologies and
agency, 100–103
contexts without context, 103–6
object relationships and networks,
99–100
objects in non-contexts, 106–7
overview, 97–99
Piedras Blancas site, 107–11, 108*f*,
109*f*
dreams, in American Indian religious
practices, 200
durability, building of by objects, 227
Durrington Walls Southern Circle,
191
dynamic assemblages, 242–43
dynamic nature of relational fields,
199

E

Early Bronze Age barrow at Crick,
260–61, 261*f*
Early Bronze Age mortuary practices
circulating reference, 239–41, 240*f*
extending assemblages, 247–48
overview, 236–37, 252–53
Early Upper Paleolithic Europe,
skeuomorphism in
materials and technology, 127–29,
128*f*
overview, 125–27, 126*f*, 126*t*
perspectivism, 129–31
earth-diver myth, American Indian,
205–6
Easter Island (Rapa Nui) *moai*,
187–88, 188*f*

Stone C, Fourknocks complex, 354*f*,
355, 356*f*
Stone E, Fourknocks complex,
357–58, 357*f*
Stone F, Fourknocks complex, 358
Stonehenge, changing architecture of,
115
stone tools, Mesolithic–Neolithic
transition in Britain, 158–59, 164
stones
Aurignacian beads made from,
127–28
in Avebury monument complex,
188–89
in Chumash ontology, 63–64
images on in Fourknocks
complex, 352–59, 354*f*, 355*f*,
356*f*, 357*f*
and topology of place, 260–63,
265–67
See also rock art
storage vessels, Saxo-Norman
Southampton, 226, 229
subject, interpreting, 18–22, 30
subjectivity, La Candelaria
miniatures, 51–54
subsistence, during Mesolithic–
Neolithic transition in Britain,
160–62, 165
substances
agentive power, in Chumash
ontology, 66–67
in essentialist view of materials,
121
subterranean landscape, 263
supernatural power, in Chumash
ontology, 64
Sweden. *See* Scandinavian rock art
symbols, material, 22–23
symmetrical archaeology, 23, 38

T

talismans, in Chumash ontology, 65
Technical Department, IoA. *See*
Repair Laboratory, IoA
technology

during Mesolithic–Neolithic
transition in Britain, 158–59, 164
and skeuomorphism, 127–29
teeth, Aurignacian beads made from,
125–26, 127
theory
context in architecture, 135–37,
147–48
in non-representationalism, 235
overview, 15–17
Scandinavian gold-foil figures,
325–27
shamanism, 60–61
visual archaeology, 282–84
therianthropic imagery. *See*
transmorphism
things. *See* objects
Thomas, J., 20, 154–55, 156, 259
Thomas Aquinas, St., 122
three-dimensional physical
models. *See* models, Institute of
Archaeology
Till, Jeremy, 145–46
Tilley, Chris, 22–23
time
and change, in non-
representationalism, 239–41,
240*f*
compartmentalization of, 157–58
Tolan-Smith, C., 163
tombs, Irish passage. *See* Irish passage
tombs
tools, during Mesolithic–Neolithic
transition in Britain, 158–59, 164
topology of place
archaeology of place, 259–60
assemblies
form and formation, 260–65
generative locales, 267–70
overview, 260
participant spaces, 265–67
propinquity of place, 270–72
overview, 176, 257–59
totality of existence, in animism, 199
trance model, 60, 61, 71–72, 75
trans-dimensional qualities of
movements

About the Authors

Benjamin Alberti
Department of Sociology, Framingham State University, USA

Growing up in the northeast of England and suffering from an early sensitivity to the grand, at times somber, material remains of the past in the region (Hadrian's Wall, Bede's Lindisfarne, and many more), I naturally leaned towards history and archaeology for my undergraduate degree. I was inspired by Peter Ucko as an undergraduate and Yvonne Marshall as a post-graduate at Southampton University, and my sensibility was nurtured by a reflection on the politics of the past and the importance of an anthropological approach. Looping back to my experiences being raised in a feminist household, my PhD was the extension of my personal reflection on masculinity into a theoretical exploration of bodies and artwork at Knossos, Crete.

I never quite settled in Cretan archaeology, however, and felt that my search for masculinity in prehistory had come to an impasse. An undergraduate exchange in Barcelona and dissertation research in Venezuela, plus subsequent trips to Argentina and a job offer to teach theory in Olavarría, Argentina, led to my current interest in bodies and ceramics from the northwest of the country. I am driven by the sense that feminist, queer, and anthropological theory should be working with such material; that we can say something new and important about the past and about theory through that encounter. I have edited two books on South American archaeology and written a number of articles and book chapters on bodies, feminism, queer theory, and ontology in Bronze Age Crete and first-millennium AD Argentina.

Ing-Marie Back Danielsson
Department of Classical Studies and Archaeology,
Stockholm University, Sweden

I had worked as an auditor for a year and as a qualified investigator at the Swedish Competition Authority for some four years when, during a round-the-world trip, I decided it was time to move on and do something else. By coincidence, I started studying archaeology at Stockholm University. It turned out to be great fun, and I also enjoyed being back in the academic environment. What attracts me the most is the subject's vast versatility in terms of methods, theories, multidisciplinary nature, hands-on experiences with material culture and remains of the past, and the chance to reflect continuously on what it means to be human in the present and in the past.

To my delight, archaeology also offers the opportunity to ponder upon these questions from a feminist perspective. This has been an interest of mine for a long time, in fact since high school. I entered the PhD program at Stockholm University, and during the extended period of time it took to finish the thesis, mainly due to maternity leave, I was fortunate enough to spend one semester at Lampeter University in Wales. As a researcher at Stockholm University I have published papers on a number of archaeological topics (all available through the DiVA/ Stockholm University search engine). They cover the archaeology of contemporary death, the history of archaeology, and in several cases archaeological approaches to sex, gender, and corporeality in Late Iron Age Scandinavia (AD 550–1050). I presently research and teach at the Department of Archaeology and Classical Studies, Stockholm University.

Sarah E. Baires
Department of Anthropology, University of Illinois at Urbana-Champaign, USA

My interest in archaeology began as a college undergrad at the University of Tennessee when my archaeology 101 professor dumped a bag full of garbage from a fraternity party onto the floor in the front of the class, followed by the statement "This is what your generation is leaving behind." From that point on I was hooked. I began to focus my archaeological interests on the pre-Columbian Southeast of North America, which led me to Cahokia, where I currently conduct research on questions of social and political complexity, religion, and mortuary practice. For me, archaeology is a unique and important area of study for uncovering and investigating our human past. Archaeology provides not only insight into the ways people lived in that past, but also allows us to investigate our contemporary practices and beliefs. Currently, I am completing my PhD at the University of Illinois at Urbana-Champaign under the direction of Dr. Timothy R. Pauketat. My dissertation focuses on the emergence of Cahokia and its relation to unique burial practices and religious beliefs.

Marcus W.R. Brittain
Cambridge Archaeological Unit, Cambridge, UK

Memories from childhood are remolded with time and experience, but I have many from my youngest days when my parents lovingly took me to fallen Greek temples and crumbling English castles and eventually had to depart with my small frame under arm, lifted from the ground with loud reluctance. These places fueled my imagination of magical worlds, and in my twelfth year some grounding was welcomed with my mother's purchase of the Adkinses' *Handbook of British Archaeology*. This provided source material for my first ten-minute presentation to my suffering classmates. The break-time bell was greeted with much enthusiasm that day.

I did eventually go on to study archaeology at the University of Manchester, although perhaps not initially with a view to a career in the subject. Manchester was, and continues to be, a fantastically vibrant city, with an ever-changing topography and a radically creative and dissenting image. Many of the ideas slicing through archaeology at this time were equally in this vein, and I found that a fantastic breadth of new imagination and magic was brimming over many other subjects. I explored as much of this as possible, and took the opportunity of deeper engagement through my PhD research, pooling together ideas from a range of standpoints. Prehistory provided the glue. During this time I was fortunate to be granted a year's sabbatical for fieldwork in the Cambridgeshire fens and in East Africa, both combining developer- and research-oriented commitments. I have continued these experiences in my present capacity in developer-funded archaeology. I no longer require physical removal from an archaeological site, but happily ancient sites continue to fuel my imagination.

Amanda J. Butler
Department of Anthropology, University of Illinois at Urbana-Champaign, USA

Before it even made sense or before I knew what it meant, I always said I was going to be an archaeologist. Beginning with a simple love of all history, but particularly the one that involves wonderfully detailed human stories, my first fascination was with Egyptology and Egyptian and Greek mythology. Growing up on a farm in extremely rural North Dakota, I often spent hours enmeshing myself in stories of great events and people of times past and then finding links of relevance to my world or my own story. Notwithstanding my early determination to be an archaeologist, the regional designation of North American archaeologist was never part of my original plan. It seemed my eyes were always looking everywhere but in my own backyard. In college, my eyes became fixed on an entirely new world of human histories and stories I had never thought before, the Mississippian period (AD 1050–1350) of pre-Columbian history.

At first, I believed I only wanted a master's degree in archaeology so I might continue to work in the applied field of cultural resource management. My plans changed when I became immersed in the archaeological theories discussing the diverse and fluid relationships and experiences between people, places, and objects. Once again, here I found the human stories of lives lived with which I had fallen in love from the very beginning. Currently, I am a PhD student at the University of Illinois at Urbana-Champaign and work on everything from provenance studies to animism and the spread of religion.

Andrew Cochrane
British Museum, UK

I originally trained as a topographical surveyor; while working at a peat extraction site, I had the opportunity to meet archaeologists excavating nearby. I liked my job—but what they were doing was far more exciting! After studying environmental science, I headed to Cardiff University to read archaeology. Alasdair Whittle was my mentor for my BA, MA, and PhD; I owe him so much. Doug Bailey introduced me to visual culture studies and taught me the art of performance. In 2004, I met Ian Russell in Lyon, and we began a collaboration to express and explore archaeology via artistic practice. We have exhibited and installed our works throughout Europe and the USA, and developed the WAC 2008 "art and archaeology" exhibitions and conference. Ian really is the best. I obtained my PhD in 2007, researching Neolithic passage tombs, and was an associate lecturer at Cardiff University between 2007 and 2008, teaching human origins, archaeology and visual culture, and British prehistory.

I have excavated with the Museum of London Archaeology and have been a research associate at the Sainsbury Institute for the Study of Japanese Arts and Cultures and at the School of Oriental and African Studies, studying imagery from both the contemporary world and deep history.

I was a consultant curator and researcher for "The Power of Dogu" exhibition at the British Museum in 2009. I was project curator for the "Unearthed" exhibition at the Sainsbury Centre for Visual Arts in 2010, and World Art Fellow at the University of East Anglia. In recent years, working with Simon Kaner, Doug Bailey, and Andy Jones has been a privilege and a pleasure. I am currently project curator at the British Museum, and I have recently worked with Jill Cook on the "Ice Age Art" exhibition (2013). I now love my job!

Chantal Conneller
Archaeology, School of Arts, Languages and Cultures,
University of Manchester, UK

I did my undergraduate degree and doctoral studies at the University of Cambridge and later held a postdoctoral research fellowship at Queens' College, Cambridge between 2001 and 2004. I also have a background in commercial archaeology and have worked at various periods for the Cambridge Archaeology Unit (CAU) as a site assistant, excavating sites across East Anglia. I have also worked as a lithic analyst for a number of commercial units in the UK. I briefly worked as a lecturer at the University of Wales, Bangor, and I am presently reader in prehistoric archaeology at the University of Manchester.

Fredrik Fahlander
Department of Archaeology and Classical Studies,
Stockholm University, Sweden

After being a technical college graduate working with electronics for a number of years, I started studying humanities in the early 1990s. I had never previously thought about becoming an archaeologist—my undergraduate years were more an excuse to finance a musical career—but the idea of working with past and partly unknown worlds gradually caught on. During my years as a PhD candidate my interest became more focused. I participated in a series of excavation and survey projects in Greece and worked for a while with genetic sex determinations from ancient DNA. I finally received my doctoral degree in 2003 at the Department of Archaeology, University of Gothenburg. For the next couple of years I worked as a lecturer and researcher, until 2009, when I began a postdoctoral research fellowship at the Department of Archaeology and Classical Studies in Stockholm. During this period I also developed an intense interest in the art of online assault game mode of Unreal Tournament 99.

My research is not restricted to any particular time period or region but is focused on social theory and methodology in general and on social practice and materiality in particular. I have mainly been working with burial archaeology and questions of social identity, including life course studies of children and elderly, but also foodways, tattoo and body modifications, rock art, and landscape archaeology (see mikroarkeologi. se). Despite the theoretical character of my research, my background in the natural sciences is still present; one of my current projects involves methodological development of 3D-analysis of rock art by photogrammetry.

Chris Fowler
School of History, Classics and Archaeology, Newcastle University, UK

I first caught the archaeology bug some time during childhood, the initial strain manifesting itself as a passion for things Anglo-Saxon and Medieval—probably acquired during family outings to castles, churches, and "open air museums" and incubated at excavations in Steyning, West Sussex, in 1989. At Southampton University I became infected by various other strains throughout the 1990s, particularly those relating to prehistoric archaeology and archaeological uses of anthropology. After eight years at Southampton I was released with a PhD, but I was later admitted to the School of Art History and Archaeology at Manchester University in 2000 to work on the person and body in the past and present. I have been working at Newcastle University since 2004.

I mainly study British Neolithic and Early Bronze Age archaeology, and have worked in most detail on the Isle of Man, southwest Scotland, and northeast England. During the early 2000s I codirected excavations at two chambered tombs in southwest Scotland with Vicki Cummings, and since then most of my research has been focused on the analysis and synthesis of published and unpublished material, including exploration of museum collections, particularly for the Chalcolithic and Early Bronze Age of northeast England. I have a particular interest in prehistoric mortuary practices, art, monuments and landscapes, and archaeological interpretation. In 2009 I was a cofounder of the Tyne-Forth Prehistory Forum, which brings together those researching archaeology in northeast England and southeast Scotland. I particularly enjoy the ongoing process of learning through engaging with other people, things, documents, ideas, and places that is a constant feature of archaeological work.

Alejandro Haber
Escuela de Arqueología, Universidad Nacional de Catamarca, Argentina

I am an Argentine archaeologist and anthropologist. I studied at the Universidad de Buenos Aires and am currently professor at the Universidad Nacional de Catamarca and researcher at the Consejo Nacional de Investigaciones Científicas y Técnicas (CONICET). My regional interest is in the Andean region, particularly the Puna de Atacama, where I have been working among the Antofalla people since the late 1980s. I have focused on the ways indigenous Andean thinking aids in the identification of colonial assumptions codified in Western disciplinary science. I am coeditor of the bilingual journal *Arqueología Suramericana* and have edited books in both English and Spanish. I have authored several books, the most recent being *La casa, las cosas y los dioses* (2012) and *Domesticidad e interacción en los Andes meridionales* (2009).

Ben Jervis
English Heritage, London

My approach to the study of material culture is a result of the various ways in which I have been fortunate to engage with it over the last ten years during my work on important ceramic assemblages in southern England, Romania, and Uganda. My undergraduate experience on the Bishopstone Valley Archaeological project was a formative one; here I had my first experience of working with pottery, under the tutelage of Duncan Brown. This work underpinned my undergraduate dissertation, which, under the supervision of Howard Williams and Carl Knappett at Exeter, became an examination of pottery manufacture and identity, still a central theme in my research. It was during my time at the British Institute in East Africa that I was able to take stock and formulate an idea that would bloom into my doctoral study, identifying a need to understand the ways in which people used, rather than made, pottery. Postgraduate study in Southampton followed by a year working at Southampton Museum equipped me with the skills and knowledge to take this study forward and enforced the need to undertake theoretically innovative research, though underpinned by a solid dataset. My choice of Andrew Jones as a supervisor has often raised eyebrows, but it was this choice that gave me the freedom to escape from the baggage of medieval archaeology and experiment with new approaches, not only trying to get to grips with how pottery was made and when, but also exploring the effects of its production, exchange, use, and deposition on medieval communities. Going forward my research and now teaching has developed to question the relationship between history and archaeology while continuing to explore the potential of relational approaches to medieval objects.

Andrew Meirion Jones
Archaeology, Faculty of Humanities, University of Southampton, UK

I never set out to study archaeology; in fact growing up in the urban sprawl of Liverpool, northwest England, archaeological remains were few and far between. I had the misguided notion that I wanted to study science and originally went to study biochemistry at Dundee University,

Scotland. After a few years the thought of leading the rest of my life in a white lab coat and learning the dull rote formulae of science caused me to rethink things; I wanted to rekindle my imaginative faculties and reawaken my childhood interest in archaeology. Luckily I managed to transfer to study archaeology at Glasgow University.

As an antidote to science, at Glasgow I gravitated toward prehistoric archaeology and archaeological theory, which were taught by John Barrett and Colin Richards. Hoodwinked by Colin Richards, I carried on to do doctoral research on Neolithic Orkney, applying petrology and lipid analysis (GC/MS) to the study of pottery to provide a biographical account of the intertwined lives of people and pots; my doctoral studies were mainly funded by working in commercial archaeology as a pottery specialist. Escaping from Glasgow on graduation, I taught at University College Dublin for a year, and was then a fellow at the McDonald Institute of Archaeological Research, Cambridge for two halcyon years. At Cambridge I met a number of key Scandinavian rock art researchers. I had long been interested in art, and I saw in the study of rock art a fresh and exciting way of understanding how prehistoric people visualized and engaged with landscapes. I haven't looked back since! I am now reader in prehistoric archaeology at the University of Southampton, and have published books on archaeological science and theory, memory, sculpture, rock art, and prehistoric materiality. My abiding interest remains the spectacular archaeology of Neolithic and Bronze Age Britain and northwest Europe.

Andrés Gustavo Laguens
Instituto de Antropología de Córdoba, CONICET- Universidad Nacional de Córdoba, Argentina

Being born in the Argentine city of La Plata, home to the Museo de La Plata, a huge nineteenth-century museum of natural sciences with large and exotic archaeological and ethnographic collections, I had no choice: archaeology was my fate. After receiving my undergraduate degree I began working in the Museo de Antropología, Córdoba, where I continue to teach archaeology and material culture studies. I have always thought that archaeology has to do with the present; at the beginning of my career my (then future) wife, Mirta Bonin, and I began working in the Argentine Andes, recuperating agricultural terraces for production. But those were not good times in Argentina for a critical social archaeology (1978–1983). A subtler and less suspicious subject provided my means of subsistence and PhD topic: Indigenous peoples' change and resistance in Córdoba during the Spanish conquest and their strategies for survival until the present, from the perspective of the vanquished.

This experience challenged me to think and do a different archeology, as I worked with ethno-historic documents that revealed dimensions of life supposedly invisible to archaeology. Consequently, in the mid-1990s I began a new project: social inequality, its emergence and reproduction in the Argentine Andes, AD 500–1000, understood on the basis of the relationships between people and things. I also research the Early Holocene peopling of Argentina; here I understand peopling as diaspora and material culture as memory in a landscape without history. I have published extensively on these subjects in books and journals. Now, with Ben Alberti, I am exploring past ontology in northwest Argentina following the approach of Amazonian perspectivism.

Gavin Lucas
University of Iceland, Reykjavik, Iceland

I have been working in archaeology since I was a teenager in the early 1980s, volunteering during the summers for the Museum of London on various developer-led excavations. It was the start of a long, if discontinuous, career in contract archaeology that has run parallel to most of my academic life—until recently. My formal education however began as an undergraduate at the Institute of Archaeology, UCL, where I was also first introduced to archaeological theory (North American, processual) by Ann Stahl. It was a very influential period, which subsequently led me to study for a doctorate under the direction of Ian Hodder at the University of Cambridge, where my horizons were broadened even further. After completing my PhD in the mid-1990s and following a half-hearted search for academic posts, I returned to full-time work in contract archaeology. My experience, particularly with the Cambridge Archaeological Unit, was inestimable. The director Chris Evans always managed to bring in dynamic and original people, and from them I learnt a different side of fieldwork and its relation to academic research. It was also during this time that I started to publish my first books and also develop my primary interest in the archaeology of the modern world. Seeking new opportunities and experiences, I moved to Iceland in 2002 to work for an independent archaeological research institution and then, in 2006, I entered my first academic post at the University of Iceland, where I remain today.

Lesley McFadyen
Department of History, Classics and Archaeology, Birkbeck University of London, UK

I am a lecturer in archaeology at Birkbeck, University of London. My main interests are architecture in prehistory and the history of ideas between archaeology and architecture. I have worked in developer-funded archaeology in Britain with the Cambridge Archaeological Unit (CAU), excavating prehistoric landscapes in East Anglia. Other projects have included: Neolithic houses on Orkney and in Normandy; Neolithic long barrows in Dorset, Normandy and Brittany; and Chalcolithic walled enclosures in the Alto Douro of Portugal.

Timothy R. Pauketat
*Department of Anthropology, University of Illinois at
Urbana-Champaign, USA*

I've been a professional archaeologist for a while, having identified archaeology as one of a number of career options by the age of twelve. I had grown up in a rural part of the American Midwest where almost every agricultural field and eroding lake edge produced pre-Columbian artifacts. Even my mother had collected Indian arrowheads as a child. But despite being a teenage artifact enthusiast and a romantic idealist, I didn't limit myself to archaeology. I seriously considered becoming a musician, paleontologist, poet, and photographer. Through my teenage years, I spent most weekends outdoors during the day—walking fields and woodlands—and drumming for a five-member dance band at night. I still have my drumsticks, a cabinet of fossils, notebooks of poems, and an old Nikon F.

An archaeology field school and an undergraduate internship for the U.S. Army Corps of Engineers solidified the archaeology career option, and graduate school ended my late-night wedding gigs. I received a PhD degree from the University of Michigan in 1991, and then taught at the Universities of Oklahoma, SUNY-Buffalo, and Illinois, where I have been since 1998. Most of my surveys and excavations—always large-scale for good reasons—have occurred along the Mississippi River. Oddly, the general lack of Indigenous cities in North America gave me an abiding interest in cities, monumentality, and agency. My fascination with politics finally if inevitably led me to religion. And my research on things and relationships almost certainly originates in my youthful enchantments with objects and oak trees.

Sara Perry
Department of Archaeology, University of York, UK

I have recently taken up a lectureship in cultural heritage management at the University of York (UK), where I am the director of studies of the department's Digital Heritage program, and the acting director of studies of its Archaeological Information Systems program. I have eclectic interests, which were facilitated by the anthropological training that I received in Canada as an undergraduate and master's student. There, I managed to tie together my prehistoric archaeology background with a fascination for visual studies and visual media; and I subsequently moved to the UK to consolidate these interests via a PhD at the University of Southampton.

Fundamentally I am concerned with how archaeologists present the past to both academic and non-academic audiences—for instance, in museums, books, journal articles, exhibitions, lectures, on television, radio, and the web. I'm working to understand how these forms of presentation feed back into the research questions that we ask as archaeologists and the funding that we receive. Intelligent use of different media has profound consequences for the discipline, both financially and intellectually, and archaeologists are only just starting to untangle the implications. Moreover, visual/media researchers and archaeologists use methods and ideas that complement, if not exactly parallel, one another. Thinking about how we might better capitalize on these relations can reshape the nature of our scholarship.

Joshua Pollard
Archaeology, Faculty of Humanities, University of Southampton, UK

I think it all began at an undefined early age with digging holes in the garden. I can't remember the rationale for this, but I do remember encounters with curious objects as a result. Perhaps a drift towards archaeology was simply a rationalization of these impulses and a means of taming a fascination with stuff. I'm not sure whether to blame my parents, the digging impulse, a raft of curious things in the world, or the remains of the distant past (I have sharp memories of a chambered tomb, hill fort, and mosaic from a Cotswold holiday when I was five). Anyway, I finally decided that it was in archaeology rather than art that my career ambitions lay, thanks largely to inspirational teaching at school from a local archaeologist, James Dyer. Then I studied (for my BA and PhD) at Cardiff University. With this came a slide to prehistory and the Neolithic in particular, under Alasdair Whittle's wonderful influence and some formative excavation experience in the Avebury landscape. The latter still has me captured, even after working on projects elsewhere in Britain and abroad.

As a number of contributors to this volume (Chantal Conneller, Lesley McFadyen, Gavin Lucas, and Marcus Brittain), I found myself working for the Cambridge Archaeological Unit. It was a great experience and I do sort of miss it. As its director, Chris Evans provided the CAU with one of the most stimulating environments in which one could work. Academia had a draw, even though its environment has always felt daunting—is it just me, or does anyone else feel like a fraud? So continued the anticlockwise progression of employment around the UK (postdoc in Newcastle and lecturing in Belfast, Newport, Bristol, and now Southampton). I remain bitterly disappointed that I wasn't born 220 years earlier and allowed to join James Cook's Pacific voyages.

David W. Robinson
Archaeology, Forensic and Investigative Sciences, University of Central Lancashire, UK

My grandparent's fiftieth wedding anniversary in 1996 bought me back to the UK and led to a memorable encounter with Stonehenge and my brother's rock band. At the time, I was studying comparative mythology, and wondered about the mythology of the Stonehenge builders. After reading my first book on archaeology, Chippindale's *Stonehenge Complete*, I realized that such questions are very difficult to answer when studying prehistory. This led to archaeology and many summers excavating prehistoric sites in Britain. Switching my major to anthropology/archaeology, I spent my time equally in US processual and UK post-processual programs, benefiting from the best of both worlds. However, after visiting Chumash rock art sites in California and reading Blackburn's *Decembers' Child*, I realized that there may well be a way of linking mythology to the archaeological record, especially where direct ethnography exists. This led to a doctorate, coincidentally with Chippindale as my supervisor in Cambridge. I now teach archaeology at the University of Central Lancashire, UK.

Having studied comparative mythology, I was very aware of the shamanic theory of rock art; however, now a trained "dirt archaeologist," I couldn't help but notice the abundant archaeology at the feet of the paintings. It simply didn't make sense that these were places of exclusion, so I began to work systematically on the fantastic rock art and archaeology of the Wind Wolves Preserve. Over ten years on now, the vibrant art of this interior Chumash landscape has made me rethink the notion of shamanism and re-appreciate the compelling mythology of Native California. Rock art sites were, and still are, places animated by living communities, both human and otherwise.

Emilie Sibbesson
History and American Studies, Canterbury Christ Church University, UK

A year into a degree course in ancient history and archaeology at Newcastle University, UK, I abandoned the Greeks and Romans to focus instead on northern European prehistory, and in particular on the emergence of agriculture. Archaeologies of the transition(s) to agriculture allow exploration of a few wider themes that also intrigue me, such as the reconciliation of scientific techniques with social archaeological questions and issues surrounding foodways in the past. Following doctoral research at the University of Southampton, I was appointed as a lecturer in archaeology at Canterbury Christ Church University, UK.

Food is not a subject that can be left in the office at the end of the day, and my research into prehistoric foodways has inspired an interest in all manners of preindustrial and modern-day food production and consumption. As a result I am exploring a couple of spin-offs of my doctoral project, including an interdisciplinary and experimental investigation into the (dis)advantages of cooking with unglazed pottery. In addition to researching, eating, and thinking about food, I have in the last few years been involved in excavations from the Channel Islands to the Outer Hebrides, and on many sites in between.

B. Jacob Skousen
Department of Anthropology, University of Illinois at Urbana-Champaign, USA

My love for history and the outdoors developed when I was young. Growing up in West Virginia, I was always outside playing sports, exploring, and camping. My family frequented Washington, DC, Gettysburg, Antietam, and other nearby national parks and monuments, which introduced me to United States' geography, history, and culture. Additionally, my family drove to the western United States every other summer to see our extended family, visiting national parks, monuments, and historical sites along the way.

Still, when I started college at Brigham Young University, I knew relatively little about archaeology and was considering a major and career in geology, physical therapy, or exercise medicine. This changed in 2004 during an Introduction to World Prehistory class, which I took as a general education requirement. This introductory class, along with an ancient history course, stimulated my interest in ancient societies, and I haven't looked back since. Over the next several years I earned a bachelor's and master's degree at Brigham Young University, studying and working in Mesoamerica, the Middle East, and the North American Great Basin/Southwest. My interest in complex societies led me to the Midwestern United States in 2009. After working for the Illinois State Archaeological Survey for a year excavating sites near St. Louis, I began graduate school at the University of Illinois in 2010 and hope to complete my PhD in 2015. My interests include pilgrimage, movement, religion, relational ontologies, and personhood.